ERSATZ AMERICA

ERSATZ AMERICA

HIDDEN TRACES, GRAPHIC TEXTS, AND THE MENDING OF DEMOCRACY

Rebecca Mark

UNIVERSITY OF VIRGINIA PRESS
CHARLOTTESVILLE & LONDON

University of Virginia Press

Printed in the United States of America on acid-free paper

First published 2014

1 3 5 7 9 8 6 4 2

Library of Congress Cataloging-in-Publication Data
Mark, Rebecca.
Ersatz America : hidden traces, graphic texts, and the mending of democracy / Rebecca Mark.
pages cm.
Includes bibliographical references and index.
ISBN 978-0-8139-3625-3 (cloth : acid-free paper)
ISBN 978-0-8139-3626-0 (pbk. : acid-free paper)
ISBN 978-0-8139-3627-7 (e-book)
1. Literature and history—United States. 2. National characteristics, American, in literature. 3. Popular culture—United States. 4. Democracy in literature. 5. United States—Social conditions. I. Title.
PS169.H5M37 2014
810.9'358—dc23 2013047222

Cover art: Visible Means of Support: Monticello, by Kerry James Marshall, 2009. Mural installation at the San Francisco Museum of Modern Art, 6 February 2009–11 October 2011. (San Francisco Museum of Modern Art, collection of the artist; © Kerry James Marshall)

To Emilie Conrad

CONTENTS

ILLUSTRATIONS

ACKNOWLEDGMENTS

This book began with 9/11 and took shape during Hurricane Katrina. I can't thank my friends, family, and colleagues enough for keeping me sane when winds were blowing inside and out. First and foremost, I thank my mom, Elizabeth, a government teacher, who raised her children in a wooded community near the nation's capital. Without her wisdom the connection between branches of oak and branches of democratic government would not have been imprinted on my brain. I wish that my father, Albert, who cheered his children on in everything they tried to do, had lived to see this book published. Somewhere in the vast universe there is a Jewish Pa kvelling about his daughter the writer. I thank all my family, particularly my sister, Katharine, and my brothers, Charles and Andrew, for their constant support and for our years exploring *the* creek and *the* woods. I owe a special thank-you to my sister-in-law Diane, an expert editor, for providing good humor at important moments. Without my friend the movement pioneer Emilie Conrad's visionary understanding of the motion of the human body and the imagination I would never have developed the concept of visceral graphism. I thank the poet and film producer Hanna Wise Heiting for her friendship and for honoring the hieroglyphic field of graphic poetics that made this book possible.

I am grateful to Linda Chrisman, Terry Cummings, Terry Dise, George Fagan, Linda Gardner, David Goodson, Cherice Harrison-Nelson, Jennifer Javonovic, Sue Josephson, Raquel Kislinger, Michelle Kohler, Charlotte Maheu, Betsy Martin, Violet Peterson, Roger Pines, Julie Raiskin, and Myra Rogers for being the best friends anyone could want. Without my friends Karen Remer and Andrea Fagan I would never have been able to mother and write at the same time. My students throughout the years have led me to discover completely new areas of intellectual exploration; for this my debt is great. I especially want to thank Kathy Amende, Michael Bibler, Sarah Ford, Evelyn Hunter, Donnie McMahand, and Kevin Murphy, whose work has challenged me in every way. A special shout-out to my Posse 2/Tulane scholars, who inspire me daily: Ghiya Ali, Wil Crary, Miaira Jennings, Nicole Kuaea, Efren Lopez, Kayla Morris, Yvonne Payne, Alexandria Rakes, Elizabeth Ramirez, Jose Rangel, and Saied Quadri.

Thanks are due to Ed Cohen for hours of theoretical conversation but most importantly for the *Futurama* tip. Had it not been for my friend the historian Sylvia Frey and the Deep South Regional Humanities Center, I would not have visited the sites of memory that defined this project. I am indebted to Luke Pickerell and Linda Chrisman for our friendship and for introducing me to the murals of Kerry Marshall. My appreciation of my life-long friends and Welty colleagues Harriet Pollack, Suzanne Marrs, Peggy Prenshaw, and Dawn Trouard is without measure. I am grateful to Jane Body, Janice Carlisle, Susan Donaldson, Barbara Ewell, Minrose Gwin, Suzanne Jones, Barbara Ladd, Mary Wood, Ruth Salvaggio, Maaja Stewart, and Larry Powell, whose friendship and scholarly work helped me conceptualize this project. I thank all my colleagues in the English department at Tulane, and a special thank-you to my colleague Michelle Kohler for reading portions of the manuscript and giving me invaluable feedback.

I am profoundly grateful to Cathie Brettschneider for believing in this work from the beginning and sticking with it through the whole process. I especially want to acknowledge Laura Helper-Ferris for helping shape the manuscript, Ann Seiber for her editorial and bibliographic work; Raennah Mitchell and the editorial and design editors at the University of Virginia Press for everything; and Joanne Allen for her tireless editing.

The following artists inform every aspect of *Ersatz America:* Jen Bervin, William Christenberry, Willie Cole, Clyde Connell, Tom Feelings, Kerry James Marshall, and Rose Powhatan. The permissions process was made bearable by the help of Dawn Bonner at Mount Vernon; Nita Cole and the Connell family; Andy Deloach and Sue Verhoef at the Atlanta History Center; Dianne Feelings Johnson; Rebecca Mei at the Jack Shainman Gallery; Paula O'Neal; and Atricia Roberts at the First African Baptist Church, Savannah, Georgia.

I am truly thankful for my coparents, Jeff Lockman and Mark Townsend, who have kept a wonderful sense of humor throughout the years of our coparenting and of my writing "the book." My love and appreciation to my son, Benjamin, for being his own person in every way, for his unique creativity and intelligence, and for all the joy and pride he brings me. He always knew what the book was about even when I questioned. Finally, my partner, Brenda Currin, deserves a hero's award for the hundreds of hours spent reading innumerable versions of the manuscript. Her excellent eye and ear and most importantly her deep belief in the argument made what often seemed insurmountable possible.

ERSATZ AMERICA

INTRODUCTION

CITIZEN ARTIST IN A CRUMBLING NATION

> I am against bigness and greatness in all their forms, and with the invisible molecular moral forces that work from individual to individual, stealing in through the crannies of the world like so many soft rootlets or like the capillary oozing of water and yet rending the hardest monuments of man's pride, if you give them time.—WILLIAM JAMES to Mrs. Henry Whitman, 7 June 1899

Between 11 September 2001 and 29 August 2005, when Hurricane Katrina made landfall, I wondered, often in despair, how, precisely, literature, art, and culture could do anything to save America, and for that matter the world. I questioned, as have many writers and artists in the past decade, whether I should quit my job and spend more time in the streets organizing for a better world. I was afraid for our democracy, and yet I was not cynical. I passionately believed in this democracy. During the long evacuation of Katrina, as I sat, pen in hand, in libraries in Washington, DC, and Alexandria, Virginia, looking out on the nation's capital, I knew that war, genocide, torture, and neglect must not be America's legacy.

Yet, as I spent my evacuation sabbatical working on this book, I saw in the streets and monuments of my childhood home of Alexandria an ersatz America, an Olde Towne sandwiched between the Washington Monument and Mount Vernon, spreading out before me. In my darkest moments I could believe only that in this ersatz America our national signs and symbols had become simulacra with no relation to democratic participation.[1] I could see the ersatz myth of America standing as a didactic sentinel with a raised, scolding finger, warning against asking any questions, holding the past enthralled, untouchable. This staged nation, performed again and again, solidified its often murderous lie. While I could have called this book *Fake America* or *Imaginary America,* I chose to use the German and Yiddish word *ersatz* because of its implication that the thing referred to—fake coffee during World War II, fake creamer used by Jewish people to keep kosher—is an inferior imitation. Unlike a pure simulation, the ersatz product holds within it the presence of a desired, if theoretically contested, "real."

In the insistent American national mythology, filled with hallucinations of John Smith and founding fathers and lost causes, this longing for the real is the crack in the Liberty Bell. Ersatz myths are vulnerable. With no historical or material substantiality, they must be perpetually reiterated, housed in museums, included in children's stories, sold and resold in schools, repackaged, reissued, and rememorialized. We must have new Pocahontas films and dolls and interactive exhibits. We must add enhanced, life-sized wax figures of George Washington to the Donald W. Reynolds Museum and Education Center at Mount Vernon, and we must forever tell the story of Lincoln's emancipation of slaves with greater reverential awe.

But as these lifeless wax and alabaster figures age, the fissures begin to show. The challenge for this book thus becomes how to recognize and ultimately read the text of a democratic America that lies not in the monuments to nation building, not in statues of our founding fathers, but in the cracks—what William James calls the "crannies"—of our national memory. This book asks how we can begin to give as much value to James's "invisible molecular moral forces that work from individual to individual" as we have been giving to the monumental hagiography of patriotic drum beating. The answer resides not just in any old crack or cranny but in the nuanced graphic inscription of human movement, seeking, tracing, and tracking the irregular fault line of our cultural imagination. It resides in Eliza Harris's wild dash across irregular green ice in *Uncle Tom's Cabin,* in the dashes and marks on Emily Dickinson's manuscripts, in the broken twigs directing slaves to secret meetings. This type of inscription maps a horizontal desire for communing over a vertical will to dominate.

The graphic scripts that I decipher in this book are the texts that result from the movement of the human body and the regenerative force of the natural world. These markings, which I call *visceral* and *biomorphic graphism,* are inherently liberatory. They are the marks left by a human gesture—a movement of the hand, the mind, and the heart—the desire to communicate, and must be distinguished from lines that simply record. Tim Ingold, in his chapter "Drawing the Line" in *Making Anthropology, Archaeology, Art and Architecture,* distinguishes between gestural and nongestural lines. He calls nongestural lines *propositional,* making statements about what is to be or what has been, while gestural lines are *non-propositional,* "meant to express the movements that generated them." Nonpropositional lines issue from bodies rather than making statements about them and "trace paths that others can follow."[2]

By focusing on visceral graphism as it relates to American democracy, I am extending Ingold's gestural line drawings to include those significant cultural marks that citizens leave as they connect to human desires and passions at unspeakable moments in American history. These traces and marks provide a visible record of the gestural act of democratic participation. Visceral graphism includes the gestural movement of hands inscribing intricate mnemonic white-and-purple beadwork for the Six Nations' wampum belts; feet tracing paths of escape through southern woods; and the feet and hands patting Juba or beating the human drum of enslaved people's freedom in the hush harbors and ring shouts of Georgia and South Carolina. The hieroglyphic marks of Clyde Connell's swamp songs, her deeply felt response to the racially violent Louisiana back country, and the line drawings of William Christenberry's *Southern Trees,* marking the intersections of religion, trees, and lynching in the segregationist South, provide clear visual examples of this kind of graphism.

By appropriating *biomorphic* to refer to these traces, I diverge from early art critics' application of this term to modern art. Geoffrey Grigson used *biomorphic* to refer to the relationship "between the history of prehistoric art and the development of modern art in its shift away from representation towards a reduced form of mark-making."[3] I too am interested in mark-making, but I apply the term *biomorphic* particularly to those marks that trace the regenerative pulse of organic forms—literally branches, filigree patterns, or what Tim Ingold calls *meshwork.* Ingold provides a detailed illustration of meshwork when he describes the lines that slugs leave on the sidewalk. He emphasizes that unlike networks, these kinds of biomorphic marks do not always end in any kind of perfectly synchronous system or closure. Instead they are infinitely expansive. In my use of *biomorphic* I expand Grigson's discussion to include specific graphic markings that perform a cultural mapping—or as Ingold reminds us tell a story.[4] These biomorphic marks do not just mimic organic forms (cells, leaves, branches), they produce an open-ended form of cultural coherence. They form a nonalphabetic linguistic inscription whose narrative core is the life force of individual expression.

By *cultural coherence* I mean a proliferation of the most precise marks of cultural regeneration, which on the cellular level can link the material world and the human artist.

By citing a wide variety of examples, I argue throughout this book that these visceral and biomorphic markings—as they track back and forth across the invisible bridge between the human imagination and the natural world—are not just interesting, not even just subversive, but a missing link, a missed clue. These markings are, I believe, an essential scripting of democracy. Precisely because these marks do not honor or value what William James calls "bigness and greatness," they provide the template for the individual to act as a molecular force within a democratic nation.

I first learned to read the script of biomorphic graphism as a child growing up in a modernist glass house community in the woods near Alexandria, Virginia. In the winter there, a child could see branches of oaks and pines forming twisted black patterns against a deep blue night sky or grey cutouts against a red morning light. Although the branches did not spell out anything, they were a script that could be read. They held the code of branches growing over time, crossing one another and intertwining. Their messages were suggestive, elaborate, detailed, complex, a limitless meshwork. The patterns were liberatory because they could not be ordered, distilled, or simplified. They were decidedly not ersatz. No pattern ever repeated itself. Each was unique.

The children in my neighborhood did not just view the intertwining branches from a distance. When we were old enough, we marked the beech trees by carving our names into their bark. Years later, the elephant skin of the beeches puckered and buckled around the carvings, and the names became unreadable as they merged one into another, forming strained lines of connection. It was no longer possible to tell who had loved whom or when, but the graphic markings spoke of other longings (fig. 1). This was a time of segregation, of racial violence, of the assassinations of John F. Kennedy, Martin Luther King Jr., and Robert F. Kennedy, of the Vietnam War. The proliferation of willow oaks, white oaks, Virginia pines, tulip poplars, hickory trees, and beeches dwarfed the houses and the cultural violence and held us in a hush harbor of condolence. We could climb a tall pine a short distance from the community and look out at the Washington Monument, which from that distance of about ten miles looked like a pencil surrounded by green. To my child's eye, the patterned intricacy of the trees—their natural crossings and our own carvings—challenged the monumentalism of the nation's capital.

FIGURE 1
Carved names on a beech tree in the woods near Hollin Hills, Virginia. (Photograph by Rebecca Mark)

In that Alexandria suburb, one could spend hours reading that script of crossing branches and winding creeks. It was not a text that was translatable into modern English, but it was a language nonetheless. Reading the woods while learning the national stories of the founding fathers in Alexandria and Washington, Williamsburg, Jamestown, Gettysburg, and Manassas, the originary sites of the nation, required that I maintain a divided historical consciousness. I was aware at once of the official discourses of nation, experiencing both a personal relationship to the landscape and monuments of nationality and a wild attraction to trees and streams that seemed to have little to do with history. Running the dog in the fields and hills at Manassas National Battlefield and Bull Run State Park, we saw and didn't see the battles raging around us, the blood of Civil War soldiers pooling at our feet, the Indian arrowheads, the footprints of escaping enslaved people.

As this book took shape, I found myself experiencing and perceiving my cultural and physical environment differently, appreciating the smallest, most intricate, and finest pattern as the perfect antidote to monumentalism. Tracing back through the most obvious points of ersatz nation-building, including Jamestown's story of Pocahontas and John Smith, George Washington as the father of our country, and even, but not as obviously ersatz, Lincoln as the great liberator, I discovered that the marks of liberation are always present both in found and in man-made forms. From Powhatan's mantle to the Six Nations Confederacy's wampum belts, to the numbered boards of Harriet Beecher Stowe's disassembled childhood home, the hush-harbor Bakongo cosmograms, the etchings on African American pottery, and the foot patterns of ring-shout rituals, the patterned graphic bridging is always making, mending, and salvaging American democracy by *becoming* American democracy. Contemporary artists, including Kerry James Marshall, Clyde Connell, William Christenberry, Willie Cole, and Jen Bervin understand the threads of this subterranean revolution and in their art unearth, and create anew a communal language of diversity, complexity, and, most significantly, condolence. These hidden-in-plain-view traces and graphic texts provide an insistent counternarrative, an alternative script for the American imagination.

Visceral graphism translates the bodily experience, the urge toward freedom, into a democratic call to action, a language of liberation. Visceral graphism demands that we hold the memory of place and body, the skin and branches of trees, as a corrective to simulation. Visceral graphism contains and salvages the pulse of culture at the moment of its becoming, the breath of life, the cellular gelling into form. In focusing on visceral graphism, the spaces in between writing and visual art, as a means of countering the mirage of ersatz America, we are looking at the human ability to step outside the boundaries of alphabetic literacy and thus of dominant national narratives.

AS NATURAL and man-made disasters terrorize our world, we have become emotionally numb to the image of people sifting through unspeakable mounds of rubble. While it is tempting to celebrate rubble as a metaphoric sign of the collapse of oppressive ideologies, a city reduced to rubble in the real world is unlivable. Rubble is more likely to invite armed guards and environmental toxins than participatory democracy and lush vegetation. Rubble is the collapse of a presumed dominant and thus ersatz relationship to our environment; as such, it is itself ersatz.

An engaged artistic response to rubble comes in many unsettling forms, but visceral and biomorphic graphic inscriptions in particular can circumnavigate the rubble, superimposing symbolic and coded graphic markings that transform old gray subway trains, flooded houses, and twisted broken fences into the material evidence of democracy at work. We can begin to truly understand the regenerative moral value of James's soft rootlets and capillaries when we have accumulated enough historically contextualized and individually marked examples. In order to tap into this fluid, constantly shifting force, it is important to proceed inductively: to find multiple examples that reveal the complexity of the individual artists' unique perspectives. This accumulation of detailed examples is precisely the antithesis of the monolithic monumental.

The most easily readable and accessible form of visceral graphism is graffiti. In what follows I begin to introduce the workings of visceral graphism by describing the difference between the graffiti-bombed (spray-painted) 1976 freedom train and the official Bicentennial Freedom Train of 1976. I then introduce the forms of citizen art produced in the aftermath of both 9/11 and Hurricane Katrina. Visceral graphism is not simply decorative. It is a direct reaction to devastating fractures in the American psyche—most significantly slavery, class stratification, war, Native American genocide, and environmental destruction—that challenge the very meaning of what it is to be human.

Freedom Trains

As a college student in Manhattan in the 1970s I witnessed the proliferation of graffiti art on the sides of subway cars. This citizen art came to me as an embodied cry against a throwaway gray and often garbage-filled city. The modern graffiti artists "bombing" the city's subway trains shape-shifted the letters of the English alphabet, making the one-dimensional plane of the city walls fly in three-dimensional extravagance. The artists' signatures burst upon the tunnels and Philip Johnson skyscrapers. All citizen art generates democratic culture, but graphic inscription, the breaking of the strict equivalency between alphabetic writing and spoken word—what graffiti artists call "wildstyle"—does something more subversive. When the graffiti artists cover the walls of the city with extravagant lettering, they humanize the skyscraper landscape by adding movement and color (fig. 2).

One particular moment of graphic explosion, entitled *The Freedom Train* by the young artists who created it, encapsulates the tension not only between street

FIGURE 2
Graffiti, Manhattan. (Photograph by Vivienne Gucwa)

art and the sanctioned art of 1970s New York but also between citizen art and national art in America. In *Taking the Train,* Joe Austin relates how on the eve of the United States' Bicentennial a group of young artists found their way into the storage yard of the Flushing-to-Manhattan subway line in Queens.[5] Theirs was not a disorganized or haphazard tag. The artists, who had armed themselves with sketches, "worked in the dark to paint all eleven cars top to bottom, in a coordinated bicentennial theme." One of these artists, DIME139, later wrote, "You have to put one foot on the train next to you and the other on the train you were piecing."[6] The artists stretched their bodies in acrobatic and gestural acts of defiance of gravity and authority. They completed a multicar work that was huge, "ten feet high and longer than two football fields."[7] Eyewitnesses said that their freedom train was spectacular. But on the morning of 4 July 1976, before the graffiti train even hit the tracks, the New York Transit Authority dismantled the masterpiece, destroying the artists' work.[8] The transit authority then tracked down the artists and arrested them.

The graffiti freedom train was not the only freedom train on the tracks in America during the 1976 Bicentennial celebration. Ross Rowland Jr., a New York commodities broker and occasional steam-locomotive engineer, dreamt up a 1976

American Freedom Train to emulate the Freedom Train from 1947. Sponsored by the federal government, the 1947 train traveled across America to stir up renewed dedication to democracy and freedom after World War II. Rowland's 1976 train also traversed the country for twenty-one months, attracting hundreds of people wherever it went. Both trains served as moving museums and propaganda machines, bringing the documents of national identity to the American public.[9]

Michael Hogan asserts that the government in 1947 was constructing "a national identity more ideal then real, in part by appealing to a traditional cultural narrative that celebrated consensus and triumphs at the expense of divisions and failures."[10] While celebrating consensus was the dominant reason for the 1947 Freedom Train, there were at least signs of dissent on the part of those who created the train. The lyrics of Irving Berlin's official song "The Freedom Train" were subversive by even today's standards: "You can shout your anger from a steeple / You can shoot the system full of holes / You can always question 'We the People' / You can get your answer at the polls."[11] Langston Hughes, in his poem "Freedom Train," a response to the 1947 train, questions who the "you" is who has these rights. Hughes asks whether there was Jim Crow on the Freedom Train and "Can a coal-black man drive the freedom train? Or am I still a porter on the Freedom Train?" He wants to know whether blacks could vote on the Freedom Train. Evoking the Holocaust, he questions whether whites went to the left, and blacks to the right, on the Freedom Train.[12]

By the 1970s ersatz history had become further established, and for this reason Ross Rowland's 1976 American Freedom Train was more elaborate, and less subject to political scrutiny, than the 1947 train. Providing exhibit space for more than five hundred iconic objects and documents, the 1976 train jumbled up such significant archival treasures as George Washington's annotated text of the Constitution and a copy of the Louisiana Purchase with Lincoln's top hat, a moon rock, and Martin Luther King Jr.'s pulpit and robes. The performing-arts display car alone contained "Rudolf Valentino's jacket, Fred Astaire's hat and cane, Charlton Heston's staff from *The Ten Commandments,* and Jack Benny's violin. John Wayne's eye patch from *True Grit* kept company with Clark Gable's script from *Gone With The Wind* and Judy Garland's dress from *The Wizard of Oz.*"[13]

The website for the 1976 American Freedom Train, indicative of the ersatz historical muddle that this train celebrates, announces: "Even as the ancient ways of Native inhabitants were lost—often savagely, and in contradiction with the American creed of individual rights and self-determination—America was building a beacon of hope for the tired, the poor, the huddled masses upon other shores who were yearning to breathe free."[14] The anonymous writers, to their credit, do condemn the deaths of the people who lived here first, but in an odd manner. To collapse and simplify four hundred years of Native American and immigrant history into such a convoluted, ahistorical statement requires significant distortion, what Jill Lepore calls "anti-history."[15] It is hard to imagine how ethnic cleansing of native peoples becomes "a beacon of hope" for immigrants. And even in 1976, years after the great waves of immigration, few Americans were breathing free. In fact, as Americans celebrated the Bicentennial, school desegregation was a hotly contested issue, and fully realized desegregation was a distant dream.

The 1976 freedom train, like the 1947 train, had its own song, "Here Comes the Freedom Train," written by Stephen Lemberg and performed by both Merle Haggard and Dolly Parton. With no sense of Berlin's 1947 ironic democratic consciousness, Lemberg's lyrics include the following lines: "The train is called America your ticket is a dream / That left the torture of freedom for all the world to see. / She left the station in Lexington in 1776 / And rode to Philadelphia where the liberty bell was fixed / George Washington was the engineer, John Adams shoveled coal / And Franklin punched the tickets / Tom Jefferson added soul."[16] It is difficult to fathom Jefferson's adding "soul" (clearly marked as African American in 1976) to the nation or Adams performing such a proletarian task as shoveling coal.

Nonetheless, the government and the contributing businessmen regarded this ersatz train, filled with the detritus of Americana, as the real freedom train—the version of America that the world should see—and the graffiti freedom train, with its spontaneous explosion of creativity and patriotism, as the dangerous counterfeit. This defies understanding only if we ignore the despotic nature of ersatz America. Since ersatz America depends on an imagined "celebrated consensus," any creative act that breaks out of this mold is dangerous.

It is not surprising that the New York Transit Authority put the artists in jail. Their form of art threatened both the steel and glass monumentalism of modern New York and the crumbling infrastructure behind the facade. The graffiti art was regenerative, connective, imaginative, and in-your-face challenging. Allowing the graffiti train to run would seem like a direct assault on America. Ersatz America had stood in as a surrogate for America for so long that few knew what a democracy by the people and for the people would even look like. That it just might look like an American flag painted illegally in wildstyle letters on the side of a subway train was more than the authorities could bear.

To make matters worse, the graffiti letters did not look like "real" writing. They were too big, too colorful, in the wrong place, and purposely explosive. They morphed and moved rather than lying flat. These young graffiti artists rejected the idea that they or their art should be invisible and silent, relegated to the wasteland of this civilization, buried by the debris that excessive capitalism generated. The graffiti artists resisted the hopelessness of a rubble world. They were not deconstructing or tearing apart the society but trying, quite literally, to piece it back together.

Missing Flyers and Refrigerator Art

The events of 11 September 2001 and 29 August 2005 have left us with a flashback of cement-filled civilizations paralyzed and turned to rubble. They brought America down on her knees sifting through the mountains of ruins. If ever two moments were defined by rubble, it was these. On 9/11, the devastating inferno of computer paper and falling bodies, unimaginable dust, and twisted steel filled our grief-choked lungs, as the symbols of towering capitalism fell to the ground. And yet what stays with us is the indelible human outpouring of fire fighters, police officers, and citizen volunteers scratching for bone fragments, teeth, and toothbrush-lifted, hairbrush-lifted DNA as they sifted through a pile of broken lives to find the codes that would link one human to another in grief.

One of the most human responses to 9/11 took the form of flyers stating that a loved one was missing. New Yorkers described seeing posters announcing missing persons all over the city, in every available empty spot—on telephone poles, trees, street lights—as many as ninety thousand posters from as few as five hundred families—immediately after 9/11. Missing. Missing. The word is so hopeful, so expectant of return, so full of promise, and yet everyone knew that the collapsed towers were final, and deadly. If someone had not heard from a loved one in the first forty-eight hours, the prognosis was not good, and yet the flyers continued to appear. Most were simply colored Xerox copies showing a loved one's face with a handwritten or typed description.

Amy Waldman wrote in a *New York Times* article: "The first wave of paper rained upon the city from the World Trade Center like death's disembodied proxy. As if in answer, a second wave rose up from the photo albums and word processors of thousands of desperate families. . . . They bore the names, smiling faces and intimate physical details—the fingers like a little girl, the titanium hip—of the missing." The posters turned the rubble of Ground Zero into a flowering of human loss, mourning, and intimacy. Waldman describes how they quickly transformed from expressions of desperate wishful thinking to memorials for the dead, from rubble to communal condolence.[17]

No monument, no memorial, no story written in conventional script will ever capture the spontaneity and intimacy of the missing posters. The nameless, faceless human beings had gone to work every day anonymously, part of a huge multibillion-dollar financial complex; they emerged from the posters as individuals, whose lives mattered, mattered desperately, to the mothers, fathers, aunts, friends, uncles, wives, grandmothers, brothers, grandfathers, daughters, husbands, sisters, and sons who were missing them so urgently.

As the rain distorted the images on the posters of the missing, the colors bled down the pages and became tears that looked like the grief itself (fig. 3). The complexity of persons and the unity of the communal need to share and grieve together become abundantly clear with these unique cultural expressions. The 9/11 site, covered with missing posters, became a memorial more passionate then the glass and cement fountains and rows of trees that now fill the raw wound of Ground Zero.

New Orleans, my home for the past twenty-five years, brought America not only the searing spectacle of people in the Superdome and the convention center begging for food and water, crying out "We do not live like this" as they demanded human respect, but also scenes of New Orleanians sifting through mold-ruined belongings and indecipherable photographs. The mountain-high detritus of 250,000 homes in New Orleans spoke volumes. Rubble swallowed communities. When people returned to the city in January 2006, a group of middle-class housewives who had never been activists set to work establishing what they called the Katrina Krewe.

At first the Katrina Krewe simply put out flyers asking people to come out and help clean up a particular street or area. Soon New Orleans realized with shock and deep respect that when these women said "clean up," they were serious. They rented dump trucks, and each weekend, along with hundreds of volunteers, they picked up piles of fallen trees, trash, the insides of moldy houses, and the mountains of garbage of the drowned city. They cleaned up whole city blocks, while the politicians sat as if paralyzed, doing little. The work of the Katrina Krewe, like that of rubble cleanup crews everywhere, is heroic, but the work is endless.

FIGURE 3
"America Weeps," from the traveling exhibit *Missing: Last Seen at the World Trade Center on September 11, 2001.* (Photograph © 2001 Bronston Jones)

It is not surprising that in 2008 Barack Obama, an African American man, and Hillary Clinton, a woman, were competing for the position of head janitor, the chief cleanup person, of a crumbling America. This kind of work is never completed. Americans have relegated the rubble of a wasteful and violent nation to a liminal space for slaves, maids, janitors, housewives, garbage collectors, and "illegal aliens" to clean up. Beyond the obvious inequity of this job description is the assumption that cleanup, preservation, and rebuilding are the backbone of a strong nation and a strong democracy. However, if people are kept busy cleaning up, they will have little time to think or create or, recalling Berlin's words, to shout their anger from the rooftops.

Years after Katrina, the house is not fully rebuilt, the people have not become fully visible, and the way to avoid rubble worlds has not been found. Rubble

FIGURE 4
Quadrant marks on a home in the Faubourg Marigny neighborhood, New Orleans, 2005. (Photograph © 2005 Cynthia Scott)

worlds make rubble out of people. Rubble worlds demand inhumane and horrendous sacrifice from cleanup crews. But after Katrina a much more exciting phenomenon emerged from the rubble. In New Orleans the maggot-infested, mold-ravished refrigerators that had been sitting in 100-degree heat for more than a month lined the streets. People started writing messages on the tabula rasa of the big blank white sides. The refrigerator art form was, surprisingly, humorous, usually with a political twist; refrigerators had painted on them "Levee Board Victim," and "Rotten 2 the Corps," or they were made to look like snowmen or monsters. People who had never been seen or heard were making themselves known for the first time.

The refrigerators eased the pain of a much more disturbing graphic inscription. When first responders arrived, they went from house to house and hastily painted *X*'s on the wooden walls of New Orleans homes, telling the world that they had come on a specific date, checked the houses for the dead, and left. These four-quadrant *X*'s were the signature script of Katrina (fig. 4). The marks in the quadrants indicated who had inspected the house; the date of the inspection;

dangers, such as gas leaks; and whether there were corpses in the house. The information in these large *X*'s had a devastating impact. The notation "1 dead" in the bottom quadrant left an indelible mark on the human psyche, an unforgettable and unforgivable one for those whose loved ones the first responders had found.

As often as not, art appears in the spaces between the broken rocks and not necessarily in or from the rubble itself. Cleanup crews in cities throughout the world have become sick with dust and smoke and mold.[18] Broken shards, cracked houses, and barren fields do not feed or house or fulfill people. The neck-high weeds growing in the cracks of hundreds of matching steps that once led to homes in New Orleans's Ninth Ward are haunting, but they are also a script that tells the story of the disaster in vivid detail. A *New York Times* article from 21 March 2012 documents the saplings and grasses winning out over civilization in the Ninth Ward. The weeds in the Ninth Ward, in what was once a thriving community, are not wanted. They are home to all kinds of creatures and do not create a livable environment for humans. They are full of snakes, rats, angry abandoned Rottweilers, rabbits, egrets, pelicans, armadillos, coyotes, owls, hawks, falcons, and even a four-foot-long alligator.[19]

The Ninth Ward recovery is a microcosm of a rudderless democratic community in action. Well-organized grass-roots organizations like Common Ground and hundreds of others, generous acts of philanthropy, and individual acts of bravery, rebuilding, and sweat equity juxtaposed with governmental corruption, individual madness, and crime reveal a society struggling between devolving into chaos and anarchy and evolving through imaginative change. It is important not to romanticize either the rubble or the excessively verdant semitropical New Orleans, but we can find a path through the thicket if we celebrate a symbiotic relationship between the two and find in nature the model for an acceptance of change and multiplicity, the biodiversity that human democratic community can achieve. While living in this overgrown environment is difficult, the relentless force of nature growing and filling in the gaps might have something to teach us. Citizen artists are not, nor would they necessarily want to be, repair people, taking the shards of the broken and making them whole again. There is no whole, and there never was. No exhibition, no apology, can keep these atrocities from happening again.

Although it is tempting from a theoretical perspective to reclaim rubble as the welcomed fragments of a crumbled oppressive regime, conceptually rubble is different from fragments. Rubble overwhelms civilization, while the juxtaposition of various fragments can provide citizens with the scraps to piece together mosaic- or quilt-style subversive art. Walter Benjamin comments that "the destructive character" will get rid of rubble or the remains of past ideologies to make room for "the way leading through it."[20] This is potentially positive or negative.

In a more metaphoric moment, Benjamin tries to recoup the word *shatter:*

> Anyone who has climbed a mountain on his own and arrived at the top exhausted, then turns to walk down again with steps that shatter his entire body—for such a person, time hangs loose, the partition walls inside him collapse, and he pushes on through the rubble of the moment as if in a dream. Sometimes he tries to stop, but cannot. Who knows whether it is his thoughts that shatter him, or the roughness of the way? His body has become a kaleidoscope that at each step presents him with ever-changing figures of the truth.[21]

The phrase "ever-changing figures of the truth" gives way to a kaleidoscope of possibility—the most optimistic way to approach both the word *shatter* and, by extension, *rubble.* Rubble has the potential to renew, but there is the equally strong likelihood of its overwhelming and actually shattering the human spirit and body. Rather than simply clearing away the rubble to make a new path, the citizen artist can reignite the shattered moment through the visceral gesture of weaving the intricate embodied details of human loss into enlivened biomorphic forms. In this case the artist energizes the human gesture rather than the pile of rubble. The man walking down the mountain actually experiences the reawakening of his body in a way that will not permit him to dwell only on the pain of the moment, but oddly enough it is the pain that exhilarates.

As the writers in David Eng's *Loss* suggest, trauma might not just be loss in need of mourning but loss itself, in want of attention. Eng contends that we do not have to assume that melancholia is pathological or even negative; instead we can understand the "insistently creative and deeply political" nature of loss. Melancholia is active, embodied.[22] One knows one is alive because one experiences the pain of loss. The propagandistic image of nation, dependent on covering up the pain of diverse moments of ethnic cleansing, a fortress of trauma "undimmed by human tears," encases and paralyzes democratic action. As Fred Moten suggests in his article on Emmett Till, "Black Mo'nin'," "when the mourning begins, or when the morning begins," or when, as he extrapolates it, "the mo'nin begins," there is "a New Word. New World." At this point democracy may emerge.[23]

The call and response, the mother's loving eye, the quiet murmurings of recognition, all enliven the first stuttered utterances. In her book *Against the Un-*

speakable, Naomi Mandel argues for rethinking the notion of an atrocity that destroys our ability to speak. Mandel maintains that when we locate an event or action in the realm of the unspeakable, "we are defining this action as 'inhuman' and hence as inaccessible to human understanding, external to the speech community that forms human culture."[24] Since a human being committed the crime and a human being experienced the assault, such marginalization diminishes our capacity for empathetic response and communing. As the fragments lie before them, artists draw threads of connection to piece them together: not to turn them into a whole but rather to create a meshwork of communal sanity.

Every American artist is inherently a member of a wounded community; those artists with any human empathy will find themselves grappling with cultural wounds. The contraction, the gasp and keening at the mutilated body of the fourteen-year-old Emmett Till, or the raised skin from the master's lash will reverberate in the citizens of this nation for generations, making any fully embodied artistic expression impossible that does not include this long-held, shattered cry of anguish. Truly transformative art calls itself into being out of the mourning, out of the loss.

In the summer of 2008, three years after Katrina, the British graffiti artist known as Banksy did a "hit" on New Orleans. Banksy came in the dark and painted at least twelve images on the walls of buildings in New Orleans. Banksy's images—drawings in blacks and grays of Lincoln pushing a shopping cart (fig. 5); a small girl with an umbrella that catches the rain so that it rains only on her; a young boy on a life-preserver swing; and a young boy flying a refrigerator kite—form a language of resistance. Banksy's graphic drawings each have a twist; they are political, touch the strings of New Orleanians' hearts, bring commentary to a broken city, and reflect mirror-sharp shards back from the drowned consciousness of New Orleans. From the fall of 2011 to the spring of 2012 in New Orleans, the artists Delaney Martin, Theo Eliwezer, and Swoon collaborated to create a group of musical houses called Dithyrambalina, where sound and image come together to revitalize the New Orleans community. Participants could literally "play" the different houses at the site by doing such things as stepping on floorboards connected to organ pipes.

In silent conversation with the musical houses, Swoon covered the old boards and fences around the houses with intricate stenciled paper cutouts (fig. 6). Swoon's art epitomizes visceral graphism by bringing bodies, souls, and a neighborhood to life in intricate filigree detail. No longer just rubble, New Orleans houses come alive and sing their odd, not-rubble songs. The overnight fragility

FIGURE 5
Abraham Lincoln, by Banksy, New Orleans, 2008.
(Photograph courtesy of Banksy.co.uk 2008/2011)

of this democratic act, of these masked bandits drawing faces on walls in a night adventure, transformed New Orleans for a moment. And when a man sprayed gray paint over Banksy's postmodern Leonardo da Vincis, the citizens felt deeply saddened. But the spark caught how many fires? And how many revolutions? Saved how many lives from the dreary? For a moment New Orleans was not a traumatized city, not a rubble city, but a living city.

Everyone remarked how wonderful it was to see the Mardi Gras Indians return after Katrina, dressed in the most pretty of pretty, but few understood the painstaking hours of labor that went into buying and salvaging beads, resewing, reweaving, reimagining wholeness out of rubble. That act was not an act of simple bravery, although it was that, or cultural renewal but an act of self-salvation and communal bonding. The thread and beads bound together to mend a tattered family and a root culture. The Mardi Gras Indians' intricately, laboriously beaded suits kept a cultural continuity, sanity, and resilience. The act of beading the tiny beads, in hundreds of colors, for hours and hours, sewing the thread that spoke from one generation to the next the code of survival, was a visceral and

FIGURE 6

Thalassa, by Swoon in collaboration with New Orleans Airlift. Paper stencils on the fence surrounding the Dithyrambalina Music House, New Orleans, 2012. (© Swoon; photograph by Rebecca Mark)

revolutionary act. As the Mardi Gras Indians walked through the blasted-out streets and past the fallen houses they signified life, pretty life, mending the catastrophic, murderous insult of a government that had forgotten how to save its own people. The nation-state had failed. The beads, full of stories, began to call out again. They did not fail.

In the Louisiana film *Beasts of the Southern Wild,* by Behn Zietlin and Lucy Alibar, the main character, Hushpuppy, finds coherence by listening to the coded voices of the beasts and by inscribing her own longing for her mother, for a cohesive community in her bayou town of Bathtub, with her black crayon on the tabula rasa of her sheets, boxes, the blank walls, and empty spaces in her room. Hushpuppy's graphic drawings mark this one little girl, the lowest person on the food chain, lower even than the crawdaddies she loves to suck on, as important, human, and alive—worthy of study by the archaeologists she hopes will discover her drawings one day.

In *Beasts,* the director finds the visual and spatial skin of the world as interesting and informative as the temporal narrative. The squirming crawfish, the hide of the alligator, the cave-drawing tattoo on the teacher's leg, the mark on Hushpuppy's mother's cheek, the upside-down letters on the walls made out of signs, the pointed porcupine sticks covering the roof of the new camp—all are examples of an alternative script that is as significant to read as the narrative of a dying, alcoholic, loving yet intense father trying to train his little daughter to "be the man," to survive after he dies. Cruel levees isolate the people of Bathtub and leave them exposed, and a terrible storm threatens to destroy them, but the visceral script marks the lives of the residents of Bathtub as visible and alive.

In both New York and New Orleans subjectivity shifts, so that the one who has been previously muted and erased becomes the agent, telling the story. The people created such an explosion of dissent in the form of unsettling art that it will take lifetimes to sift through all the images, found poetry, graphic inscriptions, music, and performances that have spilled out from every home and voice in these two wounded cities. Rubble does not just destroy monumentalism and consumer culture; it threatens to destroy community and participatory democracy. Turning one's head to find a model for renewal in the flyers and refrigerator art and in the texture of an alligator's hide is the most powerful turn of perspective anyone can make.

"We Hold These Truths to Be Self-Evident"

In America we think of nation and democracy as one and the same, but they are historically antithetical. Freedom from England, cloaked in the rhetoric of democratic self-representation, did not allow suffrage for most of the people living in the new republic. *Democracy* may be a noun, but to be a vital force democracy must depend on the constant movement of people. It only functions as a verb. Democracy is not synonymous with a nation-state, a description of a thing, but a constantly shifting hopeful possibility, dependent on an imaginative rhetorical response, an erotic gathering at every moment of its becoming.

That our "forefathers"—Benjamin Franklin and Thomas Jefferson, in particular—against their own self-interest wrote the words, "We hold these truths to be self-evident, that all men are created equal, that they are endowed by their Creator with certain unalienable Rights, that among these are Life, Liberty, and the Pursuit of Happiness" in the documents of state formation, the Declaration of Independence and the Constitution, proves that on some level they welcomed the dance between nation and democracy. These words indicate that they held on to the visionary possibility of a government of branches that could grow and transform and react to the complexities of historical circumstance. They believed, even if they did not always act like it, in a fluid form of government that could protect all the people of this country from despotism. While a nation may need a backbone, a democracy needs that backbone to be flexible and capable of movement.

Of course the two dreams, of equality for all and of individual liberty, are inherently irreconcilable. In the political realm, the tension between freedom and equality is at once productive and divisive, the source of everything, from the two houses of Congress to the Electoral College. In the cultural sphere, the tension is more interesting. The tension between equality and freedom is at the heart of the work of such iconic writers as Herman Melville, Nathaniel Hawthorne, Walt Whitman, Emily Dickinson, Maxine Hong Kingston, and Toni Morrison. As these writers struggle with the contested space of equality and freedom, they push language through metaphor and metonymy beyond the realm of the known. And like the graffiti artists, they find themselves necessarily creating hieroglyphic graphic texts—Morrison's scarred chokecherry tree, Kingston's scrolled woman warrior, Whitman's leaves of grass, Hawthorne's letter *A,* Melville's tattooed Queequeg, the scratched entry in Caruthers's Bible in William Faulkner's "The Bear," the cracked ice in *Uncle Tom's Cabin,* the scribbling of the pencil legs of Magda in Cynthia Ozick's *The Shawl,* and so on.

What cannot yet be spoken appears not in written form, not in actual words, but in the inscriptions of graphism. Biomorphic and visceral graphic inscriptions are the visible markings of the groups and individuals demanding to exist. These graphic excesses do not remain on the margins or in any preconceived liminal space but disrupt and infect the dominant texts and narratives themselves. The French philosopher Jacques Rancière affirms that democracy is an aesthetic as well as a political movement. What he calls the "police" or the "law" "implicitly separates those who take part from those who are excluded, and it therefore presupposes a prior aesthetic division between the visible and the invisible, the audible and inaudible, the sayable and the unsayable." Change occurs when "the reigning configuration between perception and meaning is disrupted by those elements, groups or individuals in society that demand not only to exist but indeed to be perceived."[25] Since visibility and audibility are everything, those who are not visible and audible must constantly bang on the gates to make themselves seen and heard. Democracy in Rancière's world is never an accomplished fact, but necessarily the aesthetic act of reconfiguring the conditions of sense perception. The graffiti letters on the unofficial freedom train reconfigure the conditions of sense perception but perhaps do not go far enough. Though they break out of known forms, they do not quite embrace the regenerative patterns of biomorphic and embodied art that other artists envision.

If democracy is based on a fragile tension between the competing desires of freedom and equality, then citizens must constantly weave the thread that keeps this tension alive. If we entertain the idea that a strong democracy comes not from an incessant focus on monuments or the rubble of their remains but from a focus on the complex membranes connecting human beings with one another and with the ecosystem, then cleanup and even dismantling old structures becomes less interesting. The graphic excesses that we might belittle as only decoration, embroidery, embellishment, and ornamentation are in reality much more interesting. If a little girl draws her longings on her bed sheets with a crayon, if the rain marks missing posters with streaked tears, and leaves of grass pierce up through the rubble, and clouds find their mirrors in skyscrapers, they draw a radically different map for rebuilding society than the theoretical concepts of either deconstruction or reconstruction allow.

The biomorphic and visceral script that can mend American democracy has no cleanup crew, no margins, no center, and it is not inherently peripheral. It is not a pile of rubble. It is not a mosaic made up of the broken pieces. It is not modern or exactly postmodern, not in many ways part of the trajectory of narrative ideology at all, but presents itself instead as constantly growing tendrils that alter the structure of the whole. These markings demand an alternative way of reading the script of the world. When, as in *Beasts of the Southern Wild,* leaves speak, cooking oil floats and glows, sparklers light up the world, the text of American democracy is infinitely liberated.

The map of democratic regeneration does not take monuments, founding fathers, the violence or the rubble they create, or the liminal space of the margins as the starting point of its imaginative reach. True democracy is a constantly shifting map of moving selves, cells reaching up, branching, reaching down, rooting, forking, splitting, diverging, converging in rhizomic multiplicity and diversity to allow visibility and equality for all. True democracy is a meshwork of connecting and disconnecting cells and can be found in the hidden traces and graphic texts that speak to us from the multiple cultures, places, and people that make up the long history of American democracy.

The three-dimensional map we will learn to trace follows democracy in its deepest graphic expression, a gathering of spirit in which no thing is less than another. To understand the graphic script at the core of this book, a script that contains the DNA of democracy, one has to imagine each human being, each plant, each blade of grass, each root in a community as linked with others by connective tissue. A self that can move freely between "I" and "we" bridges the poles of equality and freedom. The intricate and intensely personal response, the visible and detailed imaginative expression of each and every self in a democratic society, is the clearest antidote to despotism and its rubble excess.

The violent acts of humans against other humans and against nature have reduced their national monuments, parks, and houses to rubble, but they have never destroyed the fabric that connects humans to one another in community, and humans to the environment. Rubble, the crumbled remains of a civilized society, creates the garbled cells left scattered in incoherent mayhem from the most violent assaults on the land and human community. Rubble is the rambling incoherent madness inscribed onto people's homes and imagination. But at each moment, when civilization descends into the anarchy and insanity of rubble, an equally powerful human creative response contains the coherent message of renewal.

It is not the purpose of this book to list, as so many have already done, the thousands of atrocities committed in the name of the American nation.[26] Cultural critics such as Ed White, Carroll Smith Rosenberg, and Richard Sherkina have been exposing alternative American histories for years.[27] This book is not about graffiti, or 9/11, or Hurricane Katrina. It is about the language of visceral and biomorphic graphic inscription that citizen artists have sustained through every moment of reifying national history. These markings do not replace or in any way reduce the remarkable textual and rhetorical contributions of First Nation peoples, enslaved Africans, or women of all ethnicities, classes, and cultures, but they do express values, insights, and experiences that could never be expressed in the more conventional forms of the written book or even in the rhetoric of the spoken word. At the same time, artists have incorporated examples of visceral graphism in all of these forms.

This is a book about turning away from imposing monuments and mythical tales of state origin and looking instead at the hidden traces that emerge as each citizen's longing to be heard pushes the boundaries of linguistic inscription. The soul and heart and body, all in motion toward freedom, leave an imprint on the terrain and time. The tattoo of human liberation is impassioned, embodied, material, and complex. This is a book about learning to decipher and value the delicate, nonalphabetic graphic record carved into American memory. These scripts, in their complex diversity and regenerative insistence, create a counternarrative to the broad strokes of ersatz national history and in doing so dissolve the often deadly hallucination Americans call national memory.

In the town square of this book, the wailing wall, the dance of its question, the unannounced poem, the blues for America, there is a breath of life in the fields of forgotten and dry bones and in the markings left on the trees. Like Fred D'Aguiar's *Feeding the Ghosts,* this book invites the enslaved African bodies stored in the hulls of ships and thrown overboard when the cargo became too expensive, the millions of native bodies killed by disease and greed, the lynched bodies thrown into the rivers, the Chinese bodies worked to death in building the railroads, the Cherokee bodies frozen in the march west, the bodies hung from trees, the bodies left in shallow graves, the bodies beaten beyond recognition, the bodies laboring on long lines of railroad ties, the women raped and murdered for being women, the settlers' bodies starved to death in founding the nation of America, those who died from black lung disease in the mines, explosives in the wars, hunger in the cities, to speak up and join the living and invites all the living to learn to hear and see the marks of their presence.

1

A RIDDLE TO UNFOLD

> And this tattooing had been the work of a departed prophet and seer of his island, who, by those hieroglyphic marks, had written out on his body a complete theory of the heavens and the earth, and a mystical treatise on the art of attaining truth; so that Queequeg in his own proper person was a riddle to unfold; but whose mysteries not even himself could read. And these mysteries were therefore destined in the end to molder away with the living parchment whereon they were inscribed, and so be unsolved to the last.—HERMAN MELVILLE, *Moby-Dick*

The *Frieze of American History*

Tourists standing today in the Capitol Rotunda in Washington, DC, can look up at a painting on the ceiling of the dome called the *Apotheosis of Washington,* by Constantino Brumidi. The painting portrays George Washington in military regalia, with a purple throw draped over his legs, floating in heavenly ether, surrounded by semiclothed women representing the thirteen states.[1] In this mural the "father of our country" appears as a rather effeminate old man ascending to the heavens. The *Apotheosis* forces tour guides at the Capitol to gaze up to the eye of the dome and talk about George Washington not as a person but as a surrogate, godlike figure standing in for the republic itself.

Few visitors actually notice Brumidi's *Frieze of American History,* which circles the dome below the *Apotheosis,* beneath a row of windows. Painted with a technique that allowed the skilled Italian painter to create the "illusion of three-dimensional forms and figures on flat walls,"[2] the frieze, three hundred feet in length, tells the story of the conquest and colonization of America. Each panel, measuring eight by four feet, honors either a dubious hero of European occupation, specifically Christopher Columbus, Hernando Cortez, John Smith, and Hernando de Soto, or a nation-building moment of American history, such as the signing of the Declaration of Independence and Cornwallis's surrender to George Washington in 1781. In each panel the eyes of the European colonialist, whether Spanish or English, are turned to the heavens. They never look directly at the native peoples,[3] who stand with their eyes cast down.[4]

One moment of the *Frieze* would still the hearts of young people now learning about Columbus's murder of thousands of Taino people. It is quite clearly a monument to European colonization and occupation. And it is not just First Peoples that the *Frieze* colonizes; it expunges the forced enslavement of African peoples to such a degree that African Americans are simply invisible in this account of American history. The artists who finished the frieze over the years chose to represent neither Lincoln nor the signing of the Emancipation Proclamation as iconic history. In an odd visual and metaphoric twist, the human bodies in the grisaille frieze stand out in bright white against an earthy brown background. The three-dimensionality is indeed an illusion; the frieze becomes a facade for a one-dimensional celebration of European and American conquest.

Brumidi painted the *Apotheosis* in 1865, and he worked on the *Frieze* from 1877 until his death in 1879. It was a period of increasing attention to historic preservation in the United States. The preservation movement had taken off soon after George Washington's death in 1799. The most famous preservationists, pioneers of the idea of patriotic preservation itself, are the Mount Vernon Ladies. Their association, founded in 1853, and the Association for the Preservation of Virginia Antiquities, founded in 1889, formulated the intricate concepts of American patriotic memory. The present-day Tea Party, when it follows any specific ideology, takes much of its rhetoric from the nineteenth-century preservationist movement. In fact, the patriotic rhetoric of the United States is so entwined with preservationist ideals that they cannot be extricated from our national identity. On the surface, preservationists simply want to conserve the historically significant structures that define American history, a noble aim. Unfortunately, many of these organizations had and still have strong conservative agendas, desiring to isolate historical memory to include only selective iconic images of an imagined white upper class. And during the nineteenth century, groups based in the South sought to make the country's historical memory that of southern-plantation America.

FIGURE 7
"The Landing of Columbus," by Constantino Brumidi, 1878–80, 8 × 4 ft. *Frieze of American History,* Capitol Rotunda. (Architecture of the Capitol, www.aoc.gov/capitol-hill/art)

Brumidi's *Frieze* provides not a scroll of American history but a map of ersatz American history. The heroes depicted in the frieze cannot, in contemporary America or in anyone's estimation, actually be called heroes. They are, with few exceptions, conquistadors responsible for horrible atrocities. Likewise, the iconic nation-building moments that Brumidi depicts in the frieze hide, in almost every case, the bodies, screams, cries, tears, and blood of those trampled as the "heroes" appropriated the field. In the panel entitled "The Landing of Columbus," the Native American figures are stiff, leaning backwards and staring straight ahead, showing no struggle to gain the victory as the curtain of iconic memorializing closes over the moment (fig. 7).

After Brumidi's death in 1880, the artist Filippo Costaggini took over the sculpting of the *Frieze.* In his sculptures we begin to see the tension of bodies moving and in combat with other bodies. Both Brumidi and Costaggini worked on the panel "William Penn and the Indians," which depicts William Penn signing the treaty of Shackamaxon with the Delaware Indians. The artists appear to have depicted some of the Delawares, or Lenapes, in this scene with complex emotions. Silenced and previously invisible people peer out from behind the frozen icons. In the later part of the nineteenth century, Costaggini in "The Death of Tecumseh" (fig. 8) portrayed the Shawnee people as visibly fighting back.

However, when the painter Allyn Cox inherited the last of the project in 1951, suddenly the figures were entirely white men. There are no actual historical women in the *Frieze,* only symbolic figures. In the last few panels, Cox sculpted the Europeans in catatonic, memorialized poses with no gestural movement. The panel "Peace at the End of the Civil War" is the worst example of these severe,

FIGURE 8
"The Death of Tecumseh," by Filippo Constaggini, 1880–89, 8 × 4 ft. *Frieze of American History,* Capitol Rotunda. (Architecture of the Capitol, www.aoc.gov/capitol-hill/art)

immovable statues (fig. 9). In this 1950s rendition of American history it looks as if the artist was afraid that if he did not present the most controlled image of the Civil War possible, the hidden, dead, and bloody corpses and the marching-to-freedom ex-slaves, not to mention the lynching victims of the 1930s, '40s, and '50s, would emerge en masse from the background. The empty background is more interesting than the paralytic foreground.

Visible Means of Support

When the contemporary artist Kerry James Marshall painted *Visible Means of Support: Mount Vernon* and *Visible Means of Support: Monticello,* two murals each measuring twenty-seven by thirty-two feet, for the San Francisco Museum of Modern Art, he negotiated the conflicting scripts of monumental America and visceral and biomorphic graphism (figs. 10 and 11). The large-scale murals are a perfect answer to the monumentalism of the *Frieze of American History.* The installation of the two *Visible Means of Support* murals, which filled the many-storied foyer of the San Francisco Museum of Modern Art from 6 February 2009 to 11 October 2011, reimagined the Mount Vernon estate and Monticello as puzzles with mazes, hidden figures of enslaved peoples of African descent, and odd, mirror-distorted George Washington and Thomas Jefferson cartoons. The Jefferson and Washington bobble heads, with small, thin bodies and big pinched heads, are cutout figures that literally need a "visible means of support." Their support comes quite blatantly from the hundreds of African American people surrounding them.[5]

FIGURE 9
"Peace at the End of the Civil War," by Allyn Cox, 1951–53, 8 × 4 ft. *Frieze of American History,* Capitol Rotunda. (Architecture of the Capitol, www.aoc.gov/capitol-hill/art)

In the murals, Jefferson and Washington stand over larger-than-life shadow images of darkly painted African Americans looking up at them from the ground. Because Marshall portrays Jefferson and Washington as so insubstantial, they cast no shadow of their own. In some mock-ups for the Mount Vernon mural, Washington is stepping on the neck of an African American figure, visually cutting his head off from his thin, snakelike body. However, the twisted body is not destroyed but instead disappears mysteriously into the maze of the garden. The shadow, an African American head, is much larger and more detailed than George Washington's bobble head.

Peoples of African descent appear everywhere in the murals, particularly in the trees, the gardens, and the water. They stare up at Washington from behind a hill like soldiers ready for action or enslaved people ready to revolt. Geometric swimmers float in the waves of the Potomac River alongside a transatlantic slave trade schooner, representing not only those enslaved people of African descent thrown overboard to certain death but also those fully clothed and

FIGURE 10
Visible Means of Support: Monticello, by Kerry James Marshall, 2009. Mural installation at the San Francisco Museum of Modern Art, 6 February 2009–11 October 2011. (San Francisco Museum of Modern Art, collection of the artist; © Kerry James Marshall)

active people swimming toward freedom. These figures insert themselves into the sight lines of the viewer, demanding visibility. Marshall includes in the murals an image for every known enslaved African on the Monticello and Mount Vernon plantations.

The cryptic series of dots on the front lawns of both Mount Vernon and Monticello at first just look like black dots but turn out to be silhouettes of African American heads. A map of the world with a mammy figure at the center occupies the circular drive in front of the Mount Vernon mansion. The geometric swimmers, the mazelike gardens, and the silhouettes at Monticello, which form a visceral graphic, connect-the-dots pattern, challenge the dominant narrative by making visible the hidden traces of the enslaved people of Virginia.

FIGURE 11

Visible Means of Support: Mount Vernon, by Kerry James Marshall, 2009. Mural installation at the San Francisco Museum of Modern Art, 6 February 2009–11 October 2011. (San Francisco Museum of Modern Art, collection of the artist; © Kerry James Marshall)

Marshall stated that he wanted African American figures to appear in "expected" and "unexpected" places throughout the landscapes. He points out that he references childlike flowers, coloring-book-style mazes, and connect-the-dots puzzles for many reasons: "I am interested in making visible things that are not visible, and when you're having fun recovering some of the mysteries of history as well as solving some of the mysteries of visuality, then I think you have these two different levels in which you can engage with the work."[6] Marshall's people of African descent, hidden in plain view, become not just hieroglyphs, puzzles, and riddles but visible reminders of what has been left out of the story.[7] Marshall defies Rancière's "police," who regulate the "aesthetic division between the visible and the invisible."[8]

Like Marshall's Jefferson and Washington bobble-head figures, the ersatz founding fathers of America loom large and cartoonlike in the foreground of American history, while the scrolled bodies are hidden by the land and trees, the mazelike path of an American democracy for and by the people. Trees and the whole biomorphic environment are not simply convenient places to hide the heads of enslaved Africans; they are part of the missing story. As the script of American democracy expands, it embraces all life forms in a truly limitless inclusivity. In Marshall's murals the natural world modulates the dominance of man-made stories and abstract written narratives.

Alphabets, Voices, and Scripts: A Mute Voice from on High

It is no accident that Marshall is able to create a more radical critique of the founding-fathers myth with dots, lines, and mazes than others have achieved without the use of visceral graphism. Marshall employs the power of language that is not bound to the voice. Marshall's murals present a script, but it is not a script with an alphabet. In *The Darker Side of the Renaissance,* Walter Mignolo writes extensively on the colonization of memory by those who possessed alphabetic scripts. According to Mignolo, the bookmaking explosion of the Renaissance solidified remembering through alphabetic writing, allowing the European community to marginalize cultures that had nonalphabetic or ideogrammatic graphic systems, for "people without letters were thought of as people without history."[9] The alphabet also let writers create abstract ideas disconnected from land, body, and emotion. In so doing, these abstract writings could justify genocide and domination in the name of God.

When voice and graphic sign maintain their independence, they communicate vast amounts of information that exist outside dominant ideologies or nationally sanctified scripts. The voice and the graphic mark provide a link to experience that may never be expressible in alphabetic writing or narrative. Mignolo suggests that "the links between speech and writing are not necessary."[10] I would say that while they are practical and useful, they are not the only means of communication. Gilles Deleuze and Félix Guattari argue that when graphism depends on the voice, it "induces a mute voice from on high or from the beyond, a voice that begins to depend on graphism." As graphism and the voice become inextricably linked they take on a despotic power separate from human experience. Deleuze and Guattari suggest that when, through alphabetic writing, we chain voice to word, we lose the autonomous power of both.[11] Voice alone is transformative, oral, musical, and soaring. Graphic inscription freed from direct equivalency can express visual metaphors that go beyond vocal equivalencies and inscribed narrative meanings. By extension, gestural strokes of the hand, tongue, and foot express the markings of the human community in inventive ways. Dance notation is a graphic record of this gestural expression. The "mute voice from on high," on the other hand, is disconnected from body, heart, and gesture; consequently, it is the source of ersatz mythmaking.

Taking Mignolo's and others' work further, moving beyond the ideograms and hieroglyphic texts that Mignolo, Elizabeth Boone, Robert Farris Thompson, and many others explore, it is important to include markings coded as writing that might not initially appear to be so. During despotic and genocidal moments in American history, these cultural scripts often reconnect humans to their otherwise vacated bodies and blasted environments. The embodied joining of these scripts ensures that the mute voice from on high does not direct the communication. I am primarily interested in texts that are themselves biomorphic in form, expanding in branchlike or cellular patterns to create a map of biological regeneration.

From this perspective, such artifacts as Jamestown maps, the wampum belts of the Six Nations Confederacy, and the tracks of enslaved people appear as the significant cultural contributions that they are. When read as texts, these "marks" represent a field of graphic inscription that has no known alphabets but can be recognized as "writing" and represents the voices born out of the anger, grief, rage, joy, and elation of one human being reaching out to another across a field of skeletons, outside of time. Because these "writings" source the unappeased ghosts, they exist as demarcations of survival. They are encoded as a call waiting for a response.

Visceral and biomorphic graphism resists dominant ideologies by maintaining independence from voice, but unlike other forms of disconnected graphism, visceral graphism does not engage in a degenerative turn; it inherently generates new meaning.[12] Visceral graphism extends André Masson's slightly overexcited sense of "automatic drawing." Automatic writing can proceed too quickly from hand to paper for there to be awareness, embodiment, or new information (fig. 12). Visceral graphism flows directly from the passionate human need to create in the face of devastation and moves more slowly into form. Hushpuppy in *Beasts of the Southern Wild* holds on to her black crayon markings as a lifeline to sanity in a world that has quite literally been turned upside down by government neglect,

FIGURE 12
Automatic Drawing, by André Masson, 1924. Ink on paper, 9¼ × 8⅛ in. (Museum of Modern Art, New York; © 2013 Artists Rights Society [ARS], New York/ADAGP, Paris; image © Museum of Modern Art/Licensed by SCALA/Art Resource, NY)

illness, and relentless storms. As we begin to read and invite visceral graphism into our textual experience, what Barthes calls "resistance to meaning" becomes found meaning. Barthes embraces the regenerative potentiality of graphic markings when he writes that "the letter, its graphic materiality, then becomes an irreducible ideality, linked to the deepest experiences of humanity."[13]

Because the ice pattern on the window will not become the simulation of a Christmas day, seeing the ice pattern as a biomorphic visceral graphic inscription allows us to resist the ersatz story and enter the impossibly complex "meshwork" experience of ice crystal itself. By letting both the graphic mark and the voice dissolve and resolve into forms that we do not recognize as letters or words but can experience as writing, the human imagination frees itself from established narratives. The intricate embellishment of visceral graphism fills in part of the torn or never realized weave of democracy, making a healthy, ethnically diverse, democratic America at least a remote possibility. Kerry James Marshall's *Visible Means of Support* murals invite us to embrace the full regenerative nature of visceral graphism and unsettling art, returning us by way of the most gentle but devastating imagery to the site of the worst of American history. Reading slavery through winding mazes and hidden pictures opens up the past. Marshall adds humor, curiosity, and inquiry to what would otherwise be a paralyzed and traumatic history.

My focus on extraliterary texts is not an attempt to link First Nation peoples, African Americans, or any other people to "illiterate" or inarticulate markings. There were hundreds of conventionally literate people who wrote eloquently in recognizable European alphabets about genocide and oppression. There were hundreds of speakers of multiple ethnic origins whose rhetorical strategies are still models for contemporary elocution. I focus in this book on texts that could not appear in any other form than the extraliterary because what they must express in order to survive has a creative structure that demands a radical departure from dominate narrative or even alphabetic form. I address established conversations on graphism (Deleuze, Guattari, Derrida, Leroi-Gourhan) and graphic texts (Mignolo, Boone, Anzaldúa, Salvaggio, Robert Farris Thompson)[14] that explore alternative discourses as theoretically necessary means of marking democratic historical memory.

The self and therefore the art that flourishes in order to create a healthy democratic community, an always active energetic field between equality and freedom, is radically different from the self or art that exists to expand its realm of influence. In order to thrive in a democratic community, a self must be inextricably woven with the other members in an active interchange rather than a static vertical field of domination. Freedom does not mean being free *from* human community but *within* human community.

From Ersatz History to Wampum Belts

The monumentalism of the *Frieze of American History* derives from preservationists' need to see national identity not as the reality of diverse groups of people living in diverse cultures with diverse resources but as a fantasy of the white psyche. Sameness is never more than a hallucinated characteristic of America identity. In fact, the difference between the fantasy of the white psyche and America is the difference between a faux national identity and a living democracy. A democracy will, as D. H. Lawrence wrote before anyone had heard of whiteness studies, "hurt" and eventually disintegrate "the white psyche"; Lawrence's "unappeased ghosts"—and I would amend Lawrence's Eurocentric reading to change *ghosts* to the *diversity of living ethnic groups*—will demand representation.[15]

The Daughters of the American Revolution conceptualization of originary, European American identity, more extreme than Brumidi's already whitewashed frieze, is ersatz history. Ersatz history skips from Pocahontas to the Declaration of Independence with not so much as a worried or fearful glance at the debris left behind. The nation builders needed America to be constantly "new" in order to hide the history of genocide.[16] An America defined by its absolute whiteness and newness or its innocence assumes a national lineage sprouted unsullied from dubiously and impossibly white originary European colonialists.[17] But as C. Vann Woodward states, "The conquest of a continent, the dispossession and subjection of its natives, the exploitation of imported African slaves, the imposition of our will on other races and nations abroad, and the establishment of a brief Pax Americana by the world's most powerful nation are not exploits brought off without the incurring of guilt—impressive amounts of it."[18] Lawrence contends that "sometimes snakes can't slough. They can't burst their old skin. Then they go sick and die inside the old skin, and nobody ever sees the new pattern." Only if the white psyche breaks out of its hard skin of exclusion can it become a "soft, damp, butterfly," an American at last.[19]

As a nation Americans remain mesmerized by a fairy-tale story that has little or no relation to what the archival and social historians have uncovered. The twisted legends that have come to stand in for detailed archival histories have left us not actively "writhing" or trying to read Lawrence's new pattern but in a state of rigor mortis. The legends of John Smith and Pocahontas, the hagiography of George Washington as the Father of our Country, and even the adoration of Abraham Lincoln and the signing of the Emancipation Proclamation hold up the shell of a proclaimed white nation without the emerging butterfly of a democratic republic. The concept of American nation that these surrogate histories embrace murders democracy by pretending to preserve it.

An ersatz moment, because it looks back fearfully at its superior and constantly changing original, is a frozen moment, a lifeless story, no one missing person's story and thus no one's human story, nothing more than propaganda, and thus vacant. Ersatz moments are not simply innocent imitations or substitutes but anxious facades that hope that the lie, the falsity, the simplification, will forever be recorded in national memory as the "real." The ersatz moment holds the past enthralled, untouchable. It is literally an uneasy stage act. Ersatz history becomes emblematic in its paralysis. An ersatz moment is known by everyone, literate or illiterate, educated or not, street person, old or young, as it becomes part of the cultural imaginary of a nation-state. In the creation of a religion or a creed or a nation, the frozen imagery, the emblem, becomes real by the fact of its continuous performance as real. The ersatz story of America is the collapse of moving, gestating, creative individual and communal narratives into a single story repeated obsessively.

Nation building in postcolonial historical moments is not inherently genocidal or antidemocratic, as Partha Chatterjee reminds us,[20] but America is not a *post*colonial nation. America may have rejected its British rulers, but it did not reject its European colonialist hard skin. In America, the nation-building process demanded, and still demands, taking ethnic groups and people with vastly different histories and trying to make them "indivisible." An occupying people reliant on killing off native peoples and using slave labor to create a "democratic republic" must produce an ersatz myth of origins. Nationalist myths imbedded in the narratives of such popular-cultural icons as Pocahontas and *Gone with the Wind* quiet human rebellion, tears, and screams, sealing them off in a fantasy so remote and romantic that the moans can barely be heard.

Burying the rotting corpses, collecting the bones in museums, hiding the detritus of the insatiable violent nation-state, does not still the human cries of anger and sorrow that the hallucination of white supremacy at Plymouth Rock and Jamestown let loose on the world, nor does it hide or silence the always inventive and emerging counternarrative encoded on the snakeskin. Those left out of the official history have been creating, wearing, and reading the snakeskin and butterfly wing patterns all along. Discerning the exact contours of the counterfeit identity of ersatz America means learning how to hear and see the verdant scripts and allow them to emerge and speak a detailed, brilliantly original, and psychologically coherent story.

Citizen artists both at the moment of the atrocities and in the act of remembering generate a symbolic world of messages, a nonhierarchical record of longing for community that the grand historical narratives of war, heroes, and politics hide. By embracing the cycle of birth, life, and death rather than being a death-worshipping nation of war buddies, we come closer to the spirit of democracy. When we talk specifically about the patterns of Marshall's maze, we are entering a highly original artistic expression, a graphic trace that inscribes the story of the body liberating itself into regenerative, necessarily biomorphic, necessarily visceral, and inherently democratic visibility. These patterned skins regenerate the always already torn fabric of the American republic. They generate tissue that counteracts the destructive monumentalism and the equally excessive rubble in what can be thought of as the membrane separating the cultural body from dissolution and chaos. Countering the liminal, this cellular membrane fills space, is material, and insists on visibility.

Powhatan's beaded mantle and the rarely heard repetitions of the high-pitched "Hiya" sounds in the contemporary artist Alice Liu's "a.k.a. Pocahontas" dismantle the ersatz Pocahontas myth in ways that archival accounts, essential as they are, cannot. The grandfather masks (erroneously known as False Face masks)[21] carved by this confederacy in healing rituals, and the turbans seen in paintings of George Washington's slaves contain Jacques Rancière's traces open to signification, graphic information about the birth of the nation that challenges the endless repetitions of Washington biographers.

The tracks of the enslaved Africans on the move as they map out trails across the southern farms-turned-battlefields to "free" themselves at Fort Monroe, near Hampton Roads, Virginia, and the Bakongo cosmogram pattern of the ring-shout ritualized dance found on floors of slave cabins and churches in South Carolina and Georgia start to spell out a flexible human agency. These thoroughly researched but often buried stories emerge not as footnotes but as "foot" notes—tapped out, as the feet of so many people seeking freedom hit the ground. Highlighting the agency of these free people through the traces left behind charts the path of liberation more directly than does paying exclusive or primary attention to Civil War battles, Lincoln himself, the Emancipation Proclamation, or even the dead bodies of soldiers killed on Civil War battlefields.

Reading the Branches

Although the metaphoric wilderness and real nature, specifically trees, have appeared as major tropes of American literature, there has been a general resistance, even from such writers as Emerson and Thoreau, to see the trees and rocks for what they really are: trees and rocks. There has been an equal inability to extrapolate from the actual material world, the linguistic allegory of regeneration. In "A Sedimentation of the Mind: Earth Projects" Robert Smithson uses nature as a metaphor for disintegration but not for reintegration. He contends that "the names of minerals and the minerals themselves do not differ from each other, because at the bottom of both the material and the print is the beginning of an abysmal number of fissures. Words and rocks contain a language that follows a syntax of splits and ruptures. Look at any word long enough and you will see it open up into a series of faults, into a terrain of particles each containing its own void."[22]

Smithson asserts that because of this syntax of ruptures, "poetry is always a dying language but never a dead language." Referencing Poe's "Narrative of A. Gordon Pym," Smithson quotes a passage in which Poe writes about discovering chasms and holes in the ground. Smithson argues that Poe's use of these could be called "earth words," and he goes on to suggest that "the shapes of the chasms themselves become 'verbal roots' that spell out the difference between darkness and light."[23] Unfortunately, Smithson is unable to find in the splits and fissures of his words or Poe's the verbal roots that can generate as well as die and in dying regenerate. Instead Smithson focuses only on degeneration.

In Smithson's analyses nature cannot be embraced as nature, a tree as a tree, because it is inherently dangerous. In much of American literature the impending wilderness appears as symbolic of the threatening unknown hovering at the edge of civilization. From the "hideous and desolate wilderness" of William Bradford's early descriptions of the New World[24] to Hawthorne's wilderness on the edge of the Puritan village in *The Scarlet Letter* and his wild garden in "Rappaccini's Daughter," the organic world menaces civilization in these early works of American literature.

The wilderness easily peopled with "savages," the vastness of trees, and woods and trails that led to nowhere all became in American mythography "others" that not only produced real fear but also could be used by those in power to justify colonization, rape, and genocide. The etymology of the word *savage* directly connects to those who live with the trees: "wild, f. *silva* wood, forest."[25] Including both the notion of the uncivilized and its root in the wood or forest, the word *silva* reminds us that those who define *civilized* consider those who live in the woods and forests "savages." The inescapable conflict between the imagined America and the material America defines the story lines of Melville and Hawthorne and the poetic conceits of Dickinson and Whitman. The literal inability to maintain symbolic distance drives on the narrative. The trees and the expansive environment call out for linguistic innovation.

In direct contrast, texts of women writers throughout American literature invite the incursion of the natural world into the too violent, too stifling patriarchal living room. In these literary works the houses and even the characters recede as the land, leaves, and branchings overwhelm; a language of organic form fills the space of the novel.[26] In *The Country of the Pointed Firs,* a "dark clump of juniper" engulfs and protects Mrs. Todd, as well as the small village. In Eudora Welty's "A Curtain of Green," Mrs. Larkin's wild garden takes over: "To a certain extent, she seemed not to seek for order, but to allow an over-flowering, as if she consciously ventured forever a little farther, a little deeper, into her life in the garden."[27] In two stories written by Eudora Welty—"First Love" and the "Wide Net"—the slaughter of trees stands in for the genocide of human beings.

In this larger picture we begin to see not just a link between these particular authors and artists and the tree-trauma-culture matrix but a biomorphic template that ties the ability to express, the freedom of expression itself, to the graphic depiction of organic form. We can see in their insistence on the material immediacy of the thing itself—as it becomes at once metaphor and not metaphor—a morphing between appearance and materiality that ensures historical integration and, even if dangerous and engulfing, a regenerative health for individual and community.

Clyde Connell and William Christenberry: Swamp Songs and the KKK

Clyde Connell's "Swamp Songs" and William Christenberry's sketches and photographs of trees, both direct responses to the KKK lynchings in Louisiana and Alabama from the 1930s to the 1960s, emerge as if holding the metaphoric or DNA code for regenerative reclaiming of democracy after atrocity. It is not an accident that William Christenberry and Clyde Connell enter this unmarked world as they struggle to find meaning in what has become a vacated period of human despair—the segregated American South of the fifties and sixties. It is also no coincidence that these artists turn to a geographic and biomorphic imagined landscape as their culture breaks apart over white supremacist hallucinations.

The very notion of white supremacy is a disassociated "idea," a mute voice from on high, carried out through propaganda that demands a willingness to mangle, murder, hang, beat, gas, and burn the intruding body in a repetitive casting out. In many southern lynchings the mobs of angry supremacists strangled, castrated, disemboweled, shot, and burned African Americans, as if one murdering blow was not enough. The exorcising of the body and of nature from the realm of despotic "idea" demands escalating and repetitive violence. It is inherently anti-body and as such requires replacing materialized writing—the stick scratching in the sand, the chisel on the stone, the painting on the cave wall, the human crying out in the night, the song, the tone of human voice—with a hallucinated idea, a language that severs and silences human cries. The American self, the democratic self, is vacated hanging from the southern trees. Christenberry's Alabama photographs and drawings of churches and steeples—steeples turned Klan hats turned tree branches—reference these lynched African American souls.

Connell made clear that she remembered "with particular horror the lynchings that occasionally occurred in Belcher." In fact, one of her first paintings was of African Americans mourning in a cemetery. Connell had direct experience with KKK lynchings. She recalled her nurse, Susan, taking her on a walk when she was two and wailing a deep "sorrowful sound" after a posse lynched a man in her community of Belcher, Louisiana: "I can't even remember her face, but I remember those sounds and her mourning. I knew she was sad by her singing and chanting. Those sounds are where I want my art to come from."[28] While we would certainly wish Connell could remember her nurse's face, her identity was not erased, for Connell's understanding of the depth of Susan's mourning followed her for the rest of her life. The words "where I want my art to come from" are powerful, as they demand a source, and a lifeline from that source to Connell's art. Connell lived from the time she was sixty to the end of her life, at ninety-seven, in a house overlooking Lake Bistineau, where the trees and swamp vegetation overwhelmed human habitation or intercourse. There she found an open space in which to sing her mourning song of the swamp. For Connell, the trees and the vegetation and sounds of the swamp provided the material for transforming these mourning sounds into art.

At the 2004 "Unsettling Memories" conference, in Jackson, Mississippi, William Christenberry exhibited his Ku Klux Klan drawings and some of his KKK installation "dolls." The "dolls" are often faceless and expressionless but recognizable as KKK representations. The drawings include clearly identifiable, if stylized, Klan figures, with pointed hats that morph into church steeples that morph again into triangles and buildings and branches. The drawings that depict branches are at once representational and not recognizable as trees or leaves, as they appear to be the tracings of treelike figures. Some appear ghostly and skeletal. The gourds hanging from dead branches evoke human bodies hanging from trees, as well as African American bottle trees and musical gourds. While some of Christenberry's drawings of branches and trunks and leaves have no direct mimetic connection to the KKK, there is in these images still a sinister and provocative undercurrent that binds them directly to the more representative

FIGURE 13
Untitled 2005, by William Christenberry, 2006.
German ink with two brushes in tandem on paper, 40 × 30 in.
(Courtesy of William Christenberry/Hemphill Fine Arts, Washington, DC; © William Christenberry)

drawings (figs. 13 and 14). As Christenberry moved from his work of the nineties to the drawings in the next decade, he turned "steeples" and Klan hats into hidden circular and branched shapes.

When we look at Christenberry's rural Alabama photographs as a series over many years, we observe that the structures of the houses appear to crumble and eventually become completely overwhelmed by vines. In *Kudzu Devouring Building, near Greensboro, Alabama 2004,* the green, leafy kudzu covers the entire house; one cannot see the boards of a recognizable building but instead sees an odd leafy house shape. Christenberry's photographs of houses dissolving back into the natural world explore not necessarily a clear dissatisfaction with the built

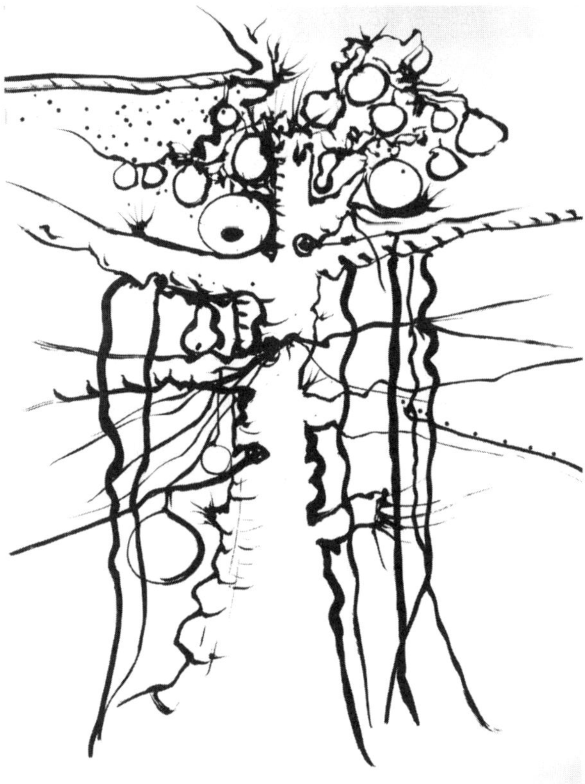

FIGURE 14
Southern Tree XXIII, by William Christenberry, 2000. Ink on paper, 40 × 32 in. (Courtesy of William Christenberry/ Hemphill Fine Arts, Washington, DC; © William Christenberry)

environment and all that we have called civilization but a recognition of its fragility and of the natural environment's power to swallow it up.

Christenberry's lifework reinscribes the terror of the racial legacy of KKK lynching in rural Alabama with the narrative of the growing vine and tree. His artistic rendering of the flowering of tree and vine over time provides an unsettling counternarrative to the deadly violence of lynching. This narrative is not necessarily positive, just a symbol of change, of time passing, of growth. The branchings of the vines and tree limbs materializes the story in a new form of inscription, markings, and symbols that provide a "written" record through repetition without the form of English letters on a page. These branchings serve as

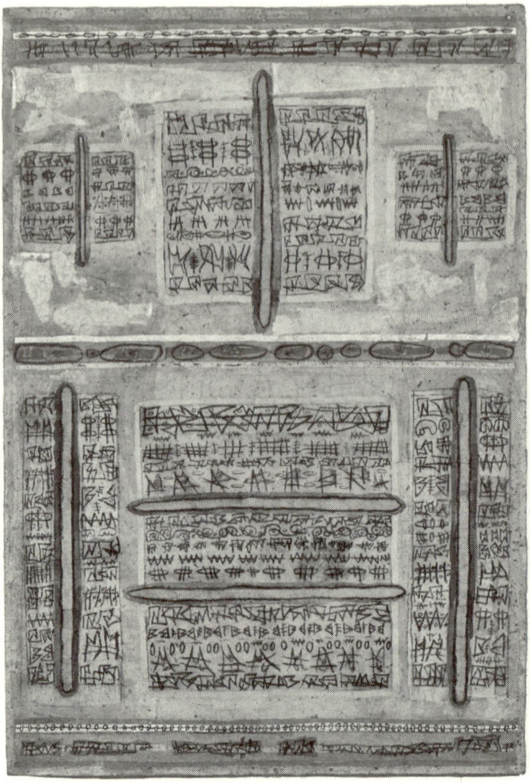

FIGURE 15
Swamp Song II, by Clyde Connell, 1979. Mixed media on paper, 105 × 63 in. (Image courtesy of Neil Johnson Photography and the Connell family)

an alchemical inscription. They are unsettling because they do not replace one narrative with another. They displace our reading. Rather than reading civilization in the turn-of-the-century progressive order from stone to skyscraper, Christenberry asks us to interrogate progress as he reverses the tale. He doesn't necessarily ask us to interpret, just to question—to see and embrace the meaning and importance of dissolution as deeply as our culture holds on to resolution.

Connell's "Swamp Song" series introduces a "written" language of the swamp that is neither visual art, writing, nor sculpture but a graphic display of her mysterious love affair with the impenetrable Bistineau swamp and her deep sorrow about the racist landscape of her life. The markings on the 1982 works *Swamp Song II* (fig. 15) and *Notations—A* (fig. 16) and the original 1968 swamp song,

FIGURE 16
Notations—A, by Clyde Connell, 1983.
(Image courtesy of Arthur Roger Gallery)

also called *Night Orchestra,* display cross-hatchings and branchings, triangles and hieroglyphic shapes. These marks follow a formal line as a text does but are not decipherable as having linguistic "meaning."

A piece called *Night Swamp Song* evokes a loosening of these formal marks toward a greater dissolution of form. Charlotte Moser explains:

> The Swamp Songs consist of random pseudo-lingual notations for individual swamp sounds. These simple shapes and patterns drawn with graphite or charcoal on the collaged papers were placed in rows within the grid of the raised ridges of paper as though lines of a manuscript. The Swamp Songs lexicon was wide, including cross-hatchings, dots, circles, flowing irregular lines, biomorphic shapes, boxes, and crosses. There is no sound "code" for deciphering meaning from the long, neatly lined scrolls of the Swamp Songs. . . . Connell cannot translate her marks into verbal language.

> Instead, as Connell explains, "no one thing means any particular thing. The differential quality of song makes the different movements. Some of the tones are strong, some not so strong." Yet something of the almost thunderous cacophony of night bayou sounds can be discerned by the sheer density and various weights of the black marks.[29]

Clyde Connell used organic material around her home to make her sculptures and paintings, from the red clay on her property to sticks, newspapers, Elmer's glue, and mud. Many of her works, including *Woods Habitat* (1979), consist primarily of twisted branches, rattan, and a special mixture of the "stuff"—soaked newspaper and Elmer's glue.

It is interesting that Connell used only the sheets of newsprint that had the most writing on them—often the classified ads—because they created the perfect color for "the stuff." Mixing the official printed word of the newspaper with glue and water and reforming it into a new kind of coded communication is a perfect visceral metaphor for unsettling and reimagining America. What is also transformative is that many of her swamp-song "writings" look like newspaper pages. By creating newspapers that tell the news of the swamp song in a beautiful hieroglyphic script, when newspapers of her time in the Deep South were telling lies about African Americans, Connell gives meaning and importance to what has been lost to most people's ears and makes a political statement in doing so. By calling many of her works songs, she embraces the separate identity of script and voice and gives each a free space.

Raised on a large plantation near Shreveport, Louisiana, Clyde married Thomas Dixon Connell Jr., who became the superintendent of Caddo Parish Penal Farm. She witnessed firsthand the violence and human misery of a racially divided South. During the Depression, she and Thomas lost everything they had, and they ended up moving to their cabin on Lake Bistineau. For Connell, unsettling and reimagining were a matter of artistic and personal survival. Her old southern plantation world was crumbling, and she picked up, quite literally, the stones and bones of its collapse. Gradually during her later years she turned from painting large magnolia blossoms to painting portraits of black prisoners at the penal colony to inventing an entirely original visual language of the grieving South. One of her most famous works from this latter period is a painting of people mourning in a graveyard called *Memorial 1955*. Connell's and Christenberry's trees and branches actually form a hieroglyphic language, telling a story that cannot be told in either word or image, but only in a hybridized combination that cannot express either culture or nature but a coupling, literally an intercourse, merging the two.

This is what Roland Barthes calls graphism in the section of *The Responsibility of Forms* entitled "The Letter, the Spirit, the Letter,"[30] what Simon Morley in *Writing on the Wall* calls "the restless energy of the body,"[31] and what Derrida extends to include all that inscribes.[32] This space animates trauma, so that it no longer paralyzes but instead moves in and through the body, in and through the wind in the trees, back and forth between human and natural world, in and out of the mouth as sound and as sound becoming word, on and off the paper as line becoming form and returning to mark, inscription, hieroglyph, bioform, and beat. Connell, with no direct visual reference to the violence of the white South, evokes the full human sorrow of this historical moment and gives us a thread of human compassion to follow through the labyrinth of time. Her abstract coded sculptures conjure the violent mourning South without ever directly telling the story of the lynching and economic starvation of African Americans.

In the visual art of both Christenberry and Connell there is a preponderance of woods, of branches, of bare sticklike forms, of patterned botany not recognizable as any particular plant. The drawings in Christenberry's exhibit on the Ku Klux Klan at the 2004 "Unsettling Memories" conference forced viewers to make a link between the representation of trees and trauma—or, more appropriately labeled, between organic forms and white supremacist violence. Connell and Christenberry invite us to think about the role that trees or organic forms play in the ability of a culture to move from the paralyses of trauma to the enlivening of mourning and eventually to the dance of regeneration. In all of Christenberry's works, the tree reads at once as its actual biological form, as the sign "tree," and as a symbolic branching. Symbolic branches represent the potentiality of metamorphoses and change. Both Christenberry and Connell created art at a moment when racism rocked the foundation of what it meant to be a human being.

Deleuze, Guattari, and Brian Massumi, in *A Thousand Plateaus,* distinguish between the tree as predetermined linear and vertical form and the root rhizome as the possibility of multiple layers of expression on a horizontal plane. In Connell's and Christenberry's work, the tree, in its many-layered and multiple branchings, acts as rhizome inverted, producing the same kind of metaphoric basis for multiple and multiplying originations.

Geographers have long cited maps, with their spatial and geographic rather than temporal renderings, as a rich location of nonlinear information. Feminist textile scholars have marked textile arts, needle marks, stitches, and quilt patterns as graphic space. Bodies in movement in space, musical notations, and drumbeats are all part of this tapestry of art, subversive in its resistance to form and its ability to name and thus inhabit space. Hovering on the edge of the known, these graphic renderings, force us to quicken and feel, without a "rational" predetermined overlay. The careful reader can find visceral graphism in established as well as unsettling art. In fact, visceral graphism appears in every artistic form, from literature to painting to opera. All one has to do is look for the location of the most intricate, textured, mysterious, and biodynamic membrane in the work of art—or in the environment, for that matter.

Deleuze asserts that writing is not the measure of "something else," that "writing has nothing to do with signifying" but instead has to do "with surveying, mapping, even realms that are yet to come."[33] With this assertion he opens the possibility that writing is not a record of what we already know, but symbolic, horizontal, even geographic, creating meaning across space, leading us back and forth between known and unknown worlds, between sign and signifier, between word and metaphor. If we follow Deleuze, then embedded in subversive writing must be this map of the unknown and a map of the unknown cannot appear in symbols that we recognize or can easily decode. Encoded in the cultural product—whether the written word, or the visual graphic image, or the dance or song with bodies and voices as the "script"—must be the as-yet-to-come-into-form inscription.

Trauma is, by definition, a moment in which the perpetrator has taken away the possibility of movement, denied escape, stolen self and agency. The lingering frozen cry is the repetitive paralyses, the exact moment reenacted without change. The source of the trauma—the murderer, the accident, the gun, the attack—long gone, but the imaginative reproduction, still appears incessantly. The cure must come in the ability to step out of the melancholic hallucination, the paralytic repetition—what has become a narrative of loss—a cause and effect with a beginning, middle, and an end—and into the organic production of newness, through the escape route of multiplying originations. The branch *and* the rhizome, both as organic material and as metaphoric form, provide just such a re-production, an unending performance of newness, and in biology, of life. This "life" counteracts the cultural and civilized demands of the traumatic story.

American elementary and secondary schools and colleges do not as a rule teach us to value or "read" Kerry Marshall's connect-the-dots drawings or tree branches in the night. The markings of citizen artists, the spaces between writing and visual art, between voice and alphabets, are as important as the great documents of American history, if not more important. Visceral graphism speaks without reproducing known narratives; the entwining lines in the margin are the "story" coming in and out of formal expression. By plumbing these depths we gain access to the realm of symbolic meaning provided by the tendriled root, the wind against a leaf, which has no equivalent meaning in spoken language but holds on to freedom of thought, constantly able to abstract the complexity of the moment. We need the equality of graphism and voice, as well as beat, line, mark, dot, step, and note, to function as a democracy. No point of entry into our human imagination should be subservient to any other. It is within the oscillating tension of democracy, this musical vibration, that graphic artistic expressions in America mend democracy.

2

POCAHONTAS FEVER

> Having seated him [Powhatan/Wahunsenacawh] after the best barbarous manner they could, a long consultation was held, but the conclusion was, two great stones were brought before Powhatan; then as many as could, laid hands on him [Smith], dragged him to them, and thereon laid his head, and being ready with their clubs to beat out his brains, Pocahontas, the King's dearest daughter, when no entreaty could prevail, got his head in her arms, and laid her own upon his to save him from death.—JOHN SMITH, *General History*

The Pocahontas Industry

When Peggy Lee sang the lyrics "Capt'n Smith and Pocahontas / Had a very mad affair / When her daddy tried to kill him / She said, Daddy oh don't you dare," she was keeping alive one of the most pervasive myths of American history.[1] It is not just Peggy Lee's Pocahontas who has a fever for John Smith; it is the whole American culture. Americans love a great romance, and the story of John Smith and Pocahontas has given us a titillating and "very mad affair" upon which to lay the scaffolding of our fantasized American nation. According to legend, Pocahontas's brave act saved Smith from her father, Powhatan, who was about to let the savages beat Smith with clubs and pointed sticks. Throughout the nineteenth and twentieth centuries the preservationist and tourist industries have added to the outpouring of movies, websites, juvenile novels, museum reenactments, plays, songs, archaeological investigations, statues, poems, and historical commentaries that continue the Pocahontas legend.[2]

The preservationist movement and the tourist industry have made the story of Pocahontas the originary iconic moment in the birth of America. In their ersatz narrative, the explorer John Smith settled in Jamestown, met an Algonquian girl named Pocahontas, and their love affair brought a merging of the native and colonial peoples: the true American identity. By coupling the first legislative assembly—the General Assembly of Virginia, 30 July–4 August 1619—with the mythical romance between John Smith and Pocahontas, historical revisionists make the Pocahontas myth the emblem of American democracy.

Legions of historians, journalists, fiction writers, anthropologists, and archaeologists have tackled the story of Pocahontas and John Smith.[3] While these accounts agree on very little, most twenty-first-century writers will agree that the woman known as Pocahontas was actually named Matoaka; that when Smith first landed in Jamestown in 1607, she was between nine and eleven years old; and that the great head-on-the-rock rescue was probably nothing more than an intricate adoption ritual, if it happened at all. But these facts have not done much to diminish the stultifying power of the myth. Throughout the twentieth century, few youths made it through elementary school in the United States without having engrained in their young minds the image of Pocahontas, lovesick and distraught, throwing herself over the exposed neck of the English colonist John Smith (fig. 17). Thanks to such movies as Disney's *Pocahontas* (1995) and Terrence Malick's *The New World* (2005), the story of Pocahontas saving John Smith has claimed the imagination of yet another generation of American children. Cultural tourism and Disney history do not erase the horror of this moment of cultural contact but simply contain it.

The counternarrative to this controlled script appears in unlikely but easily available artifacts, drawings, and contemporary imaginative responses. Inaccurately contextualized visceral and biomorphic graphic scripts, when put into proper context and allowed to speak the full complexity of their message, are able to undermine the Pocahontas–John Smith myth, adding to what archaeologists and serious archival historical narratives have already achieved.

The hundreds of artifacts from the Historic Jamestowne Fort site, John White's watercolors, Powhatan's woven and beaded mantle, John Smith's maps, Frederic Gleach's analyses of the pebbles, sticks, and corn in the Algonquian rituals,[4] the 2007 text of the Mattaponis' oral history by Dr. Linwood "Little Bear" Custalow and Angela L. Daniel "Silver Star,"[5] Rose Powhatan's totems, the lyrics of Neil Young and Alice Liu, some of the visual aspects of Malick's *The New World,* and

FIGURE 17
Smith Rescued by Pocahontas, by T. W. Knight, 1850, after Edward Henry Corbould. (Picture Collection, The New York Public Library, Astor, Lenox and Tilden Foundations)

details in James Cameron's 2009 *Avatar* challenge the nationalist diversity thesis and the romantic myth of Pocahontas and John Smith. These cultural fragments, each so radically unique, do not force us to choose between the Pocahontas myth and the rubble of bones and pottery chips. These scripts do not demand closure. Instead they slow down the ersatz machine. Human beings start to become human again. These cultural artifacts excite. They peel away the artifice.

Most historical accounts based on archival evidence introduce interesting details lost in the romantic narrative.[6] They suggest that Pocahontas and John Smith may have had some encounter, the absolute meaning of which has been lost in cross-cultural misunderstandings; that later, under Thomas Dale's governorship in 1613, Samuel Argall abducted a teenage "Pocahontas" (Matoaka) from Patawomeck, a village near her father's, where she was visiting with her husband, Kocoum, and their child; that Argall took her against her will back to Jamestown and then shortly afterward to Henrico, the settlement Dale had established upriver; that several colonists returned to Patawomeck and killed Kocoum; and that relatives of Pocahontas raised her son from her marriage to Kocoum. The archival evidence concludes that John Smith had already been sent back to London after injuring himself in a gunpowder incident in 1609 when the kidnapping took place. From 1614 to 1616 Reverend Alexander Whitaker, John Rolfe, and Thomas Dale engaged in a campaign to Westernize and Christianize Pocahontas, baptizing her in 1615. The 1840 painting of her baptism by John Gadsby Chapman is exhibited in the Capitol Rotunda as an example of the origin of American democracy.[7]

Archival records provide the information that in April 1614 Rolfe, after writing a tortured letter asking Dale's permission to be joined in marriage with Pocahontas, married her in a Christian wedding,[8] memorialized in the famous painting *Marriage of Pocahontas* (1855), by Henry Brueckner, which hangs in the governor's mansion in Albany, New York. Rolfe and Pocahontas conceived a son, Thomas, at some point in 1614 or 1615.[9] In 1616 Dale, Rolfe, and Pocahontas sailed to England with several other members of the Powhatan nation, including a holy man named Tomocomo, sent by Wahunsenacawh (Pocahontas's father, called Powhatan in most histories) to watch over Pocahontas and learn about England. Dale and Rolfe presented Pocahontas to the Queen at court. Soon thereafter Pocahontas became sick and, on the way home to Virginia, died in Gravesend, England. In 1617 Rolfe returned to Virginia without Pocahontas, leaving his sick son, Thomas, with his brother, who later sent Thomas back to Virginia. Schools in the United States are beginning to teach this historically more accurate narrative. But for economic and political reasons dating back to the second half of the nineteenth century, the assumption at the heart of the ersatz Pocahontas myth—that Jamestown, with this iconic moment at its core, is the birthplace of American democracy—has not faded away.

The Jamestown Settlement

Heading down the road to modern Jamestown, one can turn right, leading to the Jamestown Settlement and the museum and visitors' center, or left, leading to the Colonial National Historical Park, home of Historic Jamestowne. These are two very different places. A right turn lands you in the parking lot of the oversized museum and visitors' center. As you wind through the 144,000 square feet of visitor space and walk past or through a gift shop featuring Pocahontas, Captain John Smith, and colonist dolls, a cafeteria, and a movie theater showing the movie *1607: A Nation Takes Root,*[10] it is hard to imagine that this was once a struggling settlement, originally the home of the Algonquian people.

The nationalist thesis throughout the museum, promoted in the exhibits, the film, and the village itself, is that Jamestown is an exciting place where "three cultures, spanning three continents," met and contended with one another's differences. The Jamestown Settlement thesis mirrors Michael Hogan's observation that the 1947 Freedom Train created "a national identity more ideal then real" by celebrating "consensus" rather than "divisions."[11] While the diversity thesis is a step toward inclusivity and away from exclusion and complete denial, it still contains the preservationists' notions of a United America, with its implicit end-justifies-the-means attitude. The book for tourists by the Colonial Williamsburg Foundation sums up this thesis: "Jamestown Settlement provides an entertaining view of history. But this is history, not Hollywood; fact, not fantasy. A lot of people died at Jamestown—Indians, Europeans, Africans—but in the end, from this place, the United States emerged."[12] That the period during which "a lot of people died" was at least 170 years (1606–1776)—as many as 259 if we understand "the end" as the liberation of African Americans from bondage—makes the emergence of democracy a contested rather than a settled conclusion. That there is no "end" to an emerging democracy renders this statement even more problematic.

The Jamestown Settlement website boasts that "a special exhibition on display from April 2007 to April 2008, 'The World of 1607,' portrays 17th-century Virginia as part of an intellectual, social, and economic new world that brought together peoples and ideas from around the globe."[13] In the last room of the Jamestown Settlement museum complex is a large wall covered by a collage of photo images accompanied by the William Byrd quotation "In the Beginning All America was Virginia." Each of the photographs represents either a historical moment of struggle in a constructed history of America's march from conflict to unity or a moment of diversity becoming unity. Moments of American patriotism, such as of rockets taking off into space, are juxtaposed with moments of struggle. An iconic photograph of the civil rights movement has the caption "Servitude and Social Injustice," and a photograph of the Native American rights movement is labeled "Displacement of Indigenous People." This exhibition of photographs aims to create an overall impression that in some nebulous end Americans live happily together, although not one of the photographs actually encourages such an interpretation.

The shards of democratic engagement that this photo collage documents could be presented as fragments of a melancholic tragedy, in David Eng's words the "insistently creative and deeply political" nature of loss. Instead, the museum model insists on stability and wholeness. By recommending that tourists focus on the assumed thesis that "in the end" this moment in history gave birth to a proud, diverse democracy, the museum avoids dwelling on the inconsistencies and tragedies buried by the ersatz myth of Pocahontas and John Smith.[14] That "a lot of people died" is not the point. The question is, who killed whom?

What is most strikingly absent at the Jamestown Settlement museum and visitors' center is an accurate record of the systematic destruction by the English of the Algonquian people; the early colonialists' willingness to let hundreds of indentured servants die from starvation and illness in order to populate Jamestown; the British government's blind eye to the wholesale traffic of poor women and children from the streets of London and the colonies of Ireland into servitude in Jamestown; the systematic enslavement of people of African descent through the gradual and forceful establishment of the Virginia Slave Code of 1705. Desiring to propagate the diversity thesis, the Jamestown Settlement reduces the terrifying history of colonization and the establishment of chattel slavery in the colonies to a few truncated exhibits.

The devastating reality of the Algonquian demise, from the vast reductions in the native population resulting from European disease, which started many years before Jamestown, to the eventual destruction of land and habitat that led to the death of more than three-fourths of the native people on the East Coast, is not represented at the modern-day Jamestown Settlement. From John Smith to Thomas Dale, the Indian policy of Jamestown, cloaked in the language of missionary Christianizing, can only be described as one of cruelty, destruction, and violence, and yet the Jamestown Settlement gives visitors a sense of pleasant complacency as they take a walk through history.[15]

At the doorway of the Jamestown Settlement museum and visitors' center a 103-foot obelisk from 1907, the Tercentenary Monument, fills the landscape. At the base of the monument the artist inscribed the words of the London Council to the colonists: "Lastly and chiefly the way to prosper and achieve good success is to make yourselves all of one mind for the good of your country and your own, and to serve and fear God, the giver of all goodness, for every plantation which our Heavenly Father hath not planted shall be rooted out."[16] The imposing phallic statue demands "all of one mind" conformity to a European and Christian God, not democratic participation by the new colonists.

From this obelisk the map directs visitors toward a replica of early Jamestown at some imagined "moment" of stability, perhaps sometime between 1618 and 1621, when burnings, wars, famines, and massacres had not completely destroyed

FIGURE 18
Rose Powhatan and Michael Auld totems in the re-created Powhatan village at Jamestown Settlement. (© Rose Powhatan and Michael Auld; photograph by Rebecca Mark)

the infrastructure of the fort, but actually representing no possible moment, only a nostalgic hope for such a moment. In order to get to this replica of colonial Jamestown, the visitor must walk through Powhatan Indian Village, a re-creation of a Powhatan village, an Algonquian "village" built to authenticate an Algonquian community in the Tsenacommacah confederation.[17]

On the path to this "village" there is a circle of sculptures, or totems. Rose Powhatan (Pamunkey and Tauxenent) and Michael Auld (Taino) carved these figures for the opening of Powhatan Indian Village in 2007 basing the figures on descriptions from oral histories and on drawings and watercolors by the Roanoke colonist and artist John White.[18] Theodorus de Bry later made engravings of John White's drawings, so they received wide circulation. In the ersatz world of the Jamestown Settlement, the totems stand apart as powerful, unsettling art that is difficult to understand within the context of the tourist environment (figs. 18 and 19).

John White's watercolor known by the title "Indians Dancing around a Circle of Posts" depicts dancers moving around these totems (fig. 20). Each dancer has

FIGURE 19
Detail of a Rose Powhatan and Michael Auld totem at Jamestown Settlement. (© Rose Powhatan [Pamunkey] and Michael Auld; photograph by Rebecca Mark)

tree branches intertwined in his hair and on his limbs. The connections between the dancers, not just in the movement of their arms and legs but in their touching one another with branches, becomes a webbed script. In both John White's original painting and de Bry's engravings the faces of the totems are plain, almost expressionless. But Powhatan and Auld carve the faces on their totems to express pain, pride, and power: each sculpted face has become lined with the grains of wood. The red paint has turned into a red stain that covers many of the totems and over time has merged with the grain of the wood and made each face appear to be at once crying, angry, and blood streaked. The totems say more than anything else at the Jamestown Settlement about the destruction of Algonquian civilization. They express the emotional pulse of what is otherwise the sterile facade of an Indian village, what the archaeologist Patricia Ruberton so aptly calls an "empty" and "vacated" cultural space.[19] When one spends time with these

FIGURE 20
Watercolor by John White, 1585–86. (© Trustees of the British Museum)

totems, they open up and can be read and read again. Their deep silence evokes the full complexity of communication in the "contact zone."[20]

The re-created totems at the Jamestown Settlement stand silently, without dancers, as reminders of a way of life that the English settlement undervalued. They are reminders that the preservationist diversity thesis hides a much more disturbing story. Because we go through the re-creation of a Powhatan village to get to the Jamestown Settlement, it is as if this way of life were a step along the way of progress rather than the destination itself. Rose Powhatan is not just a descendent, a Pamunkey Indian, directly related to the Algonquians, she is a famous artist whose art is informed by a radical political awareness. In her portrait of Pocahontas, she shows Pocahontas removing the European "mask" that the engraver Simon van de Passe placed over her face in 1616 when he Anglicized her features. The most striking aspect of this print is that Powhatan draws Pocahontas's face with traditional facial markings (fig. 21).

Some visual displays at Powhatan Indian Village come close to rupturing the ersatz facade. Inside each of the long houses are culturally significant material

FIGURE 21
Pocahontas Unmasked, by Rose Powhatan.
Hand-colored print. (© Rose Powhatan [Pamunkey])

items, such as furs and tree limbs to create beds, walls, and shelves. The curators' careful work, an attempt at documenting how the native peoples hung dried foods, collected berries, cured tobacco, and honored the dead, becomes an unexpected visceral graphism. This cataloging type of visceral graphism is the type Holocaust museum curators create when piles of shoes, eyeglasses, and hair become a script that unveils the story of genocide. Ernst van Alphen calls this type of subversive art the "Holocaust effect."[21] At Powhatan Indian Village, piles of real animal skins in each of the long houses begin to stand in for the human lives lost. The animal skins do not actually tell the tale of European genocide of native peoples, but in this context they are a reminder of the colonial greed and killing that took place in this part of Virginia. The sheer number of dead animals and the deafening silence surrounding the real encounters creates a genocide effect. A large wolf skin with two holes that look like eyes is stretched drying in the middle of the open space, producing an eerie sense that there is an untold story here, that there is a gaping lack in search of expression. Tourists snap pictures, children run and laugh, and blond-haired actors and actresses perform the daily lives of native people.

Farther down the path through the Jamestown Settlement complex, past Powhatan Indian Village, is the ersatz version of the original Jamestown. In this faux colonial village at Jamestown Settlement, the main activities are watching an actress knead dough for bread; listening to an actor in character as a blacksmith hammers out nails; touring the two or three houses as visiting tourist children try on three-pointed hats and armor; and watching a woman dressed up as a colonial man shoot a gun. Except for the noise of the gun, this version of Jamestown is all pleasant, orderly, and excessively "Williamsburg Colonial." The repeated sound of the gun does successfully shatter any sense of easy enjoyment, while the fields of real tobacco growing around the exhibit demand an economic rather than a religious or political reading of the settlement.

Historic Jamestowne

If instead of making the right turn that leads to the Jamestown Settlement one makes a left turn, one finds oneself at the national park's version of Jamestown, Historic Jamestowne, the site of the original James Fort. This Jamestown archaeological site is equally patriotic but dedicated to a much more materially grounded "truth." Archaeologists began to uncover the fort site in 1994. By identifying the darkened soil of fence posts and using technology that measures the chemical content of the soil, they have been able to accurately define the parameters of the 1607 fort. Much of the latest scholarship on Jamestown involves the new knowledge gleaned from the many archaeological digs of the past ten years.[22] What scholars had seen as half a site, the rest previously thought to have been washed away, is now known as the full site of Jamestown Fort.

Despite the detailed, painstaking discoveries, not one hundred yards away stands the statue of a young Pocahontas by William Ordway Partridge, erected in 1922. And inside the fort stands the strikingly virile statue of John Smith by William Couper, erected in 1909. In direct contrast to the statues of the mythic figures is the Voorhees Archaearium, where the remains of the people who died at Jamestown—their bones, teeth, weapons, pottery—are set out in full view for all to see.

Tourists and students of Historic Jamestowne can finish off their day at Historic Jamestowne with hotdogs or wraps at the newly refurbished Dale House Café and cold treats at the Thomas Dale ice-cream cart. The 2007 book *James-*

town, Williamsburg, Yorktown: The Official Guide to America's Historic Triangle tells visitors that the Dale House Café is up and running and "now serving food for those facing their own personal starving time."[23] During the "starving time" at Jamestown a third of the population died, and the depth of human misery is hard to even imagine. Letters tell of colonists experiencing every type of deadly human disease. The historical and emotional denial necessary to include the above sentence about the Dale House Café exposes the deeply disassociated nature of ersatz America.

To fathom the degree of historical dislocation that it took to name the café and the ice-cream stand after Thomas Dale, one needs to understand that Dale, the governor of Jamestown off and on from 1611 to 1616, was a brutal despot who thought nothing of torturing and killing unruly colonists. His entire regime was dedicated to economic expediency at the expense of human compassion, and he was most likely the mastermind behind Pocahontas's forced kidnapping and conversion.

Head on the Rock

The Pocahontas industry's massive outpouring rests on just a few lines in John Smith's 1624 book *The General History of Virginia, New England, and the Summer Isles.*[24] Those lines, in which he refers to himself in the third person, appear as the epigraph to this chapter. Leading up to and immediately following the scene described, Smith gives intricate and detailed descriptions of Algonquian life, houses, clothing, food, and so on. Only this particular section of an extremely long descriptive and, according to recent archaeological findings, not wholly inaccurate account includes loaded words like *barbarous.*

Because John Smith made no mention of Pocahontas's saving his life in his 1608 *True Relation of Occurrences and Accidents in Virginia,* as early as 1662 skeptics, including Thomas Fuller in his *History of Worthies of England,* have doubted the veracity of Smith's Pocahontas account. Each time the debate over whether Smith was telling the truth has garnered national attention, it has been clear that debaters were using the Pocahontas story for nationalist and sectionalist ends. Whoever could prove that his or her colony was the birthplace of America could of course cash in on tourism and prestige. And in the mid–1800s, when the Mount Vernon Ladies were organizing to buy Mount Vernon, the debate could be used to sway public opinion as to whether the new "nation" would be slave or free. If it could be proved that Jamestown was the original site of the

American republic, then southern apologists and preservationists in the early nineteenth century could normalize the "peculiar institution" and legitimize southern claims that America as a union could include slave owners.[25]

It is not surprising, therefore, that in the mid-nineteenth century southern scholars launched a serious campaign to sell the John Smith–Pocahontas story. The image that the Mount Vernon Ladies perfected in the 1850s of a George Washington–style "pastoral" and paternalistic slavery was simply an extension of sixteenth- and seventeenth-century Christian and civilizing colonialist propaganda. Jamestown's claims to be the birthplace of both democracy and slavery made the peculiar institution simply part of the American landscape.

In Virginia, the Association for the Preservation of Virginia Antiquities (APVA)—incorporated in 1889 and still active today as Preservation Virginia—created what became an ethnically Anglo-Saxon-centered interpretation of Jamestown. With historians such as John Hall, from the College of William and Mary, leading the charge, APVA sought to establish a site that would celebrate an upper-class version of democracy rather then what they saw as the invasion of the immigrant-led populist view of democracy. According to James Lindgren, "Jamestown acted as a keystone in this American structure of Anglo-Saxonism, as it held 'National and Racial, not sectional' significance."[26]

In the mid-nineteenth century, at the height of sectional division (i.e., before, during, and immediately after the Civil War), John Smith was an easy target for Charles Deane and Henry Adams, whose thoroughly researched and finely articulated attacks on Smith's veracity concerning the Pocahontas incident set the terms of a debate that has not yet been put to rest. The core of their argument was that Smith was relating a worn-out tale, not a personal experience. The myth of the soldier-explorer-captive about to be killed by the king of the foreign country was already a widely circulated tale type in Europe in the sixteenth century, and it was part of the popular culture of England by the seventeenth century. The most famous version of this myth was the Lord Bateman ballad of the young man held by the Turkish king and freed by the king's lovesick daughter. This ballad had already been published when Smith wrote his Pocahontas account.[27]

The story was not romanticized in Smith's 1624 version; in fact it was not transformed into the heterosexual love story that we recognize today until 1803, with the publication of John Davis's *Travels of Four Years and a Half in the United States.* Davis fabricates the sexy romantic love story when he speaks of Powhatan (Wahunsenacawh) as an inexorable "Monarch" and relates how Pocahontas is so overcome with emotion when she sees John Smith in danger that she hangs "wildly on the neck of the reprieved victim, weeping with violence that choked her utterance."[28] These words expose almost a subconscious awareness of the cultural "violence" that had by Davis's time *literally* choked her utterance. But Davis does not stop there. He feverishly writes:

> The breast of Smith did not yield to this act of female softness and humanity; it excited an emotion of gratitude, but kindled no passion in his heart. Formed for action and enterprise, he considered love an imbecility unworthy of a great mind; and although his person could inspire tender sentiments, his mind was not ductile to them. His penetration, however, foresaw the uses to which the passion of Pocahontas for him might be converted; and his solicitude for the success of the Colony, which was much nearer his heart made him feign a return of that fondness which every day augmented in the bosom of the Princess.[29]

In this passage Davis unwittingly confesses to exactly what he is doing in creating this false history: foreseeing "the uses to which the passion of Pocahontas might be converted." Davis exaggerates the gender inequity of the original text, turning Smith's mind into a hardened phallus, "his penetration," while he creates a Pocahontas who is desperately in love with John Smith the man.

Davis's account, in all its misogynist glory, is the most repeated version of the legend. It is the one that served as the source for nineteenth- and twentieth-century dramatic performances and even for the twentieth- and twenty-first-century Pocahontas movies. The colony becomes an abstracted and distanced "nation," while the colonized stands in for human emotion, nature, procreation, and eroticism. The colony is impenetrable, unable to die, while the colonized will rise and fall at the stroke of Davis's pen. The Pocahontas myth implies that the native peoples really did love Europeans, passionately.

What is central to both the Bateman ballad and the Pocahontas myth is the dependence of the dark Turkish or native woman on the European white man. In the European trafficking economy the woman becomes symbolic, the actual signifier of the colonized land. Through the native woman, the male colonist impregnates the native land and literally, through his progeny, creates the citizens of a New World and frees himself from the yoke of the mother country. The New World has a new mother. The delight with which America embraced the myth of the native woman as the ancestral mother of America is evidence of this seminal obsession. The colonist exists in a hybrid space, no longer European yet needing to distinguish and separate himself from the "savages." The Bateman ballad consolidates the power structure of colonialism in an easy-to-accept narrative. The daughter moves from being a doting appendage of the patriarchal father to saving, loving, and becoming an appendage of the conquering hero. The woman in this patriarchal myth willfully engages in the destruction of her own people.

The Propaganda of Colonization: "Not *Meum* or *Teum*"

Francis Jennings, in his paradigm-shifting book *The Invasion of America,* sets forth the dynamics of the illusion on which American nationalists base the conquest of Jamestown: "The conquerors of America glorified the devastation they wrought in visions of righteousness, and their descendants have been reluctant to peer through the aura."[30] To peer through the aura, to destroy these early underpinnings of ersatz America, would be to dismantle the unholy and untenable alliance of a democratic nation conceived on the backs of indentured servants, slaves, and murdered native peoples. Instead the conquerors and their descendants have chosen to glorify religious righteousness.

In his first charter to the Virginia Company, King James I states clearly, "Hereafter tend to the glory of his divine majesty in propagating of Christian religion to such people as yet live in darkness and miserable ignorance of the true knowledge and worship of God and may in time bring the infidels and savages lying in those parts to humane civility and to a settled and quiet government."[31] The division between savage infidels, who lived in ignorance and darkness, and the civilized Europeans, who would bring a settled and quiet government, is the kind of extreme hallucination that the treatises and sermons from on high allowed. No invading society could have been more barbarous, louder, more uncivilized, or more savage then the first settlers of Jamestown. By using God and Christianity as justification, the colonialists could and did get away with murder. The language of religious righteousness covered up the brutality of occupation.

The justification for genocide was already in the blueprint of English colonization long before Sir Walter Raleigh's first voyage, as unveiled in the writings and sermons of Robert Gray and even Thomas More with the publication of his *Utopia* in 1516. These early writings would give articulation to the Jamestown charter. More in *Utopia* and later, after Raleigh and Smith, Bacon in *New Atlantis* (1627) began to mark the century during which Europeans legitimized the right to ownership of land. Bacon focused particularly on the right of land ownership for those with superior powers to subdue nature and realize a profit from the land. More's and Bacon's utopian views of the perfect society, the model that would eventually develop into American national identity, were pristine fantasies constructed to keep out the savage sylvan wilderness and the female or maternal cycle of regeneration. Hidden behind these lofty principles were the crude facts that colonization would bring raw goods to an agriculturally challenged England and serve as a safety valve for the disposal of the destitute from the overpopulated island.

In 1607 the enterprise of colonization was not new to John Smith, the British, or the indigenous peoples of the Americas. The tools of propaganda—which propagated the assumed right to dominate and steal the land of indigenous peoples—had been honed during the Crusades, the Spanish Inquisition, and the early colonizing, pirating, and slaving ventures of the Portuguese, the Spanish, and the English themselves. Through the writings of Bartolomé de las Casas, a Spanish bishop whose works were published in England, the critique of Spanish colonial cruelty became known as the "Black Legend." The English propaganda against the Black Legend was so intense that the portrayal of conquistadors shaped English colonial policy—not actions, but policy—particularly in Jamestown.[32]

The English wanted to make clear in their propaganda that they would do things differently. They would not kill, or harm, or coerce the "naturals" to do anything against their will. They would not, as the Spanish had done before them, commit genocide. As the first Jamestown charter states, "In all your Passages you must have Great Care not to Offend the naturals . . . and employ Some few of your Company to trade with them for Corn and all Other lasting Victuals if you have any; and this you must Do before that they perceive you mean to plant among them, for not being Sure how your own Seed corn will prosper the first Year to avoid the Danger of Famine, use and Endeavour to Store yourselves of the country corn."[33] Never mind that even in this document the well-being of the English settlers is more important than the well-being of the "naturals." The message is to make sure they are your friends, and give you corn, until you find out if your corn grows high.

One of the earliest and most famous propagandists of the New World, Richard Hakluyt, in his *Discourse Concerning Western Planting* (1584), reiterated what had become a commonplace about Spanish colonization: "That the Spaniards have executed most outrageous and more then Turkish cruelties in all the west Indies."[34] Although this seems like condemnation of the violence of colonialism, it is important to note that this is number eleven in Hakluyt's list of reasons why England should engage in an expansionist excursion. Four of the reasons in Hakluyt's top ten have to do with the fact that the Spanish were getting rich on natural resources in the New World, in particular gold and silver, while England was languishing. So while the dominant reason for colonial expansion was mercantile, the secondary ersatz reason—"That this western discovery will be greatly for the enlargement of the gospel of Christ"—was necessary because it separated Spanish violence and coercion from the gentlemanly English Christian enterprise. These English assertions of Christian good covered up the real mercantile reasons for expansionism and fueled a four-hundred-year American addiction to fake histories.

Robert Gray was one of a group of preachers—along with Robert Johnson, William Symonds, Daniel Price, and William Crashaw—who took to the pulpit in London in the spring of 1609 to argue aggressively for the colonization of Virginia. In his sermon *A Good Speed to Virginia,* delivered on 28 April, Gray stated the case so bluntly that he unmasked the whole architecture of English colonization:

> The first objection is, by what right or warrant we can enter into the land of these Savages, take away their rightful inheritance from them, and plant our selves in their places, being un-wronged or unprovoked by them. Some affirm, and it is likely to be true, that these Savages have no particular properties in any part or parcel of that Country, but only general residencies there, as wild beasts have in the forest, for they range and wander up and down the Country, without any law or government, being led only by their own lusts and sensualities, there is not *meum* or *teum* amongst them: so that if the whole land should be taken from them, there is not a man that can complain of any particular wrong done unto him.[35]

The words "not *meum* or *teum* [mine or thine] amongst them" have an eerie foreboding. Gray argues that because the "Savages"—whom he has earlier referred to as "wild beasts," "unreasonable creatures," and "brutish savages," with "godless ignorance, & blasphemous Idolatry"—have no concept of private property, no idea how to plant and cultivate, and the English do, the English should take and make use of the land. Consider the actual facts of the situation: When the English colonists landed in Virginia, they had little knowledge about what land would make good farmland, they had no idea how to grow corn in the New World, and they had very little interest in farming the land around Jamestown Fort. They were largely dependent on the Algonquian people, and they turned to them, as King

James himself had instructed them to do, for food and eventually for agriculture expertise. It is an irony that would be funny if it had not had such dire consequences for the Algonquian people.

English writers argued away theft of Indian land, the scorch-and-burn policy, and the murders and genocide of Indian peoples by postulating the righteous European ownership of an imagined utopia. As early as 1518 Thomas More contended that in his Utopia, if the natives wanted to join and become one with the Utopians, they would be accepted, but "if the natives refuse to conform themselves to their [the Utopians'] laws, they [the Utopians] drive them out of those bounds which they mark out for themselves, and use force if they resist. For they account it a very just cause of war, if any nation will hinder others to come and possess a part of their soil, of which they make no use, but let it lie idle and uncultivated. Since every man has by the law of nature a right to such a waste portion of the earth, as is necessary for his subsistence."[36] This is the meaning of *meum.* More believed that those who let their soil lay uncultivated had no right to that soil.

The construction of this narrative of domination changed very little during the sixteenth century. There was more than a century between More's *Utopia* and Bacon's *New Atlantis,* written in 1623, and yet Bacon still adhered directly to More's esoteric utopian ideals. Bacon's New Atlantis would be Christian, ethereal, heavenly, a world of angels and spirits of the mind and whiteness. Bacon solidified the image of an other too savage to exist in the newly civilized world, writing that a "poor remnant of human seed which remained in their [the New Atlantians'] mountains, peopled the country again slowly, by little and little, and being simple and a savage people (not like Noah and his sons, which was the chief family of the earth), they were not able to leave letters, arts, and civility to their posterity."[37] What one does to the world—how one cultivates one's time on earth and what possessions one leaves behind—determines one's right to exist. That the Algonquian people understood navigation and cartographic arts, developed complex governmental structures and rituals, engaged in architectural innovation, practiced advanced hunting and military techniques, possessed medicinal knowledge, spoke a rich language with a powerful rhetorical tradition, and, most of all, had expertise in cultivating the land had no bearing on the construction of the ersatz narrative.

Deeply necessary to the project of America was the rationalization of dominion over nature through ownership and cultivation of the land. The European idea of America was of an Arcadia, an imaginary place of pastoral calm and innocence, a controlled garden environment. Arcadia as a concept existed as early as the early sixteenth century, when German mapmakers named America after Amerigo Vespucci. But the concept most likely predated this. It was this dis-associated notion of a disembodied pure realm, the untouched and unspoiled virgin, that would enable the planting of an America that fed the dominion over the "savage," sylvan, living forest. As More writes, "Every man has by the law of nature a right to such a waste portion of the earth, as is necessary for his subsistence."[38] These utopian visions gave birth to the material reality of the sprawling, stolen ten-thousand-acre plantations of seventeenth- and eighteenth-century Virginia and of the plantation South in general. The white men who supposedly deserved these lands because they knew how to cultivate them in fact rarely did know how to cultivate them; nor did they cultivate them themselves. The back-breaking work of cultivation and planting fell quickly to displaced indentured servants, native peoples, and enslaved Africans.

Captive

Mapping the Pocahontas myth requires peering into a labyrinth of conflicting stories and complex firsthand documents, dispelling the aura created by early propagandists, and disengaging the impossible ahistorical rendering of the relationship between colony and nation. Rather than dislodge colony from nation, American preservationists have chosen to rewrite the colony to fit some utopian 1776 notion of an imaginary nation that never did exist and cannot exist.

By the time a group of scholars writing in the 1990s and the early twenty-first century entered the conversation,[39] the Pocahontas myth had become such a perfect mask for the lies and consuming greed that fill the firsthand documents of Jamestown that to break down the facade would seem cataclysmic, not to mention unpatriotic. There is a surprising adherence in these new popular historical accounts to the old Virginia preservationist project of claiming pre–1618, pre–General Assembly Jamestown as the birthplace of democracy and America. When John Smith injured himself in the gunpowder accident in 1609, the Virginia Company sent him back to England. In 1614 Samuel Argall kidnapped Pocahontas, acting for Thomas Dale's new regime. Dale's fellow white male colonists, including Ralph Hamor, William Strachey, George Percy, and John Rolfe, verified these facts in their firsthand accounts. English and other European eyewitnesses, who were usually biased owing to their desire to please their superiors and gratify the Virginia Company, composed the only surviving written records.

After a short stay in Jamestown, Argall took Pocahontas to Henrico, a small town Dale had "planted" upriver. In Henrico Dale had established a school to convert native peoples, as desired by the Virginia Company. However, the school had few pupils and was unsuccessful; the only pupil who "graduated" was Pocahontas, the supposedly model captive.

The accepted mythology—that these men treated Pocahontas well, that she willingly turned her back on her community, that she embraced Christianity and her new identity as a European woman named Rebecca—seems highly improbable. Paula Gunn Allen writes of Dale: "The Spanish Inquisition, still active in Roman Catholic countries in that century, had nothing on Master Dale."[40] Of the early twenty-first-century historians cited above, only Helen Rountree, in *Pocahontas, Powhatan, and Opechancanough,* and Custalow and Daniel, the writers of *The True Story of Pocahontas,* even try to imagine Pocahontas's days in captivity.

Rountree acquiesces to Eurocentric psychological interpretations, assuming that she knows Pocahontas's thoughts and motives. This colonization of Pocahontas's mind seems to be a common theme in Pocahontas studies. Rountree writes freely that Pocahontas would be worried about the difference between her "future position among the Tassantassas [Algonquian for "trespassers" or "strangers"] and her future position among her own people." She speculates freely, providing little or no evidence, that Pocahontas's future in her new home with Kocoum would not be exciting, because she would not be near the seat of power, while among the Europeans "she was the center of attention, at least among the individuals who were trying to convert her. Judging by the behavior that made her into her father's favorite, she liked being the center of attention, and she would have wanted to stay there."[41]

Rountree decides that the most important "deciding factor in Pocahontas's conversion in culture and religion was that one of her teachers was a warm hearted, earnest widower, the twenty-eight-year-old John Rolfe. All the accounts agree that she and Rolfe fell in love with each other. Rolfe, at least, also fell in lust with her, which caused those proper gentlemen no end of guilt."[42] From the firsthand documents, Rountree's only sources, all written by Englishmen, we cannot possibly know whether Pocahontas's future really would have been better or worse with the Europeans; whether John Rolfe really was warmhearted and earnest; whether Pocahontas really loved John Rolfe; whether she really had any ambition to be the center of attention; or whether that concept even existed in the Algonquian worldview. The intellectual hubris of these passages becomes even stronger toward the end, when Rountree states: "Taken all in all, by the time the governor decided to force Powhatan's hand and make him choose between his daughter and his 'prisoners' and 'stolen' weapons, his daughter was hoping that he would not ransom her after all."[43]

Ann Uhry Abrams, in *The Pilgrims and Pocahontas,* is one of the few historians who at least try to get at an interpretation more faithful to the sources, writing: "Although the marriage of Pocahontas and John Rolfe around 1613 or 1614 is often given a romantic gloss, there is ample reason to believe that it was arranged for economic and political reasons."[44] Rolfe's famous letter to Dale confessing his love for Pocahontas is highly suspicious. Since Dale was known for hanging colonists who had intercourse with Indian women, Rolfe had to ask the governor's permission, but he could have done this in another manner. He seems to have been purposely leaving a written trail to excuse what might seem odd to his peers. His real reasons were more likely economic and political.

Rolfe's letter reveals a man intent on proving to Dale that he was not marrying Pocahontas because he was attracted to her (reminding us of Davis's rendering of John Smith as impenetrable to physical attraction) but because he wanted to convert her to Christianity. He insists that his desire to marry Pocahontas in "no way led (so far forth as man's weakness may permit) with the unbridled desire of carnal affection"; instead, his marriage to her would be a sacrifice "for the good of this plantation, for the honor of our country, for the glory of God, for my own salvation, and for the converting to the true knowledge of God and Jesus Christ, an unbelieving creature, namely Pocahontas." He claims that his thoughts had been entangled with Pocahontas "in so intricate a labyrinth, that I was even awearied to unwind myself thereout."[45] He never says that he loves her, and it is unlikely that Pocahontas felt even a bitter tolerance toward any of her kidnappers after they had murdered her husband and separated her from her son, her father, and her sisters.

The Mattaponis' oral history of Pocahontas tells a completely different story of her captivity. It recounts a deeply depressed Pocahontas calling for her sister and, when her sister came, crying out to her that Dale and other men had raped her multiple times. Dale's proximity to Pocahontas throughout the whole ordeal is certainly suspicious. He is always with her, whether in Henrico or Jamestown or London. The oral history questions whether John Rolfe was even the father of her child, pointing out that it was Rolfe's job to record all births in the Bible and that he did not record Thomas's. The oral history speculates that Thomas was the result of Dale's raping Pocahontas.[46]

For most of the twentieth century and into the twenty-first century anthropologists led by such venerable figures as Robert H. Lowie and Franz Boas have battled over the reliability of American Indian oral history. Boas argued for "value neutral scientific methods," and in a fit of rage Lowie stated, "I cannot attach to oral traditions any historical value whatsoever under any conditions whatsoever."[47] In *Skull Wars,* David Thomas chronicles this battle and the way in which it deprived native peoples of control over their own history. "While we cannot accurately prove every word and fact of oral history, we can at least understand how the individual tribal historians understand their own histories," he writes.[48] In the case of Pocahontas's captivity, where there is only unreliable evidence written by English colonialists available, the oral history helps balance our perception of the moment. Until we have new evidence or a more equitable evaluation of the current evidence, this source is crucial.

We might argue about the reliability of oral history, but such atrocities are not something that a tribe forgets. No Cherokee man or woman will ever forget the *Nu Na Hi Du Na Tlo Hi Lu I* (lit., "The Trail Where They Cried"). No Jew will forget the ovens. The wound that bleeds forever does not leave our cultural memory. The descendants of the Pamunkey people would not forget the stories of the rape of their women, of their child Pocahontas. That is not something that we can discount and attribute to the forgetfulness of oral history. We read that many English colonists were "marrying" native women, but it is hard to know how many of these "marriages" were not consensual but coerced. The oral history tells of how the women had to hide their children in the woods and offer themselves in order to protect the children from rape by European colonists who wanted virgin "brides." They would cry out, "Take *me*!," in the hope of sparing their young daughters.

Particularly disturbing is the fact that Europeans mythologized Indian women, as Bethany Berger so clearly argues in her essay "Indian Policy and the American Indian Woman," as voluptuous, natural, freely sexual, exploited by native men, and easily preyed upon and open to sexual relations with white men. Even Rountree includes this stereotype when she writes, "It is doubtful that Pocahontas, coming from a culture that was far less straitlaced in those matters [their supposed mutual attraction], shared his [Rolfe's] guilt."[49] In the European mind, these overly sexualized Indian women were either asking to be raped or needed to be married and Christianized and saved by the colonists. Berger suggests that "the settlers delighted in imagining themselves as the objects of affection to these half-clothed, lustful women and believed they could use these affections as a way of gaining access to Indian people. Hence the persistent fascination of the Pocahontas story." She goes on to say that Pocahontas's "willing choice of an English soldier over her tribe remains one of the most popular images of Indians in American culture, refiguring American conquest as voluntary, a consensual seduction rather than a rape."[50]

Berger and the oral history are the only sources in any history of Jamestown that mention rape, which is surprising given that there were few women in Jamestown; the European men by their own admission were uncontrollable; and they violently attacked the Algonquians at the slightest provocation. If the native peoples did not freely and willingly initiate their own erasure, then American myths of nationhood have formulated our Jamestown origin on the rape of women, of the land, and of the Pamunkey culture.

The oral history argues that Pocahontas was pregnant when her sister came to visit many months before her marriage to Rolfe.[51] Dale was already married to an English woman at the time, and his own "Lawes, Divine Morall and Martiall" made both adultery and rape of "maid or Indian" punishable by death.[52] However, Dale went directly against his own laws when he sent Ralph Hamor to request from Powhatan permission for Dale to marry Powhatan's younger daughter, Pocahontas's sister, then just turning twelve. Dale asked that she return with Hamor so that he, Powhatan's "brother," could "by your favor gladly make her his nearest companion, wife and bed fellow."[53] Dale, who had killed colonists for far less, was willing to satisfy his own lust on a twelve-year-old girl, a desire David Price calls "abnormal even by the standards of Dale's era."[54] Wahunsenacawh refused, saying that she had already been given to another and that he could not lose her as he had lost Pocahontas.

The legend expects Americans to be so mesmerized by the iconic image of Pocahontas saving John Smith that we will believe that a man who would torture his own people and think nothing of asking for the hand of a twelve-year-old girl for his own pleasure would not violate Pocahontas or allow others to do so. Instead, we are asked to believe that Pocahontas led a satisfying and exciting life and converted happily to Christianity. That she got what she wanted. That she loved John Smith. That she loved John Rolfe. That she married a tobacco farmer and had the exciting privilege of visiting England and holding court with the Queen. Never mind that Smith was a foreigner wearing strange clothes who was three times her age, a privateer, and most likely, as Renaissance custom dictated, had not had a bath in at least a month. Never mind that John Rolfe was not an upright gentleman but a savvy politician and businessman engaged in piracy whose main interest was in the production of tobacco. This history of smoke and mirrors does not want us to remember that after Pocahontas died in England, Rolfe hurried back to Virginia, leaving their sick son, Thomas, with his brother in order to get back to his plantation and the by then successful production of tobacco. The Pocahontas myth appears to be nothing more than the first serious advertising campaign of the colonial economic enterprise. Word had already gotten back to England that the colonists were starving, that the Indians were attacking and killing colonists, and that fever and disease were rampant. What comes out in the documents from 1614 to 1616, when Pocahontas was a captive and Dale was governor, is a colony in need of economic viability, propaganda that would attract colonists, and a lucrative enterprise to appease their investors.

In defining the purpose for colonization, England had chosen the lofty notion of a divine mandate to Christianize the savages. Dale and Rolfe needed to convince the Virginia Company that they were converting the naturals to Christianity. What better way to do this than to marry one off to a Virginia planter? It cannot be just a coincidence that that selfsame planter, one John Rolfe, was also a man who required a native woman to help him learn how to grow tobacco. Strange labyrinth indeed. John Rolfe most likely would not have risked disclosure in his letter of intent to marry Pocahontas unless Dale and he had worked out a grand ruse beforehand. The speed with which Dale, Rolfe, and Whitaker carried out abduction, conversion, and marriage suggests a premeditated scheme, not a series of coincidences, and certainly not romance.

Thomas Dale

If we give up the myth of Pocahontas and John Smith as the originary narrative of our democratic nation, we are left with Thomas Dale's abduction of Pocahontas and his terrible treatment of young boys and men in Jamestown. Not only did Thomas Dale enact despotic laws but he engaged in medieval torture practices. As George Percy writes in his *A True Relation,*

> Sir Thomas Dale having almost finished the fort and settled a plantation in that part diverse of his men being idle and not willing to take pains did run away unto the Indians many of them being taken again Sir Thomas in a most severe manner caused to be executed. Some he appointed to be hanged Some burned some to be broken upon wheels, others to be staked and some to be shot to death all this extreme and cruel tortures he used and inflicted upon them to terrify the rest for attempting the like and some

which robbed the store he caused them to be bound fast unto trees and so starved them to death.[55]

Dale, as his laws indicate, punished such minor infractions as not attending church services three times a day when the minister rang the bell. Many of the people he punished were very young boys. That contemporary scholars now write Thomas Dale into Virginia history, into national history, into sanctified history, and into ersatz history, even into the fake history of *Wikipedia,* as at worst a necessary evil is a willful historical amnesia.

During the height of the preservation movement in the early twentieth century, the Anglophile historian and William and Mary professor John Lesslie Hall evoked the spirits of John Smith, Thomas Dale, and Alexander Spotswood in one of his many speeches supporting the work of the APVA and its attempts to buy the land surrounding Jamestown in order to establish a commemorative site. He told the young people in his audience that Jamestown offered valuable lessons: "Let us realize that Virginia needs living heroes; that she needs earnest and devoted Smiths to save her from drones and laggards, and from treacherous leaders; that she needs Dales to give her stern and well executed laws, and Spotswoods to develop her wonderful resources, so that the set and solitary place may blossom as the rose." He emphasized that Dale and Smith were "virile leaders, who redeemed the colony from the anarchists."[56]

We need only to read Blanche E. Hazard's *Indians and Pioneers: An Historical Reader for the Young,* published in 1897, to realize the early and pervasive nature of this portrayal of Dale. In the chapter "How the Plantation of Virginia was Saved By Dale" Hazard writes, "In less than a year after Governor De La Ware left Jamestown, it was almost in ruins for the second or third time. That was in 1611. The man who saved it was Sir Thomas Dale. He came as High Marshall of Virginia."[57] Even the northern writer Sara Pryor, who led a group of women to Jamestown for a campout and picnic to bring attention to the need for preservation of the Jamestown site, states in her book *Jamestown: The Birth of the Nation, 1607,* which she wrote in 1907, that Dale was a man of good conscience and that the governor's strictness helped turn the decaying colony around and eventually made it a successful enterprise.[58] In case we think this argument has been refuted, Frank Grizzard's *Jamestown Colony* (2007) perpetuates the same story: "Attacks by the Indians were not the only threats to life and limb of the settlers. Due to desertions, theft, and general lack of discipline, Dale implemented the *Lawes Divine, Morall and Martiall* that he, Governor Gates, and Sir Thomas Smythe had developed for the Jamestown colony. These were harsh times for the colonists; the leadership felt that harsh measures were needed in order to achieve what they had been sent to do."[59]

James Horn's *A Land As God Made It* (2005) again repeats the same tired-out line. At first quoting from Percy, Horn lists Dale's offenses: "Dale uses a variety of harsh punishments to deter settlers from running away to the Indians. Of those he manages to recover from the Powhatans, some were hanged, 'some burned, some . . . broken upon wheles. Others he had staked and shot. Men who robbed the common store he had bowed faste unto Trees and so starved them to death.'"[60] But after illuminating Dale's sins, Horn realigns himself with the dominant historical interpretation when he writes in the next paragraph that later the laws would be used "to stigmatize Dale and the Virginia Company's actions as cruel and tyrannous, 'exceeding the strictest rules of Martial Discipline,' but at the time the laws were welcomed by the venture's leaders as bringing order and stability to the colony."[61]

In *The Jamestown Adventure* (2004), Ed Southern is in complete agreement: "He [Dale] expanded the written laws of the colony, turning them into more of a martial than civil code. He and his men started the colonists on a variety of construction projects, both within and without the palisades of Jamestown."[62] Like Horn, David Price, in *Love and Hate in Jamestown* (2007), details exactly the atrocities that Dale perpetrated against the colonists but never condemns or seems horrified. Price says that Dale wanted Powhatan's second daughter primarily as a "bedfellow."[63] Karen Ordahl Kupperman, in *The Jamestown Project,* presents both sides of Dale's martial law but ends with Hamor's justification and no commentary of her own.

To see how this necessary-cruelty argument[64] has progressed and pushed out all others, we need simply go back to the words of Edmund Randolph in *The History of Virginia* (1809), before the preservationist whitewashing had become firmly established. Randolph, with some moral and ethical judgment still intact, concludes that

> Dale's powers are not distinctly known but were the more alarming as being undefined and of a military nature. Sir Thomas Smith, the treasurer, without any sanction from the Council and company in England, has armed him with articles and laws chiefly translated from the laws martial of the old countries, severe and bloody and abhorrent from the genius of a free people and the British constitution. . . . Dale . . . was himself, the despotic

dispenser of it. *And it is unfortunate for the cause of genuine freedom that any degree of usurpation, especially of that kind which affects the life of men should ever be glossed by a supposed necessity.*[65]

Arthur H. Shaffer, writing in the 1970s, shows where the preservation argument has led modern historians: "Actually Dale did not rule by undefined powers, and he was only partly responsible for the harsh steps taken to remedy the colony's disorders."[66] Even Abrams, who sees the expedient nature of Rolfe's involvement with Pocahontas, says of Dale, "The picture brightened, however, in 1611, when the new governor, Sir Thomas Dale, imposed a set of rules for organizing the colony."[67] Of course Dale and the other members of the Jamestown governing body had no obligation to democracy, but even in the England of 1607 martial law was the exception.

The early British attitude might have appeared to be one of tolerance, of doing no harm, of assimilation and conversion. However, almost upon landing and certainly as early as 1610, before Thomas Dale's reign of terror, according to documents and letters by George Percy the policy had become genocide. Percy tells of going to Powhatan to "demand certain arms and diverse men." When his request was met with what he calls "proud and disdainful answers," the Lord General sent Percy with seventy men to "take revenge upon the Paspaheans and the Chiconamians." Percy traveled to their village and killed fifteen or sixteen men and put the rest "to flight." His lieutenant brought to him the queen and her children and a prisoner, whose head Percy immediately cut off. The seventy men then burned down all the houses and cut down the corn, a scorched-earth tactic.

> And after we marched with the queen and her Children to our Boats again, where being no sooner well shipped my soldiers did begin to murmur because the queen and her Children were spared. So upon the same a counsel being called it was Agreed upon to put the Children to death the which was effected by Throwing them overboard and shooting out their Brains in the water yet for all this Cruelty the Soldiers were not well pleased And I had much to do to save the queen's life for that time.[68]

Jamestown's laws and history reveal a savagery and lack of civilization beyond anything the settlers or colonists could ever accuse the native people of, making the whole enterprise of saving the "naturals" by spreading the word of God a complete travesty. What Dale's *Lawes* tells us instead is what Dale and Strachey needed to make laws about. Article 1.29 stated that "no man or woman (upon pain of death) shall run away from the colony to Powhatan, or any savage werowance [leader] else whatsoever,"[69] which tells us that the colonists regularly ran away to the natives. We learn that the early colonists of Virginia were not religious, had to be forced to attend church services, did not like to work in this communal setting, and were committing sodomy and raping native women: "Article 1.9. No man shall commit the horrible, and detestable sins of Sodomy upon pain of death; & he or she that can be lawfully convicted of adultery shall be punished with death. No man shall ravish or force any woman, maid or Indian, or other, upon pain of death, and know ye that he or she, that shall commit fornication, and evident proof made thereof, for their first fault shall be whipped, for their second they shall be whipped, and for their third shall be whipped three times a week for one month, and ask public forgiveness in the Assembly of the Congregation."[70]

One of the great lies of the captivity story is that Dale and Rolfe would have returned Pocahontas to her father if he had come up with an adequate ransom. Part of this ransom was to be the return of English colonists who supposedly had been captured and held against their will by Powhatan. Powhatan tells Hamor that the colonists are afraid they will be punished by death for running away from Jamestown and that in Jamestown they were starving. Hamor makes it clear that we are not supposed to believe Powhatan's story, but the laws forbidding running away to Powhatan indicate that perhaps we should.

There is a distinct possibility that many of the prisoners were young English boys who fled to the Indians because their masters treated them harshly as indentured servants and they were starving. Some of the prisoners were indeed kept for leverage and negotiation, while other Europeans, such as Thomas Savage and Henry Spelman, lived with Powhatan so that they might learn native languages and customs. At times of intense animosity between the two groups, Savage and Spelman did try to escape, but they also returned to live with native peoples and became important interpreters.[71] The idea of captives was both a real necessity of war and an English fantasy that did not account for the contact zone, the merging of peoples, the voluntary alignment of oppressed and starving children, men, and women, with the stronger and better supplied Powhatan confederacy. By 1610, facing the dissolution of the colony, the English needed every last colonist to fortify their forts and plant their fields.

As the nationalist story unravels, the only possible emotional and thus artistic response becomes silence, moaning, grief, and rubble—men and women picking up the pieces. Matthew Sharpe's *Jamestown,* a modern-day retelling in novel form, tries to be funny but ends up being darkly apocalyptic.[72] We are left with the destruction of the Algonquian people; the torture of servants; Thomas Dale's despotic rule; the rise of the wealthy; the creation of a class society; England's escalation into an empire through domination, rape, beatings, and pedophilia; the establishment of chattel slavery as a Virginia institution; the black death created by the ensuing tobacco industry; and more. These stories do not make national originary myths. The moments of contact in the zone between cultures are not really stories at all. They are fragments. False starts. Exchanges.

The *Oxford English Dictionary* defines *narrative* as "An account of a series of events, facts, etc., given in order and with the establishing of connections between them" or as "part of a legal document which contains a statement of alleged or relevant facts closely connected with the matter or purpose of the document."[73] Narrative must prove a point. Whether we see narrative as necessarily ideological or not, we must see it as desiring to communicate, as desiring to be coherent. As constructed, it differs radically from the scraps of information, archaeological artifacts, travel logs, scrawled maps, and one-sided stories that are the rubble of Jamestown, in fact of any moment in history.

Sticks and Corn, or the Visceral Graphism of Algonquian Ritual

The journalistic historians Don Jordan and Michael Walsh. in *White Cargo: The Forgotten History of Britain's White Slaves in America,* and Tim Hashaw, in *The Birth of Black America: The First African Americans and the Pursuit of Freedom,* both published in 2007, dare to step out of the mold and interpret the documents to tell two devastating Jamestown histories. Two other texts that come close to unveiling the true conquest of the Powhatan nation from the Algonquian point of view are the aforementioned and contested *True Story of Pocahontas* and Allen's equally contested *Pocahontas.* These texts, as well as Rebecca Blevins Faery's *Cartographies of Desire* and Camilla Townsend's *Pocahontas and the Powhatan Dilemma,* disrupt the narrative of democratic legacy and national origin.[74]

Whether we focus on the forced labor of kidnapped indentured servants reported in *White Cargo,* or the first enslaved Africans in Jamestown, or the genocidal policies toward the Algonquian people, or the poverty-stricken English, Irish, and Scottish children compelled into child labor, the official record—comprising sheaves of letters, propaganda, and pleas for support from the Virginia Company—documents a culture that consistently denigrated humanity. Although Western historians generally have difficulty giving credence to oral history citations, recent ethnographers, particularly Frederic Gleach, have corroborated the basic tenets of the sacred oral history of the Mattaponi people, *The True Story of Pocahontas.*

The sacred history contends that Smith's life was never in danger: "Why would Powhatan want to kill a person they were initiating to be a Werowance. By Smith's own admission Wahunsenacawh gave Smith his word that Smith would be released in four days. Smith's fears were either a figment of his own imagination or an embellishment to dramatize his narrative."[75] Allen argues that Pocahontas might have been one of the beloved women, the sacred white-feather women, coming of age into the role of counselor to her father and protector-teacher of the new members of the tribe.[76]

The anthropologist Frederic Gleach's account in his groundbreaking *Powhatan's World and Colonial Virginia: A Conflict of Cultures* (1997) is in complete agreement with the oral history. Gleach concludes that the incident Smith describes—being ambushed, taken prisoner, his head put on a rock, and being saved by Pocahontas—*could* have taken place but that if it did, Wahunsenacawh was initiating Smith into the tribe so that he could make him and the other colonists useful members of the Powhatan nation.

In Gleach's description of this ritual we begin to find a world not of words or stories but of graphic markings that denote holistic spiritual "maps," to which the Algonquian people gave more meaning than they did to any particular sequence of daily actions by earthly men:

> The ritual to which Smith was subjected lasted "eight, ten, or twelve hours without cease" . . . and was repeated three times on successive days, with feasting each evening at the conclusion. The principal action, repeated each day, was the creation of an elaborate diagram. . . . This diagram was likely created by a much more complex active process, like the mimetic processes of the *Gamwing* where the creation of a "map" has effects in the universe through its use in a ritual context. The intent seems to have been to control the way in which the English (represented by the sticks) entered from beyond, through the boundaries (the grains of corn), into the Powhatan world itself (the cornmeal). Rather than divination, this is better understood as a ritual of redefinition, establishing the forms of the relationship between the colony and the Powhatans.[77]

The sticks and grains of corn plot out the Powhatan belief in the power of designing a physical and material model, a map that will not just mirror changes already occurring between the Powhatan and the European colonists but also, more importantly, "establish the forms" and thus effect changes in the power dynamic between the two groups. The patterns in the dirt made by sticks and grains of corn form a graphic inscription. Most contemporary Americans are not accustomed to understanding visual or performance art as politically and economically transformative, but from the Powhatan cultural perspective the design of change was the change itself.

Smith himself writes that Wahunsenacawh "came unto him and told him now they were friends, and presently he should go to Jamestown to send him two great guns and a grindstone, for which he would give him the country of Capahowosick, and forever esteem him as his son Nantaquoud."[78] Because Smith so grossly misinterpreted—or chose to misinterpret—what had just transpired, he never sent the guns and the grindstone, and he never honored his role as Wahunsenacawh's son. Wahunsenacawh took it no more kindly when later the English held a ceremony and presented him with an English crown and all the other accoutrements of a European king to make him part of sovereign England, but at least he understood (and totally rejected) what they were trying to do. But Gleach reminds us that just because Smith misunderstood or misrepresented the meaning of the events does not mean that he described them inaccurately.

When one is introduced to a new culture, with little linguistic understanding on either side, the senses become dominant. If we read Smith's text as a weaving in which the actual colonization story takes up only about a tenth of the telling (italicized below), then we allow for the fragments of information to come forward.

> At last they brought him to Werowocomoco, where was Powhatan their emperor. Here more than two hundred of those *grim* courtiers stood wondering at him, *as he had been a monster;* till Powhatan and his train had put themselves in their *greatest braveries.* Before a fire upon a seat like a bedstead, he sat covered with a great robe made of rarowcun [raccoon] skins, and all the tails hanging by. On either hand did sit a young wench of 16 or 18 years, and along on each side of the house two rows of men, and behind them as many women, with all their heads and shoulders painted red; many of their heads bedecked with the white down of birds, but every one with something, and a great chain of white beads about their necks. At

his entrance before the king, all the people gave a great shout. The Queen of Appomatoc was appointed to bring him water to wash his hands, and another brought him a bunch of feathers instead of a towel to dry them. Having seated him after their best *barbarous* manner they could, a long consultation was held, but the conclusion was, two great stones were brought before Powhatan; then as many as could laid hands on him, dragged him to them, and thereon laid his head, and being ready with their clubs *to beat out his brains,* Pocahontas, the King's dearest daughter, *when no entreaty could prevail, got his head in her arms, and laid her own upon his to save him from death.* Whereat the Emperor was contented he should live to make him hatchets, and her bells, beads, and copper; for they thought him as well of all occupations as themselves. For the King himself will make his own robes, shoes, bows, arrows, pots; plant, hunt or do anything as well as the rest.[79]

Foregrounding the physical senses rather than any glorified story, we see that the towels, the women's red paint, the white feathers, and the sound of the cry all figure prominently.

While John Smith's narrative of Pocahontas is most likely delusional, his descriptions give us valuable firsthand information about Powhatan ceremonies, dress, sex and gender systems, architecture, and division of labor that historians have authenticated. As Gleach argues, "Smith's interpretations of meanings and reasons are far more likely to be wrong than the simple facts he chose to record."[80] I would amend Gleach's "facts he chose to record" to read "details he chose to observe."

Again, when we look at the shape of the text, we begin to see that more of the words on the page are about the visual details of the setting, clothing, and lists such as "robes, shoes, bows, arrows, pots" then about plot. If we read Smith's text not as a story but as a map, as a text of visceral graphism, we enter a completely different liminal space. In the raccoon tails hanging down, the red face paint, the beads and feathers, the two great stones, and the list of things that Powhatan will expect Smith to make once he becomes a productive member of their society we can see both potentially stereotyped images gleaned from the propagandistic literature that Smith surely read and the distinct possibility that beneath all the layered misconception we are being given accurate information.

If we follow Allen's analyses of the white-feather ceremony, the feathers provide important information. That the Indians used feathers instead of a towel,

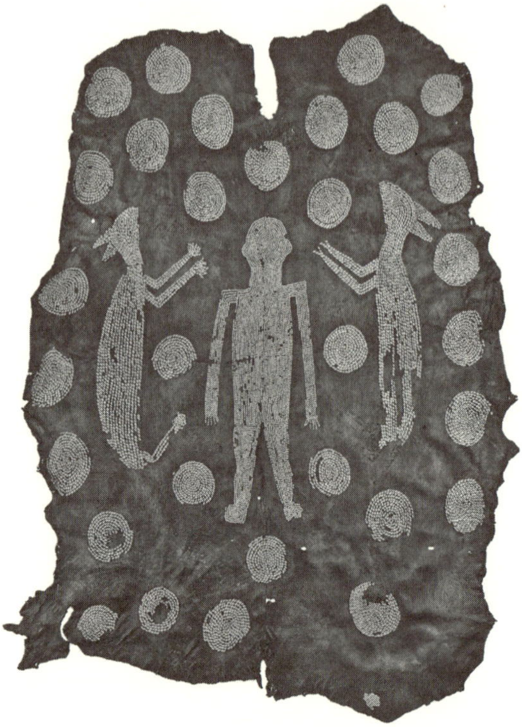

FIGURE 22
Powhatan's mantle with shell map, 1608. Four pieces of tanned buckskin, 2.35 × 1.5 m. (Ashmolean Museum of Art and Archaeology, University of Oxford)

that the seating was like a bed, and that many people were crowded around Powhatan are all details that bleed through the mythic plot. Gleach affirms Allen's analysis when he writes, "The details Smith reported also support this account; they fit with the Powhatan world-view too well to be made up by an outsider. Washing Smith's hands and drying them with feathers is a cleansing act typical of Algonquian rituals; the formal organizations and attire of the Powhatans also supports this view."[81]

The last sentence of Smith's description immerses us in the material world and transforms a legend of savage brutality into a flattened revelation of native ingenuity and self-sufficiency. Smith recognizes that the Powhatan chief makes the things he needs himself, while the British explorer depends on artisans to craft them for him.

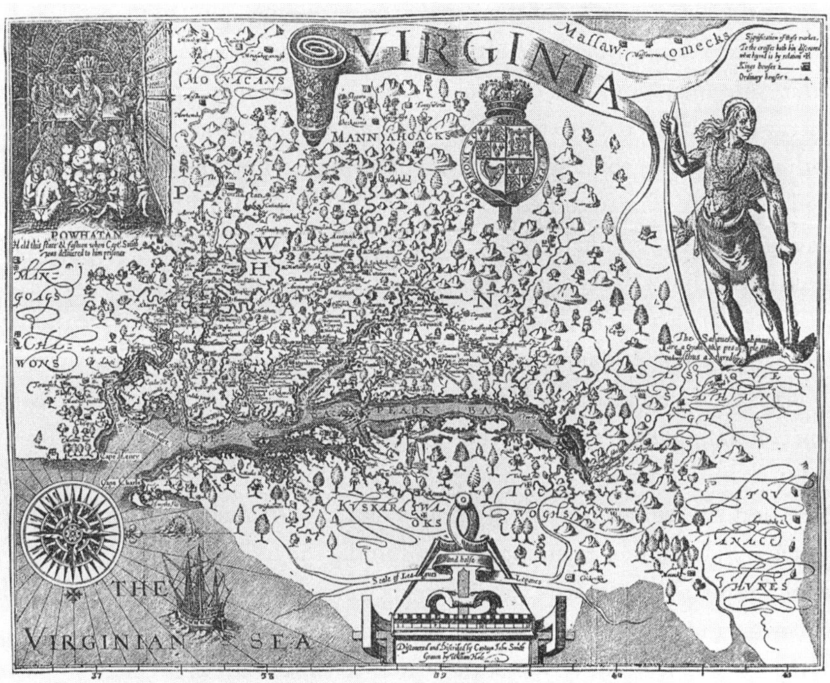

FIGURE 23

Virginia Discovered and Described by Captain John Smith, 1606, by John Smith. Copperplate engraving by William Hole, 1612. (Library of Virginia)

Maps

The visual record of Jamestown is quite extensive, including the paintings and sketches by John White; the etchings of Theodorus de Bry; the maps created by John Smith, Don Pedro de Zúñiga, Johannes Vingboons, and later Sir Robert Dudley, John Farrer, and Edward William, to name just a few; and in a completely different medium, Powhatan's mantle (fig. 22). Smith had a visual acuity that allowed him to remember in minute detail everything that he saw, as witnessed in his intricate descriptions of his travels and in his fairly accurate maps. The medium of Smith's textured drawing in his famous map of Virginia, which combines line drawings, flora and fauna, crude maps of the surrounding villages, and almost comic-strip-type drawings of native peoples, destabilizes the colonialist sequential narrative (fig. 23).

The beaded mantle is a representative map of the Powhatan nation, reminding us that the native peoples of the East Coast were accomplished mapmakers by the late sixteenth century. The anthropologist Gregory Waselkov argues in *Powhatan's Mantle* (2006) that many of the maps we ascribe to European cartographers were actually copied from maps by native mapmakers and that this mantle, with its thirty-four spiral shell circles, actually represented the many groups that made up the Powhatan confederation. As a spoil of war or a gift, the mantle cuts through the conventional story of John Smith and Pocahontas, offering not an interruption but a shattering of form.[82]

Powhatan's mantle is a map that traces circles within circles, with the human at the center. The Algonquians honor the deer, their source of food and survival, by placing a deer on either side of the human. The beaded circles of shells represent communities bound together by kinship and agreement. This is a nonlinear script. While there is definitely a sense of a growing Powhatan confederacy, it is a world that spirals inward; in Smith's narrative of almost having his brains beaten out, he cannot even imagine subsuming the individual within a greater whole. Smith's "going native," as it were, becoming part of this family of circles as Powhatan expects, is as far from any reality Smith could envision as flying to the moon. He is not traveling the waters to expand his knowledge of native peoples, although he certainly does so. He is traveling to find a passage to the Indies and to find much-needed food for the colonies. Smith's map is directive, looking toward a goal, while Powhatan's circles inward and outward.

According to Zbigniew Bialas, "a major function of colonial cartography was to give tangible presence to what could only be imagined." Whereas we think of mapping as a way of tracking the already explored territory, colonial mapmakers mapped what they imagined to exist. Bialas argues that maps as "imitative information grounded in terrestrial substance" were the first "proof of the new world, followed later by botanical, and zoological gardens and ethnographic collections."[83] The botanical and zoological gardens and ethnographic collections were archival and additive rather than narrative. Large books with thousands of drawings of plant leaves, stems, and bark began to prove to Europeans that the New World really was different. These are the texts that Terrence Malick references in the opening sequences of *The New World.*

We might question Virginia backed up against the "Sea of China and the Indies" on John Farrer's *Mapp of Virginia discovered to ye Hills,* as he maps the fantasy of finding a passage to the Orient, but his point of focus predetermined his perspective. In 1507 Martin Waldseemüller depicted the New World as a thin strip separating what we now call the Atlantic Ocean from a mythical Sea of

China.[84] What is interesting is the cartographer's certainty, the drive to discovery that would lead him to place the object of his desire so assertively on the blank paper. The native maps of the time are quite plain, while the colonial maps of the same time period and territory decorate or embellish every inch of the space. Bialas contends that even beyond the terror of the unknown, colonial cartographers had a "fear of the magical." He proposes that "to secure and perpetuate a stability that the original does not possess, blind spots had to be eliminated, otherwise they would either suggest non-being or provide space for alternative readings."[85] While I agree with Bialas that absolute certainty and the elimination of blind spots was the desire both in Smith and other colonialists' writings and maps, the maps themselves and the writings reveal a slightly different story. These texts and maps open up a space of magical and even decorative inscription that belies reason, knowledge, or any scientific evidence. On Farrer's map, for instance, there is a little merman blowing what looks like a shofar into the empty space of the sea.

On Smith's map of Virginia, not only are there sea monsters in the Chesapeake but these monsters are the same size as the English ships. Smith's drawing of Powhatan presents him as the most important person in Virginia, belying any dismissals of the savages that occur in his narrative embellishments. Crosslike symbols show where the known world ends and where Smith is depending on what people have told him. These symbols indicate that what he calls "the land of the giants" is outside the world he has explored. A large giant and Powhatan on his bedlike platform with a council of native peoples are under a banner that reads "Virginia" in huge letters, unfurled over and disconnected from the whole.

Fear, mystery, and recognition of the unknown can be seen everywhere on Smith's map. The map is in fact more unknown than known, the true state of English exploration of the New World. Such maps represent a strange no-man's-land, a holdover from the medieval practice of putting monsters or sea creatures in the unexplored far reaches of the map. The phrases *hic sunt dracones* (here be dragons), found on the Lenox globe (ca. 1507), and *hic sunt leones* (here be lions), found on many fifteenth-century maps, indicated that the cartographer did not know what lay beyond.

It is true that Smith's map covers the lands around Jamestown with the names of all the native towns in perfect English script surrounded by cartoonlike trees and hills, decorative rather than botanical or scientific, out of proportion and repetitive. There is no empty space. Emerging from behind this cluttered juxtaposition of Indian names and cartoon hills and trees is the name Powhatan written in a weird, twisted way, so that the letters appear to be hiding in the trees. To make matters even more mysterious, on one side is a larger-than-life native person who seems surprisingly meek, perhaps effeminate. Under this strange hybrid of a human being clothed with the skins of animals, the inscription reads: "The Sasquesahanougs are a Giant like people and thus attired." The sentence itself is wonderful. We are lifted into the magical and fearful realm of the giant people and then grounded in the ethnographic certainty of vestments. The textures and quilted clothing suggest that the artist tried to piece together a figure who was part man, part beast. By presenting the figure as gentle, and by making a museum exhibit of him or her, the mapmaker colonizes the giant. The giant is not an Algonquian "savage" whose towns are neatly marked as civilized habitations, but one of many creatures outside the contact zone. What this indicates is that by the time Smith drew this map, he was comfortable with the Algonquian people and saw them not as others, not as savages at all, but as part of his world. The worrisome others were the giants and the monsters. But what also must be noted is that Smith's depiction is not original but comes instead directly from the cartographic convention of the fifteenth century. On the Lennox globe, the words *hic sunt dracones* appear near the southeastern part of Asia. On the Borgia map (ca. 1430), in the Vatican Library, there is a dragonlike figure in the upper left quadrant, exactly where Smith locates his giant.[86]

On Smith's map we see the colonizing process not as a finished enterprise, a done deal with no blind spots, but as a dynamic occurring even as he draws the map. There are far too many Indian names. They crowd out the whole. And the native images are too big and all-pervasive, threatening to take over the conceptual frame of empire, for this map to do the work of propagating the colonies as well as it should. Smith tries to partition the native presence of Powhatan on his "bed-throne" off in the corner. But in its framed-painting style, the drawing of Powhatan imbedded in the map becomes European, not other at all, as if Smith is trying to say, "These people are not the same as the giants and dragons and lions of old, nor like my odd little mermaid men in the China and Indies seas." The picture of Powhatan reveals so much real observation; it is not a cartoon and not sketchy, but full of intricate detail. Smith has seen this scene and knows it well. Where there are no names, there are trees and twisting and turning tortured streams and inlets. The streams are different from those on a modern cartographer's map, but similar to those on a navigation map, for a boatman like Smith must have know every little turn and nook. This is not a calm or resolved map. It does say, "This New World exists," but it does not yet believably say, "Virginia exists."

What potentially comes out of this foregrounding of the geographic terrain in opposition to the temporal narrative of the contact zone is a necessary abandonment of the dominating European self, a weakening of the power of the tale itself, and an eventual equalizing that could bring the two cultures into communal understanding rather than conflict or dominion. A horizontal rendering, in which spatial awareness keeps expanding, is metaphorically aligned with community and with freedom. In contrast, a vertical temporal rendering, in which the hierarchy of time demands sequential cause-and-effect relationships, is structurally much more in line with the self and with the formation of a sovereign or despotic state.

By paying attention to what we commonly see as background information, we can begin to distinguish between a narrative rooted in ideological concepts and ideas, the source of colonial illusion (and delusion), and a less stable, more multivalent, experientially based text of visual and sensual materiality and textuality. Powhatan's mantle, the paintings of John White, and the maps of John Smith suggest that there is a way out of this maze of mirrors.

Hollywood Pocahontas

The Disney *Pocahontas,* produced in 1995, took into account much of the most recent historical work on Pocahontas and Jamestown. Directed by Mike Gabriel and Eric Goldberg, it portrays the colonists as greedy, wasteful, and gold starved, cutting down hundreds of trees. The mother spirit of the tree is the voice of sanity in the film, a voice all too similar to the fairy godmother in *Cinderella.* The natives are portrayed with ambiguous dignity, and Pocahontas is a strange mixture of Asian, Mexican, and generic ethnic otherness, an American everywoman, all-powerful, almost a Superman figure, able to jump tall waterfalls in a single bound. What destroys the Disney *Pocahontas,* a film that for once gives young girls a strong and intelligent protagonist, is its unrelenting insistence on the John Smith–Pocahontas love story. This adherence to the myth takes away as much autonomy and power as the filmmakers give to Pocahontas. Instead of being a seven- to ten-year-old girl, she is a nineteen- to twenty-year-old woman. John Smith is handsome, blond, a perfect Aryan hero, and they are in love. John Rolfe does not appear until the sequel. No one talks about tobacco. In the end, Smith leaves for England, but all is well in the colonies.

While we might expect narrative distortion and a complete lack of historical accuracy from Disney, we would hope to find a more unsettling and exciting take on Pocahontas from a filmmaker as famous for subtle artistic and poetic films as Terrence Malick. Malick's *The New World,* filmed in 2003–4 for a 2005 opening, adheres to the romantic legend of a love affair between Smith and Pocahontas even though by the time he was filming, the oral history, Paula Gunn Allen's book, Gleach's book, and many others had already been published. *White Cargo* and *The Birth of Black America* had not appeared by 2003, but historians had completed and published the close archival work on which they are based. The fact that Malick's *The New World* is merely poetic—or more accurately, prosaic—and politically embarrassing testifies to the power of the ersatz legend over the postmodern artist.

Although Malick obviously tries to make his film historically accurate, from the detailed models of the ships to the elaborately rendered period costumes, the narrative that dominates the excruciatingly long film is the same old worn-out romance between Smith and Pocahontas, with even greater emphasis on the sexual attraction between the two. One astute critic who goes by the name Zettel rejects both the typical bored moviegoer's and the awestruck aesthete's reactions to *The New World* and tells it like it is: "This empty, patronizing, sentimentalized farrago of historic lies is scandalously ethnocentric."[87]

Malick fills whole scenes with the historically impossible sexual attraction and consummation of Smith and Pocahontas's love affair at a time when she could not have been more then ten. That Q'orianka Kilcher, the actress portraying Pocahontas, was herself fourteen at the time of the shooting is even more disturbing. Several of the people working on the film were horrified that Malick repeatedly shot sexual scenes with this underage actress, take after take, underlining in a frightening moment of art mirroring life the pedophilia at the core of the myth. Rather than filming the probable sexual assault that Pocahontas experienced as a captive of Dale and Rolfe, Malick engages in his own sexual harassment of a young actress and covers up the treatment of Pocahontas in Henrico. What is most troubling about this omission is that it allows Malick the luxury of lyric dreaminess. While Malick films the starving time and makes it quite horrific, he overlays Smith's odd whisperings about Pocahontas.

Given the terrible choices that Malick makes in terms of plot and narrative, what is fascinating about the movie is that someone, either an art director or Malick himself, was aware that there was another way to tell the story. There is something different going on in this film that seems to mesmerize the audience and the critics so that they focus on the visual aspects of the film and take less interest in the narrative. Ethan Alter, of the *New York City Film Critic,* calls the movie a "gorgeous, moving, messy and utterly unique visual poem," and Mark Collette, of the *Tyler (TX) Morning Telegraph,* calls it "a poetic, fluid painting." The visual space is indeed where Malick makes his greatest critique of the Pocahontas myth. Opening sequences that include long shots of waving grass with big guns cutting through the land are aesthetically engaging. Behind the opening credits old maps of the territory animate, in a truly extraordinary display of visceral graphism, the language of these maps. We watch as the branching rivers come alive. In the opening sequences the waters dance and shimmer as if to say, "This is where the secret lies." In fact the opening to this unrelenting narrative of heterosexual romance is this awareness that graphic maps and the natural world tell a diametrically different story. Pocahontas and Smith's gaze turns to the natural world as if they are trying to find the answer, to interpret, to decipher the codes of the branching trees and rivers, and the camera points directly to the branchings as if to tell the audience, "The answer is here. Here."

But instead of trusting this impulse, Malick almost immediately layers the predictable romantic narrative on top of the fabric of geographic and natural erotic voicings. Before the movie starts, Pocahontas lifts her hands to the sky and evokes the spirit goddess and the power of her people's land, and we have hope. But Malick gives up his political commentary when he turns Pocahontas's eyes, her whispering, and her entire consciousness toward Smith, never to leave him. From that moment, he sells the soul of his movie to a misogynist and Eurocentric Hollywood.

When the camera cuts to Pocahontas in the field with Smith during their first encounter, we see her as a deer, playing an innocent game of make-believe. At first the audience hears only crickets and the wind—the unsettling text—but as Smith looks at this forbidden fruit, Malick chooses to play Richard Wagner's *Vorspiel* from *Das Rheingold.* In Wagner's *Ring Cycle* anyone who will renounce love may steal the Rhine maidens' gold. And if he who steals it makes it into a ring, he will become master of the universe. This music plays in the first love scene between Smith and Pocahontas, as well as at the end of the movie, when Pocahontas is dying. By 2007 the connection between Hitler and Wagner was well established, and the notion of Wagner as a strong German proponent of Aryan Christianity was well known. Malick made a conscious and potentially liberating choice to mark and signify white supremacy, the search for gold in this moment. As a conscious choice this would be brilliant, but it is a terrifying choice embedded and hidden beneath the unrelenting love story. Left to the audience to decipher, Wagner appears neither dangerous nor overbearing but simply hauntingly beautiful.

In two short scenes Smith becomes, not the potential Wagnerian thief, but the American everyman, planting the seeds of a democratic nation. While he is exploring upriver, we hear him speak as the camera pans over the grasses, the water, the boat full of men rowing toward a Powhatan village: "What voice is this that speaks within me, guides me towards the best? We shall make a new start, a fresh beginning. Here the blessings of the earth are bestowed upon all. None need grow poor. Here there is good ground for all and no cost but one's labor. We shall build a true commonwealth. Hard work and self-reliance our virtues. We shall have no landlords to rack us with high rents or extort the fruit of our labor. . . . None shall eat up carelessly what his friend got worthily or steal away that which virtue has stored up. Men shall not make each other their spoil." John Smith did not actually speak these words. Instead he wrote: "And here are no hard Landlords to racke us with high rents, or extorted fines to consume us, no tedious pleas in law to consume us with their many years disputations for Justice: no multitudes to occasion such impediments to good orders, as in popular States. . . . Here is ground also as good as any lyeth in the height of forty-one, forty-two, forty-three, etc., which is as temperate and as fruitful as any other parallel in the world."[88]

Malick's interpretation of John Smith's words reads like a manual for democracy and equality, while Smiths' words themselves read like a manual for individual gain and fortune hunting. The line that is most telling is Smith's "no tedious pleas in law to consume us with their many years disputations for Justice." A man can be a man without worrying about laws. Smith's actual writings have little to do with equality or freedom for all. They have much more to do with a kind of frontier mentality. Here, in this colony, anyone can make it. When freedom means license to do whatever one wants, there is no democracy. Malick either mocks Smith or mocks his own ignorance of Smith by having two native people sitting tied up in the boat with Smith when he says these words. Is Malick forewarning us about the hypocrisy of American slavery and genocide, or is this simply a mistake?

After Smith has been taken captive, we move quickly to the scene of Smith's rebirth and adoption. But here Malick makes the most bizarre—or what we might concede to be the most brilliant—choice of all: he tells both versions. First Smith's, briefly, with whooping Indians in the most stereotypical manner coming at Smith with clubs ready to "beat his Brains out." Then the screen goes black, and the next time we see Smith, he speaks the words, "At the moment I was to die, she threw herself upon me." Then we see Pocahontas ask of her father, "Spare his life," and the scene switches completely to a mutant narrative combining Gleach's rebirth-and-adoption story with the Pocahontas love story. There are even signs of Paula Gunn Allen's beloved-women narrative, as the women are wearing white feathers, and Powhatan says that he will let Smith teach Pocahontas about his land across the sea. She might be read at this moment as Allen's diplomat, or spy, if the romantic tale of love did not overpower and silence all other readings.

Allen was not a consultant for the movie. Had she been, the plot might have been quite different. Even though Gleach is listed as a consultant, the ritual that Malick films has no resemblance to Gleach's detailed description of Algonquian society mapping its path into a transformation of power. In Malick's rebirth-and-adoption ritual it appears as if a woman is giving birth to Smith. We see the confusion on Smith's face. Malick makes the scene fearful and fast instead of reflecting the prolonged amounts of time, days even, on which both Allen and Gleach insist.

Quickly Smith and Pocahontas move from playing childish games in the woods to teaching each other their respective languages in a highly sexualized fashion, touching lips and hands, to having sex and falling madly in love, to the point where Pocahontas is ready to give up all to be with Smith and Smith is ready to live in this Powhatan village permanently. We watch as an underage actress makes love to a middle-aged actor and no one arrests anyone. We are only 30 minutes into a movie that will go on for 145 minutes. Music heightens this foreplay to erection and sexual intercourse. The men protecting Pocahontas are impotent in the face of Smith's sexual prowess. Like the many depictions of Algonquian men as effeminate, including White's paintings of the dancers, Malick emasculates them. "He is like a God to me," Pocahontas tells her spiritual, ancestral, and real mother. For a while Smith "goes native," but gradually he is pulled back to the starving, neglected men and boys at Jamestown and finally to his real work: exploring the world.

Powhatan tells Pocahontas: "You will put your people before all else." Pocahontas puts Smith before all else. One of the weirdest aspects of the movie, one that many critics fall for as esoteric and beautiful, is the muted "whispers" that emanate from the head of John Smith and occasionally from Pocahontas. Rather than a cacophony of inner voices, or Powhatan's or any or all of the other characters' inner voices, we hear almost exclusively that of the leading man. When we first hear Pocahontas's inner thoughts, she is speaking to her dead mother, first asking where she is but then immediately speaking of John Smith, saying that she is not two with him but one: "One I am." Almost every other time we hear her inner thoughts, she is thinking about Smith. Thus in Malick's fantasy she becomes a Jezebel, an Eve, the one to blame for the death of her village. Smith tries to resist her, but she is too forward, too sexual, too beautiful. He addresses her as "Love" and justifies his passion: "Love, shall we deny it when it visits us? Shall we not take what we are given?" Although Pocahontas turns to her mother to ask, "Where do you live in the sky, the clouds, the sea?" it is only to tell her about John Smith, who has taken over her world, her brain, her whispers in the night. He has taken what he has been given.

As if Pocahontas has not been blamed enough for this tragedy, her father blames her for giving the colonists the seed that will allow them to grow a crop and stay another season. Malick asks us to believe that Pocahontas betrays her people for Smith and that the English burn the Algonquian villages because of her betrayal. The script does not blame Smith. She is a temptress, and he becomes a God: it is his voice we hear, and it is his voice that is the righteous one. Powhatan tells his daughter, as he never did in any historical account: "You are no longer my child." Lost, she is dependent on the white men before she is even captured—an absolute historical distortion.

When Pocahontas is captured, we again hear her inner thoughts—never about herself, always about her longing for John Smith. The audience never has to suffer a moment of guilt over her capture, because she is glad to be captured and finally see Smith. She wonders at the moment of her capture, "Oh mother has he sent this ship for me?" She is not afraid or angry for being taken captive. She has a smile on her face, and she is excited. Henrico and Thomas Dale are conveniently left out of Malick's narrative. The footage that is most insulting to the Algonquian people shows an English servant who probably had not had a bath in months teaching Pocahontas how to bathe. She fits her with shoes and a corset, and Pocahontas obeys because she wants to make herself more attractive to Smith. She even asks him, "Am I as you like?," and she tells him, "I belong to you."

Pocahontas does not go mad when she is kidnapped, or when her father disowns her, or when she is made to wear horrible shoes. She goes mad when she hears (falsely) that Smith has drowned. She says, "You have gone away with my life—killed the God in me." Smith is her God. She is so distraught that she makes no attempt to warn her people that the English colonists are going to burn the villages. In an even worse inversion than in the Disney movie, the English servant woman teaches Pocahontas about nature: "Think of a tree how it grows round its roots. The branch breaks off, it don't stop but keeps reaching towards the light. We must meet misfortune boldly. Not suffer it to frighten us."

Meanwhile, John Rolfe has been lurking about watching Pocahontas, and he does come right out with the truth: "She has accepted my invitation to work in the fields; she understands the culture of tobacco." Pocahontas does all the work and shows him how to farm tobacco, the real saving of the colony. Malick includes footage of the native people working in Rolfe's garden, but it is an idyllic pastoral moment, not the forced work of those whose homes have been burnt down. Rolfe expects her to want him. He asks, "Why do you shrink from me? Won't you say yes?" She looks sad and confused and says, "If you like." Here there are echoes of her kidnapping and forced sexual relations, but Malick makes Rolfe so good and so perfect that we cannot imagine him hurting her in any way. He says instead, as if scolding a child: "This is not what I expected Rebecca. Why are you crying?" She thinks, "He is like a tree, he shelters me. I lie in his shade."

Malick makes his strongest political comment when Pocahontas goes to England with Rolfe, but again he achieves this in the background, with props and scenery, not in the dominant plot. When Pocahontas goes to meet the Queen, there are animals from America in cages, including a raccoon and a bald eagle, implying that Pocahontas is one of these animals, a curiosity to show the Queen. Later, at the castle, she wears a patterned print, and her hair is tied back. She is no longer wild but civilized, no longer interested in the adventurous Smith but instead interested in the sedate, safe husband John Rolfe. In a taming-of-the-shrew moment, she is now ready to be Rolfe's wife. She wears a dress that in its manicured, stiff shape is exactly like the clipped, shaped trees; she dies soon after this.

In many of the nationalistic narratives a heroic figure overpowers or kidnaps the female figure. Whether it is *Gone with the Wind, Superman, Woman of the Year,* or *Pocahontas,* the myth is the same: the struggling female other is overcome by the powerful heroic and American figure who courts her. What creates the nation is not the regenerative coupling of male and female but the masculine ability to overcome the powers of the female to resist and put nation before lust. Rhett must overcome Scarlett after the war to bring North and South together. Superman must be the dominant red, white, and blue figure, saving—and outsmarting—Lois Lane to prove his superpowers. And John Smith must overwhelm Pocahontas in order to justify colonial dominance. The entertainment born of this myth, such as *The New World,* is really not much better than soft porn, based on a masculinist fantasy of dominion over rather than a joining with. Dominion over requires silencing the other's reality.

The New World's historical dramatization of the ersatz myth produces a monstrous hybrid—the head of romance and the body of starvation. As the art director of *The New World* must have realized, the hieroglyphic odd maps and the animated drawings of imaginary New World flora and fauna at the beginning and the end of the film titrate trauma, slowly make the reality and the full imaginative potential of the moment live and move.

Marlon Brando, Pocahontas, and Me

One of the lesser-known unsettling versions of the Pocahontas myth is Neil Young's song "Pocahontas." Sung in various versions by Johnny Cash, the Savages, Gillian Welch, and Everclear, "Pocahontas" exposes the core sadness and the core fascination of the Pocahontas myth. The multiplicity of perspectives in Young's "Pocahontas" deconstructs the Pocahontas myth by questioning all the positions of domination and subordination. In this song Neil Young shape-shifts from native to colonialist, from outsider to insider, from male to female. He is both the Indian in the canoe fleeing from the white man and the sixties rocker with his blanket and pipe.

With the lines "I wish I was a trapper / I would give a thousand pelts / To sleep with Pocahontas / And find out how she felt," Young critiques the dominant positioning of the Europeans. Young quietly asks us to realize that neither being a trapper nor sleeping with Pocahontas would help us figure out "how she felt." One does not know how another feels even if one is sleeping with or having sex with that other, especially if one is buying sex with her by giving a "thousand pelts." Writing that maybe he and Marlon Brando and Pocahontas will smoke a pipe together and talk of Hollywood and "The good things there for hire," Young makes it clear that America perceives the native peoples through the screen of Hollywood. If we are Americans, we are the sons and daughters of Pocahontas, both native and colonialist at once. Murdered and murderer. We live on a Hollywood set, in a homeland we have never seen. The "me" here echoes the self of America. Neil Young, yes, but also any "me." The notion of a self. It is the self of America, the concept of individualism that demands that we smoke our pipe with Hollywood. The "me" separated from society lives false stories. So in this moment we have only, as Young knows, "the homeland we have never seen." To remind us of this homeland, he evokes the "aurora borealis," the northern lights, called the "dance of the spirits" by the Creek, as a new graphic script that will tell a story as yet unread. Between the green field and the dance of the spirits are only the sound of the song and the pattern of the lights.

Young mentions Brando because on 27 March 1973 Marlon Brando asked Sasheen Littlefeather to decline Brando's Oscar for Best Actor for his performance in *The Godfather.* Brando could not be at the Academy Award ceremonies because he was at Wounded Knee supporting the uprising there. Littlefeather gave the press a short statement and then read parts of Brando's prepared speech, which included the accusation that "the motion picture community has been as responsible as any for degrading the Indian and making a mockery of his character, describing him as savage, hostile and evil. . . . When Indian children watch television, and they watch films, and when they see their race depicted as they are in films, their minds become injured in ways we can never know."[89] Although many claimed that she was just an actress with no Indian heritage, Littlefeather has since confirmed that she is an activist with an Apache and Pueblo heritage.

Young might also have mentioned Marlon Brando because Brando was purported to be bisexual and closeted, so that when Young talks of "the good things for hire in Hollywood" he may be talking about young men. His implication would be that Marlon Brando, Pocahontas, and "me" have all been taken by strong white men. Although he is ostensibly saying that he would sleep with Pocahontas to see how she felt about being taken by a strong white man, he in fact may know in some way how she felt. But the desire to know is what matters. The longing for empathy is a far cry from domination. Young is willing to put himself in the position of the native peoples and of the woman to discover how the "other" felt.

While Young's song opens the myth up to new interpretation, Alice Liu's "a.k.a. Pocahontas" taps into her pure rage at the cover-up. Liu directly addresses Mr. Disney, telling him to keep "his hands away" from the little child Pocahontas, whom he has in fact called by the wrong name. But where Liu breaks through the narrative entirely is in a long plaintive chant of the word *hiya.* The sound of the "hiya hiya" is haunting and terrifying at the same time that it is excruciatingly beautiful. That Liu repeats this sound, this chorus, over and over indicates that she knows that the language we have to talk about this story is overused. She does not evoke a particular native language or her own modern language, but the sound of outrage and grief connected to an alphabetic rendering and at the same time freed from that connection. *Hiya* could be seen stereotypically to evoke an Indian chant or war whoop. *Hiya* can also be heard as *Hi ya,* meaning "Hey you," or as a stereotypical sound made in karate when someone is about to attack his or her opponent. All these readings work here. Liu sings "hiya hiya" in a heartbreaking, high-pitched call. She breaks our silence and also breaks the fantasy: Hiya. Hiya. Pocahontas is not yours. You cannot have her. Hiya. Hiya. Hiya. I will sing only this sound. I will pour sound into the space where the wound lies. I will fill this corrupted place with this sound and reclaim this territory. Hiya. Hiya.

Avatar

The most recent cultural representation of Pocahontas is James Cameron's epic 2010 film *Avatar*. This 3-D visual extravaganza rewrites the Pocahontas myth from the native point of view, but the natives in this film are the Na'vi, a group of blue, science-fiction Algonquian-like humanoids from the planet Pandora in the Alpha Centauri star system. Pandora's box is an apt reference, as this planet seems to let loose every weird, horrible beast known to James Cameron's mind. The Na'vi, both male and female, worship the earth as mother; they are ten feet tall, evoking Amazons, although there are as many male as female Na'vi. One of their dwelling places, Home Tree, is a magnificent, miles-high, layered tree with thousands of branches. Every element of the planet Pandora is an exaggerated version of actual biological flora and fauna found in various places on earth.

Humans are on Pandora because the RDA Corporation wants to mine a precious metal called *unobtainium* (a wonderful play on words). They have half-heartedly launched the Avatar project, an attempt by the corporation to get a group of scientists to work with the Na'vi so that they will trust the company and not fight back. The Avatar project is the equivalent of Dale's school to Westernize and Christianize the Algonquians. The difference is that the scientists working on the project have become fascinated by what they are discovering and feel protective of the people and their world. The RDA Corporation is supported by a hypermilitary group of mercenary thugs who have the latest, most overdone weapons that Cameron's more than four hundred artists and producers could think up. It is almost as if they said to themselves, "If we are going to make a film in which the touchy-feely feminist, goddess-loving people win out in the end, we have to have so much shoot-em-up-gun-fast-space-ship-explosion-fighting-intergalactic-hyper-super-techno-guy-warfare overwhelming the whole movie that no one notices that the women actually are in power and win." The scientists are much more dedicated to the project than the corporation is. The scientists are interested in finding out as much as they can about the Na'vi and the flora and fauna of Pandora.

We enter the story as Jake Sully, a paraplegic ex-Marine, appears on the scene after his brother, a scientist, has died. Because Jake's DNA is a match for his brother's, he is able to take on his brother's position in the Avatar program. He is assigned as a bodyguard to two of the scientists as they go into Pandora and conduct experiments. By actually creating surrogate hybrid bodies that can be inhabited by humans, the scientists hope to gain the Na'vi's trust and learn more about their civilization.

In this film the producer and writers turn the Pocahontas myth around. As in the historical "real" story, the shareholders on earth (the Virginia Company) threaten the Na'vi (Algonquians) with extinction and destruction of their home because they want to mine the unobtainium (gold) under Home Tree and particularly under the Tree of Souls, where the spirit of the Na'vi world has its powerful spirit home. On one mission wild beasts attack Jake, and he becomes lost in Pandora after dark. He meets Neytiri, a strong Na'vi female of Pandora, who (like Pocahontas) saves him from the attack and begins to introduce him to the quieter, gentler ways of Pandora.

Like Powhatan, Neytiri's mother tells her to teach Jake their customs. Many of the warriors are suspicious. Jake ends up becoming closer to his Na'vi friends and Neytiri than to his human contacts. Although he has been asked by the ultra Marine character Miles Quaritch to spy on the Na'vi, Jake now knows that he will be spying on the humans and warning the Na'vi about their actions. Quaritch ends up bulldozing Home Tree. When the tree goes down, there is sadness precisely because it is a tree and will not be able to grow back in all its magnificence. At this point the movie veers into the realm of gratuitous violence, showing image after image of the bulldozing of the tree, creating a pornographic orgy of destruction. Ironically, it is an ersatz tree invented by the *Avatar* artists, so they take as much pride in being able to destroy their own invention as they did in being able to build it in the first place. In the violent assault the military forces for the corporation kill many of the Na'vi as they destroy the environment. The Na'vi lose hundreds of their loved ones. After Jake and Dr. Grace Augustine, the chief scientist on the Avatar project, are arrested and then freed, they go to help save Pandora. Grace dies when she loses contact with her human body. But Jake, in an elaborate ceremony to save the Na'vi's Tree Souls home and their planet, is able to transfer into a Na'vi body permanently.

In the end the Na'vi survive because the animals and beasts communicate with one another and with the plants through a telepathic neurobiological system, enabling them to fight back against Quaritch and his supermilitary machines. That everything in the nature-centric world of Pandora is actually ersatz and a machine and created by machines is an irony that the film does not investigate. In a doubling of the ironic nature of the production of *Avatar,* it is a reversal of the ersatz myth.

Avatar is the height of simulation. Cameron and his legions literally created a virtual world, down to the minutest detail. They waited for and invented technology that would be able to produce the most believable and intricate "fake-out" imaginable. But in order to do so, rather than project some hypertech world, they went back to nature—to the most unknown of unknown places, the actual rain forests and beautiful natural habitats of the earth. For young people today, high tech is nothing. Earth, the natural world, is what is exotic. Because Cameron and his team were trying to be as realistic as possible, they studied every movement of thousands of animals to imagine how six-legged invented creatures would run; every leaf of the plants; every color and variation of tone. These techies and art geeks studied every aspect of fauna and flora in every nature book they could find.

For Cameron as for Malick, accuracy was everything. Cameron even insisted that the actors fly to Hawaii and experience a real rain forest so that when they did the scenes for the motion-capture photography (which turns human movements in a flat-black cement rehearsal room into animation in a rain forest), they would actually know what it felt like to walk through mud, over branches, through the rain. The actors had to train and use their bodies so that they appeared as strong and energetic as they were portrayed to be in the film. So Cameron had to turn for models to the natural world, which had been devalued by the very virtual technology on which he depended.

Cameron became an expert on women, feminism, spirituality, trees, biology, diversity, and regeneration. He presented a movie that is really about the fight between the masculinist, hegemonic military industrial complex and Pandora, the lush, womanist, biomorphic rain forest that hyperindustrialism is busy destroying. It is a bit upsetting that as millions of dollars are spent re-creating a rain forest and human movement, the real rain forests perish and the children of today sit watching *Avatar.* One is quite sure that Cameron's animators, predominantly white men, created, as did God, a whole world, and yet they remembered to connect back to the real world, to nature, and mostly to the branchings of root and limb. The first time one watches *Avatar,* one would think one was back in the same frozen imagery of the old Pocahontas myth. But in *Avatar* the woman is strong and the man is wounded by a society at war. The imagery is pure Hollywood, with fancy effects, big explosions and horrible weaponry of war, and the whole romance plot. But rather than the visceral, branching graphism's taking a back seat, it is actually the primary player.

When Jake goes into the land of the Na'vi, floating illuminated plant life surrounds him. These creatures are the perfect embodiment of the narrative structure that Virginia Woolf called a point with rays stroking out, tiny and jellyfish-like with tentacles that surround him and cover him with a floating, fluttering light. The Na'vi are decorated in a visceral graphic fashion, with tiny dots in intricate illuminated patterns all over their bodies. The glowing beings are spiritually powerful and accept Jake. He holds still and lets the plant life surround him. Neytiri tells him to slow down, and he does. Jake allows her to introduce him to her world. Unlike Pocahontas coming to Jamestown, then to England, and then dying, the male figure comes to Pandora and heals, is able to walk again, and sloughs off the skin of the old world.

While in *The New World* John Smith rejects the return to nature and the love of a woman because he prefers to continue on his colonial excursions, in *Avatar* the male explorer lets himself dissolve into the natives' world. He does have to fight off large adversaries and to take part in a full-fledged war, but he is protected and surrounded by enormous trees with thousands of branches and roots. In the scene in which he makes himself whole by combining his DNA with the DNA of the Na'vi people, he runs with his newfound legs. In some ways he runs for all who are confined to offices and cubicles and inactive lives and all who have lost their limbs in the never-ending wars in Iraq and Afghanistan. This merging with the people of Na'vi is the direct opposite of the individualism of the American hero. He saves the whole by becoming the whole.

The regime of Gates, Dale, Argall, and Rolfe was one of martial law and what we would today call dictatorship. The Jamestown of 1611–14 had little to do with any future democracy. The first representative assembly was indeed held in Jamestown as early as 1619, but this was three years after Pocahontas's death. Embedded in the Pocahontas legend is the success of the democratic vision. The Pocahontas legend, from the earliest record of John Smith's fantastical account, in his 1624 text, to the most recent misrepresentation, by Malick in *The New*

World in 2005, ignores the fact that the contact zone within one hundred years almost destroyed a people who had lived on the banks of the Chesapeake Bay for thousands and thousands of years. What is exciting is that in John Smith's fantastical maps, in Gleach's description of the adoption ritual, in the lyrics to Neil Young's "Pocahontas," and even in *Avatar* the texture of the contact zone becomes more nuanced, more communal, and more democratic.

3

GEORGE WASHINGTON'S HEAD

His head is well shaped though not large, but is gracefully poised on a superb neck. A large and straight rather than a prominent nose: blue-gray penetrating eyes; which are widely separated and overhung by heavy brows. His face is rather long than broad, with high round cheekbones, and terminates in a good firm chin. He has a clear though rather colorless pale skin, which burns with the sun. . . . His mouth is large and generally firmly closed, but which from time to time discloses some defective teeth. His features are regular and placid, with all the muscles of his face under perfect control.
—CAPTAIN GEORGE MERCER, letter to a friend in Europe, 1760, as quoted in Baker, *Early Sketches of George Washington*

Larger Than Life

In the Donald W. Reynolds Museum and Education Center, a 66,700-square-foot complex opened in 2006 on the grounds of Washington's Mount Vernon home, and in the gift shops at the estate Washington's head figures prominently. If you count the Houdon bust, the new sculptures of Washington at various ages, the enormous new floating head of Washington, and Grant Wood's Washington, there are quite literally Washington heads to the right of us and Washington heads to the left of us.

On one side of the Reynolds complex is the museum that houses Jean-Antoine Houdon's bust of Washington, sculpted in 1785. On the right is a rather strange addition: a glowing white, six-foot-high sculpture of Washington's head. No matter which direction you turn, the Mona Lisa eyes of the alabaster

FIGURE 24

Concave head of Washington, 6 feet high, by StudioEIS, Brooklyn, NY, in the Donald W. Reynolds Museum and Education Center at Mount Vernon. (Courtesy of the Mount Vernon Ladies' Association)

sculpture, "lit with special effects to make the head appear to be a normal, convex, three-dimensional object, protruding outward," follow you around the room (fig. 24). The official Mount Vernon website celebrates the many Washington heads as normal and exciting: "If the Houdon bust is the literal Washington preserved forever in unyielding terra cotta, the larger-than-life head symbolizes the intangible Washington, intriguing and alive."[1] What the site does not explore is why Mount Vernon has such a clear fascination with George Washington's head.

The six-foot head at the entrance to the Reynolds Center is not the first depiction of Washington's head that floats in space. Gilbert Stuart's 1796 unfinished portrait of Washington is a careful, realistic study in which Washington's head floats in whiteness, with no discernible body. In direct contrast to the heads in Kerry James Marshall's mural of Mount Vernon (see fig. 11), these floating heads are not pinched but full blown and alone. There are no shadow figures and no hidden enslaved people, no puzzles or mysterious mazes, no biomorphic or graphic traces. In fact, a tiny fraction of the space at the Mount Vernon estate is devoted to depictions of African Americans, while Mount Vernon's singular emphasis on George Washington's head is quite remarkable. This large floating mask is simply the apotheosis of America's George Washington head fetish. As with John Smith in the Pocahontas myth, George Washington is not the only or necessarily the most important figure in eighteenth-century American history. The Native American and African American counternarratives were more visible and easily accessible than at any other time in American history.

The members of the Six Nations Confederacy (also called the Iroquois Confederacy or the Haudenosaunee, translated as "people of the long house") marked their intricate negotiations over land rights with beaded wampum belts, which, with their patterns of purple and white beads, make visible a viscerally and biomorphic graphic space that transformed the contact zone of European imperialism. These beaded belts served as intricate reminders of how the meeting of cultures was a conjoining not just of economic interests but of deep values and ethics. These belts, with their insistence on complex rhetorical rituals and listening, slowed down the process of genocidal erasure and violence against indigenous peoples at this moment of American nation building. As trained native leaders voiced the desires of the people through the wampum, they simultaneously mourned the loss of ancestors and the native customs of living that this moment threatened; the belts preserved the values of their ways of creating community, values that became, through contact, imbedded as some of the best elements of our democracy. An equally important form of Six Nations cultural practice, the grandfather masks (sometimes erroneously called Iroquois false face masks), carved from trees, pour their wood-grained messages into the script of eighteenth-century American history. These masks rewrite the narrative of American democracy from one of monumental heads to one of healing masks. If we follow the viscerally graphic record of wampum and grandfather masks to modern popular-cultural texts, including Matt Groening's "The Day the Earth Stood Stupid," episode 7 in season 3 of *Futurama,* the iconic head of Washington shrinks from Mount Vernon's omnipresence to Kerry Marshall's insubstantial.

Sculptors and painters made likenesses of Washington throughout his life and have continued to do so since his death in 1799. From Gutzon Borglum's 1927 highly controversial colossal head of Washington carved into the side of a cliff at Mount Rushmore on sacred Lakota land, to the super-sized postmodern steel head of Washington near a highway in Michigan made by Thomas Moran at Moran Iron Works, artists seem hell-bent on creating the biggest, most hyperbolic Washington head imaginable. It is hard to determine exactly why the monumentalizing of George Washington has focused on his head. We can speculate the obvious—that George Washington, as the father of the country, was quite literally the head of the new nation. But there seems to be more to the head fetish.

The preservationists, beginning in earnest with the Mount Vernon Ladies' Association, desired an America unchanged from the moment of the Declaration of Independence. In order to freeze "the nation" as an identifiable commodity, they needed a symbol that was indisputably American. George Washington's head would serve as a perfect surrogate for this frozen moment. Patriotic America must constantly reify the myth of national origins with no deviation. Creating a reproduction or facsimile demands at least the illusion of sameness. Nations defined in this fetishistic marble-headed manner must remain impenetrable or fortified. The head, George Washington's head in particular, is the closest one can get to an abstraction such as "the American nation." A nation so conceived cannot degenerate. Bodies decay; only minds can be imagined as inviolate. Conservationists and preservationists hold on to a dream of nation that has no body—*nobody*—and thus, ironically, no relation to democracy. For the preservationists at Mount Vernon to worship an exact replica of Washington is to locate the meaning of American nation in the identity of one man.

Deviation would transform reproduction into regeneration and would mean progressive change. Regeneration, in biological term creates a diversity of species; in terms of national memory it means a diversity of individual experiences, a diversity of Americas. Democracies are constantly changing, necessarily regenerative and never stagnant. Not only are democracies mobile, they are multiple and multiplying. They cannot be represented by the singularity of one personality. Democracies are stages where new identities, new faces, performing new roles constantly challenge the status quo. Democracies exist only in the liminal space where those who are unseen and unheard struggle to break down the barriers that demand their invisibility. Thus democracies depend on the appearance and visibility of bodies, exactly as Marshall insists throughout his murals, where hundreds of African American heads contest the dominance of Washington's and Jefferson's big heads.

Even during Washington's lifetime sculptors and painters clamored to get his exact likeness on paper or in clay. Washington was inundated with requests to paint his portrait: "I am so hackneyed to the touches of painters' pencils that I am now altogether at their beck, and sit 'like patience on a monument,' whilst they are delineating the lines of my face. It is a proof, among many others, of what habit and custom can accomplish."[2] Washington *was* a monument to habit and custom while he was alive. Jean-Antoine Houdon, the only sculptor who actually made a plaster cast of Washington's face and sculpted his famous bust from this cast, was fanatical about producing a "likeness." Interestingly, the likeness Houdon chose was from a moment when George Washington became particularly enraged at a horse trader who he thought was trying to swindle him. When the horse trader stated his price, Washington "reacted by throwing his head back and uttering a strong but indecipherable sound of outrage." Houdon found his pose in the moment when he saw "the mask crack."[3] Unfortunately, what Houdon sculpted as an expression of vitality has become a monument to lifelessness. The terra-cotta bust of Washington is located in the hushed Houdon Bust Gallery at Mount Vernon. This gallery and the prominently displayed photograph of the original Mount Vernon Ladies' Association, including Ann Cunningham, the founder, standing around the Houdon bust on the back porch of the newly purchased Mount Vernon in 1860, demonstrate how important Washington's likeness was, and still is, to their organization.

What is particularly disturbing about the iconization of George's head is what it says about the body politic in this newly formed democracy. Adriana Cavarero reminds us that in medieval writing and certainly in popular understanding long before this, "the state *(res publica)* is a sort of body modeled on the human figure. The prince is its head, the senate its heart, and the judges and governors its ears, eyes, and tongue; soldiers serve as its hands." John of Salisbury identified financial experts with the belly and intestines, and farmers, "who are in constant contact with the ground," with the feet.[4] In Constantino Brumidi's *Apotheosis of Washington* and in Mount Vernon's multiple hydra heads, the public has disappeared completely; all that is left is the head of state.

In the exhibit at Mount Vernon there is a surround-sound video of schoolchildren of many races singing "America the Beautiful," whose lyrics include the line, "Thine alabaster cities gleam undimmed by human tears." Again, preservationists ask us to celebrate diversity through a gleaming alabaster oneness. If the sanctified white male head is the defining symbol of American national diversity, if identity itself is reserved for the commander in chief, for the president only, then there is no democracy. The individual, or self, in this American context becomes the man who stands out from the rest, whose being depends on the subservience of others (who serve as his hands, arms, and feet), and whose sanctity cannot be violated in any way. The individual in this formulation is thus a fully formed, immutable self incapable of transformation or change. In this body politic the community of citizens would be formed of unidentifiable parts—legs, arms, feet—that could easily mutate one into another to be subservient to the head.

If Washington did not understand the people who worked on his plantation to be human beings with distinct identities, but only appendages of his all-important self, we should not be surprised that he did not protect the people of the Six Nations Confederacy and the Algonquian nation, free his slaves, fight against the early fugitive slave acts, or legislate for universal emancipation. If those around him were only his appendages—the farmer feet that made his grand agrarian experiments possible and the warrior hands that fought his wars—the conceptual shift from the medieval paradigm of the body politic to the modern paradigm of the body political had not, and perhaps still has not, taken place. What would visitors think if Mount Vernon were "peopled" as in Marshall's art, with statues honoring the roughly 318 enslaved humans who worked and lived there?

The ersatz production of George Washington as cultural capital blocked any real progress toward a socially just, slave-freeing democracy. It is one thing to decry the power relations of Jamestown, at a moment when there was no real democracy or democratic rhetoric. It is another to see the same expedient and covetous forces at work when the rhetoric of liberation defined the moment and the man. The monumental George Washington has so thoroughly taken over Americans' imagination that his biographers sometimes write as if there were no other people living in the eighteenth century.

The Cherry Tree

In 1939 Grant Wood painted a satiric portrayal of a six-year-old George Washington, hatchet in hand, being confronted by his father next to a desecrated cherry tree.[5] Called *Parson Weems' Fable,* the painting depicts Washington with the body of a boy but the head of an adult, namely, the head as it appears in Stuart's familiar portrait, on the one-dollar bill, so like the floating head. When *Life* magazine reprinted the painting on 19 February 1940, it reported that when the painting first appeared in 1939, "literal-minded patriots" "bombarded" Wood with angry letters for "debunking" Washington.[6] In the painting, Wood shows an oversized Weems as the magician in front of the curtain revealing the scene. Wood claimed that he was not actually dismissing the story, but instead bringing light to the importance of democratic art at a moment when despotic nations were using their nationalist mythologies to take over the world. Whether or not

Wood was debunking Washington, he was certainly calling attention to the power of art to mold the national imaginary.

Twenty-first-century historians who dismiss the cherry-tree myth as a fabrication risk, as Wood tried to point out, going head to head with the power that this particular fabrication has had over the American psyche from the early nineteenth century to the present. Even in this apocryphal but constantly repeated legend of George and the cherry tree we find the seeds of a contest between national memory as truth and national memory as a lie. In order to be the surrogate head of America, George Washington must be truthful and moral. This man, who was, according to Colonel Henry Lee, "first in war, first in peace, first in the hearts of his countrymen,"[7] had to stand for something. The fact that the whole scaffolding of George Washington's America—a slaveholding nation with slaveholding founding fathers fighting for liberty from British tyranny—was morally inverted and certainly not truthful did not matter. The fatherly head of George was what mattered.

Parson Mason Locke Weems published his first version of *The Life of Washington* in 1800, immediately after Washington's death, and presented it to a public that was eager to embrace any myth of their great leader. In the 1809 version of *The Life* Weems claims that George Washington "one day in the garden, where he often amused himself hacking his mother's pea-sticks," came upon a young "English cherry tree" that he knew his father loved. He tested his hatchet on the trunk of the tree and injured the bark so badly that the tree died. When his father saw the dead tree, he asked George what had happened, and George cried out the famous line, "I can't tell a lie, Pa; you know I can't tell a lie. I did cut it with my hatchet." Rather than getting upset, his father responded, "Run to my arms, you dearest boy . . . glad am I, George, that you killed my tree; for you have paid me for it a thousand fold. Such an act of heroism in my son is worth more than a thousand trees, though blossomed with silver and their fruits the purest gold."[8] Weems could have proved this same moral by using any possible incident, but the story of the cherry tree contains an illuminating folkloric history. Weems's fable was not simply a figment of his imagination. In constructing this story, Weems borrowed freely from the European folk tale that we now know as "Cinderella."

In Jacob and Wilhelm Grimm's version of the tale, when Cinderella's father asks his stepdaughters and Cinderella what they would like him to bring back from his journeys, Cinderella asks that he carry back home "the first branch which knocks against your hat." He showers his stepdaughters with dresses, pearls, and jewels, but for Cinderella he brings a hazel twig[9] that "brushed against him and knocked off his hat" in a green thicket. Cinderella plants the branch on her mother's grave and weeps "so much that the tears fell down on it and watered it. It grew, however, and became a handsome tree." Although the mother is dead, she is able, in her manifestation as a tree, to protect and nourish Cinderella. Cinderella asks the magic mother tree to let her go to the dance and to provide her with clothes. At the dance, she dances until evening and then wants to go home, and the king's son, who finds her beautiful, asks to see her home.[10]

The Grimm brothers' *Cinderella* and the many other cinder-girl stories are not nice tales of a princess who finally finds and falls in love with her prince. They are instead, as Maria Tatar in *Off With Their Heads* explicates, tales of a young woman trying to escape the incestuous pursuit of a brother, father, or uncle figure after her mother has died.[11] In almost all of the many versions of the cinder-girl tale a young woman loses her mother, and then her father either marries a woman with two wicked daughters or himself is interested in marrying Cinderella, his own daughter, in an incestuous union. In the Grimms' version Cinderella, who is afraid of the prince, runs from him and springs "into the pigeon-house." The prince waits for her father to come home, and then they both go to the pigeon house. The old man wonders, "Can it be Cinderella?" and the prince brings "him an axe and a pick-axe that he might hew the pigeon-house to pieces, but no one was inside it . . . for Cinderella had jumped quickly down from the back of it."[12] In most early versions of the tale, Cinderella runs away, covering herself with furs or smearing cinder on her skin in order to conceal her identity. The cinder-girl tales chronicle the transition from matriarchal to patriarchal power, replacing the earthly, fur-covered tree woman with the captive forced into the glass slipper of civilization.

In Parson Weems's story the references to the old tale have become fragments, but the desire to do away with the maternal connection to the tree and the male violence lingers on. Weems includes: the peas (the pea-sticks of George's mother); the fertility image of Cinderella's desire for a twig in the form of George beating the tree with a branch to produce more fruit; and the death of the mother who has turned into a tree, in this case symbolized by the English cherry as mother England. In the Grimms' tale, when Cinderella wants a wish to come true, she goes to her mother's grave, where the hazel tree grows, and cries out: "Shiver and quiver, little tree, silver and gold throw down over me." Weems includes this allusion in the phrase "though blossomed with silver and their fruits the purest gold."

By referencing this patriarchal tale, however obliquely, Weems unknowingly creates the perfect blueprint for an already thriving fairy-tale America. The fraternal bonding between father and son gives birth to an America free from the yoke of mother England. In the process, the father and son sacrifice all that the living tree symbolizes: the mother, future generations, biological integrity, and a direct physical connection to a living communal web. The father and son will kill off the tree and agree to support each other in covering up the "truth" in order to embrace the abstraction "honesty." The father would rather have an honest son than a living tree. Earlier in the tale the father even threatens to kill George if he does not tell the truth. He values their constructed bond above all else. Pacts between fathers and sons are carefully woven into the cultural myths and children's stories of America in order to reinforce the rules of patriarchal domination. They are handed down in oral storytelling from generation to generation.

Weems wrote and rewrote his two-hundred-page hagiography of Washington to ensure that the American cultural imagination would remember Washington and lionize him as a truth teller. That the story itself was a fabrication that successfully distorted the historical truths of Washington's contribution to American democracy did not dilute the impact of this mythic invention on American memory. The appellation "father of our country" became common parlance soon after Washington's death on 14 December 1799. Weems sold more than fifty thousand copies of his Washington biography,[13] an unheard-of number at the time. Weems's fabricated story about who could or could not tell a lie is not just a small lie but a significant contribution to the construction of ersatz America. Washington was not the father of a democracy; he was the father of a union of white, male American landowners.

Land-Surveying Teenager

Unfortunately for Mount Vernon, Gilbert Stuart's famous portrait and Houdon's well-known bust both depict Washington in his later years. Even though the estate proudly presents Grant Wood's painting, it seems to have been so disturbed by the image of the aged statesman, which the painting mocks, that in order to present a younger Washington, Mount Vernon spent millions of dollars and hired a team of forensic scientists to measure Washington's dentures, take digital photographs of the paintings, and gather any other available evidence to determine jaw size and identify bone structure and skeletal features in order to digitize Washington's head so that he might be depicted at earlier moments in his life.[14] The museum displays what it calls a forensic lab (fig. 25). These scientific methods allowed artists to sculpt the head of the young and middle-aged Washington at what they considered certain heroic moments during his life.

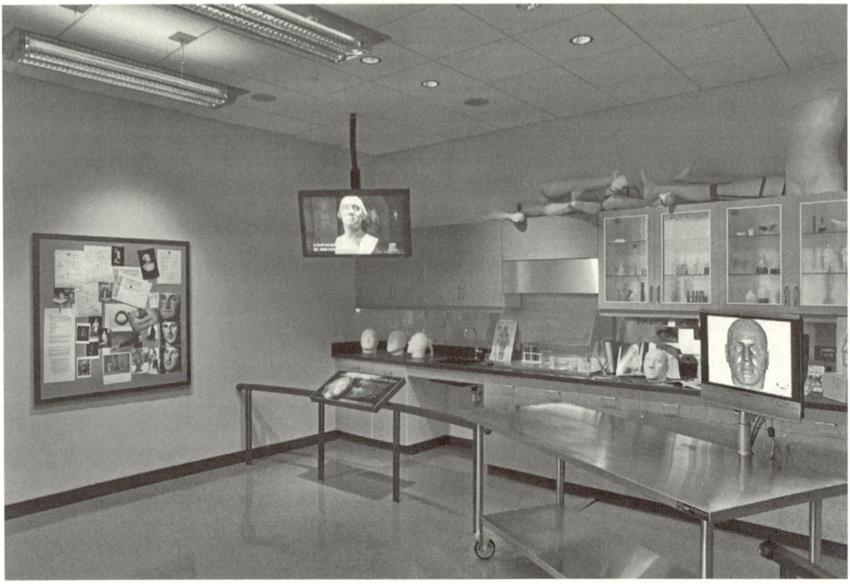

FIGURE 25
Ultraviolet forensic lab in the Donald W. Reynolds Museum and Education Center at Mount Vernon. (Courtesy of the Mount Vernon Ladies' Association)

Adjacent to the gallery that houses these new sculptures is a video nook where visitors can learn how artists crafted the "life" masks. The museum website description reads:

> Three life-size models created by a forensic anthropologist and a team of interdisciplinary experts depict Washington as never before seen at three significant stages of his life—including as a land-surveying teenager. This will dispel the elder statesman icon and encourage people to think about Washington in a new way: an incomparable American hero who evolved from a young man of modest means into this country's first and greatest president.[15]

In this nook there are oddly discarded plastic manikin parts that the artists must have used to determine realistic poses for Washington's body.

This exhibit and the resulting statues do present Washington as "never before seen," even in his own lifetime. These life-sized statues of Washington commemorating his career as a surveyor at nineteen, his role as commander in chief at Valley Forge at forty-five, and his being sworn in as president at fifty-seven in

FIGURE 26
Life-sized sculpture of George Washington as a nineteen-year-old surveyor in the wilderness, in the Donald W. Reynolds Museum and Education Center at Mount Vernon. (Courtesy of the Mount Vernon Ladies' Association)

1789—take a broadly sketched icon, a copy, and make a copy of a copy. Washington was never the innocent teenage surveyor "of modest means" playing with his surveyor's tools that these curators want us to imagine (fig. 26).

Surveyors in Washington's time were not humble workers but highly paid professionals with access to the best tracts of land. The young Washington was a privileged Virginia planter being trained as a surveyor by his brother and his brother's rich friends to become part of the Ohio Company. The Ohio Company was a group of Virginia landowners who looked west to Ohio and north to Pennsylvania with the aim of acquiring for the Crown and for themselves as much land as possible,[16] what amounted to hundreds of thousands of acres of Indian land.[17] Barbara Alice Mann writes about the Ohio Company's "presumptuous, and rather preposterous claim to Ohio lands, which had long belonged to the Iroquois, Cherokees, Lenapes, Shawnees, Miamis, Ottawas, Potowatomis. . . . Ohio was not 'empty lands' or mere 'hunting grounds.'"[18] Although they met with difficulties and competition, Washington and his business partners' desire for this land was clear throughout the period. Indeed, Washington's father, his grandfather, his great-grandfather, and in time his brothers were landowners who had all the resources of Virginia planters, including slaves.

Land speculators in colonial Virginia depended on surveyors to back up one of the most massive land grabs in history. They achieved their enormous landholdings in many ways: through complex treaties that were constantly broken; by plying the First Peoples with alcohol to make them sign their names to bogus land gifts; through the simple assumption of ownership; by use of force justified by trumped-up indignities; by infecting large populations of First Nation people with disease; or simply by burning the native dwellers' fields and massacring them. England gave out royal land grants as if it owned the whole territory and had the right to dispense such grants. George Washington personally received twenty thousand acres for his services in the French and Indian War.[19]

Washington learned how to play the land-grab game at a young age, from the legacy of his great-grandfather John Washington and his grandfather Lawrence Washington and directly from his father, Augustine Washington, and his brother Lawrence Washington. Although the Washingtons were not always directly involved, they benefited enormously from the stealing, swindling, and appropriations of land from native peoples—the daily, accepted, normal practice of the Virginia landowning elite. Many of Washington's male relatives held initially hundreds and gradually thousands of acres of land in northern Virginia and Pennsylvania, which most of them worked with slaves.

During the years of their greatest power, between 1650 and 1870, elite landowners in Virginia initially made up only 20 percent of the colonial population, but by 1750 they owned as much as 70 percent of the land. Small farmers made up approximately 20 percent of the population and owned the remaining 30 percent of the land; the majority of the population, including slaves and indentured servants, owned no land at all.[20]

John Washington already owned land through the headright system, and he received an additional seven hundred acres of land when he wed Anne Pope in 1658. The National Park Service initially used the copy on the website of Sulgrave Manor, George Washington's ancestral home, and concluded that "by 1668 and in a span of ten years, John Washington by use of head right and shrewd investment had amassed his land holdings to 5,000 acres"[21] The National Park Service later invested in one of the most thorough studies of the settlement of Virginia, Kathleen Bragdon's *Ethnographic Overview and Assessment: George Washington Birthplace National Monument.* Bragdon does not give John Washington credit for "shrewd investment." Instead she writes that "John Washington and his contemporaries participated in the common colonial strategy of dispossession, undermining Native claims to territories on the Northern Neck, and in the establishment of 'reserves' that effectively reduced Native mobility and access to their ancestral lands."[22]

The National Park Service rightly understood that to call acquisition of lands from the Dogue, Piscataway, and Susquehannock Indians around the area that is now Alexandria, Virginia, and Washington, DC, a "shrewd investment" is to ignore the fact that in order to "acquire" these lands, Virginia planters systematically pillaged native villages, or "retaliated" for attacks on settlers with out-of-proportion violence. Thousands of native peoples lost their lives, thousands more lost their homelands and communities, and by the late eighteenth century, there were only a scattering of native peoples left in the region. The Dogue, Piscataway, and Susquehannock Indians declined 95 percent from 1585 to 1685 and another 95 percent from 1685 to 1790. John Washington was not a man of modest means—nor was his great grandson.

John Washington received this land from the Crown through the headright system in partial payment for forcing poverty-stricken English and Irish youths into indentured servitude. No part of this story makes him a model ancestor for George Washington unless we count investing in the project of colonialization and Indian genocide heroic. Ersatz America at Mount Vernon takes what was a greedy, self-aggrandizing legacy in Washington's life and the life of his family and turns it into the seeds of a young general's courageous youth.

Visceral Graphism in "The Old Mount Vernon"

The erasure of slavery at Mount Vernon began shortly after the Mount Vernon Ladies' Association took over in 1858, whereupon Miss Sarah Tracy ran the estate with Upton Herbert. When northerners accused the Mount Vernon Ladies' Association of using slaves to run the plantation, Tracy responded: "All the Negro employees here have been freed, and as much as possible, are those descended from the old stock, who have been free for generations."[23] What we know from Eastman Johnson's paintings—of the kitchen at Mount Vernon (1857) and of the back side of Mount Vernon (1857)—is that there were many enslaved and some free people of African descent living on the property when Louisa Dalton Bird Cunningham, a slave owner herself, the matron of the Rosemont Plantation in South Carolina, took a steamboat ride down the Potomac in the summer of 1853 and first laid eyes on the dilapidated plantation.[24]

Louisa wrote to her invalid daughter, Ann Cunningham, after seeing Mount Vernon: "I was painfully distressed at the ruin and desolation of the home of Washington, and the thought passed through my mind: Why was it that the women of this country did not try to keep it in repair, if the men could not do it? It does seem such a blot on our country!"[25] Ann Cunningham, confined to her home with a severe spinal-cord injury since falling from a horse at fourteen, found meaning for her lonely life in marshaling the forces of women throughout the country to save Mount Vernon from certain decay and desecration. As she took on this ostensibly self-sacrificing project, she raised herself and the underemployed and undervalued women of the South, as well as some from the North, to a position of national prominence. In many ways, they influenced the historical memory of America more directly than they might have if they had been elected to positions of power.

Under the auspices of the Mount Vernon Ladies' Association, Ann Cunningham and her vice-regents raised two hundred thousand dollars over a five-year period to buy Washington's home from John Augustine Washington (George Washington's great-grand-nephew and the owner). They worked to turn Washington's Mount Vernon from the blighted property of 1853 to a vision of the perfect home of the father of the country. Tracy was concerned about northern detractors, since Ann and Louisa Cunningham, both slaveholders and southerners, were fixing up Mount Vernon to prove to the rest of the country that George Washington, the symbol of the Union, could be proliberty, a general of the American Revolution, and a benevolent slaveholder at the same time. No one could put forth the image of Washington as a benevolent slaveholder if poor and half-starved slaves and ex-slaves lived on the premises. The Ladies' Association desired to restore Mount Vernon, not to any actual time in the past, but to an idyllic and Arcadian ideal of pastoral bliss.

Thanks largely to Ann and her mother, this utopian vision of a gardenlike slave plantation would take comfortable hold in the American imagination, presented full blown in the 1939 Hollywood production of *Gone with the Wind* and found carefully preserved in almost every plantation home opened to the tourist industry. Louisa Cunningham's allegiance to "our country" in 1853 would be more to the South than to America as a nation. Mount Vernon only made sense in the sectional split occurring in the 1850s between slave and nonslave states if it could be presented as propaganda, the symbol of a nation conceived in gentleman farming, and dedicated to the principle that the slave owner would be benevolent and paternal, a kind father.

The Mount Vernon Ladies' Association has continued to raise money to restore and rebuild the historic home. In fact, the renovated Mount Vernon turned out to be one of the most lucrative tourist businesses in the world and one of the largest successful businesses run by women of that generation or indeed any generation.[26] But Mount Vernon is not just a business venture; it is an actual and metaphoric shrine to George Washington and supposedly to the idea of a democratic nation that he helped establish. From the outside, if one does not delve too deeply, it appears that the Mount Vernon Ladies' Association is honorable, and there is no sense that theirs is anything but a sincere attempt on the part of patriotic ladies to preserve the home of the father of our country—certainly a noble undertaking. However, the association was not just cleaning up the grounds; it was cleaning up the image of a slave-owning president. The pastoral imaginary allows visitors today to experience Mount Vernon with no guilt and no sense of the profound hypocrisy of Washington's position as slaveholder and revolutionary general.

Two painters, Junius Brutus Stearns and Eastman Johnson, visited the property during the 1850s, which was the period in which Cunningham started her campaign. Their interpretations of Washington's home reveal the underlying tension in the nation's relationship to the great hero at the time. John Michael Vlach argues that paintings like Stearns's *Washington as a Farmer at Mount Vernon* (1851), showing the famous general and former president out inspecting his lands (fig. 27), render slavery as a gentleman's pursuit:

> Presented in a relatively casual moment, Washington converses with an overseer, while several slaves are shown diligently gathering in the wheat harvest. Washington displays his authority by dispensing advice that we assume will be followed. Yet, his slaves seem not to pay him even the slightest bit of attention; the two who are closest to him even stop for a drink of water. Washington seems a fair and generous master, and slavery appears to be a benign practice, a position that the artist emphasizes by including in the foreground two children at play.[27]

Stearns's painting shows cherubic African slaves who look like gypsies engaged in romantic love trysts and children putting flowers in each other's hair. This is

FIGURE 27
Washington as a Farmer at Mount Vernon, by Junius Stearns, 1851. Oil on canvas, 36.83 × 57.47 cm. (Courtesy of the Virginia Museum of Fine Arts, Richmond; gift of Edgar Williams and Bernice Chrysler Garbisch; photo by Katherine Wetzel, © Virginia Museum of Fine Arts)

a picture of Arcadia, not a southern plantation run by a master and worked by enslaved people. The South wanted to claim for Washington the role of yeoman farmer working alongside his slaves. Slavery and democracy could coexist. Vlach emphasizes that this type of "romantic idealization" lifted plantations above the intensifying sectional debate over slavery.

In stark contrast, Eastman Johnson's *The Old Mount Vernon,* painted just six years later, in 1857, presents the back side of the pastoral image (fig. 28). As Vlach so accurately asserts, "When he painted Mount Vernon, he dared to ignore the eminence of the estate's revered founder and moved deliberately toward the margins of the property."[28] In Johnson's painting there are at least four people of African descent, but the vastness of the broken-down plantation dwarfs them. Johnson's painting shows enslaved people living in dark and obviously deteriorating conditions on a plantation that is shadowed in poverty. The trees overwhelm the house itself, and the details, including cracks in the paint, create a visceral and biomorphic graphism that dismantles the old story and begins to allow a new story to emerge. In one of the most original paintings of the estate,

FIGURE 28
The Old Mount Vernon, by Eastman Johnson, 1857.
Oil on board, 14 × 24¾ in. (35.6 × 62.9 cm).
(Courtesy of the Mount Vernon Ladies' Association)

Kitchen at Mount Vernon, Johnson uses visceral graphism to unsettle the ersatz myth. The details of crumbling walls and exposed bricks, as well as the complex folds in the African American woman's dress and her turban, begin to reveal the complexity of a graphic narrative. Johnson critiques a democracy that allows this kind of poverty as the result of slavery at the home of the first president of the republic. He exposes the hidden Mount Vernon.

The Mount Vernon Ladies' Association has never embraced the buried truths of Johnson's paintings. No Johnson paintings are referenced in the exhibits, although they are chronicled on the website. Even as late as 2006, when the current Mount Vernon Ladies' Association built the Donald W. Reynolds Museum and Education Center, they relentlessly pursued the pastoral image of Mount Vernon. The official website proudly states that the architects "tucked 65 percent of the 66,700 square foot complex under the four-acre pasture just inside Mount Vernon's main gate, a design which guarantees that the pastoral setting and viewsheds [areas of land seen from a particular perspective] to and from the Mansion will be preserved. Traditional Hogg Island sheep, like those Washington raised 200 years ago, will graze in the pasture, invoking a bucolic setting similar to the Mount Vernon of Washington's day."[29] As of this writing, sheep graze in several locations at Mount Vernon.

Unfortunately, the more than three hundred enslaved people, the overseers, the forced labor, the inhumane housing conditions, and the scarcity of food and clothing—all conditions that archival historians have documented—contradict the idea of a "bucolic setting." The emphasis on such a setting, the sheep, and the four-acre pasture suggests the original desire of southern preservationists to rewrite the slave plantation as a pastoral farm. And far from Stearns's romantic gentleman farmer, George Washington was a tough taskmaster. Mount Vernon's own Mary V. Thompson, the one on-site historian who consistently breaks down the official script, writes that George Washington was not "above blowing up at a servant, white or black, who didn't meet his standards."[30] Richard Parkinson, an Englishman, remarked that "it was the sense of all his [Washington's] neighbors that he treated [his slaves] with more severity than any other man."[31]

Neighborhood gossip may well have hinged on Washington's strict management of the estate, which became more modern and scientific over the years. By increasing the scope of supervision, Washington tracked the amount of time each person spent on each type of work, the number of days they lost due to illness, the amount of corn each farm used, and hundreds of other minute observations and calculations. Fritz Hirschfeld quotes a letter that Washington wrote when he became unreasonably angry about "The Laxness of Sewers":

> It is observed, by the Weekly reports, that the Sewers make only Six shirts a week, and the last week Caroline (without being sick) made only five; Mrs. Washington says their usual task was to make nine with Shoulder straps, and good sewing; tell them therefore from me, that what *has* been done, *shall* be done by fair or foul means; and they had better make choice of the first, for their own reputation, and for the sake of peace and quietness, otherwise they will be sent to the several Plantations, and be placed as common laborers under the Overseers threat.[32]

Washington was rapidly taking on the behavior of a modern industrialist or efficiency expert rather than that of a traditional gentleman farmer.[33]

While according to the ersatz myth of Mount Vernon the subsequent toll that Washington's scientific urge toward improvement took on his slaves was simply a necessary sacrifice to progress, we know from other sources that he did not have this same desire for cleanliness and obsessive orderliness in either the clothes he provided for his slaves or the buildings that housed them. The Polish revolutionary writer Julian Ursyn Niemcewicz wrote after visiting Mount Vernon in the 1790s that "there was no peasant in Europe who lives as poorly as the slaves in the New Republic."[34] One cringes at the thought that each of the numerous innovations Washington supposedly put in place on his plantations may have caused the enslaved people to work even harder. However, it is equally possible that these innovations, credited to Washington, might instead have initiated from enslaved Africans who began to understand the agricultural intricacies of their daily work.

Ann Cunningham and her vice-regents formed an elaborate organization that succeeded in tapping into the patriotic fervor and manipulating it to further the southerners' express desire to form one nation with slavery and plantations and George Washington busts for all. One must wonder why, at a time when white women had not yet won the right to vote, they would be so blindly patriotic. Maintaining the colonists' sense of entitlement—of Christian righteous dominion over the Indian barbarians and the savage Africans—was not easy. As the third, fourth, and fifth generations of European landed gentry sailed to America, establishing the ascendant position at each step of the way took repeated efforts. As these Europeans took up residency, stole more and more land, and enjoyed a wealth previously unheard of except by the very few, the women enjoyed a vicarious but eerie leisure. While the rich European men were grabbing land from the native peoples and able to offer a semblance of equality to the ever-increasing number of colonists, male and female, coming from Europe to settle in America, wealthy women were still appendages. As disturbing as this might be from a feminist perspective, their place as upper-class women depended on their maintaining the scaffolding of ersatz America.

Privileged women from aristocratic southern families who were accustomed to living on the excesses of this privilege became active players in the fantasy, demanding of the society their secondhand ownership in the rights of property and entitlement. To hide the trickery and extortion that their men were engaging in on a daily basis meant lives devoted to "preservation," building up a scaffolding to protect the fantasy, cleaning up the bones and blood, and putting on the finishing touches of the facade. If they were going to step onto this playing field, it would be in the manner of the rubble women in Germany after World War II, cleaning up the mess German and American men had created. Not, unfortunately, the metaphoric moral and ethical mess but the actual ruins of the homes, plantations, and burial sites that marked the creation of "nation" as they imagined America should be. When Lady Cunningham saw Mount Vernon in ruins, weeds growing on Washington's grave, the house crumbling, and people of African heritage living in squalid conditions on the premises, she had to act.

How could this be the reward she had been promised for membership in the upper class?

Homage to this fantasy demanded that these upper-class ladies devote their lives to protecting and refurbishing, redecorating and preserving, the icons of the story that was becoming America. If they were not the deserved heirs of the estate of America, then they had no identity. If they were not the ladies in waiting to honorable lords, then who were they, and why had so many native peoples and enslaved Africans died to allow them to live in luxury? The story had to be preserved, or they would die of the revulsion at what had been done, often in their name.

By the nineteenth century, as the colonial plantations of the forefathers began to crumble, memories began to fade, and the reality began to seep through, women took up the cry of preservation. The sites of memory of the expedient nation that had been fed so freely and so expensively on the backs of native peoples, poor white European immigrants, indentured servants, and enslaved Africans was crumbling; the cancer of slavery was eating away at all the great hopes and dreams, and the "nation" was dividing along lines of pro- and antislavery. To allow the foundational symbols of America to disintegrate in the mid-nineteenth century would have been to risk exposure of the emptiness at the core.

To understand why women would take up this mantle is not hard. In the nascent American patriarchy women were responsible for the home, and in the hierarchy of the nation women still felt responsible for the home, even if this home was their prison. To admit that the home was a prison and the nation a madhouse would be to go mad oneself; to look at the cursed lives that empire had left on the road to power would be to implode with the awareness of the catastrophic disaster of it all. The only course the women saw for dealing with the mess was to clean up the rubble and move forward, stepping over the rubble and building back up the monuments to empire that the Jamestowns and Mount Vernons had become.

Cracks in the Marble

Accumulating cultural capital by achieving the rank of commander in chief of the Continental Army in 1775, fighting for the noble cause of freedom in the Revolutionary War from 1775 to 1783, and then winning Congress's endorsement as the first president of the United States in 1789, all conferred power and impenetrability on Washington far beyond his person. The plaster white mask was so suffocating, and Washington performed the role for so long, that he himself would have had trouble distinguishing the myth from the reality, the person from the performance. Several times he tried, telling his supporters that he was not up to the job. In sad and cataclysmic ways he was not up to the job, and in equally sad and cataclysmic ways he *was* up to the job. The problem was not always the man, who had the good sense not to become a king and take the charade into the realm of the ridiculous, but the job definition itself. The republic, which had not become a democracy, needed its first president to keep the fabricated facade from crumbling. Unfortunately, Washington *was* up to this job.

If the northern and southern states would only form a "democratic" union on the land of native peoples and the sweat labor of Africans, then a man who was up to the job had to live a lie, both a personal lie—as George did by holding slaves and making no real attempt to fight for their manumission—and a professional lie—as he did by assuming that he could become the father of a nation that professed to be both democratic and slaveholding. For Americans in the first part of the nineteenth century to deconstruct the image of George Washington was to threaten the fragile threads that held together a deeply contested North and South, the same union that made up American nationhood. Washington was not just representative of the fledgling American nation. People poured the fervor of their patriotism, of their revolutionary pride, into his image. He was not just the emblem of the nation; he *was* the nation.

The emerging nation held its originary documents and symbols of nation close and dear. The 1776 Declaration of Independence maintained a high place of honor. However, less known to the contemporary consciousness was the value placed by the young democracy on the papers that documented George Washington's commission as commander in chief. As the official history of the Department of Archives proudly chronicles, government officials mounted these two documents together in the Patent Office from 1841 to 1876 "in a single frame and hung in a white painted hall opposite a window offering exposure to sunlight."[35] So closely associated are the two events in the public's mind that we link them in history as well as in importance.

But Washington did not become president until thirteen years after the signing of the Declaration of Independence. During this long space of time, which included six years of war and the drafting of the Constitution, many of Washington's actions were reprehensible. During this time he was still an exacting slaveholder. As commander in chief of the revolutionary forces, he ordered the destruction of the homes and land of the peoples of the Six Nations. If we add to this list the now very real possibility that Washington fathered a son named West Ford with a slave named Venus from his brother's plantation, the man we have idolized as Washington was not actually a god or a cardboard cutout but a human being.[36] The hidden truths that lie behind the carefully constructed mask of Washington are not small oversights; they are not anecdotes that can be winked at or, as in biography after biography, given two pages or a footnote. In each case, it took decades of work by meticulous archivists, brave historians, and disenfranchised ancestors to break down the barriers of official discourse.

After the Crops Are Harvested

While Washington fought for a democratic government that would guarantee freedom, equality, and liberty for all, he owned not only the 8,000 acres at Mount Vernon but 64,000 acres on his Virginia, Pennsylvania, and New York plantations and 317 slaves. Washington could have been a leader moving the colonies away from dependence on slave labor and toward greater and greater democracy; instead he became the standard-bearer for the status quo, benefiting economically and politically from his position as one of the richest landowners in Virginia. He could have followed the advice and model of his dear friend the Marquis de Lafayette and started a process of freeing his slaves, educating and helping them find useful work in a rapidly expanding, newly formed national economy. Instead Washington waited until he died to free his slaves (but not those of his wife, Martha), and while he was alive he treated them, except for a few favorites, as little better than useful workers on his vast farms and plantations. In his lifetime and when he died he was not anything as intangible or romantic as the figurehead for democracy but instead the overseer and architect of a deeply divided slavocracy.

Nonetheless, the people who served him existed and inserted themselves into the cultural imagination. John Trumbull reveals a subversive subtext to the iconic imaginary in his painting of Washington standing beside his horse with, in the background, one of his favorite slaves, William Lee (commonly known as Billy Lee), whom Washington called his *val de chambre* in his 1786 inventory (fig. 29). If we can get beyond the fact that Washington lists Lee in his inventory, we can see ways in which Lee asserts his own autonomy in his dress and demeanor.

Trumbull portrays the enslaved William standing in the shade, behind the horse, looking with what we assume to be a stereotypical expression of surprise and adoration at his master, who is decked out in full military regalia, illumi-

FIGURE 29
George Washington, by John Trumbull, 1780. Oil on canvas, 36 × 28 in. (Metropolitan Museum of Art, New York; bequest of Charles Allen Munn, 1924; image © Metropolitan Museum of Art; Art Resource, NY)

nated by the shining sunrise. In terms of perspective, the painting adheres to the dominant social construction of monumental art, with Washington out in front, the horse next, and then the enslaved *val de chambre* far behind. All would be according to order but for William's red turban and the golden ornament fastening it in the front, which lead our eye away from Washington as we become engrossed in these more interesting elements. William's red turban forces us to ask questions that the iconic picture does not. We are so used to the man in uniform that we do not wonder at anything on his person. We are much more intrigued by William. The ornament on William's turban is what Muslims throughout Turkey, India, and Iran call a *sarpech—sar* meaning "head" and *pech* meaning "fastener." This jeweled fastener would attach the turban to itself or to strings of pearls hanging on the headdress. The jeweled sarpech was often a form of reward for exemplary service or a gift one diplomat would present to another.[37] Not only do the red turban and the sarpech call attention to William but they confirm that the enslaved African of this period adorned himself according to Muslim custom; that he may have come from noble ancestry; and that he held on to his own cultural markers.[38] The best work on the subject of enslaved Muslim peoples is by the historian Sylvianne A. Diouf in her book *Servants of Allah: African Muslims Enslaved in the Americas.* Diouf argues strongly against the accepted narrative that enslaved Muslims quickly lost their faith: "On the contrary, systematic research throughout the Americas shows that, indeed, the Muslims were not absorbed into the cultural-religious Christian world. They chose to remain Muslims, and even enslaved, they succeeded in following most of the precepts of their religion."[39]

William Lee's head quickly becomes more important in this painting then Washington's. William takes center stage, when the artist is supposedly trying to make Washington appear dominant. One wonders, however, whether Trumbull had a subversive agenda. One of the most basic rules in painting and drawing is that the eye will be drawn to the point of greatest contrast. The greatest contrast in this painting is between William's flaming red turban and the dark background. William's person gives off more markers of dominance than of subservience. The turban actually expands the subject, creating an egalitarian field in this painting of supposed iconic superiority. Trumbull uses William's turban and sarpech to tell a graphic story that could not be recorded openly in narrative form. Artists and slaves were making themselves visible.

Trumbull *is* being subversive, even if he only trusted in verisimilitude and painted the vestments that William actually wore. Because William is marking and performing his own manhood as quickly and ingeniously as Washington is trying to take it away from him, he steps out of the frame of master and slave. That Trumbull paints William's turban as red and literally flaming off the top of his head, matching the tiny detail of the ship in flames far in the background, right in front of the horse's face, confirms this subversive subtext. This repetition of flaming red places William on the side of revolution, squarely in the fray, expectant of battle and liberation. While Washington has a calm look on his face, appearing almost to be wearing a mask, both William and, interestingly, the horse look troubled and expectant. Washington is an iconic cutout, while William and the horse are alive.

In this painting William is not just dressed in decorative garb; he wears the clothes of a comfortably well-off Muslim merchant. If William is asserting his own identity and cultural heritage, Washington does not own him body and soul. He is not an appendage but the head itself. After sifting through hundreds of Washington's letters, bills of sales, registers, newspapers of colonial Alexandria, and recent historical sources, Thompson provides ample evidence that Washington's slaves adorned their bodies with Muslim clothing and body markings, and that they even gave their children Muslim names. Her evidence confirms Trumbull's depiction of William with a turban and sarpech. Thompson writes that in letters written to Washington and about his estate, visitors describe Sambo, one of the Mount Vernon slaves, as having a tattooed face and earrings made of "real guinea gold."[40]

Thompson cites eyewitnesses who confirm that Sambo had "two or three scars or cuts on each side of his face, high up" and that "Jack, who was about thirty years old in 1761, was said to have 'a small face, with Cuts down each Cheek, being his Country Marks.' Neptune, who was twenty-five to thirty in that same year, had filed teeth and his back was decorated with 'many small Marks or Dots running from both Shoulders down to his Waistband.'"[41] In these marks we find not just a degree of self-agency but cultural continuity and selfhood that cannot be achieved by simply adorning oneself.

Jennifer Putzi's book *Identifying Marks: Race, Gender, and the Marked Body in Nineteenth Century America* addresses the complex negotiation that women and enslaved people faced when masters' tattoos and beatings or diseases and birthmarks patterned their bodies in distinct ways that they had not chosen or desired. She explores issues of agency, the gaze, and methods in which individuals transform and take control of how they are seen and interpreted. In the case of the small dots running along the slave Neptune's shoulders, these marks were chosen and contain a narrative of cultural power and pride. Neptune's markings, deliberate and precise, are the exact opposite of the scars and tattoos, the branding of ownership, that Putzi describes. Although as Putzi relates so clearly, individuals transformed their relationship to their scars, the marks of abuse are radically different from the markings of cultural continuity. When the master looks at the self-marked slave, he can never fully own him.[42]

Thompson relates that even the names corroborate a direct Muslim inheritance. Thompson states in an essay written for the Mount Vernon website that "two women, presumably a mother and daughter, named 'Fatimer' and 'Little Fatimer' were included on a 1774 list of tithables at Mount Vernon, a document prepared for local authorities listing the people for whom George Washington was responsible to pay taxes. These names appear to be a variation of the popular Muslim woman's name Fatima, meaning 'Shining One' in Arabic, and the name of the Prophet Mohammed's daughter." She also found evidence that a woman named Letty named her child Nila. "This unusual name," according to Thompson, "is a known variant of an Islamic woman's name 'Naailah,' which means 'someone who acquires something' or 'someone who gets what they want.'"[43]

Thompson argues that people were actively practicing the Muslim religion at Mount Vernon for a period of at least thirty-five years and that for a great deal of time afterwards Muslim religious practices, cloths, and names were part of the culture of the slave community there.[44] Trumbull's painting and Thompson's accounts of individual slaves on the Mount Vernon plantation bear no resemblance to the ersatz image of slaves at Mount Vernon or of colonial slavery that we have been taught in contemporary American schools to imagine. Any man or woman at Mount Vernon who had a marked body could not identify as "a slave": they had a history, a cultural identity, and personal volition. Sambo's, Neptune's, and Jack's marked bodies are a powerful form of visceral graphism, a script that tells a story of heritage, and cultural roots that are radically different from those of the fox-hunting, landowning Virginia lords and ladies.

After the war and Washington's bloody baptism defending the rhetoric of freedom and liberty, he did begin to change his opinion on slavery. This may have been driven as much by economic necessity as it was by humanitarianism. Washington realized in the late 1780s that the decreasing proportion of useful slaves to dependent slaves at Mount Vernon and other farms, partially the result of his decision in 1786 not to engage in the buying or selling of slaves, was leading him to economic difficulty. If he could not buy or sell slaves, then he could not get rid of dependent and no longer useful slaves or buy young, healthy, productive slaves. The promise to himself and the country not to engage in the slave market might easily have come from his awareness that his legacy, already fully emblazoned on the national consciousness, would be tarnished by such lowly practices. But there may have been other, more personal reasons as well.[45]

If West Ford was indeed his son from a sexual liaison with an enslaved woman named Venus from his brother John's plantation in Westmoreland, as Henry Wiencek argues, then Washington might have feared his son's being sold at auction.[46] Before Wiencek provided the timetable that would vindicate Linda Allen Bryant's stories, she wrote her controversial 2004 fictional account of the Ford family history, called *I Cannot Tell a Lie,* based on a liaison between Venus and George Washington. At first historians could not confirm the dates that would have made such a liaison possible, but Wiencek validated a visit by Venus to Mount Vernon that would make this association conceivable.

Wiencek's latest historical research makes the idea that West Ford was George Washington's son a real possibility, if not a known fact, and pinpoints the year of Ford's birth as 1785. Wiencek uses travel records and letters to argue that Ford could easily have been conceived when Hannah Washington and her slave Venus visited Mount Vernon in the late fall or early winter of 1784. Wiencek argues that it is also quite possible that Ford at age four or five accompanied George's nephew Bushrod Washington on a visit in January 1789. "Perhaps it is not a mere coincidence," Wiencek writes, "that Bushrod's January 1789 visit occurred at the same time that Washington declared to David Humphreys his regret over slavery and confided his plan for emancipation and his intention that the children of slaves should have 'a destiny different from that in which they were born.'"[47] The Ford family has always argued that these visits and the fact that West Ford was George Washington's child are accepted truths in its oral history.

For Washington, the birth of this son into slavery could have been a powerful incentive for disengaging himself from the slave trade.[48] But if he was not going to sell slaves, the question remained in the late 1790s, then how could he get rid of the slaves who had become a drain on his family economy and would be a stain on his legacy after he died? Manumission was one way out. He might have expressed his desire for manumission in his will in order to solve the financial and emotional riddle of these extra slaves.

Washington wrote clearly in his will, dated 9 July 1799, that all slaves in his name be freed after his wife's death:

> And I do moreover most pointedly, and most solemnly enjoin it upon my Executors hereafter named, or the Survivors of them, to see that this clause respecting Slaves, and every part thereof be religiously fulfilled at the Epoch at which it is directed to take place; without evasion, neglect or delay, after the Crops which may then be on the ground are harvested, particularly as it respects the aged and infirm; seeing that a regular and permanent fund be established for their support so long as there are subjects requiring it; not trusting to the uncertain provision to be made by individuals.[49]

While Washington's desires concerning manumission are unequivocal, his insistence that this manumission take place without evasion, neglect, or delay, "after the Crops which may then be on the ground are harvested," reveals the ambiguous nature of his convictions. While he is writing the most important lines of his life, still in the forefront of his mind is the need for these enslaved human beings to finish the work at hand before they walk away from the plantation.

In his defense, Washington filled almost three pages of his will with explicit instructions concerning the manner in which his slaves were to be freed. He specified that the children should be educated and trained so that they could support themselves as free people, and in his own methodical way he predicted the exact difficulties that would in fact face enslaved Africans after manumissions in 1865. He left money to support his manumitted older or feeble slaves who could no longer work; he gave William Lee a pension for life and allowed him to stay on the plantation; and he tried, with the strong encouragement of Lafayette, to imagine a scheme for supporting and educating the freed slaves. His will is firm on this point.[50] There is also some speculation that he did not emancipate his slaves sooner because so many of them had intermarried with his wife's slaves and manumission would have broken up families.

What both Lafayette and Washington realized was that to free the slaves would mean instituting schools, work programs, and education in self-sufficiency—an experiment that they often discussed but that neither had the support of the community to carry out. Washington went so far as to try to rent out his neighboring acres to tenants who would hire his manumitted slaves, and Lafayette bought an estate to house freed slaves. But Washington did not take a stand early enough, and when he did take a stand, it was not strong enough. He did not fight against the Fugitive Slave Act of 1793, and, in fact, he was trying to capture his own runaway slave Oney Judge in 1796, just three years before he died. Nor could he understand why his cook, Hercules, and his family would want to run away; his escape both angered and wounded Washington. Thompson documents that these and many of Washington's other slaves did try to run away. While Washington led a life devoted to the fantasy of the yeoman farmer plantation owner who could fight for democracy while forcing hundreds of enslaved people to build his empire, he could not get beyond what Lincoln would face years later, namely, that preserving the Union and the abolition of slavery did not go hand in hand. Southern plantation owners would not have followed Washington if he had decided to free his slaves to set an example for the rest of the nation. His last act was perhaps a good one, but it was far too little, far too late.

Nor were the Mount Vernon Ladies as innocent and pure as they might at first appear to have been. It does not seem odd that they made the renovation of Mount Vernon their undying cause in the early years, but it is somewhat surprising that generations of women since then have continued to do so, eventually endowing a website, an inn, the shops at Mount Vernon, a large interpretive center, and, in the last five years, the Donald W. Reynolds Museum and Education Center and the Ford Orientation Center, which, the website boasts, includes 25 new theaters and galleries. Mount Vernon, unlike most struggling museums, is open to the public 365 days a year. One can still hear rumblings of Washington's highly questionable decisions and actions in the bucolic scenery of present-day Mount Vernon.

While the researchers in the library at Mount Vernon, particularly Mary Thompson, have done an admirable job trying to bring Billy Lee, Venus, West Ford, Sambo Anderson, Simon Washington, Austin, Frank, Oney, Charlotte, and many more enslaved people out of the shadows to fill in the contours of Kerry James Marshall's silhouettes; while there is now a memorial, organized by Dr. Judith Saunders Burton and designed by architecture students at Howard University, to the enslaved Africans who gave their lives to service at Mount Vernon, with a plaque that reads: "In Memory of the Afro Americans Who Served as Slaves At Mount Vernon This Monument Marking Their Burial Ground Dedicated September 21, 1983 Mount Vernon Ladies' Association"; while Mount Vernon celebrates Black History Month; while there are reenactments with actors representing enslaved people; while there is a new slave cabin far away from the main house—still, throughout the Mount Vernon plantation the adoration and whitewashing continues. Not only at Mount Vernon but also at the Washington Monument and before all the numerous statues of Washington, we cannot actually see, feel, touch, hear, grieve, or mourn the lives of those who served Washington.

To open up this bandaged wound of American history—Washington the wound, not the icon—is not that difficult. So much of the research has already been done. How can we know the facts and yet continue to adore and adorn the false image? Here lies the cause. We, the American public, have refused to let ourselves be appalled and angry. We have let Mary V. Thompson, alone in the archives, or the descendants of West Ford carry that banner. For years the descendants of Venus and West Ford listened to the oral tradition that their ancestor was the son of George Washington. And for years mainstream academic historians and the Mount Vernon Ladies' Association went on National Public Radio to declare this an impossibility, stating that there was no evidence that West Ford could actually have been Washington's son. Now that a respected historian has provided evidence that it is factually possible, West Ford's descendants may finally receive some attention.

The United States has never recovered from the fact that propagandists like Parson Weems and the Mount Vernon Ladies' Association were blindly willing to sacrifice the possibility of a truly noble and exciting liberty, a land free of slavery, for the holograph of a gentlemen farmer quietly farming his land. The preservation of an ersatz liberty, one for white landowners only, meant taking this simple man with all his faults, the very faults of the faltering democracy, and anointing him as the great hope of union. The fantasy of union that this act put into motion allowed the fledgling nation to continue to deny its own hypocrisy and cost thousands of lives, not just because of the continuation of slavery for another three-quarters of a century, not just because of the thousands who died in the Civil War, but through segregation, lynching, economic starvation, and the violence in the troubled cities of our current nation.

That the Country Might Be Not Merely Overrun but Destroyed

One of the ersatz images of George Washington is that he was a distinguished general whose leadership during the French and Indian War and the Revolutionary War guaranteed Americans' freedom. George Washington in his youth was actually a fairly mediocre soldier: "Washington returned to Virginia a defeated man, even more a bungler who had been at times overly daring and at times indecisive, and who had been unable to enlist Indians to offset the French advantage. He might have had 'courage and resolution,' General Lord Albemarle, the British ambassador to France, commented, but he simply had 'no knowledge or experience in our profession. And yet miraculously the twenty-two-year-old soldier was greeted back home by fellow Virginians as something of a hero, if only for his determination and valor under fire. He allowed others to take the burden of blame for the defeat."[51]

If we measure George Washington's military prowess not by his participation in famous revolutionary battles but by his decision to order the Sullivan-Clinton campaign, a devastating destruction of Six Nations (also called Five Nations) homes, lands, and peoples, a different general emerges. Washington appears crueler, much more volatile, and more interested in adding acreage to American landholdings—opening access to the Great Lakes and to trade routes for new European settlers—than in engaging in any Revolutionary War concept as esoteric as freedom or democracy or a new republic. The need in 1607 to prove the economic viability of the colonies had turned into the drive in 1779 to build the grandest empire in the world with a few powerful men in control of vast acreage. In the early eighteenth century, the colonists' campaign to push farther and farther west was met by a strong push on the part of the Six Nations Confederacy to stay put, at times even to settle farther east. There was only one way to secure the lands for British interests, land speculation, room for new settlers, and access to trade routes: drive out the First Nations.

The colonial period in American history was one of exciting interdependence, when disparate peoples learned how to live with one another, becoming fluent in one another's languages, customs, and rituals, while battling for land, negotiating peace, engaging in trade, articulating the rhetoric of a hundred treaties, and weaving the wampum belts and carving the grandfather masks of compromise and reconciliation. David L. Preston provides a detailed account of the intersecting communities that crisscrossed the Ohio Valley during this period. Preston's map fully supports Mary Pratt's assertion of early America as a zone of contact and interaction rather than one of conqueror and conquered. Preston writes:

> The convergence of three rivers, Native trails, and British military roads produced an extraordinary confluence of cultures in the Ohio Valley. Thoroughfares such as Braddock's and Forbes roads began to overlay an even more complex network of Indian trails (Braddock's Road, in fact, was once Nemacolin's trail). The Catawba Path, which ran from Iroquoia to the Southeast, came through the heart of the Redstone Country and other Euroamerican settlements along the Cheat River. The east-west Mingo Path facilitated daily contact between the Mingoes and the Monongahela colonists. Hundreds of Iroquois, Delaware, Shawnee, and Mingo warriors going to fight their Catawba enemies came through the colonial habitations weekly, bartering with or demanding supplies.[52]

The crisscrossing paths and roads on which native and European peoples intersected with each other on the way to war and trade carved a clear graphic pattern in the landscape, a visceral map of feet etching out paths that inform us of a complex, multilingual community in a constant state of cultural interchange.

Rather then learning the textual language of intersecting life paths, a kind of language a surveyor would have no trouble explicating and even composing, George Washington chose instead to fight first and ask questions later. From his first battle, the battle of Jumonville Glen, through the Sullivan-Clinton campaign,

Washington gloried in his military experience, but he had little skill in, or did not choose, diplomatic nuance. At Jumonville Glen he ambushed, and some claim massacred, a diplomatic party of Frenchmen under the command of Jumonville who were calling for a cease-fire.[53] The fact that Washington emerged from this period of western expansion, land acquisition, and empire building as a "hero" reveals the compromised values of colonial America. As long as the Indians were necessary to the British forces for purposes of war with France and trade in the interior, the British and later the Americans courted and sometimes "appeased" various groups. But whenever the Indians stood in the way of settlement and empire building, they became expendable. Washington could have joined with the confederation of the Seneca, Onondaga, Oneida, Mohawk, Cayuga, and Tuscarora peoples—the Six Nations Confederacy—to form a complex community of diverse cultures. Instead he chose to commit himself to a military campaign of ethnic cleansing.[54]

It is this act, Washington's decision to order a scorch-and-burn attack on the Six Nations Confederacy, that should give us pause. When he wrote the orders to attack the Six Nations, he was following the worn-out colonialist policy of Indian removal. Sadly, for Washington and his generals, this act was simply one of expediency. These Six Nations peoples, who had established centuries-old, proven forms of representative government; who had helped European settlers accommodate and often assimilate into native communities; who in the opinion of an entire school of historians influenced the formation of the colonies as a confederacy; and who had been, and could have continued to become, natural allies and friends, fell instead, by the stroke of Washington's pen in 1779, to the flames and gunshot of his militias.

Before the Articles of the Confederation, drafted in June 1776, were ratified, George Washington ordered the destruction of the Six Nations' villages and towns. On 31 May 1779 George Washington penned the following orders to General John Sullivan:

> The Expedition you are appointed to command is to be directed against the hostile tribes of the Six Nations of Indians, with their associates and adherents. The immediate objects are the total destruction and devastation of their settlements, and the capture of as many prisoners of every age and sex as possible. It will be essential to ruin their crops now in the ground and prevent their planting more. . . .

> I would recommend, that some post in the center of the Indian Country, should be occupied with all expedition, with a sufficient quantity of provisions whence parties should be detached to lay waste all the settlements around, with instructions to do it in the most effectual manner, that the country may not be merely overrun, but destroyed.[55]

Washington would use the "massacres" of settlers at Pennsylvania's Wyoming Valley (32 killed) and Cherry Valley by the British colonel John Butler and Seneca forces to justify the campaign. Seneca forces had agreed to join with Butler in these so-called massacres in retaliation for encroachment on native lands, specifically the burning of the Tioga and Onoquaga villages. But Washington ordered this campaign not primarily because of these attacks or because the Senecas, the Cayugas, and the Onondagas were siding with the British—the usual justifications—but simply because these people were in the way of the tsunami of American settlers moving into the western territories. George Washington and New York governor George Clinton ended up purchasing several hundred acres of the conquered land for themselves.

The Sullivan-Clinton campaign was, in fact, the largest campaign of the Revolutionary War and the most massive attack on Native American peoples in the many years of colonial occupation. American generals and colonels, including Major General John Sullivan, General James Clinton, Colonel Daniel Brodhead, Colonel Goose Van Schaick, Brigadier General Enoch Poor, Colonel Peter Gansevoort, and Colonel William Butler, with between 4,500 and 6,000 troops, attacked, burned, and pillaged every native village in what is now western and middle New York State. Many Seneca, Onondaga, and Cayuga peoples were captured, kidnapped, beaten, raped, and killed on the spot. The troops burned hundreds of thousands of acres of corn, fruit trees, and homes. While some of the Native Americans had time to flee because of an intricate system of messengers and warnings, thousands who escaped to British forts died of starvation and exposure during the following autumn and winter.

Although we rarely hear the number of Senecas, Onondagas, and Cayugas killed in the Sullivan-Clinton campaign, we do know that there were many deaths. Sullivan and almost every other officer tells of an old squaw who came to tell them of the dead and wounded. They all say that they gave her a warm blanket and a bit of food. But in most cases vulnerable people were either killed, taken prisoner, or left to starve. Barbara Alice Mann argues that the campaign was a systematic, highly destructive, and genocidal attack. She cites evidence of multiple rapes of the female captives—even asserting the possibility that the women were taken captive for this reason—and the murder of toddlers who were too small to walk and thus a nuisance to the movement of captives from town to town.[56] The American generals and lieutenants in their written record make a point of recording every captured white child, but only once does an officer report finding a small Indian child. This is a bit suspicious, because they report speaking to abandoned old women, the infirm, and all who were left behind. Captain Jabez Campfield writes in one entry only that "here was left a child of about two years old."[57] In all his other descriptions of children he tells who adopted or cared for the child, but in this case he is silent. Wayne Lee writes in *Barbarians and Brothers: Anglo-American Warfare, 1500–1865* that "the Iroquois pointed out that when the Americans took British prisoners, 'The Rebels don't put them to death; But we have no mercy to expect, if taken, as they will put us to death immediately, and will not even spare our Women and children.'"[58]

If biographies and histories of Washington mention the Sullivan-Clinton campaign at all, they minimize its importance, defining it as a sideshow to the real battles of the Revolutionary War. Yet, this was the violent and deadly act of aggression that effectively ended the possibility of peaceful coexistence between native peoples and Europeans, split families and mixed communities, and ensured the poverty and continued second-class citizenship of hundreds of groups of native peoples. That there is still a vibrant and strong political community among the Six Nations is testimony to the strength of these peoples and of the confederacy. The Mohawks, in addition to their many other accomplishments, are known for being the most skilled high-beam steelworkers and have built hundreds of skyscrapers in New York City and other cities.

Mann and Max Mintz in *Seeds of Empire* present the most thoroughly researched day-by-day accounts of the campaign, and they both pull open the curtains to reveal the full calamity of the moment. Mann reveals that "too few scholars know that the term 'holocaust' was previously used by the Iroquois, from the eighteenth century onward, to label the horrific destruction visited upon them in 1779 by Van Schaick, Brodhead, Clinton, and Sullivan."[59] Mann exposes the fact that scholars during the nineteenth and early twentieth centuries presented "these orchestrated despoliations as great victories over a ferocious foe." Towns throughout New York State have plaques commemorating Sullivan and Clinton, Brodhead, and Van Schaick: "They glorified in Washington's ordered destruction of the food supply, housing stock, and habitability of the Iroquoian homeland, certain as it was to bring about conditions of starvation and exposure, not to mention the transfer of land from the Iroquois to the Americans."[60] For at least two centuries there have been elaborate parades, speeches, and town gatherings to commemorate what was seen as a day of liberation for the settlers.[61]

To believe that Washington had a right to do this, as an act of aggression against Indians who had been attacking settlers, is to distort the years of contact. While native people did attack and kill settlers, at times violently, they did not do so without centuries of provocation; they knew by 1779 that they were fighting for their lives and their lands. The European settlers were encouraged by wealthy landowners to project their own violence and aggression onto the native peoples even though they had engaged in a 170-year unabating attack on Indian peoples.

The officers of the Sullivan-Clinton campaign wrote openly in their journals about scalping Indians, as if it was common practice. William Barton wrote on Monday, 13 September 1779: "The men then went to scalp him, which caused some dispute who should have it."[62] In fact, the Europeans—French, English, and Dutch—from as early as the first half of the seventeenth century offered pioneers, settlers, and militiamen a bounty for every head or scalp of an Indian returned to them. As Ward Churchill confirms,

> Payment listed for native scalps was £50 each, regardless of age or sex, if the killer were an average civilian or professional scalp hunter; £20 each as a supplement to the meager pay of militiamen; and £10 each to regular soldiers. These rates were modified in 1704 so that an incredible £100—*four times* the annual income of a good New England farmer—was paid per man's scalp, £40 per woman's, and £20 per child's. "Men" and "women" were defined as being any Indian over ten years of age.[63]

When Washington's command gave legitimacy to this rampage, the militia needed no encouragement; many militiamen were already experienced Indian hunters. There was always a fringe element willing to kill and destroy if given an economic incentive to do so. This particular raid was not so much the exception as the general policy.

The English and the French took to scalping with a vengeance out of all proportion to the scalping native peoples might have engaged in prior to contact. Churchill relates that in 1779, "during the Sullivan Campaign against the Seneca, the soldiers of the Continental Army weren't content with merely scalping their foes, living or dead. Not uncommonly, they skinned them from the hips down in order to make leggings from the tanned hides."[64] Churchill is not exaggerating. Sargent Thomas Roberts writes: "31st. This morning Our trupes found 2 Indians and Skin thear Legs & Drest them for Leggins."[65] The English did not learn scalping from the native peoples. The beheading and scalping takes the concept of personal identity and the iconization of George Washington's head to a whole new level. His head is regarded as precious to the nation, a prize that should be saved. But for the privilege of that one prized head to represent our nation, thousands of heads had to roll.

Often one European group would dress up as Indians in order to attack another European group and put the blame on the Indians; the twisted aspect of this performative dressing up is disturbing. Even as they were exterminating native peoples, the immigrant Europeans adopted not just the dress but also the symbolism of the natives; to be American was to embody some strange hybrid notion of Indian. After all, what separated European settlers in America from those who remained in Europe was their newfound cross-cultural interchange with the Algonquian, Mohawk, Iroquois, and Delaware peoples. It is not surprising, then, that Europeans not only stole the land but also have stolen the eagle from the top of the Six Nations Tree of Peace, the image of an Indian maiden as Liberty for gold coins in 1849, the story of Pocahontas, and much more. In fact, cultural cross-dressing was a common practice in a society whose members crisscrossed one another's paths daily, intermarried, and traded everything and anything. What is surprising and ironic is that colonialists and newly minted Americans chose to murder democratic American hybridity in order to claim diversity as a defining aspect of the new nation.

Colonization was to be total, involving body and soul, taking over, literally ingesting, the "other" body, cutting off the scalps and skins and stitching them into hats and tanning them into leggings. On a less gruesome level, Robert Griffing's paintings of the Six Nations peoples show Iroquois men wearing British uniforms and British soldiers adorned with Indian blankets and feathers. The European settlers stilled the democratic and egalitarian mixed racial and ethnic identity within themselves to become white. To kill was to become. This self-loathing was incomprehensible because it was the spark of interchange, of difference from the European, that fueled the revolution. The new American became a cannibal who invigorated his waning Anglo-Saxon roots through the intake of native strength and resilience. The invented American with Indian blood became the genetically superior brand of whiteness, but whiteness nonetheless.

George Washington's ordering the destruction of the Six Nations Confederacy was terrible in its own right. But that the people whose destruction he ordered were the same people who had been neighbors, friends, husbands, wives, trading partners, and teachers of English, French, German, and Dutch settlers over a 170-year period, betrayed the hidden desire, no matter how subliminal, to establish the righteous Christian and white ownership of America. Rather than embracing the reality of an ethnically diverse nation that had become—and still is becoming—stronger and more richly layered every year, Washington continued on the path of land acquisition and ownership. America persisted under his leadership in a delusional search for purity, the alabaster monument of nation rather than the permeable body of democracy.

During the campaign, many soldiers kept journals or wrote letters home. These records reveal that most of the soldiers killed native peoples with no sign of remorse. In the hundreds of pages of published journals from this war, the officers and enlisted men talk with pride about the excellent job they are doing razing Indian villages. All six of the generals followed trails through Indian country and destroyed everything in their path—fruit trees, corn, livestock, houses. Sullivan, with the precision of a surgeon, methodically records the actions of his military force: "At Kanadaque we found twenty-three elegant houses mostly finished and in general, large. Here we also found very extensive fields of corn, which having been destroyed, we marched for Hannayaye, a small town of ten houses, which we also destroyed."[66] Sullivan talks about death, murder, and burning with detachment, showing no sign of morality, Christian brotherhood, or a guilty conscience.

Major Jeremiah Fogg and Sullivan both calculate future use of the captured land quite blatantly, assessing its quality, the ways in which they could plant the land, the number of fruit trees, and so on. Fogg writes:

> The land between the Seneca and Cayuga lakes appears good, level, and well-timbered; affording a sufficiency for twenty elegant townships, which in process of time will doubtless add to the importance of America. The communication of the Seneca with Cayuga is passable with boats and is about twenty miles.
>
> Whether the God of nature ever designed that so noble a part of his creation should remain uncultivated, in consequence of an unprincipled and brutal part of it, is one of those arcana, yet hidden from human intelligence. However, had I any influence in the councils of America, I should not think it an affront to the Divine will, to lay some effectual plan, either to civilize, or totally extirpate the race. Counting their friendship, is not a

> disagreeable task, but impracticable; and if obtained it is of no longer duration than while we are in prosperity and the impending rod threatens their destruction. To starve them is equally impracticable for they feed on air and drink the morning dew.[67]

Fogg's accusation that "so noble a part of his [God's] creation" is "uncultivated" because it is in the hands of "unprincipled" and "brutal" people assumes that if the right people, meaning elite Europeans, had the land, they could cultivate it properly. In Fogg's reasoning we see the ersatz rationalization set forth by the original propagandists for English colonization of Virginia.

It is hard to understand how Fogg, standing on Indian land and describing perfectly cultivated fields of corn, hundreds of exquisite fruit trees, and beautiful houses, can call the Onondagas, the Cayugas, and the Senecas uncivilized. One wonders exactly why he feels he has the right—while in the midst of scorching and burning, driving people from their homes, and destroying life—to call them "unprincipled" and "brutal." In this and in most of the military journals concerning the campaign, there is a complete dislocation between mind and body, action and heart, language and reality. Fogg has no problem burning fields and fruit trees with one hand while writing about uncultivated lands with the other; mentioning God and his creation in one breath and in the next breath advocating the total starvation, destruction, and extirpation of the First Peoples. The word *extirpate,* which is not in common usage today, implies a total removal by tearing up the roots of a community or people.[68]

Sullivan reports to General Washington with pride, listing every tree, bush, bit of corn, and animal that the generals have had their troops destroy. He proudly asserts that he has accomplished his task and that "every creek and river has been traced, and the whole country explored, in search of Indian settlements, and I am well persuaded that, except one town situated near the Alleghany, about fifty miles from Geneseo, there is not a single town left in the country of the Five Nations."[69] The website Sullivan/Clinton Campaign Then and Now provides a terrifying interactive map that traces the six generals' converging paths of destruction as they marched from village to village.[70] This map of annihilation is the antithesis of the regenerative crisscrossing trails and the forts and houses built to connect the paths that joined one culture with another. The meshwork of connection took hundreds of years to weave, the extirpation a matter of weeks. The most disturbing quality of all the generals' and enlisted men's journals, diaries, and letters is their detachment. The word most repeated in the journals and diaries is *destroy.*

The Influence Thesis

One of the most disturbing aspects of Washington's campaign is that the peoples of the longhouse were the very peoples who—through the words of intricate, slow and steady treaty negotiations, through the threaded and knotted beads of hundreds of thousands of yards of wampum strings and belts, through the communal and sanctioned oratory of negotiators from all sides—had not just worked out a largely peaceable coexistence with the European colonists but in many instances helped these communities begin to create a governmental structure for their new communities. Accumulated evidence proves that the peoples living on the land when Europeans settled the country were integral members of a hybrid, multiracial, multiethnic society and that as members of this society they attended hundreds of treaty sessions, participated in the discussion about the formation of the Americas, supported colonists in their war against the British, supported the French against the British and the British against the French, and in every other way were involved in this formative stage of American democracy.[71]

What allowed the peoples of the Six Nations to come up with the notion of a confederacy in the first place and what then made the "founding fathers" understand and take this gift of a complex democratic form into the writing of the Articles of Confederation and finally into the Constitution is known as the Influence Thesis. This thesis has been richly debated but largely misunderstood in historical accounts. These were not some far-off, exotic Indians. According to many historians, they were the people who helped Benjamin Franklin formulate the principles of confederation that led to the balance between state and federal government found in the Constitution.[72] Those who argue against the influence of the Six Nations Confederacy forget that it was the only working model of a confederation of states at the time. For Jefferson and Franklin, the proximity of the Six Nations Confederacy made the native people's words, ideas, and political insights highly likely sources for the founding fathers' formulation of a government. To assume otherwise is to construct an odd confinement of ideas that could not have existed in this highly porous community between the colonists, new settlers, and the Six Nations Confederacy. Thanks to Franklin in particular, the treaties were a matter of public record.

The Albany Plan is often regarded as the first proposal for a united colonial government, Benjamin Franklin being the chief architect. What few realize is that England had asked the delegates to gather in Albany in 1754 to work out a strategy for appeasing the Six Nations Confederacy, which in 1753 had declared that the Covenant Chain between the Six Nations and the British was officially broken as the result of rash and unabating violence, settlement, and disregard of native treaties, native lands, and native alliances. Not wanting to lose this military and trade alliance, the royal forces asked the colonies to come up with a plan.

Thus, at the first moment of defining a confederation of colonies, the Six Nations were foremost on everyone's minds. In addition to this underlying agenda, the Albany Conference was in no way a carefully thought-out attempt at colonial rule. As Fred Anderson writes in *The Crucible of War,* each of the groups at the Albany Conference was scheming in direct and indirect ways to claim as much of the empire for themselves as possible. Even Franklin, according to Anderson, was positioning himself for power in the newly configured colonies. He understood, as all the other participants did too, that a united colonial force would be able to stand strong against the native peoples and extend settlement farther into the interior. But even given this understanding, there were factions and in-fighting. This display of self-interest on Franklin's part did not preclude his having gleaned the blueprint for unity and confederation from the Six Nations Confederacy. He had spent years printing the intricate treaty negotiations of the Six Nations, and he knew the precise values and strictures that held the confederacy together.[73]

During the negotiations for the Lancaster Treaty of 1744, Canassatego, speaking for the Confederacy, had advised the colonies to come together in confederation:

> We have one Thing further to say, and that is, We heartily recommend Union and a good Agreement between you our Brethren. Never disagree, but preserve a strict Friendship for one another, and thereby you, as well as we, will become the stronger.
>
> Our wise Forefathers established Union and Amity between the Five Nations; this has made us formidable; this has given us great Weight and Authority with our neighboring Nations.
>
> We are a powerful Confederacy; and, by your observing the same Methods our wise Forefathers have taken, you will acquire fresh Strength and Power; therefore whatever befalls you, never fall out one with another.[74]

When, Canassatego spoke these famous words, they were not, as would become blatantly obvious, in his or his people's best interest. If the colonies had not come together in union, they would have been much less powerful. But he obviously felt comfortable enough, close enough to the assembled governors, deputies from the Onondagas, the Senecas, the Cayugas, the Oneidas, and the Tuscaroras, as well as to his good friend the interpreter Conrad Weiser, to make this suggestion.

Franklin himself referred to the model of the Six Nations Confederacy as the perfect example for the young colonies to emulate. In March 1751 he wrote to his friend James Parker: "It would be a very strange Thing, if Six Nations of ignorant Savages should be capable of forming a Scheme for such an Union, and be able to execute it in such a Manner, as that it has subsisted Ages and appears indissoluble; and yet that a like Union should be impracticable for ten or a Dozen English Colonies."[75] Franklin was not just modeling the Union on the Six Nations'; he was also, ironically, insinuating that not to understand the importance of this model would be a grave strategic mistake. In this missive Franklin shows no love for the native peoples but a great deal of respect for their system of government. When Franklin drafted the Articles of Confederation, he used much of what was in the original Albany articles, and much of the Constitution stemmed from them.[76]

The early peace and war negotiations between 1736 and 1762, led by such a formidable diplomat as Conrad Weiser, are evidence of a complex, unbroken, and mutually informative contact zone of political exchange. Certainly such small tribes as the Tuscaroras needed the protection of the Six Nation Confederacy against the encroachment of European settlers. Likewise, the early colonial governments were living in a multiethnic, multiracial scattering of colonies that had to learn how to act in a manner that was most beneficial for all concerned.

Given the sheer number of governors and gentlemen of prestige and power present at the treaty meetings, not to mention numerous other negotiations, it cannot be claimed that those in power knew nothing of the political ways of the Haudenosaunee. Cadwalder Colden's *History of the Five Indian Nations of Canada,* describing the exact nature of the Iroquois political system, had already been published,[77] and too many men in power had read the book to claim ignorance of the overlapping political theories. The similarities between the Six Nations Confederacy and their constitution, the Albany Plan of Union, and the Articles of Confederation were too great to be merely coincidental.

It is unfortunate that academics have spent so much time arguing against

Iroquois influence—such a belittling word—and so little time imagining how much was lost by not letting the Six Nations influence America more. Americans should not fight the idea that the colonies learned from the Six Nations Confederacy. Eighteenth-century interpreters, fur traders, politicians, and land speculators understood some of the nuanced and deeply spiritual contributions of Six Nations oral tradition, arts, and government better than we can ever hope to do.

As ersatz America progressed, colonialists had to refute the influence theory in order to sustain not just the concept of a savage "other" but also that of the exceptionality of the European over the barbarian. Historians of a patriotic nation would have found it difficult to justify the murder of millions of First Peoples if they could not argue for a superior, more civilized race. That Europeans could be equally or, as seen in the Sullivan campaign, more savage than the savages and that the First Peoples already had a more sophisticated system of government would undermine the whole justification for colonization.

The Condolence Ceremony

The Six Nations Confederacy differs from the Algonquian nation in that the former's myth of origin focuses directly on a legend of peace. This legend of peace gave birth to the condolence ceremony, which originated when Deganawida, the "peacemaker," who was called upon during the Second Epoch to heal his people after a period of deep decay, civil war, and, some say, cannibalism (although this may be a metaphor for civil war) first visited Tiskonsase (also known as Jingonsaseh), a woman who had been feeding the warriors. He convinced her of his message of peace, and she joined with him, becoming known as the Mother of the Nations. Then Deganawida went to the chiefs of all the nations and convinced them of his message of peace. Only one of the Onondagas, a man named Atotarho, would not accept the message of peace, so the Mother of the Nations came up with a plan to sing him a song that would help him to hear the message.[78]

Susan Kalter tells a version of this same origin myth that connects the condolence belt directly to the wampum:

> In one version of the story, as Hiawatha pursues negotiations with Atotarho, all three of his [Hiawatha's] daughters and his wife die at the mercy of forces only implicitly, and yet quite evidently, linked to the mad, power-hoarding Onondaga chief [Atotarho]. Bowed low by grief, Hiawatha finally retreated south. Finding shells at the bottom of a lake, he threaded them on

> strings to make the first wampum and, as he journeyed east, talked to himself about how with these strings he would console a person in grief such as his own. Upon reaching the edge of a Mohawk village, he was approached by Deganawida, who took up the word strings of condolence that would shape Iroquois diplomacy for centuries to come.[79]

The peacemaker sang to Atotarho, and gradually his twisted, snake-ridden hair and the fearful look on his face softened, so that Hiawatha was able to comb the snakes from his hair, and his mind and body became straightened.

Mann adds to these narratives the insight that the story of Deganawida and Hiawatha repeats the origin story of Sky Woman, who fell to earth to create Turtle Island. Sky Woman, who lost her daughter Lynx when Lynx gave birth to male twins, was so overcome by grief that she rejected her grandson Flint, who became unbalanced because of this rejection. The condolence ceremony therefore becomes a myth of national origins.[80] The great law of peace, the condolence ceremony, and the Hiawatha condolence belt grew out of this myth and strengthened the joining together of these groups in a federalist confederacy.

The condolence ceremony, which reenacts the peacemaking this myth introduces, is remarkable because it addresses issues of mourning and post-traumatic stress by actually listening to all that the survivor is trying to say in every form that it takes. The condolence ceremony is just that—a prolonged, ritualized form of condolence, or empathy and sympathy, to ensure that an individual in a community will not turn his or her grief into revenge and war. Kalter expands our understanding of condolence when she writes:

> Perhaps the most striking words are those of the first, second, and third "articles" of the requickening part of the ceremony. In the first, the condoler, who reenacts Deganawida's role with Hiawatha, wipes away the mourner's grief in recognition that an excess of tears can blind the mourner to the world and his responsibility to live in it. In the second, the condoler clears the passages of the ears that have become obstructed from so much crying and caused the mourner to lose his hearing. "It comes to pass where a great calamity has befallen one's person that the passages of the ears become obstructed and the hearing is lost. One then hears not the sounds made by mankind, nothing of what is taking place on the earth."[81]

"Ears filled with tears" is a metaphor for the way in which the mourning person closes himself or herself off from all mankind. The person who does not grieve at all can become equally deaf to the living. Perhaps ersatz America is the calamity that has befallen an America that has not allowed its people to grieve, that has not engaged in condolence. If ersatz America has obstructed our ears to what is taking place in the world of the living, then this condolence ceremony is a lifeline back to American humanity. A political system that constantly stayed current with the grief and violence of the world would have created a powerful democracy, a community of different peoples in which no one's tears would have gone unnoticed.

The symbol of the Haudenosaunee is the great white pine, returning us to the importance of branching in regenerating community. According to the *Encyclopedia of the Haudenosaunee,* "Its branches are said to shelter the people of the confederated nations, and its roots spread to the four directions, inviting other peoples, irregardless of race or nationality, to take shelter under the tree."[82] From the base of the tree, a snow-white carpet of thistledown would cover the surrounding countryside, protecting all the peoples that it covered. The thistledown is a tiny copy of a tree with seeds, the point with rays stroking out that Virginia Woolf actually draws at the top of each chapter of *The Pargiters* as a counterdiagram to the rising action, climax, and falling action of the traditional narrative model. The point with rays stroking out mirrors *Avatar*'s floating, illuminated plant life. As a metaphor, thistledown tells a story that is connected to the physical and humane well-being of the Haudenosaunee peoples. A point with rays stroking out is a universal symbol of connection and regeneration, a graphic symbol that has no end but is constantly in a state of growth and diversification, connecting all things in one community. On top of the Iroquois tree sits an eagle. When contemporary Iroquois planted a tree of peace on the National Mall, detractors scorned what they saw as a presumptive claim to influence, when in fact the Iroquois were acknowledging their American identity; they were asserting their right to have a place on the National Mall.

Wampum

After every treaty agreement, the parties on both sides exchanged intricate beaded belts and strings. Not being a conventionally literate society with an established written alphabet and vocabulary, the Haudenosaunee remembered their history through oral storytelling and the use of what we know by the European name *wampum.* Beaded wampum belts were an ancient, sacred form of mnemonic communication combining the written word and the spoken word.

The wampum served as a mnemonic device that the speaker could "read" to recover the original message entrusted to him by his community. The beads linked the speaker to the message, and the message contained the history of a condolence, an easing of grief, a means of connecting to the lost ones and of making things coherent.[83]

The intricacies of these messages linked Europeans and native peoples for centuries. As Kathryn V. Muller makes clear, this wampum passed back and forth to ensure a continuous and long-standing relationship: "The Friendship Belt represents the Covenant Chain alliance, established between the Haudenosaunee and the English in 1677 to guarantee an everlasting peace between brothers. Both the Haudenosaunee and the Europeans presented a number of these white wampum belts with two purple figures, united by the metaphorical chain, at many conferences in order to remind each other of their steadfast friendship."[84]

That the memory of the Six Nations' culture is so linked to a ritual of condolence is the greatest gift that we can receive from the Six Nations Confederacy. After every agreement, long speech, moment of accord or disaccord, or giving of recognition or promise, the speakers for the various Indian groups and those for the European groups exchanged beaded belts to record and verify the proceedings. That both sides engaged in this way of marking and recording the proceedings is remarkable. As early as 1610 the Europeans recognized the importance of these exchanges to negotiations with Indians. That the condolence ritual was punctuated with the use of wampum strings and belts provides a direct connection to a forgotten language of peace and forgiveness. The treaties are liberally punctuated with phrases such as "gave a belt of nine arrows," "gave a string," "gave two strings of black and white wampum," and "gave a belt and a string" or the longer explanation "To enforce what had been said, the GOVERNOR laid down a Belt of Wampum; upon which the Indians gave the Yo' hah."[85]

But while the Europeans may have misread or minimized the importance of these exchanges of beaded belts, calling them currency or money, the wampum readers and writers knew their full significance. Wampum writers actually communicated with the symbols of the wampum, understanding the subtleties of the messages. The wampum "writing" is a perfect example of voice in a symbiotic but not co-dependent relationship to graphism. Rose Palmer, in her book *The North American Indians,* suggests that wampum writers were speaking their thoughts into the wampum. Once spoken into the wampum, the message could be read, with considerable confidence as to its accuracy.[86] John Heckewelder, an eighteenth-century Moravian missionary who lived with the Confederacy, stated that a good messenger was "able to point out the exact place on a [wampum] belt which is to answer to each particular sentence, the same as we can point out a passage in a book."[87] This relationship to the wampum meant that the written tradition did not dominate and take over the visceral relationship that the reader had with the beaded message. The message therefore retained its communal coherence. Voice and graphic inscription held an autonomous, albeit symbiotic, relationship.

Wampum—the name given by the Dutch to the beaded strings and belts made of woven and knotted purple and white whelk shells—was not, as so many critics have assumed, a form of monetary exchange or in any way related to economic or commercial concerns. Because the beads to make wampum were so sought after by the Six Nation Confederacy, Europeans, who did not know the ancient stories of Hiawatha and the condolence ceremony, could only think of exchange in terms of currency. Because the native peoples preferred to be paid in wampum rather than gold, silver, or, for that matter, any coin, the Europeans assumed that this was their currency. The Dutch, living in an area where the purple and white whelk shells were readily available, particularly in the late seventeenth century, took over production of the beads and in many cases flooded the markets with counterfeit beads carved out of conch shells or manufactured glass beads.[88]

The wampum was the reminder to speak from the heart, because the heart was the heart of the speaker's whole community. In an exchange between the Six Nations negotiators Tokahayo and Teedyuscung and English negotiators, Teedyuscung

> spoke from the Heart, in the same Manner they used to do in ancient times, when they held Councils together. They wished they could say as much of the English; but it was plain the English either did not understand Indian affairs, or else did not act and speak with that sincerity and in the manner they ought. When the Indians delivered belts, they were large and long; but when the English returned an answer or spoke, they did it on small belts and trifling little strings. . . . And yet the English made the wampum, whereas the Indians were obliged to buy it. But the reason was, the Indians spoke from the heart, the English only from the mouth.[89]

But even if the English answered with small belts and trifling little strings, the interesting fact about these interchanges is that the English actually tried to adopt the Six Nations Confederacy's way of negotiating. That the Dutch and then the English controlled the production of wampum was much more problematic. The original way of making wampum took an enormous amount of patience and a direct biomorphic understanding of the tiny purple and white shells. The beads produced in this painstaking manner were by all accounts beautiful. The European variety were mass-produced and held much less biological and human capital. The hours spent making the beads was part of the peace process, engaging people's time in the act of production rather than destruction. The creation of the beads, as well as the making, exchanging, and "reading" of belts and strings, helped maintain the sanity and peace of communities and the whole confederacy.

Grandfathers

George Washington saw fit to destroy a culture that understood the importance of condolence to peacekeeping, that was able to form warring groups into a working confederacy, and that carved grandfather masks to honor the ancestors and heal the sick. These masks are sacred and powerful. The *Encyclopedia of the Haudenosaunee* tells us that "these masks when used properly, are said to be associated with healing physical illnesses, restoring mental health, and maintaining harmony between humankind and nature in Haudenosaunee society."[90]

The Haudenosaunee thought of them as living and breathing. Misunderstanding the masks as objects, William Fenton collected hundreds of them, and collectors put them in museums and behind glass. Fenton's book *The False Face Masks of the Iroquois* caused a reaction from the contemporary Indian community, who believed that he should not have collected or photographed the masks for his books. Indian leaders felt strongly that the masks were living ancestors and should be "fed" and allowed to "breathe," not kept behind glass in museums. According to a statement of the Haudenosaunee Grand Council of Chiefs, "The exhibition of masks by museums does not serve to enlighten the public regarding the culture of the Haudenosaunee, as such an exhibition violates the intended purpose of the mask and contributes to the desecration of the sacred image."[91] These masks live not just in their cultural context but in the graphic inscription of the hundreds of crooked facial expressions they present and in the movements that performers bring to them.

The original story of the grandfather masks is as follows:

> According to tradition, the Creator met a being who walked across the earth carrying a turtle rattle and a wooden staff. Called the Great Doctor, the Hunchback, Gagohsa, the Face, Or Hadui, this being lived on the rim of the world and controlled the winds and disease. Both the Creator and

Hadui claimed to be more powerful than the other. Agreeing to a contest to decide, each commanded a nearby mountain to move toward them. The Creator was so successful that Hadui struck his face on the rock. As a result, he consented to give humans power to cure illnesses by blowing hot ashes over patients. In return, the Huadenosaunee carve and wear False Face masks in his likeness prepare feasts and conduct ceremonies that include singing, dancing, and tobacco offerings. Masks are to be treated with respect, and they are periodically offered corn mush and tobacco.[92]

Those who dreamt that they should make a "grandfather," a tree mask, in honor of the protector would carve the mask out of a living tree, and the living tree would speak to them as they carved. The masks, all different, are intricate and beautiful. Almost all of them have some form of crooked face, usually a bent nose or crooked smile. These masks perfectly express the language of both visceral and biomorphic graphism, deriving from the gestures of the body of the one called upon to carve and of the body of the tree itself. The masks insist that the health and healing of the human community is intricately and inextricably connected to the health and healing of the natural world.[93]

When we compare the multiple statues of Washington with the Six Nation Confederacy's grandfathers, we find a radically different conception of identity and community. While the American colonies were solidifying their power around the image of one heroic white man, the Six Nations Confederacy expressed value for the dimorphous, shape-shifting mask carved from the living tree, the power of the tree still known to live within the mask. By masking, the members of the native society were problematizing the very idea of identity. This ability to shift power, to move in and out of formal structures, to negotiate with the spirit world and the ancestors, kept the Six Nations Confederacy alive and well throughout the first period of European invasion. Preservationists want to capture identity in a formaldehyde solution, while the people of the Six Nations carve faces from living trees to confuse and morph identity. Almost every bust or image of Washington has been created with the aim of making him an everyman, with no emotions, no expressions. Only one painter dared paint Washington's mouth as swollen and painful from bad teeth. In contrast, the masks of the Seneca people were full of humor, expression, laughter, sadness, confusion, hilarity, and sorrow.

By ordering the Sullivan-Clinton campaign against the Six Nations Confederacy, Washington tried to destroy at least one hundred years of delicately, painstakingly, often violently negotiated peace and cohabitation between German, French, English, and Six Nations peoples. Just as Thomas Dale is the hidden horror in the Pocahontas story, the Sullivan-Clinton campaign is the hidden horror in the Washington myth. Ironically, Washington himself had many contradictory faces. He was a masked and performative shape-shifter, not a godlike figurehead; a hieroglyph, not the alabaster head of state or the phallic Washington Monument that we have demanded he become. Rather than celebrating difference and multiple, life-giving and healing grandfathers, Americans worship a George Washington mask of death, conformity, and singularity.

The Day the Earth Stood Stupid

To break out of the phantasm of Washington the god, a strange role for a man who did not even want to be king or to stay in power for long, we have to look outside state-sanctioned tourism, state-sanctioned history, and even academic history. Few dare to tread on the Washington icon. It is no surprise, then, that one of the funniest and, ironically, most culturally sophisticated critiques of America's idolization of the "head" of state and the dangers of such idolatry can be found in "The Day the Earth Stood Stupid," an episode in season 3 of *Futurama* that was shown in February 2001. Created by Matt Groening, *Futurama* is an American animated science-fiction sitcom that addresses politically quirky and sometimes radical issues. *Futurama* may be the closest one can get in contemporary American society to the Six Nations Confederacy's grandfathers. While the part about Washington's head does not occur until midway through the episode, the whole *Futurama* episode assesses social and governmental idolization of heads and brains over hearts, minds, and bodies. In an earlier episode, Fry, a main character, saw famous heads from the past in a museum where a whole room was devoted to past presidents, including Washington. They were lined up, ready to impart wisdom to those who would listen. All the talking heads were suspended in formaldehyde in identical jars. The museum housed only the talking heads—no bodies, no material objects, no landscapes, no trees.

Not uncoincidentally, one month after George W. Bush was inaugurated for the first time, Groening presented an episode titled "The Day the Earth Stood Stupid." Playing on the 1951 movie *The Day the Earth Stood Still,* the *Futurama* episode warns humans about the impending threat to earth from giant brains invading the planet. In the 1951 film, Klaatu, an alien from a distant planet, visits Washington, DC, in a flying saucer to warn the people of earth that if they continue to make dangerous nuclear weapons, they will threaten the solar system, and other, less violent planetary societies will have to eliminate humans for the good of the whole system. The warning in the *Futurama* "Stupid" episode is more subtle: humans have to start thinking in imaginative and mysterious ways, as the character Fry does, if we are to outsmart the giant disembodied brains that have invaded the planet.

The episode starts at a country fair of sorts, with a pet show in which a giant hypno-toad with weird eyes is busy hypnotizing the sheep, then the judges, then the audience, who all clap in unison in an eerily Nazi-like scene. The commentary on people in America, who, like sheep, follow a dubious leader, Bush II, is quite obvious. Nibbler, a small, black petlike creature with three eyes, whom the judges and his owner, Leela, assume to be cute and stupid, is actually acting undercover as a spy from the planet Eternium, whose superintelligent species end up saving earth. When Nibbler realizes that earth has been invaded by giant brains and that they are making everyone on earth as stupid as Leela says (he corrects her and says "stupider"), he gets in his space ship, taking Leela with him, and heads home to Eternium. Meanwhile, the disembodied brains are sucking the delta brain waves out of all humans, leaving them incapable of logical reasoning.

Besides being a commentary on the state of the electorate after George W. Bush, this episode is a subtle statement about the damage that is done by giant, disembodied brains, whether they are powerful CEOs and politicians or unethical scientists and professors. Disembodiment is a serious problem that causes racism and dominance. Abstraction, or the ability to understand complex associations and abstract reasoning, can save us, but disembodiment is lethal. Hyper-big-brain disembodiment is not the same as intellectual engagement, theoretical analyses, or simply using one's grey matter. Nibbler is capable of highly abstract thought. Giant brains are not capable of abstract reasoning. The giant brains are perpetually "floating," with no connection to life, animals, the planet itself, or any other reality.

Not only are the disembodied brains everywhere but the image of invading "whiteness" occurs throughout the episode. Leela keeps Nibbler as a "pet," or slave, infantilizes him, puts him in diapers, and talks down to him. Nibbler is black, while the brains are white. Nibbler's only moment of difficulty occurs at the state fair, when he mistakes an ersatz balloon pig for a real one. When he tries to eat it (Nibbler can eat animals twice his size), he falls into a pail of white milk, splashing milk all over the faces of the bystanders. The potential danger of whiteness is shown throughout the episode. Fry, regarded by everyone as stupid, is in fact the only one who can fight against the giant brains, because only Fry has cobbled together a brain, quiltlike, from different brain waves that can resist the delta-wave-sucking big brains. Fry's brain is, as in Leela's words, "a brain made like a carpet fragment prom dress"—a post-sixties example of visceral graphism.

After Fry tries several times to destroy the giant brain that has taken up residence exactly where Fry thought it would, in the New York Public Library, he realizes that if he thinks, it weakens the giant brain. Fry reaches for books to help him think, rejecting the Hardy Boys books as too easy and the Nancy Drew mysteries as too hard and choosing instead *Bonfire of the Vanities,* which has the right mix of racial violence, intrigue, and perplexing problems to invoke thinking. This attempt at stimulating thought starts to work but does not weaken the big brain enough.

The giant brain fights Fry to imprison him by making him reside forever in the mental realm of particular classic books. The giant brain's choice of books is interesting: *Moby-Dick, Tom Sawyer,* and *Jane Eyre.* When Fry lands in the textual world of *Moby-Dick,* he is in a boat with Queequeg and Ahab trying to find the white whale. Instead of the whale, Queequeg spies the big white brain: "That no white whale, that gray thinky whale." As Fry tries to spear the brain as he would a whale, the brain calls back, "You will all be trapped in this dense symbolist tome forever." Disembodied brains and whiteness, the same evasive and ever-present enemy, are making everyone stupid. In case we have any doubt about this, the next book the giant brain forces Fry and Leela into is *Tom Sawyer,* at the moment of the famous whitewashing scene. Tom Sawyer has employed the big brain to help him. When Fry sees the big brain painting the fence white, Fry and the whole crew suddenly land in *Pride and Prejudice,* and they travel through this literary time-space continuum by throwing Tom Sawyer's white paint at the giant brain. However, neither the white paint nor the spear of Ahab and Queequeg kills the brain. The symbolism and the slice of corny Americana do not do away with the racism of the big brain. Only by writing his own account of the events that are transpiring does Fry, in his strange way, write the giant brain out of the narrative.

Every image of the other, the Nibblonian planet's headquarters or castle, and Queequeg appears fully scrolled. In the picture of the Nibblonian fortress there are two obelisks that resemble the Washington Monument, covered with the same kind of hieroglyphic scrolling found on Queequeg. Only by writing the big brain out of the narrative in his own form of hieroglyphic writing—namely, bad spelling—does Fry win. In Fry's version the big brain flies out the window saying that he is going to leave earth for "no *raisin*." As silly as this may seem, Groening is highlighting the power of language that is no longer bound to the written inscription. The phrase "no raisin" reformulates meaning as the disassociation of sound and graphic—something new. Groening celebrates the power of his own medium, the animated cartoon, which complicates the visual and the vocal.

Now that he has banished the giant brain, Fry decides that he will try to make his now stupid friends smart again. He gives them a lesson in American history, starting with the presidents. From the cryogenic museum, he has taken the preserved heads of two presidents: George Washington and Chester Arthur. These are presidential preserved talking heads, *Futurama*'s version of the disembodied brain. When everyone asks who was the first president, none of Fry's now stupid friends know. Even Washington's disembodied head has gone stupid, saying, "Thomas Jefferson." Fry drops the preserved heads of Washington and Arthur on the ground, and the water or formaldehyde leaks out disabling the former presidents and revealing how fragile these icons actually are.

Matt Groening simply follows the lead of so many artists, sculptors, and the industry we call Mount Vernon in fetishizing Washington's head as if it were the nation itself. With the giant brain in power, there is no value placed on the body, or more importantly the whole person, functioning as both body and brain. By equating giant brains with pervading whiteness, Groening exposes the lie of ersatz America, a lie that assumes the superhallucination of power as real power encapsulated in small jars in museums. What this means is that even when we do dig into the archives, as so many valiant historians have done, and find the fallible, human George Washington, the ersatz curtain closes again, and we are left with a placid Houdon bust and head. The *Futurama* episode on George Washington's head provides the best modern counternarrative to Mount Vernon's obsession with the head of the great white father.

NO MATTER HOW deeply or how passionately, and with what skillful care, we unveil the imperfect man, the larger-than-life looming disembodied head still grows larger. The great balloon-head image blocks our view of the truly frightening human toll that the enormously wealthy barons of colonial Virginia wreaked on the general populace, white, native, and black. On this stage, at this moment in history, because Washington was not simply a supporting actor but playing the leading role, he must bear a greater share of the responsibility for their avarice and inhumane actions than the coupling of Washington and America allows.

The details of Muslim clothing, jewelry, and body markings that George Washington's slaves used to adorn their body and the intricate beaded wampum belts of the Six Nations Confederacy provide the visceral graphic inscription that does not simply refute what has become a monolithic and stupefying myth of national origins but painstakingly rewrites the years of the Washington presidency as a more fully representative community of diverse peoples.

4

"BLOOD MARKED EVERY STEP"

The dogmas of the quiet past are inadequate to the stormy present. The occasion is piled high with difficulty, and we must rise with the occasion. As our case is new, so we must think anew and act anew.—ABRAHAM LINCOLN, annual message to Congress, 1 December 1862

Lincoln Portraits

LINCOLN PORTRAIT I: "THIS IS WHAT HE SAID"

There is little doubt that George Washington's life and death, seized upon by the likes of Parson Weems, added height to the already sky-high scaffolding of ersatz America. While the Mount Vernon Ladies' Association and the Association for the Preservation of Virginia Antiquities were busy preserving an America built with enslaved labor, the nation was falling apart. Trying desperately to solidify an image of an established, nation resting comfortably on the head of George Washington's pastoral slavery, these organizations ignored the fact that slavery's incompatibility with democracy was becoming blatantly obvious. Just as Washington's slaves in the late eighteenth century had outnumbered his resources and strained his powers of denial, so now did the nation's.

From 1810 to 1860 the slave population in the United States grew from a little more than six hundred thousand to nearly four million. While Virginia and the Atlantic coastal states were reducing their slave populations by selling slaves, Louisiana, Mississippi, Alabama, and Texas were buying and "growing" as many slaves as possible to create a labor force for their ever-expanding estates.[1] The increasingly grand plantations with hundreds of slaves—in South Carolina in the eighteenth century and in Louisiana in the late eighteenth and first half of the nineteenth—made the concept of paternalistic slavery not just a pleasant fantasy but an impossible lie.[2]

In the colonial and even the revolutionary era, slavery could possibly have been seen as a temporary evil or a pastoral gentlemanly necessity. But by 1850 enslaved labor was the economic backbone of the nation, in no way paternal or pastoral. A master could hold as many as two hundred slaves on a single plantation. The explosive and performative violence necessary, or imagined to be necessary, to keep African peoples from armed revolt and resistance was indeed gruesome—from starvation to head collars to allowing dogs to dismember runaways. The South's fear of rebellion was a combination of reality and paranoia run wild. On big plantations, the "kind" master did not even know, let alone "love," his hundreds of slaves. Between 1790 and 1860, as slaveholders in Maryland, Virginia, Georgia, and the Carolinas sold 835,000 slaves downriver to Alabama, Mississippi, Louisiana, and Texas, they broke up families, communities, and cultures, and as they did so the last vestiges of paternalistic slavery should have dissolved.

The abolitionist movement in America gained formal structure with the establishment of the American Anti-Slavery Society in 1833. There was certainly strong opposition to slavery long before the founding of the society. The American Anti-Slavery Society depended directly on the rhetoric and strategies of the British abolitionist movement. As the abolitionist movement grew, few Americans could claim to be ignorant of slave abuses. As early as the 1820s, John Rankin's *Letters on American Slavery* detailed the atrocities occurring on many plantations. While Henry Lloyd Garrison, the Beechers, Frederick Douglass, and Harriet Beecher Stowe were not the primary force behind emancipation,[3] their speeches and writings supported the enslaved people's own powerful fight for freedom.[4]

By 1831, when Garrison published the first issue of the *Liberator,* the tide of public opinion in the North was turning toward emancipation, and the debate over whether new states would enter the Union "slave" or "free" was tearing at the fabric of national unity. But it was the Fugitive Slave Act of 1850 that broke the house apart and let loose a torrent of literary and oratorical attacks on slavery. It was a true awakening for abolitionists and just people with hearts and minds of their own to see that no states, not even the "free" states, were safe for enslaved people. The radical abolitionist literature and the fiery righteous oratory brought the degrading treatment of slaves and the conditions under which they lived to the attention of the citizens of northern towns and villages. In speeches at town halls, in pamphlets, newspaper articles, paintings, and, eventually, mid-century photographs, the reality of slavery gradually became part of the public imagination.

If we attempt to extend the timeline of ersatz America to the period of nation building from 1861 to 1865, the clear battle lines between the "real" story and the ersatz mythography become much less coherent. To even question Abraham Lincoln's motives concerning the Emancipation Proclamation or the inevitability of the Civil War, as many historians have done in the last five years, is to tread on predictably unsettled ground.[5] Lincoln lives in the American cultural imagination as a fairly uncontested hero, and the cultural monuments in his honor are so numerous that it would be impossible to name them all.[6] Americans may willingly put John Smith's or even George Washington's head on the mythical rock in a revisionist reading of American history, but they are protective of the man they perceive as their savior. They stand in awe in front of the larger-than-life Lincoln in the Lincoln Memorial. However, the America of today, the troubled result of a halfhearted emancipation, an uncivil bloody war, a tortured reconstruction, and a failed attempt at equal educational or economic opportunity, leaves the American cultural psyche with an uneasy relationship to Lincoln.

Understanding this relationship means paying attention not to the monumental memorials to Lincoln or to the myths surrounding his person but to the more subtle portrayals in modern cultural history. In 1942 André Kostelanetz put out a call to musicians for "portraits" that would celebrate "the qualities of courage, dignity, strength, simplicity and humor which are so characteristic of the American people" and inspire Americans as they entered World War II. He asked Aaron Copland in particular to write a piece, and this progressive Jewish composer wanted to honor Walt Whitman. But because his fellow composer Jerome Kern had already chosen Mark Twain and Kostelanetz did not want only writers, Copland instead agreed to compose a musical portrait of Abraham Lincoln. His *Lincoln Portrait* is a strange and haunting musical dialogue between bombastic nationalism and popular folk songs. With the flourish of his virtuosity, Copland frees liberty to become a moving force clashing against the solidity of the rampant nationalism of both World War II and the Civil War.[7]

By the time Aaron Copland was writing *Lincoln Portrait,* Margaret Mitchell had written *Gone with the Wind* (1936)—following the lead of Thomas Dixon, whose 1905 novel *The Clansman: An Historical Romance of the Ku Klux Klan* was made into the 1915 movie *Birth of the Nation*—and Hollywood had produced a full-blown Technicolor version (1939), a glossy apologia for slavery and white supremacy. The very words *gone with the wind* demand that America become once again newborn and wipe the slate clean of past atrocities as Americans welcome the unity of national whiteness—this time all Irish, and any other now designated "white" minorities might apply. The veneer of southern gentility and Hollywood slickness that the book and the movie version of *Gone with the Wind* invent would define America's memory of slavery for at least a generation. The damage that its stereotypes and historical distortions do to historical memory could fill the pages of a second volume on ersatz America. But at least introducing the book and movie here can remind us of the backdrop of nationalistic "forgetting" against which Copland composed.

By interweaving folk music, the spoken word, and bombastic nationalist music, Copland demands that his audience rethink blind adherence to a cause. As the trumpets, tympani, and trombones battle it out with the flutes, oboes, and bells, Copland inserts a short libretto comprising quotations from Lincoln, which he introduces each time with the words, "This is what he said," followed by "He said," or "Lincoln said," or "Abraham Lincoln said," or "Abe said." In the short libretto, which takes up only two single-spaced pages, he repeats the phrases "This is what he said" and "He said" a total of eleven times. Copeland's close friend and fellow composer Virgil Thomson suggested that Copland add Lincoln's words, but it was Copland who chose the text. Thomson wrote two operas with Gertrude Stein, *The Mother of Us All* and *Four Saints in Three Acts,* and in the repetition of "This is what he said" and "Abraham Lincoln said" we hear a Steinian influence.[8] For Stein, the way to bring attention to language was to repeat phrases in multiple combinations. At this time Stein was also writing portraits of famous people, such as Picasso. In the contested space of "not music" and "not narrative," Copland's *Lincoln Portrait* captures the ongoing drama of Lincoln's contribution to American history. The rhythm of the phrases "This is what he said" and "He said" transforms words into musical notes, and the interplay of instruments and musical styles transforms musical notes into graphic portraits.

Copland was not the only artist who recognized the necessity of memorializing Lincoln's words. What distinguishes Lincoln's monument from George Washington's is that the architect, Henry Bacon, chose to cover the walls surrounding the statue with Lincoln's words. Bacon recognized that what Lincoln said was as important as the body of the man himself, if not more so. If George Washington was an iconic head, Lincoln was the mouthpiece, the oracle of democracy.

Since the Cincinnati Symphony's 1942 debut of *Lincoln Portrait,* every major American symphony and many international symphonies have performed the piece. More than fifty celebrities, as varied as Barack Obama, Katherine Hepburn, James Earl Jones, Coretta Scott King, Margaret Thatcher, and General Norman Schwarzkopf, have spoken Copland's script. As the speaker voices Lincoln's words shortly before he issued the Emancipation Proclamation—"The dogmas of the quiet past are inadequate to the stormy present. The occasion is piled high with difficulty and we must rise with the occasion. As our case is new, so we must think anew and act anew. We must disenthrall ourselves and then we will save our country"[9]—Copland's complex orchestration emphasizes that to "think anew and act anew," to "disenthrall" to free oneself from a ruling force, is not a passing fancy but the real work of the citizen in a democracy.

The score and libretto perform democracy rather than memorializing the democratic man. The archival copies of the musical notation and libretto for this piece present an animated visceral graphism that transcends the scripted page. The double-dotted note (a note with two dots following it) increases the length of the note by three-quarters, and the stressed marcato rhythms that separate the spoken words not only give greater emphasis to Lincoln's insistence on a democracy based on equality for all but enact and trace a longing, a literal reaching for a way to think anew and act anew. If we imagine conventional thought as one side of a crevice and the hope of democracy as the other, we can imagine thinking anew and acting anew as bridging the distance between them. The only problem with this metaphor is that democracy is not a fixed point to which one might build a bridge but is constantly shifting. For Copland in *Lincoln Portrait* the simple note will not do; it needs to be double-dotted, to stretch forward, to be held a little longer and create the tissue that will not just critique nation building but perform democratic longing.

Copland chooses to quote Lincoln's most radical words:

> He said: "It is the eternal struggle between two principles, right and wrong, throughout the world. It is the same spirit that says 'you toil and work and earn bread, and I'll eat it.' No matter in what shape it comes, whether from the mouth of a king who seeks to bestride the people of his own nation, and live by the fruit of their labor, or from one race of men as an apology for enslaving another race, it is the same tyrannical principle."[10]

Copland includes in his libretto the following words:

> Lincoln was a quiet man. Abe Lincoln was a quiet and a melancholy man. But when he spoke of democracy, this is what he said.
>
> He said: "As I would not be a slave, so I would not be a master. This expresses my idea of democracy. Whatever differs from this, to the extent of the difference, is no democracy."[11]

Elizabeth Bergman Crist points out that "all of his [Copland's] selections evoke the political and moral challenges to American democracy posed by slavery in the Civil War and fascism in World War II."[12] While Crist's analysis is correct, Copland's approach tells a more artistically troubled story, one that positions Lincoln and the historical moment of slavery, as well as America and entry into World War II, in a contested relationship. As we look carefully at how Copland attends to repetition and counterpoint in the music, we see that he is recuperating old "Africanized" rhythms and setting them against European musical forms to remind his 1940s audience that the complexities of racism exist on American as well as German soil and that it may have been the slaves themselves who drove emancipation.[13] Copland was well aware that the expostulation of fascist Germany's racial superiority was not that different from the white-supremacy and eugenics movements of 1940s—and, for that matter, 1860s—America.

Like any president forced to declare war, Lincoln, when he had to choose the aggressive nationalism of the Civil War in order to protect the democratic values of freedom and democracy, risked the very values of freedom and democracy that he was trying to protect. As Copland's music vacillates between disjunct melodies and a deep, conjunct bass line made up of adjacent notes in a scale, it underscores and juxtaposes the seriousness of the two historic moments and this same impossible choice. Rather than forcing his music to speak for the inevitability of war, he allows his score to display the innate discord of a divided republic, held in check by the steadying influence of the words: "As I would not be a slave, so I would not be a master." By putting himself in the place of the slave and assuming an empathetic rather than sympathetic position, Copland's Lincoln bridges the power gap in this one coordinate sentence. The sentence itself is symmetrical. Lincoln sees enslaved people as just like himself. Human beings. Empowered.

In *Lincoln Portrait* Copland includes two well-known folk songs, "Camptown Races" and "Springfield Mountain," creating a hidden intertextual commentary that is much less patriotic and bombastic than most productions of the piece would like to admit. Few critics pay attention to the lyrics of these songs, but Copland warns us that we must pay attention to what the words say. These two songs are not easy or obvious choices. The lyrics in "Springfield Mountain," one of the oldest American folk songs, speak of a young man who goes down to a field to mow the grass and is bitten by a serpent. He returns to his lover, who kisses him to remove the venom and dies herself: "And so the poison killed them both." In this last line we can recognize the almost clichéd abolitionist understanding of the way in which the infection of slavery, often portrayed in nineteenth-century political cartoons as a serpent or snake, destroyed both the slave and the master. No one is immune. In one of Lincoln's most famous rhetorical moments he compares slavery to a snake in a child's bed: "If I saw a venomous snake crawling in the road, any man would say I should seize the nearest stick and kill it; but if I found that snake in bed with my children that would be another question. I might hurt the children more than the snake and it might bite them."[14] Here Lincoln asserts that all the people of the Union are his children and that he cannot violently destroy slavery without injuring his children. Unfortunately, this was the choice he had to make.

Crist notes that the inclusion of the black minstrel song "Camptown Races," which is written "in dialect," could be seen as a nostalgic turn to an earlier pastoral America or a nod to Lincoln's youth in the country. But she argues that there is an overlying racial commentary in the choice of this song: "With its gapped melody and rhythmic syncopations, 'Camptown Races' perhaps even preserves some traits associated with African-American music in the antebellum South. These have already passed through Stephen Foster's white, commercial filter and are now subject to a process of modernist abstraction."[15] She contrasts Copland's accurate rendition of "Springfield Mountain" against his fragmented version of "Camptown Races": "It is easy enough to recognize the quotation or at least sense its familiarity, but the melody is so changed that it is difficult, if not impossible, to hear the actual song or its derogatory dialect. Thus is Copland able to exploit the song's connotations without becoming complicit in its offensive racial politics."[16]

Copland could easily have seen a minstrel show in which the actors sang "Camptown Races," for the song was an American favorite from the mid-1800s up until the 1950s. Stephen Foster based his version on songs he had heard in the camp towns and shantytowns of African American workers; he allowed the syncopated rhythm of instruments such as the banjo to preserve the polyrhythmic beat of drums from the Senegambia area of Central Africa.[17] Foster mimicked those songs in his tunes and in many cases created a minstrelized orchestration. The juxtaposition of Copland's version of "Camptown Races" with Lincoln's words is not just a strong commentary on minstrel racism but a reminder of how an artist can liberate the beat from the word and the word from the beat.

Copland, by linking Lincoln to the history of white supremacy in America, goes far beyond honoring the man for his role as the great emancipator. African Americans may have been liberated, but they were not freed from the dominance of white America. Segregation, eugenics experimentation, sterilizations, lobotomies, lynching, and economic violence were the law of the land in 1940s America, as the country self-righteously sent thousands of young men and women of all races and classes off to stop Hitler's ethnically based genocide. This hypocrisy is not lost on Copland. Nor is the struggle between the tangled rhetoric of democracy and the pomposity of a nation at war.

Copland ends with Lincoln's words, "that government of the people, for the people, by the people, shall not perish from the earth."[18] In emphasizing Lincoln's words Copland plays a trick with his score, with our cultural imagination, and with our memory of Lincoln. Rather than returning to the troubled man—who sometimes acted in the best interest of the enslaved and sometimes did not, who sometimes spoke with the racially problematic assumptions of nineteenth-century America and sometimes did not—Copland keeps coming back to the steady drumbeat of Lincoln's best words. Just as someone in an argument would say, "This is what you said." It is as if he is reminding Lincoln, reminding the nation, "This is what you said." This is what the great man said. This is what America is supposed to stand for. Liberty and equality for all. This is what the founding fathers said.

As Copland orchestrates a cacophony, he makes no note in his composition more important than another, no note the master and no note the slave. He builds a gathering of voices that often drowns out or minimizes the heroic call to battle. The narrator begins to speak as the orchestration is teetering on the edge of complete dissolution. At this moment, the orchestra quiets and opens a space for Lincoln's rhetoric. The only calming antidote, antinode, or anecdote at this moment is the narrator's voice reading Lincoln's clear, intelligent prose, which Copland punctuates with instrumentation.

Copland, following Gertrude Stein's word portraits, makes the spoken words short and human, in direct contrast to the heavy orchestral waves and to the nation's desire for a propagandistic arrogance that would build a cultural appetite for war. The spoken words stay the impending chaos. Copland does not include any of Lincoln's ambiguous pronouncements about race or his deliberate political compromises. Copland brings forth only the words that still matter, the words not of ersatz nationalism but of democracy and equality—a delicate and fine distinction. He connects the dots back to America's best democratic self.

Copland makes it clear in *Lincoln Portrait* that Lincoln, a man of his time, is through his own words trying desperately to talk himself and his nation out of their enthrallment with slavery. The cultural history of the nineteenth century has several hydra heads. On the one side of the drive toward emancipation are the white abolitionist writers and rhetoricians, who are struggling to shed what Lawrence would call their white racial snakeskin to meet the moment. It could be argued that the people whom the Civil War and the Emancipation Proclamation freed were not enslaved Africans but the white men who thought they owned them. The proclamation freed them from the delusion of ownership but not, unfortunately, from their own prejudices. Freeing from their own prejudices people who defined themselves as superior because of the lightness of their skin and their European heritage was a long-drawn-out job.

On the other side are the enslaved and freedmen, writers and orators, artists and artisans, articulating an unflinching knowledge of selfhood and an uncompromising fight for freedom. The syncopated "Africanized" camp-town beat tracks this self-awareness from the first day on the first slave boat to the "last" day, listening to the Emancipation Proclamation under the freedom tree in Hampton Roads, Virginia.

LINCOLN PORTRAIT II: "CHAINED SIX AND SIX TOGETHER"

In 1838, in a speech before the Young Men's Lyceum of Springfield, Illinois, Abraham Lincoln admonished the people of America that they must avoid and abhor mob violence and obey the laws of the land: "As the patriots of seventy-six did to the support of the Declaration of Independence, so to the support of the Constitution and Laws, let every man pledge his life, his property, and his sacred honor—let every man remember that to violate the law is to trample on the blood of his father and to tear the character of his own and his children's liberty."[19] The only problem with this admonishment is that evolving democracy requires dissent, violating the memory of the father, and, as Henry David Thoreau reminds us, civil disobedience.

When a man's property includes human beings, pledging this property to the cause of freedom is a form of insanity. Throughout his presidency Lincoln favored constraint and abiding the law over rebellion and division. His language, vacillating between eighteenth-century restrained prose and nineteenth-century

Byronic soaring, found meaning in a careful progression marked by adherence to historical precedence. Unfortunately, this adherence to order set him at odds with abolitionists, who had to defy the "law" of the land in order to free slaves, and made him a confusing savior. If the law of the land is abhorrent, then following the law of the land while sustaining a democracy is impossible. As Henry Louis Gates points out in *Lincoln on Race and Slavery,* Lincoln warned against violence toward black people, both lynchings and murders, as a form of mob control of the government, but did not rid himself of his own prejudices.[20]

This is the deepest contradiction in Lincoln's life, and it is what makes understanding the time period so difficult. It is why only the most sophisticated artists—Walt Whitman with "O Captain, My Captain" or Aaron Copland with *Lincoln Portrait*—could begin to reveal the full intricacy of the moment and the man. And Copland could only do this in a form that included but gave autonomous expression to voice, movement, sound, and script. The notes of double-dotted rhythms, the layered rewriting of minstrel tunes, and the juxtaposition of voice and orchestra distill the moment to the essential—this is what he said—and animate this essence. In 1942 Americans could not stand still; they had to learn to move forward, with Lincoln's words stirring them.

It took Lincoln himself a long time to recognize his own racism and his habitual responses to slavery, and longer still to act on his own words. Old ways of thinking, old ways of using language, kept so many reciting the stereotypical and inhumane racism that allowed the continuation of human bondage. It took hundreds of thousands of words and the endurance of African American cultural forms and beliefs over several centuries to untie the devil's knot of slavery. It has taken another century and a half to begin to expose the knot of racism. In 1838 Lincoln was still mystified, living in a nationalist bubble.

In a letter to Mary Speed dated 27 September 1841, Lincoln writes that he has witnessed slavery up close in St. Louis, seen slaves "chained six and six together. A small iron clevis was around the left wrist of each, and this fastened to the main chain by a shorter one at a convenient distance from the others; so that the negroes were strung together precisely like so many fish upon a trot-line." The use of the words "fish upon a trot-line" is odd because, as we must force ourselves to remember, fish on a trotline are dead. Lincoln's description is so vivid as to be almost photographic, but like the image and the chain itself, his words are strung together in such a way as to avoid the full humanity of the twelve people about whom he is talking. It does not escape Lincoln's notice that slave drivers are selling these slaves away from family, friends, and wives to a place where "the lash of the master is proverbially more ruthless and unrelenting than any other." But he protects himself by asserting that the slaves were happy, that they "danced, sang, cracked jokes," played the fiddle and engaged in various games. He chooses what will become the Stephen Foster minstrel version of "Camptown Races" over the rhetoric of liberation. He does not actually allow the individual human beings chained together on this boat into his sight or his heart.[21]

What is most disturbing is that Lincoln achieves this distance by chaining himself link for link to the Declaration of Independence, the revolution, and the founding fathers. Lincoln's speeches and legislative initiatives attest to the fact that most European Americans, even radical abolitionists, never fully extricated themselves from the white-supremacist concepts of their forefathers, even as they recognized the moral evils and economic impracticability of slavery. Thomas Jefferson's appalling and now infamous reasons in *Notes on the State of Virginia* why freed African Americans should not be incorporated into American society and why, after they were shipped off to colonies, Caucasian citizens should be imported to fill their places were not only the ravings of a brilliant but deluded forefather but a blueprint of late eighteenth- and early nineteenth-century racism.[22]

If we have any doubt that Lincoln was himself tied to this Jeffersonian trotline, we only need recall that in July 1852 he justified his colonization position on slavery by referring directly to Jefferson's argument for colonization. Eulogizing Henry Clay in 1827, Lincoln commended him for his deep attachment to the American Colonization Society, "founded in the halls of Congress in December 1816," and proudly quoted Clay as saying in a 1827 speech before this society, "There is a moral fitness in the idea of returning to Africa her children, whose ancestors have been torn from her by the ruthless hand of fraud and violence. Transplanted in a foreign land, they will carry back to their native soil the rich fruits of religion, civilization, law, and liberty."[23] Clay's words provide evidence not just for some vague "racism" but for the utter dislocation of and disassociation from rational thought—even by the most logical and eloquent of statesmen—when it came to understanding or even seeing the freed people of America as people. Once they were free, the enslaved people had to be gotten rid of because, as Jefferson pointed out in excruciating detail, they were worthless to society. But they should be sent to Africa to uplift her people. Never mind asking why Jefferson would think that people who were enslaved, beaten, chained, and treated like cattle—whom he considered morally and intellectually inferior—would be able to or would want to take a message of religion, civilization, law, and liberty to Africa, an assumption that borders on the absurd.

The only explanation for why the likes of Henry Clay and Abraham Lincoln would create an intertextual genealogy back to this argument is that they were still hanging themselves on the same trotline, a deluded fantasy of the supremacy of whiteness and masculinity. When one considers that Thomas Jefferson's own love, Sally Hemings, and his own children were of African descent and that he had enslaved people at his home who were unparalleled craftsmen, scientists and innovators, architects and artists, his argument is emotionally dishonest and mean-spirited, as well as scientifically incorrect.

That Lincoln and Clay quoted Jefferson and looked up to him reveals how deeply the founding fathers were entranced by their own ersatz projection of an American nation. Even more disturbing is that cultural scholars have defined the period during which Jefferson scripted his calculated racism as the age of reason. The kind of rhetorical strategies that Jefferson and Lincoln used were rational and scientific only if seen within the ersatz filter of white patriarchal power. But outside of this fantasy, such reason appears as madness. This very ability to balance fact and fiction is what gives Lincoln's rhetoric its power, but it drives those of us who see that the emperor had few clothes to distraction. There is little doubt that Lincoln had trouble really understanding racial issues, as did almost all upper-class or powerful white men and women of his generation. It is also now almost an accepted commonplace that while he became progressively more pro-emancipation as the war dragged on and the division of the nation became more dire, he never let go of his desire for colonization as the final solution.

Indeed, Lincoln held on to his plan to colonize slaves as the best solution to the "problem" of how to assimilate freed people into the American economy and society long after delivering the Emancipation Proclamation and fighting for what would become, after his death, the Thirteenth Amendment to the Constitution.[24] These historic documents become lifelines that will allow him to avoid asking himself what real revolution would look like at this moment. By binding himself to the chain of this ersatz "story," he insulates himself from the actual experience of slavery. The documents throughout *Lincoln on Race and Slavery* unveil a careful, calculating, practical, and political Lincoln who would have liked to wean American society from its reliance on slavery, but with as little disruption to an eighteenth-century rationalism and social peace as possible.

This balancing act between the "freedom" of anarchy and mob violence and the equality of "ordered government" marked Lincoln's presidency; for better and for worse, he patiently tolerated moral and ethical positions that were intolerable to the survival of democracy. Lincoln was always antislavery, but his understanding of political possibility made him prudent and patient.[25] In bill after bill—from Lincoln's time as a state legislator to his time in Congress to his presidency—he followed this careful approach, a course of action that was philosophically and morally contradictory but politically savvy. The conventional biographical reading is that Lincoln became a progressively more passionate liberator. But as odd as it might sound to twenty-first-century audiences, Lincoln was consistently antislavery, consistently procolonization (i.e., insisting that the best strategy would be to send freed people back to Africa), and consistently unable to embrace the full humanity of African American people. Lincoln's stance on slavery was not radical or original but in harmony with the twisted logic of ersatz America. What did change, however, was his rhetoric—what he said.

Even as historians such as Allen Guelzo and Eric Foner expose Lincoln's less than stellar racial politics, Americans will feel strangely sacrilegious, on the wrong side of what most would view as a finished discussion, mainly because of what he said. Abraham Lincoln said, "As I would not be a slave, so I would not be a master." The Emancipation Proclamation, while certainly the least noteworthy of Lincoln's writings in terms of literary flourish, was one of his most daring rhetorical acts. With it, Lincoln brought together action and word, so that word had power. The president simply said:

> That on the first day of January in the year of our Lord one thousand eight hundred and sixty-three, all persons held as slaves within any State or designated part of a State, the people whereof shall then be in rebellion against the United States, shall be then, thenceforward, and forever free; and the Executive Government of the United States, including the military and naval authority thereof, will recognize and maintain the freedom of such persons, and will do no act or acts to repress such persons, or any of them, in any efforts they may make for their actual freedom.

The Emancipation Proclamation was a rhetorical gamble, and it worked. He said: it will be so because we have said it will be so. Ironically, Lincoln punished the rebels by taking away slavery and rewarded the Union supporters by allowing them to continue to hold slaves. This was not a moral position but a tactical one. But what Lincoln knew was that sometimes the tactical position leads to the moral outcome. The Emancipation Proclamation took on this power not because it brought the country together and not because it freed all the slaves. It did not. But the enslaved people heard words that matched the reality of a personal liberty that they had sustained throughout the years of bondage. The word (not yet the law) of the land and the soul of the people were in harmony for one short, miraculous moment. Rhetoric in this case was more liberatory, and achieved more change, then all the guns and cannons combined. For one reason and one reason only: the Emancipation Proclamation tore down the scaffolding of the ersatz American nation and promised the full reality of democracy to a people who already understood this possibility.

Neither the calcification of these historical moments, the hagiography of great men, nor the desecration of these historical moments and the revisionist appraisal of heroes heals the human wound that slavery inflicted on the American nation.[26] We cannot even say that slavery inflicted a human wound on American *democracy* because Americans had only the *idea* of democracy until slavery ended. Whether we are vilifying or glorifying Lincoln, when we keep our attention on Lincoln himself and on what becomes, even in such fine portrayals as Stephen Spielberg's and Daniel Day Lewis's nuanced *Lincoln, his* Civil War and *his* Emancipation Proclamation, we once again ignore the people most affected by this moment. Because Lincoln said in his Gettysburg Address, "Of the people, for the people, by the people," the people, both black and white, understood one thing from his words: freedom.

LINCOLN PORTRAIT III: "PROCLAIM LIBERTY THROUGHOUT ALL THE LAND"

The famous Currier and Ives lithograph from January 1863 of the great patriarch Abraham Lincoln freeing the slave who is on bended knee (fig. 30) predicts the relationship of nineteenth- and twentieth-century America to the freemen and freewomen during Reconstruction, as entrenched racism trumped antislavery sentiments. The crouched slave *receives* his freedom in a position of perpetual gratitude, inactive rather than active, object rather than subject, dependent rather than autonomous; he is a passive recipient, as Marcus Wood discusses so thoroughly in *The Horrible Gift of Freedom.* The anonymous slave in the Currier and Ives print expresses no retaliation, no fury, and no ability to stand up straight, only appreciation for the little that is thrown to him. Northern abolitionists, Abraham Lincoln, and the nation as a whole legalized liberty but never fully recognized manhood and womanhood. By embracing this stooped figure, they set the stage for another hundred years of the desecration of the democratic principle of liberty for all.[27]

In the print, not only does Lincoln seem to be lording it over a half-clothed, newly freed (not free) African, while he himself is fully dressed in a three-piece

FIGURE 30

Freedom to the Slaves, by Currier and Ives, 1863.
Hand-colored lithograph, 13⅜ × 17¹⁵⁄₁₆ in.
(Prints & Photographs Division, Library of Congress)

suit, but his hand is raised as if to say, either "I proclaim you free," "Look up to God because you are free," or, as most read the gesture, "Stand up man, you are free." The male figure and the woman and two children, much smaller behind him, do not look like they could ever be Lincoln's equals. The artist clothes the diminutive people in rags of a slightly "Africanesque" style, a bit odd for the time period. The vestments suggest a possible colonization overlay. The newly freed man kneels in a position that is impossible for a human body to sustain, one knee bent and almost touching the ground, the other only slightly bent. He is a crouched animal, a falling body, anything but a man about to step up to his own freedom and stand as an equal with Abraham Lincoln. In fact, it looks as if he will fall forward onto Lincoln. His whole body is curved toward Lincoln's in a position of supplication—or as an animal about to leap—as the tiny family looks on. The inscription at the bottom of the print reads, "FREEDOM TO THE SLAVES / Proclaimed January 1, 1863 by ABRAHAM LINCOLN, President of the United States. / 'Proclaim liberty throughout All the land unto All the inhabitants thereof.' ______LEV. XXV 10." Equating Lincoln with God, the 1863 print creates a larger-than-life, stagnant image of emancipation.

This Currier and Ives image of Lincoln as the great emancipator became the model for the Freedmen's Monument in Lincoln Park, in the Capitol Hill area of Washington, DC, erected in April 1876 (fig. 31). Formerly enslaved people, under the leadership of Charlotte Scott, paid for the monument, which was sculpted by Thomas Ball in the period between his renditions of George Washington and Henry Clay. The monument repeats the scene depicted in the print, except that the women and children are gone and the enslaved man is dressed only in a loincloth, making him look Roman rather than African. But the people endowing this statue insisted that the man, who was sculpted after a real free person who had once been a slave, have African-style hair and that Lincoln's hand not actually pull him up from the ground. As the pastoral does for George Washington, the classical references transform slavery into an unavoidable phase in the progressive development of Western civilization. Henry Bacon consciously modeled the Lincoln Memorial as a replica of the Parthenon to evoke what he saw as the original site of democracy. It is interesting that when Pierre Charles L'Enfant designed the city of Washington, he thought of this square, now called Lincoln Park, as the point from which all distances on the American continent would be calculated.

LINCOLN PORTRAIT IV: "HE STRANGELY TOLD US"

Frederick Douglass's "Oration in Memory of Abraham Lincoln," spoken at the dedication of the Freedmen's Monument, is one of the most nuanced and most accurate portraits of Lincoln. Douglass argues throughout his speech that Lincoln was primarily "a white man's president" and that his motives "were never for the true recognition and liberation of the African American race as equals." Douglass also concedes that Lincoln was the right man at the right moment to deliver the Emancipation Proclamation and set the stage for the ratification of the Thirteenth Amendment, saying that for this his people are respectfully and

FIGURE 31
The Freedmen's Monument, by Thomas Ball, 1920, Lincoln Park, Washington, DC. (Prints & Photographs Division, Library of Congress)

eternally grateful. Nothing more, nothing less. No glittery patriotism, no hagiography. No horrible gift:

> Our faith in him was often taxed and strained to the uttermost, but it never failed. When he tarried long in the mountain; when he strangely told us that we were the cause of the war; when he still more strangely told us that we were to leave the land in which we were born; when he refused to employ our arms in defense of the Union; when, after accepting our services as colored soldiers, he refused to retaliate our murder and torture as colored prisoners; when he told us he would save the Union if he could with slavery; when he revoked the Proclamation of Emancipation of General Fremont; when he refused to remove the popular commander of the Army of the Potomac, we were at times grieved, stunned, and greatly bewildered; . . . but by a broad survey, in the light of the stern logic of great events, and in view

of that divinity which shapes our ends, rough hew them how we will, we came to the conclusion that the hour and the man of our redemption had somehow met in the person of Abraham Lincoln.

As Douglass tells the crowd, when they, with all their immense resources, build the memorials to Lincoln that they will surely build, they should remember this memorial, because it was built by the people whose lives he changed forever: "For while Abraham Lincoln saved for you a country, he delivered us from a bondage."[28] *Delivered* is a far different word than *freed.* Deliverance is a hand held out along a horizontal trajectory, to help one cross, not a decree from above. When a postman delivers a package, he puts into our hands what was ours to begin with, the epistolary receipt by the person designated as the receiver. Douglass builds national memory through rhetoric of complex negotiation and forgiveness. Douglass's speech is a woven condolence belt.

"With One Wild Cry and Flying Leap"

As I will argue in chapter 5, slavery ended because of the pressure of people of African descent on the people of European descent. However, the insanity could only stop when enough right-minded white people began to dismantle their own entrenched nineteenth-century racism and complacency. By the 1850s, the evangelical awakening in the enslaved communities had given voice to backwoods preachers, to increased activity in the melding of African and Christian religious creolization that fueled the liberation rebellions on the plantations. Those who escaped brought their stories, their battered bodies, and their liberation theology to the receptive ears of the now fully institutionalized abolitionist movement, and northern writers were listening.

During the entire period of enslavement in America, from 1619 to 1865, there were free people of color living in the United States who were writers, poets, orators, activists, storytellers, and readers, participating in and contributing to the reading community. These literate and articulate free people of color, along with the outspoken among the enslaved and free(d)men and free(d)women, were a minority, but they drove the rhetoric of abolition and liberation. They provided the metaphors—and urgency—to the literary renaissance of both African American and European American letters in the nineteenth century.[29]

But I do not aim in this chapter to explore African Americans' literary output at this stage in American history. I want instead to look at the ways in which African American aesthetics transformed white literary America. By specifically examining iconic and canonical works by Harriet Beecher Stowe, Nathaniel Hawthorne, and Emily Dickinson, I will go so far as to suggest that the metaphors and sourcing behind the renaissance of literary output in the 1850s came from the realization, often unconscious, sometimes troubled, that slavery had to end. An enslaved democracy had equally enslaved language. As the authors, pressured by the voices of enslaved peoples, began to free themselves to conceptualize a true democracy, their language shifted and began to pulse with forceful metaphors. These metaphors—Queequeg's scrolled body, Eliza's leap across the ice, Whitman's leaves of grass, and Hawthorne's letter *A*—expressed a visceral graphic response that came directly from the voices of those still enslaved.

In fact, the many hundreds of books on slavery, both literary and historical, from the earliest to the present, can be read from the point of view of visceral graphism. And in many, if not all, the reader will find the dots, points, lines of connection, weavings, and beats of visceral graphism that have allowed survivors to speak the tongue of regeneration. While African American writers understood this line from the graphic inscription of cultural retention to the oratory of Frederick Douglass, white writers were struggling to break down their enthrallment from within the dominant culture to inscribe their new linguistic bridge to freedom.

The conditions of enslavement were no longer invisible. They were the fully sketched tales of horror that the abolitionist propagandists peddled. In answer to this fervor, for the first time, white writers were speaking out in every way imaginable, and their voices were cryptic, an odd echo of Lawrence's tortured skin shedding. In 1851–52 Harriet Beecher Stowe composed *Uncle Tom's Cabin;* in 1851 Herman Melville finished his masterpiece *Moby-Dick* and Hawthorne wrote *The Scarlet Letter;* in 1855 Walt Whitman wrote *Leaves of Grass;* and in 1861 Emily Dickinson wrote eighty-six poems. In fact, the years 1860–64 were Dickinson's most prolific. We could never prove that the rhetorical fabric these texts wove helped Lincoln, a man of words, envision a real democracy. But these writers, whom Lincoln read, insisted on an attention to a new conceptual space.

As this democratic spark took hold, Hawthorne, Melville, Whitman, and Dickinson began to engage symbols that forever changed the way America could be imagined. And each did so, not by inventing a new visual, visceral, and graphic metaphoric textual universe, but by following the lead of free and enslaved rhetoricians, writers, and activists. Hawthorne's letter *A,* Melville's scrolled script on

Queequeg's body, Dickinson's buzzing fly, and a hundred other minute details became the templates of a new American alphabet. This American alphabet allowed the erotic, the embodied, the natural, and the female to enter the dialogue of the American imaginary. While these scripts tried desperately to reconcile the irreconcilable tension between equality and freedom, they often fell short. Melville's story line constrains the text so much that Queequeg literally disappears and Pip does not take on as full a voice as we might desire. It is clear that Queequeg knew exactly what the scrolled symbols on his body meant. And Dickinson and Whitman do not completely embrace a full-blown narrative of social liberation from slavery *and* racism, but their poetry quickens the metaphoric field of linguistic possibility necessary for white America to imagine a slave-free nation. Hawthorne never even pretends to be an abolitionist or a suffragist, but his transformation of linguistic possibility, from the overdetermined symbol to the multitudinous metaphor, provides a potent linguistic field for democratic imaginings. All of these writers created this space by freeing the graphic from alphabetic equivalency.

These graphic inscriptions were not in and of themselves liberatory, buried as they often were in conservative texts. But they held the potential for liberation. In a society that had not taken the time to fully embody and give value to the kind of woven wampum belt of condolence that these symbols represented, the graphic codes of the nineteenth-century literary giants have, in many cases, been buried, ignored, or simply misinterpreted by critics. If white writers of this time and the society as a whole had understood the revolutionary potential of their own moment of linguistic invention, any number of Elizas could have safely crossed the water.

In a perfect, utopian universe—one in which wealthy white planters did not identify so passionately with their role as slave masters and in which Americans had trusted the weaving process, learned to read the code—northerners and southerners could have slowed down the nation's traumatic, frightened, and paralytic response to centuries of slavery, embraced a universal emancipation, and saved 620,000 people from death on the battlefields and in the sick wards of the Civil War. If there had been more patience, more ability to read the signs and symbols of this new metaphoric language, a slowing down of thought, and a matching of action to imagination, one footstep following another across the widening path, liberation could have been achieved in civil dialogue rather than uncivil war. The mending of democracy, the ice melting, had already begun, and the ersatz nation of the founding fathers was cracking wide open, becoming, in a tide of human insistence, for a moment at least, Frederick Douglass's flowing river of democracy.

The assumption in the field of American studies is that American exceptionalism explains the prolific and powerful period of imaginative outpouring in the mid-nineteenth century. The nation had come of age. Writers were defining a truly American style of writing, depending less on European models, even as the literacy rate had increased, offering a greater readership, pointing to a democratization of reading as a leisure activity. But there is something much more important going on in these particular works. Following the lead of African American abolitionists, as each writer expands the way we can conceptualize meaning, embracing spatial and visual metaphors that join the known material world with the unknown, each extends the power of fiction not as aesthetic delight only but as cultural and political work. They weave the metaphoric rope that allows their readers to rappel down the narrative cliff and find their way through the mute terrain of social dislocation and change. But they do so because they can finally begin to hear, however faintly and with whatever heavy cloak of prejudice, the voices, and with them the values and artistic choices, of those they had assumed did not have a voice.

HARRIET BEECHER STOWE'S CABIN

No social change as profound as emancipation occurs because of the actions of one man. Lincoln did not come up with his rhetoric on his own. Lincoln was a reading man and a listening man, deeply influenced by the great outpouring of abolitionist, transcendental, and literary rhetoric in the first half of the nineteenth century. In fact, Lincoln was probably more affected than any other president has been by the cultural giants of his time. Rather than being outside of the mainstream of his historical moment, Lincoln represented the troubled relationship toward race that marked his countrymen. Even if he did not say to Harriet Beecher Stowe, "So this is the little woman who started this big war,"[30] he could have, for he had read not only *Uncle Tom's Cabin* but also Stowe's explanation of the sources for the book, *A Key to Uncle Tom's Cabin.*

While we do not know whether Lincoln actually said these words to Stowe, we do know that her work had an enormous effect on popular opinion concerning slavery. She wrote and serialized her famous novel *Uncle Tom's Cabin* in 1851; when the novel came into print in 1852, it sold three hundred thousand copies in the first year. Attacked for being sentimental, for plagiarizing from the 1849 *Life of Josiah Henson, Formerly a Slave, Now an Inhabitant of Canada, as Nar-*

rated by Himself, and for perpetuating and creating damaging, infantilized racial stereotypes, *Uncle Tom's Cabin* was nonetheless a clear indictment of slavery. In the first year, Stowe sold more than a million copies in England alone, and it was the best-selling book of the year in the United States.

With all the hoopla about George Washington's home, one might expect that the United States would also embrace and preserve the birthplaces and childhood homes of its great writers, especially one credited by Abraham Lincoln with starting the Civil War. But in fact, in 1998 the town of Litchfield, Connecticut, refused to allow Harriet Beecher Stowe's childhood home to be rebuilt in a prominent location in town. Her home had been moved and reduced to a pile of boards. The boards, carefully numbered, lay in a garage behind the historic Tallmadge House, built by Elijah Wadsworth, a Revolutionary War hero. In 2002, when I visited Litchfield along with others attending a conference on slavery and freedom in New England, Tallmadge House was owned by Chandler Saint, the founder of the Beecher House Center for the Study of Equal Rights, who calls his home the Wadsworth-Beecher House. The boards are from the house that was home not only to Harriet Beecher but also to the Reverend Lyman Beecher, a prominent member of the Litchfield community, renowned for his antislavery sermons; Henry Ward Beecher, a famous preacher who, from his pulpit in Brooklyn, New York, advocated an end to slavery; Catherine Beecher, who founded schools for young women; and Isabella Beecher, active in the suffrage movement. Each one was renowned enough to justify preserving their childhood home. That the most famous among them is Harriet Beecher Stowe makes the pile of boards and rubble odd at best. At the moment of this writing, after many lawsuits and complicated negotiations, the house has not been reassembled.

According to Chandler Saint, the town would not let him build on the site because of zoning ordinances. One wonders why the town selectmen would pass up the opportunity to include Harriet Beecher Stowe's childhood home among Litchfield's historic attractions at a time when cultural tourism was so lucrative. Although Stowe was certainly controversial to academics concerned about her stereotypical depictions, she was a well-assimilated symbol of American dissent, fighting for the union of North and South and the abolition of the peculiar institution.

The Beecher house had become a dormitory for Spring Hill School, the same school that Pete Seeger, the 1960s activist folksinger, attended. For a town that insists on its conservationist position, Litchfield has been home to many radicals. In 1997, when the school, then named the Foreman School, decided to tear down the Beecher house, Chandler Saint and Stephen Solley bought the home for one bicentennial silver dollar. Saint and Solley decided to return it to near its original site, a quarter of a mile from the Tallmadge House. But the neighbors wanted no part of their plan. Neighbors told Elizabeth Maker, of the *New York Times,* that they had moved to Litchfield from Westport, Connecticut, precisely because of Litchfield's "uptight" zoning laws. A member of the Litchfield Historical Society called the plan "a disgrace." She pointed out that the proposed site for the museum lay in Litchfield's historic district, "where you're not allowed to change a window or a door or put a fence up" without a special permit, "yet Chandler and the state have done an end run around every local ordinance to push through a project that is totally wrong for this zone."[31]

It is strange to think that in a town that prides itself on its colonial heritage, it would be considered "totally wrong" to return a revolutionary-era house, the Beecher house, to a location only a few hundred yards from where it once stood, in the historic district no less. It was apparent that the citizens were not interested in actual historical accuracy or architectural preservation, but in maintaining the image of an ersatz antebellum history. The neighbors sued Saint to stop him from constructing the house so near their property. That lawsuit sparked a long-drawn-out fight between local and state factions—the state overriding local zoning ordinances in order to make the project possible—that has kept the Beecher home sitting in Saint's garage and in several trailers for many years.

Today Litchfield is a tourist town where New Yorkers and former residents of Connecticut have moved to get away from the city. But it has a strange architectural history. The Litchfield Historical Society website relates that at the turn of the nineteenth century "the town embraced the colonial revival movement, transforming itself into an idealized vision of the colonial past. Colonial, federal and Victorian era homes were renovated to capture a vision of traditional architecture loosely based on the most elegant styles of the colonial and federal periods."[32] While this desire to become an idealized vision of the colonial past seems harmless enough, it is a perfect metaphor for America's relation to memory. Much better to go back to a period when Americans imagined that they were all one as a nation than to have to talk about slavery, abolition, or the Civil War. It is the same preservationist impulse that moved the Mount Vernon Ladies' Association. If slavery posed a difficult problem to the notion of a perfect union, then one simply pretended that slavery had never existed. And certainly, a town aiming to represent itself as a perfect colonial masterpiece would not want to admit that some of the most famous abolitionists had been born, preached, and lived there.

Having grown up in an Alexandria, Virginia, turned Olde Towne Alexandria,

I know the impulse well. However, Litchfield's colonial revival, unlike Alexandria's, created some fairly ridiculous and weird architectural grotesques—Victorian mansions turned into colonial homes but twice the size that a colonial home would have been. The desire to return to an antebellum national memory was so strong that people ripped down or covered up Victorian facades to replace them with "colonial" white wood and black shutters. The anachronistic quality of the town's architecture becomes evident to anyone visiting the town center. But if Alexandria still had architectural integrity as a colonial town in the 1830s, what Alexandria would later call "Olde Towne" was "the largest port for the coastal slave trade in the upper South,"[33] and certainly few tourists visit the Frankland and Armfield slave jail.

If it seems surprising that at the time of this publication there is not one mention of the Beechers on the Litchfield History Museum website, we need only note that the town's museum does not concentrate on any history after about 1830. The advertisement for the museum reads: "The museum's seven galleries highlight family life and work during the fifty years after the American Revolution, a time when Litchfield was a bustling commercial, political, and educational center." Litchfield was at the height of its wealth and power during the period chronicled in the museum, so it is perhaps understandable that the town's preservers of historic memory would like to return to that moment. The museum exhibits "antique" "colonial" furniture made in the early 1900s by taking apart Victorian furniture and reassembling it. It becomes clear that a town so dedicated to things' staying the way they never were might resist putting Harriet Beecher Stowe's home back where it belonged.

Even though the town had gone through this aggressive colonial revival obliterating the Victorian homes that had dominated the community in the late 1890s, it is difficult to believe that it would actually want to obliterate its post–1830 history as well. But during the first decade of the twenty-first century, when this controversy unveiled itself, the ersatz revival had come even further than the colonial revival. Many real-estate advertisements for Litchfield and Litchfield County describe the area as pristine, with covered bridges and sugar maples, old barns and stone walls, untouched by time. The *Oxford English Dictionary* defines *pristine* as both ancient (returning something to its "pristine" past) and brand-new (never having been sullied by the past), which we could say is the same crisis of identification that plagues ersatz America itself.

The Litchfield Historical Society barely mentions the nineteenth century. Litchfield is rich only in colonial and revolutionary history. The town advertises itself as a utopia, a place to get away from New York and all its problems, a place to escape urban crime (read racial and class), a place to forget about all that complicated American history, about all that represented dissent and messy democracy—slavery, Stowe, the Civil War, the sixties, Pete Seeger. Democracy is definitely not pristine. Litchfield is at once brand-new and clean and ancient and perfected. There are two ways to have no history: one is to be so old that everyone has forgotten it, and the other is to be newborn. Maintaining either state requires complex gyrations. One demands an untimely death to the present, and the other a false claim of innocence.

At the time of my visit to Litchfield, a group of African American teachers from New Orleans persisted in questioning Chandler Saint about why the boards from the Beecher house had been ignored. He seemed a bit reluctant to hazard a guess, but finally conjectured that the town selectmen did not want the kind of people that the house would attract. He suggested that certain townspeople did not wish to have the Wadsworth-Beecher House in their backyard because it might attract African American schoolchildren from Hartford. They needed to maintain the sense of Litchfield as a "pristine" (read white) colonial village. Litchfield is not adverse to tourists; in fact the whole town, particularly the "historic district," is set up to welcome tourists, but the "right" kind.

The fact that Litchfield excludes the Beecher and Stowe stories from its town history is more important than it might first appear to be. As the town's website announces with pride, "Beginning in 1784, Litchfield lawyer, Tapping Reeve, systematized his law lectures for young students, creating the Litchfield Law School. . . . The list of graduates includes two Vice Presidents, Aaron Burr and John C. Calhoun, over 100 members of the House of Representatives, 28 senators, 14 governors, 14 cabinet members, 34 State Supreme Court Justices, and 3 Justices of the United States Supreme Court."[34] Litchfield was home to many of the earliest members of the U.S. government, and the systemization of the law that Tapping Reeve put into place gave them a particular mind-set about America. The fact that Litchfield was also home to a budding feminist movement is minimalized: "Established in 1792, Sarah Pierce's Litchfield Female Academy [which Harriet Beecher Stowe attended but which goes unmentioned] was one of the first major educational institutions for women in the United States." As Bruce Mason, writing in a local Connecticut newspaper, so accurately puts it: "There is flat refusal from some to see the goodness of what that house [the Beecher house] offers to the community, state, nation and world. The teaching of that house serves to free all people from bondage. It represents the beauty of the United States of America in that she recognizes a great wrong, and continues to work to set it right."[35]

Chandler Saint himself argues that the town ignores Harriet Beecher Stowe, not even capitalizing on her value as a tourist attraction, as a cultural icon, an abolitionist, and early feminist. One town selectmen told Maker that it was "fine" by him to keep the home in Litchfield, but the educational programming should be located elsewhere. Litchfield residents' main complaint against the Stowe house was that the state had interfered in local zoning ordinances, an all-too-familiar argument.

At the very bottom of this argument, as always, was racism, the ever-present desire to keep America white, the kind of racism that made small southern towns refuse to integrate and made southern states tell the federal government that it had no right to interfere in states' rights. The conference attendees had been on the *Freedom Schooner Amistad* the previous day, but even boarding a replica of a slave ship had not been as upsetting as realizing the calcified racism at the heart of Litchfield's decision not to save the Beecher house. Underlying our extreme emotion was the fact that we had spent two days learning that the slave history of the North—of Rhode Island, Connecticut, and Massachusetts—was a history of businessmen who had made enormous sums of money on the slave trade. The response of the teachers in the group, who were furious and saddened and silent, made me realize that perhaps I had underestimated the power of Harriet Beecher Stowe's language. From the garage, the boards with the numbers beckoned me to rethink Stowe's work.

The iconic image at the heart of *Uncle Tom's Cabin,* Eliza crossing the water, is depicted with symbolic language that merges the struggles of both the suffragist and abolitionist movements, but in doing so it creates something much more profound:

> In that dizzy moment her feet to her scarce seemed to touch the ground, and a moment brought her to the water's edge. Right on behind they came and, nerved with strength such as God gives only to the desperate, with one wild cry and flying leap, she vaulted sheer over the turbid current by the shore, on to the raft of ice beyond. It was a desperate leap—impossible to anything but madness and despair; and Haley, Sam, and Andy, instinctively cried out, and lifted up their hands, as she did it.

> The huge green fragment of ice on which she alighted pitched and creaked, as her weight came on it, but she stayed there not a moment. With wild cries and desperate energy she leaped to another and still another cake; —stumbling—leaping—slipping—springing upwards again! Her shoes are gone—her stockings cut from her feet—while blood marked every step; but she saw nothing, felt nothing, till dimly, as in a dream, she saw the Ohio side, and a man helping her up the bank.[36]

This scene has captured the imagination of many generations. Readers anxiously wait to see whether Eliza, jumping across the floating ice of the Ohio River with her child, Henry, clasped in her arms, running from the fugitive slave catchers, will make it to safety. Readers embrace the impossible hope that she will indeed escape to freedom. Each time, we are ecstatic that she has escaped, only to learn that because of the Fugitive Slave Act of 1850, it is just the beginning of her trial. The image is so exhilarating that artists have made it an icon (fig. 32). Yet with all the paint and ink spent on this passage, it is possible that we have read and depicted this section of *Uncle Tom's Cabin* too literally and missed the point of the moment Stowe creates.

Of course no one could actually leap barefoot from cake to cake of cracked green ice with one's child in one's arms and make it safely to the other side of a raging river. But if we read the floating ice cakes as a graphic script, another story emerges, written not in the plot but in the forms of this image. This is the story that Stowe learned from the autobiography of Josiah Henson and by talking to Sojourner Truth; it is the story of the personal and communal passion of the enslaved people for liberation. As Stowe somehow understands, this is a script marked out by bloody feet, both literally and metaphorically.

In 1851, at the very moment when Stowe was writing *Uncle Tom's Cabin,* at the Woman's Rights Convention in Worcester, Massachusetts, Abby Kelley Foster spoke the words that would define the women's rights movement for years: "I do not rise to make a speech—my life has been my speech. For fourteen years, I have advocated this cause by my daily life. Bloody feet, sisters, have worn smooth the path by which you have come hither."[37] Anyone listening to this speech would have known that although Abby Kelley Foster and many other suffragists had walked miles gathering signatures, their feet were not literally bloody. The bloody feet deliberately echoed the feet of the runaway slaves of the other political movement of the time. The reference empowers Foster. Reverend Henry Ward Beecher was in attendance at this conference. That same year, at the Wom-

FIGURE 32
"Eliza's Escape," from *Uncle Tom's Cabin,* printed as an advertising poster. Color lithograph, 72 × 53 cm. (Prints & Photographs Division, Library of Congress)

en's Rights Convention in Akron, Ohio, Sojourner Truth gave her famous "Ain't I a Woman" speech, making clear rhetorical connections between the antislavery and women's rights movements. The rhetorical power of Truth's speech comes from her reference to the strength of her body to lift and haul and carry. Her feet and arms and back and legs all defy the esoteric notion of the frail, weak "lady." Harriet Beecher Stowe met Sojourner Truth during this period.

By connecting Eliza's bloody feet and the bloody feet of both liberation struggles, Stowe empowers embodied feet connected to intelligent heads over disembodied heads as the agents of change. She creates a gestural, graphic trail of Eliza's footprints. But African Americans' feet were not just bloody. They were moving, escaping, and beating out a steady demand for freedom. African Americans maintained their personhood and their freedom throughout the dehumanizing torture of slavery by remembering a precise and exacting "Africanized" beat of liberation through talking drums, dancing juba, and numerous other cultural retentions.

Whether she knew it or not, Stowe acknowledged the source of her writing and the defining fact of the years between 1850 and 1865: in fifteen years, America was able to turn from the horrifying prospect of the Fugitive Slave Act of 1850 to the liberatory demands of the Emancipation Proclamation, not only because of the acts of abolitionists, not only because of the Civil War, not only because of Lincoln's actions, not even because of what he said, but primarily because enslaved people had marked themselves free with the resounding sound of feet being placed firmly on the earth and the sounding board of wooden floor and body turned drum. Stowe understood on some deep level that Eliza's ability to find firm footing in the most violent of circumstances was the real story.

The enslaved person's intelligence was in his or her ability to escape enslavement, both to run and to place feet firmly on the ground whether still enslaved or not. Not to be free in some nebulous "soul" but to be free in one's own body fully integrated with one's mind. The intelligence of the feet, rather than being the lowest form of intelligence, is in fact the highest. The jagged, black-lined pattern between the pitching and creaking cakes of green ice creates what artists call negative space, a hieroglyphic of gaping crevices, and exposes, not unrepresentable or unimaginable spaces, but the dark water of the river. The river is change; the ice is the status quo. That these lines mean death is only because Eliza is trapped in a world that cannot tolerate change.

Stowe's search for a language to express one woman's passion for freedom takes her into unknown linguistic territory, not just the spatial and graphic domain between written narrative and visual expression but the nowhere space of black water. The difference between frozen water and rushing water is that the latter moves. In this case, black water moves the white ice cakes. As the frozen ice of the memorialized nation breaks open, the river flows, and Eliza can hope to make it across to freedom. The path is not the ice itself but is the black lines, the river directing Eliza from one cake to the next, one stable footing to the next, her feet finding a ground to walk on. That there are bounty hunters lurking on both sides and dogs barking at her heels underlines the fragility of this momentary freedom. The image of Eliza crossing the Ohio, mass-produced in drawings and plays, did not depend on a citizen's access to the written word or even on an accompanying narrative. The icon told the whole story.

Stowe wrote and published installments of *Uncle Tom's Cabin* in direct response to the passage of the Fugitive Slave Act of 1850, imploring all people, particularly women, to speak out against slavery, which she knew many saw as an abomination. Under the act, slave catchers could seize any runaways and return them to their master, but the slave catchers were just as likely to capture free people and return them to some assumed master for substantial profit, as the movie about Solomon Northup, *Twelve Years a Slave,* documents. Though the act's sponsors sought to solidify the southern hold on slavery, the effect was to create a union in which no African American was truly free. During the 1850s, it became increasingly clear that holding a union of slave and not-slave states together was virtually impossible. America was literally choosing between what Frederick Douglass called "the withered branch of slavery" and the "flowing river of democracy." The Fugitive Slave Act of 1850 mobilized abolitionist opposition. As the tension increased, the fervor on both sides grew. The facade of a plantation republic, George Washington's legacy, could not hold.

A few months before Lincoln penned his initial Emancipation Proclamation on 16 June 1862, he borrowed Stowe's *Key to Uncle Tom's Cabin* from the Library of Congress—not the novel itself, but the *key* to the novel, in which Stowe gives historical evidence to support her fiction. It is almost as if Lincoln, removed from the daily realities of slavery, had to see it for himself, to get as close as he could, in order to have the strength to go through with writing the Emancipation Proclamation. Our assessment of Stowe's legacy and of her words' ability to affect political action would be stronger if it could be shown that Stowe was the powerful woman responsible for the great emancipation rather than for the Civil War. Unfortunately for Stowe, *Uncle Tom's Cabin* probably sent more young men off to war and death than any other propagandistic recruitment tool. What Stowe did for the nation is arguably momentous. How Stowe influenced our image of African American people could be called disastrous. Uncle Tom and Mammy, ersatz American stereotypes, die hard.

When, however, we read *Uncle Tom's Cabin* through the viscerally graphic image of the black lines in the ice and Eliza's bloody feet, a much more subtle, subversive Stowe emerges. When we break down the stereotypes of the glorious Civil War soldier in his Currier and Ives frame and bring the kneeling, praying Uncle Tom up from his knees, it will be through the art and words of many who have tried. The regenerative branching line, the textured web, emerges once again as the transformative site of change in literature as well as other cultural forms.

These metaphors and images can appear in texts that are in other ways more conservative. Bloody feet and cracked ice. To paraphrase Copland: This is what enslaved people lived. This is what she wrote. Harriet Beecher Stowe wrote this.

As Eliza jumps from cake to cake of ice, she knits together the space between her desire for freedom and the possibility of gaining that freedom. She speaks a language that dance theorists would call embodied narrative; her legs speak. She weaves her path to freedom with the language of her own body moving in space. Even in the midst of the turmoil of breaking ice and barking dogs and slave catchers on both sides of the river, Eliza is able to run across the ice-clogged river toward freedom because Stowe literally writes this path into being. The white writers and orators of the abolitionist and transcendental periods were not so much inventing freedom as translating the liberatory embodied acts of the disenfranchised into narrative language. They took up the thread handed to them by the Elizas and Josiah Hensons, who mapped the way through the labyrinthine historical moment.

Eliza's plight cannot be presented as gentle or easy. She makes her way through the minefield of slavocracy. White racism will necessarily break apart violently and temporarily implode. A nation that has allowed its identity to rest on the forced labor of millions of enslaved people cannot emerge easily. It will break open, splitting at the seams, and women who love their babies will have to run wildly to find a path across the cracking ice. Stowe's metaphor is potent and one that applies to the iconic battles of the Civil War, the Emancipation Proclamation, and finally the surrender at Appomattox. Because Stowe is a self-consciously political writer, the metaphor is written with broad strokes.

In this moment, writers such as Herman Melville, Emily Dickinson, and Nathaniel Hawthorne began, both consciously and perhaps in some cases unconsciously (as in Hawthorne's case), with a more nuanced brush than Stowe's, to write a script of democracy. Because the country had never actually lived the impossible dream of democracy, they began to weave a metaphoric language that could help them imagine the possibility of a nation dedicated to the proposition that all men and women are created equal. The word *imagine* is itself a visual term, acting along spatial and graphic lines rather than through temporal, established narratives.

American literature during this period was powerful because the great minds of the time were called upon to provide a weaving of condolence unlike anything that had ever been written before. For the first time, democracy was a possibility, and writers could not help but address this issue. Rarely, if ever, in American history had literati and politics been so close together. As orators, poets, essayists, and novelists provided outlines for the dream of democracy, they sketched what a union conceived in liberty could be in the "white imagination," not what it was politically or economically. Writers turned not just to the work of Frederick Douglass and Sojourner Truth but to the life experiences of hundreds of fugitive slaves who had brought their stories into the public imagination. The enslaved and recently freed were not living in a dreamlike world or struggling to imagine freedom. Those who had not gone mad, become the living dead, or succumbed to the brainwashing of the master were living an embodied footprint of freedom. As the ersatz facade began to fall apart, the imaginative voices of enslaved and freed people—written, spoken, and visual—increase in volume and intensity, building and gathering in metaphoric and linguistic brilliance a new reality to replace the ersatz one. The literary response to this human wave of liberation created a linguistic renaissance, not always politically radical but culturally radical in its ability to open a jagged space for democratic possibility.

So whether or not the story of Lincoln giving Stowe credit for starting the war is true, at no time in history was literature's impact on the political scene more direct. Likewise, at no time was the impact of enslaved rhetoric, life stories, and scourged bodies on the literary imagination more direct. Harriet Beecher Stowe, as well as writers of European descent such as Ralph Waldo Emerson, Margaret Fuller, Henry David Thoreau, Herman Melville, Emily Dickinson, and Walt Whitman, began to articulate a distinctly American cultural imaginary that was at once geographic, visual, and spatial. Their words at this time were less dependent on law and order and temporal narratives of national self-interest. They explored the edges of the unknown in the American experience. A writer on a cliff must find a language to reach across and throw out lifelines, tendrils, to bridge the divide between what he or she knows and what he or she has never spoken before. Americans of European decent in 1862, having always lived in a nation dependent on slavery, did not know true democracy or the language of liberation. They were reaching, stretching, leaping across a great chasm. For this reason, the literary giants of nineteenth-century America wrote desperate fiction, as with Eliza: "impossible to anything but madness and despair." Their language is taut, caught between the poles of equality and freedom. Lincoln's emancipatory rhetoric did not spring fully formed from his own head. These metaphors of a new American language helped create the graphic space for Lincoln's Emancipation Proclamation, with all its faults and obviously expedient military necessities.

NATHANIEL HAWTHORNE: THE LETTER *A*

In 1850 Nathaniel Hawthorne, scorned by abolitionists for his racist statements, his support of the southern sympathizer President Franklin Pierce, and his antiabolitionist position—wrote *The Scarlet Letter,* followed by *The House of the Seven Gables* (1851), *The Blithesdale Romance* (1852), and *The Marble Faun* (1860). While these novels are not consciously antislavery or prosuffrage, they reveal the extraordinary attention to the language of the margin that the times demanded of even the ever-cautious Hawthorne. The visual pull of a new imaginary intrigued Hawthorne to such a degree that he entangled himself in the web of *The Scarlet Letter,* introducing the potential of a truly unusual and viscerally graphic American *A,* the start of an alphabet of liberation that Hawthorne, unfortunately, did not have the heart to see through. The letter *A,* caught in an obfuscating, deeply conservative text, reveals what a powerful force visceral graphism can have on the cultural imagination and inadvertently unveils the ways in which writers like Hawthorne could silence liminal textual inscriptions.

In the opening section of *The Scarlet Letter,* "The Custom-House: Introductory to the Scarlett Letter," Hawthorne goes into great detail about his discovery of a document that provides proofs of the authenticity of the story he is about to relate. This introductory section is an attempt to give verisimilitude to the fictional account, a common practice in nineteenth-century novels. He claims to have discovered a fragment of red cloth shaped as a letter *A.* This biographical section about the Custom House, quite literally full of descriptions of old men who have long given up lives of sea travel and military and political service, bothers many readers, as it is dull in comparison with the rest of the text. A young narrator, forced out of financial necessity to work as a customs officer, claims that he gladly left his old pursuit of letters behind and enjoys the predictable company of these old men, but he seems to be eager for something that will make him start writing again.

In case we doubt whether *The Scarlet Letter* is about America and about the American cultural imagination at this moment in history, Hawthorne's long description of the deteriorating colonial-style Custom House—anticipating by just a couple of years the description of the decaying Mount Vernon with which Ann Cunningham rallied the Mount Vernon Ladies' Association—with the banner of the republic floating or drooping from the "loftiest point of its roof, during precisely three and a half hours each forenoon,"[38] points us toward a more political reading. His description of the "enormous specimen of the American eagle . . . [with a] fierceness of her beak and eye"[39] clues us to the fact that the meaning of the American nation to its people was foremost in Hawthorne's mind. That he had been fired from his post in the federal customhouse might have led to this criticism of the American eagle and the patriotic trappings of the Custom House, but the book reveals a more complex critique of the nation.

Whatever Hawthorne's political views might have been, the moment the nameless narrator wanders away from the old sea captains, soldiers, businessmen, and politicians of Old Salem who are the other customs officers and into the space of the upper vaults of the Custom House, he finds the large room of his imagination. He writes a text that is almost a blueprint for how to move from ersatz iconic history to an embodied history of liberation and individual experience. Earlier in the text he refers to his own family history when he describes a particularly mean-spirited ancestor:

> His son, too, inherited the persecuting spirit, and made himself so conspicuous in the martyrdom of the witches, that their blood may fairly be said to have left a stain upon him. So deep a stain, indeed, that his old dry bones in the Charter Street burial-ground, must still retain it, if they have not crumbled utterly to dust! I know not whether these ancestors of mine bethought themselves to repent, and ask pardon of Heaven for their cruelties; or whether they are now groaning under the heavy consequences of them, in another state of being. At all events, I, the present writer, as their representative, hereby take shame upon myself for their sakes, and pray that any curse incurred by them—as I have heard, and as the dreary and unprosperous condition of the race, for many a long year back, would argue to exist—may be now and henceforth removed.[40]

By referring back to his ancestors and their guilt, Hawthorne-cum-narrator seems to take upon himself the responsibility of righting the wrong, but instead he simply asks for the stain to be removed "now and henceforth." What follows, however, is a much more complex engagement with the stain and the guilt.

On the rainy day when he goes up to the rafters of the Custom House and starts sifting through the rubble piled up in the corner, "poking and burying into the heaped-up rubbish in the corner," he "chanced to lay my hand on a small package, carefully done up in a piece of ancient yellow parchment. This envelope had the air of an official record of some period long past, when clerks embossed their stiff and formal chirography on more substantial materials than at present. There was something about it that quickened an instinctive curiosity, and made me undo the faded red tape, that tied up the package, with the sense that a treasure would here be brought to light."[41]

As the narrator unwraps the package there is a quickening inside him, and he hopes for a treasure. "Unbending the rigid folds of the parchment cover, I found it to be a commission, under the hand and seal of Governor Shirley, in favor of one Jonathan Pue, as Surveyor of his Majesty's Customs for the port of Salem, in the Province of Massachusetts Bay." He remembers that the only material objects left of Jonathan Pue are a skeleton, some pieces of clothing, and "a wig of majestic frizzle."[42] The reference to Pue and the wig is a direct allusion to the founding fathers, and in this section he seems to dismiss them quite readily. They embody the official record. All that is left of them are bones and wigs. They are not interesting. The stiff parchment and the formal chirography are not interesting. They are substantial but dead. Not the stuff that inspires a writer.

At this point Hawthorne focuses in on what we will come to know as the scarlet letter:

> But the object that most drew my attention, in the mysterious package, was a certain affair of fine red cloth, much worn and faded. There were traces about it of gold embroidery, which, however, was greatly frayed and defaced; so that none, or very little, of the glitter was left. It had been wrought, as was easy to perceive, with wonderful skill of needlework; and that stitch (as I am assured by ladies conversant with such mysteries) gives evidence of a now forgotten art, not to be recovered even by the process of picking out the threads. The rag of scarlet cloth,—for time, and wear, and sacrilegious moth had reduced it to little other than a rag,—on careful examination, assumed the shape of a letter. It was the capital letter A. By an accurate measurement, each limb proved to be precisely three inches and a quarter in length.[43]

As the wig is the mark of a founding father, this red fragment of cloth is the mark of those who are left out of the national script: the women and the artists. Hawthorne even refers to a woman's handiwork. The fact of a red rag cannot help but produce images of blood, and menstrual blood at that. As Hawthorne unwraps and frees the rag from the rigid parchment, the known alphabet, he turns the potential language of bloodstains into a new script, worthy of being read. As he holds the scrap of cloth in his hands, it becomes a letter with three perfectly shaped limbs, a letter *A,* an American nation, reduced by time and wear and sacrilegious moth to a rag. This letter, as a red rag, could easily be the bloodstain of the murdered women hallucinated as Salem witches. It could be so many of the stains upon the crumbling bones of Washington's America. It is a rag that is literally wrapped in stiff parchment and hidden from national consciousness. To read this living, pulsating heart of America, the real story, the script he is enfolding, the alphabet of dead women, enslaved Africans, and Indians deceived, is antipatriotic, antinational, when so many were trying to preserve the frizzled wigs and stately customhouses of the past. For a fairly conservative Hawthorne, it is not surprising that the letter would be red-hot: "I happened to place it on my breast. It seemed to me,—the reader may smile, but must not doubt my word,—it seemed to me, then that I experienced a sensation not altogether physical, yet almost so, as of burning heat; and as if the letter were not of red cloth, but red-hot iron."[44]

Unfortunately, in *The Scarlet Letter* Hawthorne transforms this potentially embodied "red-hot" text of Indian genocide and the bloody stains of witch-hunting back into a memorialized "dead" text. By having Hester embellish and embroider the letter *A,* so that we see only the letter *A* and never go to *B* or *C* or *D*—or more to the point, to the graphic world that hides within the embroidered letter *A*—he hides behind his imagination, letting it rest in a place of indecision rather than a place of action. He gives the whole story away when he wonders "whether the letter might not have been one of those decorations which the white men used to contrive, in order to take the eyes of Indians."[45] He literally takes *our* eyes. He wants us to take our eyes off Indians and off slaves and off the treatment of women in this so-called democracy, and he does so through the contrivance of the letter *A.* Throughout the rest of the novel he embellishes this letter with Hester's needle so that it becomes an embroidered imaginary that successfully "takes our eyes off" the real atrocities that it represents. The letter *A,* which in all its multiplicity should stand for freedom, for passion and possibility, in the hands of Hester and the townspeople, stands only for a paralytic guilt that never progresses beyond survival. The guilt of America becomes the conventionalized guilt of one woman's adultery and rests only on her breast. While Hawthorne makes it clear that her crime is no worse than the crimes of all those around her, he never exposes those other crimes. There is no real change or movement in *The Scarlet Letter* except—and this is an important exception—in the symbol itself. The symbol, as Hawthorne embroiders it throughout the text, takes on a multiplicity of meanings. It is only Pearl who moves, and her movement is wild, so wild that she must return to Europe to be pacified.

Hawthorne remembers 1640 not to unearth the buried bones of his ancestors but to hope and pray not only that they have turned to dust but that he can fabricate, literally fabricate, textile letters embroidered in golden thread, stories that will hide and decorate their tombs. He embroiders the stain rather than delve into the mystery of where and how this stain appeared. The stain is the visceral graphism. The embroidery in this case hides the coded trace. He successfully erases the stain without investigating the crime. He is renovating his ancestral memory in exactly the same way that Cunningham renovated and cleaned up Mount Vernon. This is the Hawthorne who told his abolitionist Concord that the Union was more important than individual liberty and human kindness.

In Hawthorne's hands, the writer-magician details his textile red letter *A* with a craft that invites us into a world of intrigue and passion and yet demands that we keep this passion under wraps. In doing so, he hides so much else that should be told. Hawthorne, rather than condemning his ancestors for the atrocities that they perpetuated in the witch trials, as he claims to do, minimizes the crimes of his and the country's founding fathers. As Laura Doyle explicates in her article "'A' for Atlantic: The Colonizing Force of Hawthorne's *The Scarlet Letter,*" it is colonization, the taking of native land, and the related taking of African people to work this land that are the hidden crimes in Hawthorne's text.[46]

But the gestural act of embroidering still has a subversive power in the story. As Hester Prynne embroiders the letter *A* on her bosom, she speaks her passion to a society that has made passion and the voices of women unspeakable. She speaks her passion as a prisoner in a society that lets her live but forces her into hard labor to earn her daily bread. The labor that she must engage in is embroidery, both needlework and storytelling. She is on her scaffold, an emblematic slave, waiting for the judgment of the crowd. If Hester could speak for women, for America, she could speak for all those left in the margins of Hawthorne's text. But as she wanders to the edge of the settlement with Dimmesdale, she only toys with the idea of escape.

Meanwhile, Hawthorne plays with the power of the imagination, with the power of his own symbol, and he does so on the backs of the native peoples of 1640, whom he barely mentions and keeps on the fringes of society, and of the African American people of the 1850s, to whom he does not allude at all. Hawthorne engages in a favorite exercise of masculinist American writers, what Henry James will do in *The Portrait of a Lady,* that is, to explore his own desires, imaginations, and what Laura Doyle calls "interiority"[47] through that of a woman. Hawthorne explores his own guilt and his ancestors' guilt through Hester. It is only Hester, after all, who has to expose herself to the world, never

Dimmesdale or any of the other male characters. Their crimes remain hidden, the stain erased.

Like Hawthorne, Hester can "experiment" with an individual artistic expression, with liberty, if she does not go beyond the bonds of law. Hawthorne made a now-infamous apology for racism and slavery in his 1852 biography of Franklin Pierce, arguing that abolitionists should not fight against slavery because the day would eventually come when God would end the admittedly unpleasant institution. Patience would solve the problem without human intervention. Hawthorne believed that when the time came, and God was willing, slavery would end. Hester on the scaffolding chooses to hold on to her symbol of sin until the day might come.

Hawthorne seems to engage in covering up the actions of his forefathers in the same way that he does the actions of Pierce and the evils of slavery. In *The Scarlet Letter* he creates creaky old magistrates who do not treat Hester nearly as severely as the law would have demanded, with public whipping or worse. These over-the-hill (and thus harmless) magistrates do not seem capable of stoning, drowning, or burning witches. Hawthorne takes the old men of the past, the criminals, and makes them harmless Nazis like those portrayed in 1960s sitcom *Hogan's Heroes,* buffoons incapable of doing harm, thus erasing and minimizing their historical atrocities.

When Hawthorne uncovers the letter *A* in the Custom House, there is rightfully great hope that he is writing a new kind of script. As when he examined the letters and documents detailing his family's past, Hawthorne unfolds the potentially liberating rag from the parchment in a room at the top of the Custom House that is open, large, and not yet finished by painters and carpenters. The space is a tabula rasa in which anything is possible. But Hawthorne imprisons the fragment on the chest of Hester, letting her experience a moment of fancy but not a freedom of bodily movement. He tames his shrew as effectively as James does Isabel. Both artists invent women characters to relieve themselves of the tedium of, for Hawthorne, a job at the customhouse or, for both James and Hawthorne, a house full of boring men. Just as Stowe's Tom, the moment he could free Jim, instead wanders in a fog of his own imagination, Hawthorne and James, the moment they could free their characters to autonomy and independence, wander in a limited fog. Hawthorne even says that the art of the embroidery had been lost and that "certainly there was some deep meaning in it, most worthy of interpretation, and which as it were, streamed forth from the mystic symbol, subtly communicating itself to my sensibilities, but evading the analysis of my mind."[48]

In letting the prize of their imagination, their muse, their burning letter *A,* free, they would lose their identity as authors of their narratives. Hawthorne enjoyed writing about women, pinning his alphabet on their chest, not allowing them to tell their own stories. And he does so by "evading the analysis" of his own and their minds. He does not ultimately erase the stain from his ancestors' bones but instead turns what should be a bloody letter *A* of colonial guilt and repentance (Doyle) into an embroidered letter in which gilt covers guilt. Hawthorne writes into the cultural imagination of America such a powerful symbol without allowing its power to manifest.

He does this again in an essay called "Chiefly About War Matters," an account of his trip through the war zone of the Civil War, when he suggests that African people and Puritans are brothers and sisters, having come over together on the same boats, and then cannot bring himself to see the contrabands that he meets on the street during his trip as more than picturesque, "like fauns."[49] Although he is fearful about what will happen to them as they march north to freedom and wonders if their lives will be better there, he does nothing to make their present lives better. A paternalistic attitude toward women and children and blacks keeps him from following his own alphabetic map.

The letter *A* breaks the confines of symbolic language that held Hawthorne's imagination hostage in the short stories "Young Goodman Brown" and "The Minister's Black Veil" and lets loose the possibility of symbolic indeterminacy. With his attention to the letter *A,* the first letter of *America* and the first letter of the alphabet, Hawthorne introduces the possibility of a new American literary language, a language ostensibly of sexuality, eroticism, and behavior that can move inside and outside the prison walls (the stiff parchment), appear embodied in the physical appearance, actions, dances, and cries of the young Pearl, take over the clouds in the sky, infect and alter the actions of all the people in the Puritan town, and burn in the breast of the guilt-tormented Dimmesdale. But Dimmesdale's ability to endure Hester's torture in silence for pages and pages is only topped by Hawthorne's ability to constrain his own and thus Hester's imagination. At a time when the meaning of America was in the most profound and powerful moment of moral crisis, when every writer in the country faced his or her own demons and convictions, Hawthorne gave birth to a new language and then demanded that it die a stillbirth. Pearl kept breaking away from this fratricidal impulse and ended up back in Europe, confined like Claire in James's *The American.* When confronted by the reality of female sexuality, many male authors, like William Faulkner with Caddy Compson in *The Sound and the*

Fury, end up kicking their female characters out of the narrative or locking them up.

One cannot help but note in reading Hawthorne's biography that he wrote *The Scarlet Letter* after marrying Sophia Peabody, herself an artist and intellectual. Her sisters were both well-known abolitionists. Hawthorne describes her as his best friend, so it would have been hard for him not to appreciate the depth of her intellect and the disparity between his position of power in society and her lack thereof. But Hawthorne's horrendous comment about women writers—"America is now wholly given over to a damned mob of scribbling women, and I should have no chance of success while the public taste is occupied with their trash—and should be ashamed of myself if I did succeed"[50]—would never earn him feminist credentials.

Nonetheless, by telling the tale of a woman who, condemned by society to a life of shame, turns that shame into personal power, Hawthorne could have begun to speak for all imprisoned, enslaved, silenced people, and in many ways he did. The obvious parallel between Hester on the scaffolding and slaves on the block could not have escaped a man as astute as Hawthorne. By his own admission, he did not have sympathy for slaves or believe in the necessity of human activism to end slavery. His comment about John Brown that "no one was more justly hanged"[51] is inexcusable. Hawthorne's views did mellow during the war. His sympathies turned toward fighting to preserve as free a union as possible, not returning out of war weariness to a divided, slaveholding nation. Many northerners liked the idea of freeing African Americans but barely tolerated African Americans as individuals. But whatever one might say—and condemn him I do—there is the troubling matter of the potentially liberating, viscerally graphic letter *A.*

EMILY DICKINSON: "NO RACK CAN TORTURE ME"

Emily Dickinson enters the space of the slave consciousness most directly in her poem 384, "No Rack can torture me." The trope of the trapped body appears often in her poems, and what she names the "soul" must negotiate between ambiguous and multiple masters. In "No Rack can torture me," Dickinson grapples with the concept of self-liberation. Her poem makes it clear just how difficult maintaining self in the face of bondage can be. Like most Dickinson poems, "No Rack can torture me" can be read as self-confession or political commentary. Dickinson wrote the poem in 1862, when the North was teetering on the edge of embracing the Emancipation Proclamation, without actually having won the war. On a personal level, as a woman genius battling for time to write in the face of domestic responsibilities, Dickinson knew a form of bondage.

No Rack can torture me—
My Soul—at Liberty—
Behind this mortal Bone
There knits a bolder One—

You cannot prick with saw—
Nor pierce with Scimitar—
Two Bodies—therefore be—
Bind One—The Other fly—

The Eagle of his Nest
No easier divest—
And gain the Sky
Than mayest Thou—

Except Thyself may be
Thine Enemy—
Captivity is Consciousness—
So's Liberty.[52]

What this poem would seem to parrot is the clichéd division of bonded body and free soul. Abolitionists often touted this rhetorical division, to the point of advocating suicide as a way for enslaved people to free their souls to join God. What is different in Dickinson's poem from the more conventional version of this equation is that while she starts with the idea of a liberated soul, she expands a simple duality, tortured body/liberated Soul, into the more complex "Two Bodies." For Dickinson, if one's body is actually captured, enslaved, or jailed, one cannot be tortured, because behind the mortal bone that the master abuses is another body—not a soul, but another body. This other body is more visceral, a "bolder One," meaning an identity, but a bolder b/one.

Another body, rather than an ephemeral spirit, is more able to resist because it has the physical power to fly, transform, transmute, and is able to *knit.* The *Oxford English Dictionary Online* definition of *knit* reads: "To interlock, interlace, intertwine; to twine, weave, or plait together." The bolder bone is not departed or dead but actively knitting, regenerating its own boldness. A bone that is broken heals by knitting. From Dickinson's letters we know, of course, that she and, in fact, all the women in the Dickinson household were constantly sewing, knitting, and engaging in the domestic chore of producing clothing, blankets, sweaters, and so on, for the household. In this poem, as in many others, Dickinson elevates knitting from a domestic chore to a lifesaving metaphor. As Aife Murray informs us in *Maid as Muse,* Dickinson had close friendships with women servants in her home, both African American and white, with whom she engaged in household chores and whom she trusted with her art. She often wrote her poems on menus, scraps of paper in the kitchen, and receipts.[53] When Dickinson uses the word *knit,* she knits herself to the act of her writing and to the world of the domestic. She is of two bodies, the one that can be sawed, tortured, and stabbed and the one that can "fly."

Many of Dickinson's biographers have wondered about her "illness"—about what kept her confined to her room and to the house so much of the time and drove her to doctors and cures. Lynda Gordon argues in her 2010 biography *Lives Like Loaded Guns* that Dickinson might have had epilepsy, but we must be suspicious of any diagnosis of Dickinson, in fact even of the desire to diagnose or pathologize Dickinson. Gordon argues that Dickinson was not by nature a recluse and did not choose solitude but that in a society that did not understand and often shunned people with epilepsy, she was forced to live a less social life than her peers. She reads many of Dickinson's poems, including "My Life has stood—a Loaded Gun—," as the work of a person who knows how it feels when one's brain is not predictable. While Gordon's reading is interesting, if we simply substitute *woman genius* for *epilepsy,* we would have a similar reading. Dickinson knew the torture of a captive or divided body, whether it was because of epilepsy or some other disease or the choice of a genius that needed time to work. But the very existence of her writing, given the struggles we know she faced, indicates that she knit together another, bolder self, another body, another somebody, that could not just withstand but fly from the eagle's nest.

There is no real indication in "No Rack can torture me" that Dickinson is writing about slavery, emancipation, or the Civil War. But there are strong markers that she was speaking of a conflict that went beyond self. As in Hawthorne's Custom House description, the eagle, a symbol of America itself, can leave the nest and "gain the Sky" only if it imagines itself free. Given the way Dickinson has constructed "No Rack can torture me," in order to believe that the eagle can gain the sky, we must believe that "Thou" the reader, "Thyself," can fly—an endorsement of democratic individualism. Captivity is consciousness, and one can be one's own "Enemy," making it impossible to find the bolder one, the second body, the divestiture of the domestic nest. She can fly from the constraints of the nest. The second marker that indicates that Dickinson might also have been referring to enslaved people is the use of the word *liberty* twice in the poem. If there were anything on people's minds in the early part of the year 1863, it was liberty, both for the slaves and to save the Union.

The question remains how easy it really is to "divest," to fly, to gain the sky, to knit a bolder bone. An eagle can only leave the nest for a moment and then must return—to safety, to children, to home, to rest. But if one moves from bone to bone, from body to body, one never loses oneself and will never fall. One can only leave one body, and knit a bolder bone, another body, if one has a thread, a safety line. Dickinson's safety line is her writing. Even if one must move back and forth from liberty to captivity, the movement itself is liberty. The liberty is in the back and forth. Liberty is the tension between equality and freedom, between the sameness of being and the distinctiveness of individuality. Dickinson's eagle is ultimately defined by the pairs—the two bodies, the nest and flight, captivity and liberty—and the ability to morph from one to the other.

Dickinson accomplishes this flight back and forth by literally using her punctuation to create a graphic bridge. The poem itself "knits" in that there are fourteen dashes moving the meaning from torture to liberty. Poem 384 was written in 1862, at the exact moment when writers had to imagine the emancipation as real in order to make it become so. In *Touching Liberty: Abolition, Feminism and the Politics of the Body,* Karen Sánchez-Eppler confronts the doubleness in texts by Walt Whitman, Harriet Jacobs, and Emily Dickinson as she traces the abolitionists' impulse to proselytize that enslaved people should forfeit their bodies in order to return to heaven, where there would be no bodily enslavement. For the enslaved, unfortunately, freedom would mean death. Sánchez-Eppler argues that for Dickinson the doubleness is irreconcilable: "From this middle place Dickinson does not aim, as Whitman does, to mediate between body and soul. The divisions within identity that her poems chart are not, for her, reconcilable. Indeed, what interests her about identity is precisely its unresolvable doubleness. Instead of forging mergers she seeks to describe a 'Double Estate,' one in which human identity is suspended between the irreconcilable but inseparable requirements of a body and a soul."[54]

If we followed Eppler's reasoning, then Dickinson's two bodies in "No Rack can torture me" would be irreconcilable. But in fact that is not exactly what we "see" in the poem (I use the word *see* here because the poem itself has a shape that can be seen). The fourteen dashes actually create connectors that suggest not only movement forward but stitches that connect images and words that have no way of being connected together with known or existing linguistic symbols. As Deirdre Fagan proposes in "Emily Dickinson's Unutterable Word," "The dashes become a thread between the sayable and the unsayable, a caesura between life and death, a pause, a gasp, sometimes a chasm over which one must make a leap of understanding."[55] Fagan disagrees with Paul Crumbley, who, in *Inflection of the Pen: Dash and Voice in Emily Dickinson,* takes a complex look at the dashes in terms of length and fine differences. Fagan argues that the dashes, whether long or short, are a moment of silence, the unutterable pause.

I would suggest that the dashes represent neither a silence nor the unspeakable but instead express potency and passion. They are embodied, physical; they exist and take up space. They are another kind of bone. They express the actual stroke of Dickinson's hand, the gesture of writing, the speed and fluidity, and thus are a part of her embodied world. Thus, while Dickinson might turn to absences, disappearances, and silences in her writing, the dash keeps the work always on the page, vibrant, connected to the depth of her imaginative moment. The dash always reminds the reader of the act of creation itself—that the poem is not just a product but also a process, the wildness of the imagination coming into form. Reading the dash as the stroke of the hand, the flourish, the rush, disturbs the image of Dickinson as quiet and secluded and brings her into the world as an artist on fire. Rather than representing any absence or silence, any unknown, unspeakable word or thought, the dash is just that—a dash, an energetic pulse of the hand, a heartbeat, a handclap, a patting jubalike drumbeat. Dickinson's dashes are like Ingold's nonpropositional lines, expressing the direct gesture of the body. In this reading the length or number of dashes reflects energetic movement rather than calculated intention. The dashes do not indicate words that cannot be expressed, but a graphic inscription, a form of writing separated from alphabetic equivalency. To turn the dashes into anything else makes Dickinson a poet of negations, negations that we have too often projected onto her life. She was ill. She was a recluse. She was different. In "No Rack can torture me" Dickinson knits her words together with her dashes. But more accurately, she keeps herself going through difficult territory, heart beating, picking up momentum as she writes.

Dickinson referred to poems as "marking/signing/sewing."[56] If we read these dashes and the convoluted manuscripts written upside down and sideways, interspersed with recipes and shopping lists and other domestic papers, we begin to see a graphic form that marks, signs, and sews its way into an interesting relationship to nation and democracy during the Civil War. Dickinson was not apolitical, nor was she an abolitionist. Instead she was writing her way into subversive and liberatory spaces by creating a language of mark and line, expressing what the world was not yet ready to understand. "Captivity is Consciousness— / So's Liberty." The dash represents Dickinson's choice to be free and to write the language of liberty.

Three artists for whom Dickinson has been a muse are Aaron Copland, in *Twelve Poems of Dickinson;* Jen Bervin, in her art series *Dickinson's Fascicles;* and Lesley Dill, in her opera *Divide Light.* Each, with his or her own unique art, responds to Dickinson with viscerally graphic gestures. In doing so these artists take her small, hidden fascicles and write them large. In their hands she becomes the diva she was: large, embodied, operatic. Bervin expands Dickinson's universe to make her fascicles embroidered works that take up large canvases.

In Copland's *Twelve Poems,* her poems become passionate, excited, marked. Copland has Phyllis Curtin hit a triple forte to match the intensity of the lines, "Why—do they shut Me out of heaven? / Did I sin—too loud?"; and she repeats the line over and over again at this feverish pitch. In Copland's work one can hear the leaps, the dashes. Brian Wise expresses the fullness of the marriage of these two visionaries:

> Copland's settings are enormously varied, alternately melancholic, sardonic, and wistful in tone. His distinctive and often demanding vocal writing contains numerous bold leaps, jagged melodic lines, declamatory rhythms, and extremes of range that require a singer with a particular ease and flexibility in both the soprano and mezzo-soprano ranges. Copland expressed a special liking for "Sleep Is Supposed to Be" and "The Chariot"—indeed, two of the cycle's most gripping songs. Still, the whole is larger than the sum of its parts, and presents a compelling, complementary, and multifaceted portrait of what Copland called Dickinson's "unique personality."[57]

Copland matches the power of Dickinson and in no way prettifies or sentimentalizes her. She is full force, full throttle, and the whole range of the keyboard.

Jen Bervin, a contemporary artist, takes the dashes and stitches to their wildest conclusion with her *Dickinson Fascicles,* described on her website as "six large embroidered works based on composites of the punctuation and variant marks of Emily Dickinson."[58] Bervin, by combining on one canvas many of the marks, reveals the movement and fluidity of Dickinson's punctuation (fig. 33). Each of Bervin's embroidered works is six feet by eight feet and combines all the marks in

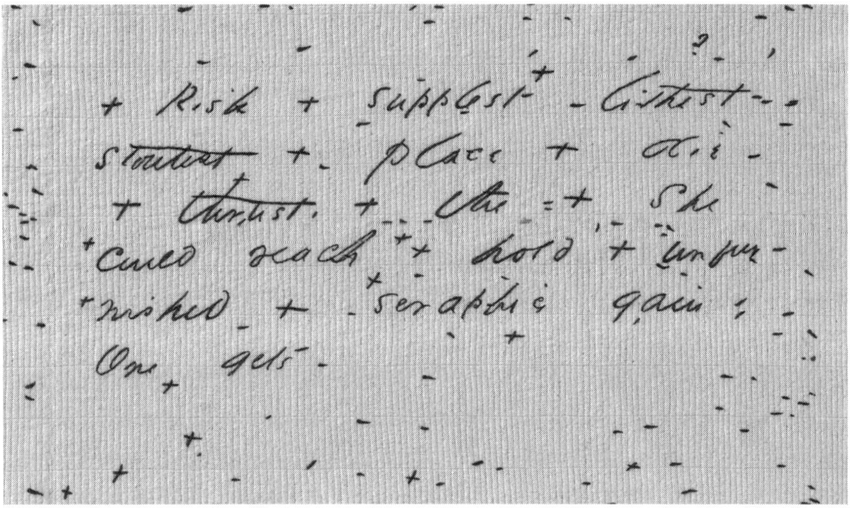

FIGURE 33

Detail of *The Composite Marks of Fascicle 28,* by Jen Bervin, from *The Dickinson Composites* (Granary Books, 2010). Machine-sewn cotton thread and hand-sewn silk thread on cotton batting backed with muslin. (© Jen Bervin)

one fascicle. Bervin creates these works by using pieces of muslin that she threads with cotton and silk thread and cotton batting. The thread is often red. Bervin writes about her own process: "I have come to feel that specificity of the + and – marks in relation to Dickinson's work are aligned with a larger gesture that her poems make as they exit and exceed the known world. They go vast with her poems. They risk, double, displace, fragment, unfix, and gesture to the furthest beyond—to loss, to the infinite, to 'ecstasy,' to extremity."[59] Bervin's understanding that Dickinson's marks gesture to the furthest beyond reveals the potential transformative power of these types of graphic inscriptions.

To say that Dickinson's poems exit and exceed the known world is a beautiful way of saying that they move beyond conventional discourse. By using the word *exceed,* Bervin reminds us that the marks express a force rather than a fixed, mathematical, or systematic meaning. To gesture is to point to something that is not right in front of a person and to use bodily movement instead of language to do so. They unfix. Bervin's interpretation of *Fascicle 16* is truly breathtaking. She writes: "Fascicle sixteen contains the first insert page, a smaller sheet pinned in with a straight pin. The hand-embroidered black text is taken from this insert page and reads: And could I further/'no'? Emily Dickinson wrote in a letter to Judge Otis Lord, 'And don't you know that "no" is the wildest word we consign to language?'" The no is the outer boundary, the edge of language. But it is also the most powerful way of saying yes to something that has not yet been seen.

Lesley Dill's opera *Divide Light,* which premiered on 13 August 2008 at the Montalvo Art Center in Saratoga, California, could also be said to exit and exceed the known world. One critic wrote that

> Dill has made *Divide Light* into a spare and closely developed theatrical presentation, layered with a haunting visual element which features large projections on a back screen and multiple scrims. The images are a combination of Dill's stark, edgy and evocative black-and-white photographs and projected text from Dickinson's poetry. Poems stream, scroll, flash, swirl, twirl, pop out, edge in, seep out, fade in, fall down, and rise up on the screen and scrims. The performers sing Dickinson's words and wear them scrawled across their costumes. Poems appear in unusual places throughout the opera, interacting with the audience in unexpected ways.[60]

All three of these responses—Copland's, Bervin's, and Dill's—"gesture to the furthest beyond." They transform the conventionalized image of Emily Dickinson—a frail, sickly, shut-in spinster—into that of an operatic diva, a "bolder one."

THE TEXTS OF Stowe, Hawthorne, and Dickinson reveal the importance of visceral graphism—the cracked ice, the letter *A,* the dash—in the formation of new liberatory narratives. In each of these cases the overpowering drive is toward a democratic vision of America. The degree to which the writers can move beyond established narratives, beyond ersatz stereotyping, is the degree to which they invite into their imaginative universe the graphic displacement of established alphabets. Copland's double-dotted notes, Christenberry's cross marks, Hawthorne's golden threads, Frederick Douglass's deliverance—all push language to the abyss, to a liberty that has never been known. The United States of America, and thus every citizen in America in 1863, was torn in half—half-free, half-enslaved—and the chasm between the two halves was vast. The dash is Eliza leaping with bloody feet over the black river from ice cake to ice cake to a fragile freedom on the other side.

5

"IN THE SOLITUDE OF MY SPIRIT"

> What have I, or those I represent, to do with your national independence? Are the great principles of political freedom and of natural justice, embodied in that Declaration of Independence, extended to us? . . . This Fourth [of] July is yours, not mine. You may rejoice, I must mourn.
>
> In the solitude of my spirit, I see clouds of dust raised on the highways of the South; I see the bleeding footsteps; I hear the doleful wail of fettered humanity, on the way to the slave-markets, where the victims are to be sold like horses, sheep, and swine, knocked off to the highest bidder.—FREDERICK DOUGLASS, "What Is the Fourth of July to a Negro?" 5 July 1852

Self-Liberation

The writers of the Emancipation Proclamation and the generals of the Civil War never intended to endow true liberty and selfhood to African American people, nor were they capable of doing so. As the poet Audre Lorde would say, the master's tools never dismantle the master's house. If enslaved people had not lived as human beings despite the dehumanizing extremities of the slave institution, there would have been no selves left for Lincoln to declare free.[1] Ira Berlin argues in *Freedom* that "no one was more responsible for smashing the shackles of slavery than the slaves themselves."[2] But he does not define liberty as coming from the slaves themselves. Liberty is still something that must be conferred upon an enslaved person. Marcus Wood, in *The Horrible Gift of Freedom,* theorizes that liberty as the gift bestowed on the slave creates a fantasy liberty: "Such fantasies represent liberation or emancipation as an enforced donation from the empowered possessors of freedom to the unfree and disempowered slave."[3]

Those who subscribe to the self-emancipation school believe that enslaved people's active and persistent involvement in the Civil War, their economic impact on the North, and their movement toward freedom pushed Lincoln to sign the Emancipation Proclamation.[4] In response to his fellow historian and self-emancipation doubter, James McPherson, Berlin concedes that in the political and economic realm slaves could not actually free themselves:

> Still slaves could not free themselves. . . . Slaves could—and they did—put the issue of freedom on the wartime agenda; they could—and they did—make certain that the question of their liberation did not disappear in the complex welter of the war; they could—and they did—ensure that there was no retreat from the commitment to emancipation once the issue was drawn. In short they did what was in their power to do with the weapons they had. They could not vote, pass laws, issue field orders, or promulgate great proclamations. That was the realm of citizens, legislators, military officers, and the president.[5]

By momentarily surrendering the term *self-emancipation,* Berlin, one of the most ardent advocates for self-emancipation, reveals his adherence to the basic tenets of state history, precisely the idea that only a president can liberate an enslaved people—the Currier and Ives model. In doing so, he inadvertently concedes that only laws, field orders, or great proclamations determine human agency. Because, as Wood so adeptly reveals, this model can be found in so many of the visual representations of emancipation, emancipation itself, liberty itself, becomes suspect and a "horrible gift."

If we embrace instead the notion that an enslaved person is never actually enslaved and therefore in no need of emancipation, then the term *self-emancipation* becomes meaningless for very different reasons than those Berlin lists. In order to "free" slaves or even colonize "ex-slaves," the populace has to believe that a person can be or has been a slave. Before he could suggest, let alone adhere to, colonization as an option, Lincoln himself had to believe in the ownership of human bodies and the right of the state to move these bodies from one location to another.

A shift in our philosophical understanding of slavery away from identity toward human agency requires that we make a distinction between freed slaves and free people. Freed slaves, people freed by someone else, are still theoretically conceptualized as once having been property. They are dependent on, rather than independent of, the rhetoric of the state. Free people were never property. Slaves are not slaves; they are enslaved human beings. Bondage is not only a shackle on the foot or a whip on the back but an internal state, an assumed surrender of selfhood as the result of the violent destruction of a community and cultural history that selfhood needs in order to thrive. In an overwhelming number of cases, enslaved people preserved their selfhood by designing new communities, creating fluid, shape-shifting, masked identities, and finding ways to practice cultural and religious continuity.

The vast slave network of seventeenth-, eighteenth-, and nineteenth-century European colonialism and American expansionism captured, imprisoned, raped, demoralized, tortured, beat, denied knowledge to, and murdered people of African descent, many of whom, the record shows, did not identify themselves as slaves. Enslaved people from Virginia to Louisiana engaged in radical acts to preserve their identity on their own terms by creating independent communities and protecting African forms of spirituality. From the 1620s until the Emancipation Proclamation, against all odds, hundreds of human beings—on slave ships, at slave markets, in the fields, and in the houses—took on rebellious identities, including those of insurrectionist, arsonist, poisoner, outlier, runaway, artisan/artist, author, sculptor, blacksmith, cook, carpenter, designer, dancer, and preacher, rather than of slave. These resilient individuals demonstrated, over and over, the human ability to deny the master the right to name them property, and they did so largely through marking the national imagination outside of the halls of power.[6] Walter Johnson, in *Soul by Soul,* insists on the agency of enslaved people in New Orleans during slave auctions and throughout the entire enslavement process.

Many outlier communities in Florida and South Carolina maintained their connections to the enslaved people still on plantations, surrounding them, offering them food, military support, and help planning escapes. As the historian Vincent Harding points out, "The outliers represented a hidden submerged black power that the masters could not break. They were a radical presence, challenging blacks and whites alike."[7] Sylvia Frey writes that "there were always roving bands of runaways hiding in the swamps but grand marronage, the formation of permanent, independent settlements, marks the growth of rebelliousness among slaves in the eighteenth century. Men, women, and sometimes children, established villages in plantation hinterlands and survived by raiding plantations for cattle and crops. Their camps often served as staging grounds for subversive activities."[8]

One of the most famous outlier groups was the community established in what is now called the Negro Fort (Fort Gadsden), in Apalachicola, Florida. More than three hundred free Negroes and those escaping slavery—men, women, and children, as well as twenty Choctaw warriors—lived at or near the fort. The inhabitants had built farms, houses, and viable communities up and down the Apalachicola River. These communities supported those still held on the plantations in surrounding neighborhoods and thrived until 1816, when General Edmund P. Gaines of the U.S. Navy quite literally blew up most of the population with an errant red-hot cannonball during a siege. By forming communities, these outliers preserved themselves and their sanity.[9]

But an enslaved person did not have to go off the plantation to preserve his or her selfhood. Harding asserts that the enslaved populations who stayed on the plantations, "with great but silent determination, were learning how to re-create their religious experience, in order to possess their soul in the midst of a destructive and soulless situation."[10] In order to possess one's soul in the midst of destruction, one had to create a communal home in America, most often with a creolized connection to homes in an ancestrally imagined, if not experienced, Africa.

The enforcement of slavery in ersatz America is not subtle. Ersatz America is monumental, abusive, and above all else physically violent. The marks of nation are broad and clumsy, repetitive and large. Violence may be unpredictable, but it cannot be described by such words as *complex, delicate, refined, intricate,* or any of the words that would define the markings of enslaved resistance. Dominance belittles detailed filigree and the gestural fine lines of regenerative tissue as weak, feminine, other. The slavocracy ruled not by using subtlety but through the crudest robust forms of physical intimidation. Slave masters and their right arms, the slave drivers, hoped to keep slaves in a constant state of terror and trauma by using every means of taking over their bodies and inhibiting their ability to move and speak. Ironically, the enslaved people who saw themselves as distinct autonomous actors, mothers, fathers, artists, and in many cases warriors, rather than passive objects or beasts of burden, were practicing their art under the nose of the master without being suspected.

Because they did not understand the subtleties of the forces of resistance that were passing in front of them, masters resorted to trying to still the body of the slave. The invasion of the body was the primary means of maintaining slavery. The slave owners tried to cut off human communication by amputating limbs and fingers, tongues and ears. They forced people to wear metal neck collars with bells on them, locked them up in attics, woodsheds, or closets, often hanging them by the thumbs or arms above the ground so that their feet would not be able to touch and relieve the unbearable pressure. Completely free, if not by law, by social acceptance, to do whatever they wanted to their "property," the masters beat, kicked, and branded with fists, paddles, and hot irons.

Masters tortured enslaved people by forcing them to witness loved ones' being humiliated, prodded, touched inappropriately, poked on the block, and, worst, sold away from family, familiar plantations, and loved ones. One of the most heinous crimes was to cut out or slit in half a person's tongue so that he or she would be unable to speak. In *Meridian,* Alice Walker tells the story of a slave woman named Louvinie who had her tongue cut out.[11] But as horrible as all of these punishments are, the two most common forms of torture were whipping and rape. Domination was not creative or fluid; it was simply repetitive, brutal, and horribly painful to body and soul. No one created any cultural capital by perpetuating a culture of violence and fear. Repression in any form, but particularly slavery, is inherently unimaginative, culturally flat-lined, static, and destructive to human ingenuity.

But because people of African descent as a whole maintained their connection to cultural singularity, sometimes through pan-Africanization[12] and sometimes through historically continuous cultural preservation from specific countries and regions, the assault on their bodies did not destroy their souls. Archival historians have recorded evidence that enslaved people incorporated African patterns and traditions in basket weaving,[13] architecture,[14] agricultural techniques,[15] quilting,[16] martial arts,[17] cooking and food preparation,[18] music,[19] dance,[20] pottery, funeral rites,[21] and creolized language patterns.[22] They brought African plants and African methods of gardening, seed preservation, and cultivation to North America.[23] In most cases these influences overlapped and interpenetrated.[24]

Writers such as Harding often define this period as one of "silent determination," and while silence certainly played an important survival role, especially for house slaves, there was an equally vocal and inscripted resistance as well.[25] In each of the areas of cultural continuity listed above, from the formation of communities to the continuation of cultural practices, the available evidence benefits from a reading of graphic elements.[26]

One of the best-known stories of such inscripted resistance is that of an enslaved potter named David Drake, who made large bowls and not only signed his own name but wrote verses of poetry on the bowls, allowing all to see that he was an outstanding potter as well as literate and aware of his own worth. Many of his poems were enigmatic, strangely worded, and full of double meanings. They appeared in a looped, full-scripted handwriting along the circular shoulder of the large pots. One of them, written 9 November 1836, reads: "a better thing, I never saw / when I shot off, the lions Jaw."[27] Drake's reference to the African lion in America reveals not just cultural retention but the possibility of a subversive, metaphoric sleight of hand. By presenting himself as a hunter with a gun, capable of shooting a lion, and particularly of shooting off the lion's jaw, thus stilling the beast's roaring and his ability to attack, Drake steps out of the role of slave and becomes dangerous to the roaring power of the slave master.[28]

"Feet Don't Fail Me Now" I

One of the famous songs of the Mardi Gras Indians in New Orleans is "Feet Don't Fail Me Now." This song could be the national anthem of enslaved people. The most potent forms of resistance came from the slaves' unwillingness to stand still—both metaphorically and literally. Bodies that are not moving can be imprisoned more easily than bodies in motion. Moving bodies resist incarceration and paralysis and slip freely from space to space. Because punishment was repetitive and stagnant, subversion embraced movement. The people who escaped to the North and to Canada carved the paths of liberation into the actual land, their feet and their feats wearing down the ground, and by extension the geographic imagination of the American continent, so that the divisions of slave and free, North and South, became instead a crisscross of trails and escape hatches.[29] As runaways pushed north to freedom and back and forth across the border between slave and nonslave state, they left hanging in the air the echoes of their voices, whistles, songs, and coded riddles, and they left on the land hidden graphic messages, paths, and footprints as they spoke to one another, to missionaries, to many different Indian groups, and to Quakers and abolitionists, all of whom tracked one another and traded as they reached for the safety of human dignity.

These paths to freedom remind us that the history of freedom should be read not from an abolitionist's standpoint, as the North against the South, but as a complex network, a contact zone of abolitionists, enslaved Africans, and free people of color creating a geographic meshwork of connection across regional, ethnic, gender, and racial lines. Judy Livingston, in *Routes of Freedom,* suggests that if we examine the locations of resistance and transformation occurring in the field of literary geography, we might very well read a nation already poised to end slavery without the bloodbath of the Civil War. If we read the markings of visceral graphism, we come to a similar conclusion. Slavery as a cultural system that divided North and South, the greatest ersatz facade ever invented, was collapsing from the pressure of enslaved bodies in motion. Marcus Wood would argue that by making the Emancipation Proclamation the signifier of liberty, we perpetuate that facade for generations to come.

As early in the Civil War as 1861, in Hampton Roads, Virginia, three enslaved men who had escaped—Frank Baker, James Townsend, and Sheppard Mallory—rowed a boat across the harbor and presented themselves to Major General Benjamin Butler at Fortress Monroe for asylum. Instead of sending them back to their "owners," Butler decided that they should be called contraband of war, and he put them to work building fortifications. Since they had been building fortifications for the Confederate troops, Butler saw a military advantage in retaining this increased manpower. Butler's decision to call the escaped slaves "contraband of war" opened the floodgates for thousands of enslaved people to escape across Union lines. They were still property, but now they belonged to the Union as a result of a strange bill of sale that had no easy resolution.[30]

Butler was no enlightened liberator or even particularly kind to escaped enslaved people, but his decision was monumental. The phrase "contraband of war," a rhetorical sleight of hand, gave a federally sanctioned and thus protected identity (however demeaning) to those who had already begun the long walk to freedom, and it was in many ways the turning point in the war. The 1989 movie *Glory,* about the African American Fifty-fourth Massachusetts Volunteer Infantry, makes us believe that only a small number of black soldiers served, but 179,000 black soldiers served in the Union forces (a full 10 percent), and many more served in the navy. For Lincoln, with recruitment of white soldiers slowing down and the knowledge that enslaved men were being put to work for the South, military expediency and economic reality made both the Second Confiscation and Militia Act of 17 July 1862 and the Emancipation Proclamation of 1 January 1863 practical, military necessities. But the real impetus behind both the act and the proclamation was the fact that enslaved people were freeing themselves by the thousands by walking across Union lines. By moving their own bodies along trails of their own making, enslaved people chose and marked out trails of movement over stasis.[31]

In Hampton Roads, at first there were only a few hundred "contrabands." But by 1865 ten thousand enslaved people had walked out of bondage into what was now called the Grand Contraband Camp, and thousands more lived in camps throughout the country. When thousands of people choose freedom, they dictate policy and determine the direction the country will take. As the historian Barbara Fields states in Ken Burns's *Civil War,* "The slaves understood that war was about slavery before there was a war. The fugitive slaves made a nuisance of themselves the army had to deal with and if the army had to deal with it then the War Department had to deal with it and if the War Department had to deal with it, Congress had to deal with it and that meant that every fugitive slave that made a nuisance of himself to the local commander eventually made a figure of himself to the Congress of the United States."[32] No Union general, especially in the border states, could forget that he was fighting for liberation. The African American free(d) people inserted their newly liberated selves into the view of the Union army and never moved out of the frame. The war began on 12 April 1861, and Townsend, Mallory, and Baker appeared before Captain Butler on 23 May, just forty-one days later. They scripted the narrative and put themselves squarely in the middle of the action.

The Union army continued to call them contraband, reacted, used and abused these self-proclaimed free people, and at the same time had to provide them with necessities. Missionaries taught them and gave them books and helped with food and hygiene and medicine. Men like John Eaton, the general superintendent of contrabands, worked with an open heart and a skillful precision. But for all his goodwill, he could not alleviate the suffering of many of the newly free people who came under his command. Jim Downs, in *Sick from Freedom,* exposes the horrible conditions the ex-slaves experienced in the contraband camps.[33] But the story that emerges in the firsthand accounts is of the astounding fortitude of the people put in this situation. The free(d) men and women designed their own new lives. When they heard the Emancipation Proclamation read under what is now called the Emancipation Tree in Hampton Roads, Virginia, they interpreted emancipation with a much more fully human response than did those who supported the document. These people who had fought so hard for freedom wanted above all else, more than food and clothing, education.

When the camps became overcrowded, and many suffered disease, hard labor, and hunger, the disappointment was palatable and real, but the desire was still for freedom of the soul, for books, for learning, for knowledge. The human stories of the people in such contraband camps as Camp Shiloh (Corinth, Mississippi), Slabtown (Hampton Roads, Virginia), Freedom's Fortress (Fort Monroe,

FIGURE 34

"Cumberland Landing, Va. Group of contrabands at Foller's house," 14 May 1862. Photograph by James F. Gibson from the main eastern theater of war, the Peninsular Campaign, May–August 1862. (Prints & Photographs Division, Library of Congress)

Virginia), Grand Junction (Grand Junction, Tennessee), Freedman's Colony of Roanoke Island (North Carolina), Camp Chelsea (Memphis, Tennessee), and Federal City (Washington, DC) are just a few of the hundreds that are documented for contraband camps. In oral histories we find that prominent people visited the contraband camps in Washington, DC, almost as if they were visiting an exotic other. Mary Todd contributed to the contraband camp through the work of her friend and seamstress Elizabeth Keckley, and the Lincolns visited the people in the contraband camps near what is now Howard University. But while the contrabands walked to freedom, their bodies were marked by the assault of slavery. One can see an unimaginable exhaustion or sadness etched on the faces of newly free(d) people in documentary photographs from the second half of the nineteenth century. Although it was the custom of the time not to smile for the camera, most have a deeper, grimmer, more downward curve to their set faces than was usual (fig. 34).

There is no denying that the Union fear of and prejudice toward free(d)men and free(d)women reenergized schemes of colonization; fueled contraband camps, which looked more like southern plantations and forced labor camps; and kept a stranglehold on free(d) people's hopes for autonomy, liberty of movement, and participation in a free market economy. There is no denying that these "camps" and newly staffed plantations were often breeding grounds for disease, particularly smallpox, which killed thousands of newly free(d) people. There is no denying that Union generals fitted shackles on the feet they had just unshackled. There is no denying that a newly resurrected nation, which had just agreed to unite as a slave-free nation, proceeded to build upon the toppled heads of the 246-year-old hallucination of power, from the still stinking and deteriorating bones of the six hundred thousand dead Union and Confederate forces, a new racist edifice, a new country of white, male talking heads. Ersatz America was and is alive and well. This is the undeniably sad and devastating truth.

But if this is the only story we tell, then we give no credit, no honor, to the incredible human beings who demanded first and foremost access to written language and books. Mary Smith Peake started a school under the Emancipation Tree in Hampton Roads for the children of people who had once been slaves. At first she taught outside, but later she moved into the building that became the Hampton Institute and then Hampton University. Mary Peake's students survived, spoke out, imagined another world—a democracy—and worked to make it real. It is that force—the force of the living against all odds—that is democracy. W. E. B. Du Bois argues convincingly in *Black Reconstruction in America* that the free(d)men's push for literacy and education laid the groundwork for American public education.[34]

As early as 1915, Du Bois insisted that American politicians, scholars, and artists should recognize the full manhood and womanhood of Negroes and the cultural contributions of their race to the worlds of industry, letters, and the arts. Before Du Bois wrote his paradigm-shifting book *The Negro* in 1915 and Carter Godwin Woodson wrote *The African Background Outlined,* on the contribution of the African Americans to American culture and society after Reconstruction, in 1936, the free(d)man and woman had, according to conventional wisdom, no history, no past, no accomplishments, and no culture. To admit otherwise would have destroyed twentieth-century notions of racial hierarchy. From Reconstruction through segregation and even up to our present economic inequality, white supremacy has depended on this erasure of African cultural contributions. Without the assumption of a nonexistent past, the plight of enslaved people would have overwhelmed the delicate construction of racial superiority in America and allowed a flood of reality to overpower the ersatz *Gone with the Wind* construction of slavery in the American imagination. From New Orleans Mardi Gras Indians, to Maroon societies, to Gullah Geechee culture, traces of these continuous Africanisms are still visible in the Atlantic world today.

Possessing One's Soul

The narrative of the self-determination of African American people belongs not just in the story of resistance, not just in the movement of people toward freedom, not just in the arsons, poisonings, armed rebellions, and escapes, but in the ways those who never left the land of their bondage found, to repeat Harding's words, to "possess their soul in the midst of a destructive and soulless situation."[35] The story of emancipation belongs in the realm of the creative artist who turns his and her memories of ancestral spirits and whispers into a fabric of civilized democracy.

The story of liberation is not to be found in the Currier and Ives depiction of the kneeling supplicant waiting for the "horrible gift" of freedom. Those who carved out traces to freedom, who learned to decipher the written words of the European alphabets, who designed and stitched intricate quilts, who passed the word of the ancestors to the children through Arabic writing and elaborate storytelling, who found a spoken-word voice by embracing the evangelical Christianity of backwoods preachers and rejecting the organized written liturgical Christianity of Anglican ministers, who developed elaborate linguistic schemes and jokes to trick the masters, actually lived life free in their own beings and brought freedom to themselves.

Others have examined the many creoles that could be heard in this diasporic linguistic community as peoples from all over the world created a rich pool of patois throughout the seventeenth, eighteenth, and nineteenth centuries. The creole languages were as diverse and layered as the origins of people in these mixed communities, and equally rich were the shared forms of graphic communication. The story of liberation belongs in the complex ideogrammatic writings called *nsibidi,* seen carved on the trees in the hidden Maroon communities of West Florida. The graphic languages, freed from the necessity of direct vocal equivalency, communicate different values and morals; they knit together communities in ways that abstract alphabetic languages do not.

Crossmarks of African cosmography on the bottoms of water pots, coded messages on quilts, broken twigs revealing the path to hush-harbor meeting places in the woods, intricate burial altars, holes drilled in the form of Bakongo cosmograms in the subfloors of churches and cabins, graphic inscriptions in fine woodwork carved by freed slaves in the First African Baptist Church in Savannah, Georgia, the talking drumbeat, the patterns in basket weavings, the insistent footpaths that marked out a language of resistance, the fingerprints of African workers who pushed the mud into the cracks between wooden planks in the plantation homes of Louisiana[36]—all form a democratic and resonant script of liberation.

This is not to say that enslaved people did not bring written languages with them. But from what we know at this moment, other than those of the people on the East Coast who could write Arabic—and there were some famous examples, particularly in the Georgia and South Carolina Sea Islands communities—these scripts tended to be ideogrammatically based rather than alphabetic. People stitched maps, stars, directions, and codes to the Underground Railroad in their quilts. There are those who doubt that the quilts hid codes and directions and secrets and that enslaved people could read the quilts. But instead of asking *if* there were secret codes and messages and *if* they can be deciphered, they should ask instead how there could *not* be codes and messages that were indecipherable to onlookers.

Only if the slaves had lost all desire to communicate could there not have been secret languages within enslaved people's communities. Quilts, with their intricate needlework and their juxtaposition of shape and color, provide a perfect tablet for hidden inscription. In the vast history of enslaved people of African descent in the United States, there were inevitably plantations where the abuse was so bad, the surveillance so intense, and the punishments so severe that the human urge to live was severely muted. But even in such cases, individuals metaphorically escaped enslavement through circuitous routes. If the conditions were too awful, they escaped into madness or suicide. If we assume that for the majority of the human beings jailed on plantations the primary goal was freedom, then the only way to hope and plan and plot and journey forth was to speak to one another in a common language. The layering of communication within an isolated community results in what to other people appears to be indecipherable, but to those in the know is only a linguistic sleight of hand.

West Africans and the people from the Congo region did not have to learn to retain their cultures through graphic markings. Ideographic signs on pottery, cloth, beaded headdresses, and jewelry; elaborate scarification on faces and bodies; and complex funeral altars and patterns on the walls of houses had always defined their personhood and their cultures. An intimate photograph of a recently captured young woman from the eastern United States, with the leather yoke still around her neck, shows intricate piercings with grass reeds through them on her lips, revealing the degree to which women engaged in body marking.[37] These designs scripted their age, marriageability, status, ethnic heritage, and in some villages which boys could not be sold into slavery.

Mary Thompson's detailed accounts of letters describing body markings on enslaved people at Mount Vernon confirms that African people came to the Americas with fully scrolled bodies. The horrible scars left by the whip are in direct contrast to the cicatrization of the skilled artist.[38] That Queequeg is scrolled is no accident. It is most likely that just as Melville had seen the dances of enslaved people that he includes in *Moby-Dick,* he had also seen examples of this elaborate body art.[39] These marks on and off the body move the discussion of self-emancipation out of the realm of the political, legal, and economic and into the realm of artistic self-expression. The enslaved stayed alive by marking themselves as free, using coded languages to escape and to plan intricate means of resistance.

Enslaved people who could not write any European or Arabic alphabet had access to graphic inscriptions. We only think of enslaved people as illiterate because we do not "read" the nonalphabetic script of these coded languages. Nigerian *nsibidi* hold secrets of warfare and power. Enslaved people from West Africa, the Congo Basin, Sudan, and New Guinea brought these values and arts with them.[40] *Nsibidi* pictographs and ideograms, carved on trees and pottery, painted on clothing and houses, scarred onto faces and bodies, recorded the most powerful moments of life and death for secret martial societies. They were directly entwined with the governing and socializing of the citizens.

That the traffickers in the transatlantic slave trade were bringing human cargo from Senegambia until at least 1808 and to certain areas of the United States illegally much later meant that these people were transporting African religions, foods, burial practices and language practices to the continent much later than we often imagine. In some areas of the country this would mean cultural continuity rather than retention. Each slave ship from West Africa, legal or illegal, brought people with specific traditions to the Americas. These newly enslaved people introduced a multitude of "African" practices and languages from a variety of West African areas to the mainland. By holding on to what we now see as substantial "Africanized" elements of culture and community, by creating hybridized forms of linguistic, artistic, and spiritual expression, enslaved people preserved a self-representation that even the most devastating violence could not destroy.

These marked forms of communication and communal memory sustained human health in a nightmare of cataclysmic proportions. In each case, the marks of liberation are marks of movement beyond or within the limits of captivity and reveal the refusal to stay in one place, captured and shackled in mind, spirit, or body.

Bakongo Cosmogram

Sterling Stuckey and Robert Farris Thompson have traced crosses and circles that archaeologists observed on pottery, subfloors, doors, and household objects in South Carolina and Georgia to depictions of the cosmos traditional among Bakongo priests from the southwest coast of Africa.[41] The basic form of the Bakongo cosmogram is a simple cross with one line representing the boundary between the living world and that of the dead and the other line representing the path of power from below to above, as well as the vertical path across the boundary. One of the most remarkable discoveries of a Bakongo cosmogram occurred at an archaeological site in South Carolina. While cataloging thousands of colonoware shards, archaeologists began noticing marks on the bases of some bowls, which, after many false starts, led them to the Bakongo cosmogram.

In his article "The Cross Is a Magic Sign," Leland Ferguson suggests that the crosses within either a circle or a square found on the bottom of many of the colonoware bowls in the rivers near the plantation site most likely represented the Bakongo cosmogram. Ferguson suggests that "in South Carolina some pieces bear marks similar to those used in Central African religious expression. They appear to represent material aspects of African religion incorporated into the creolized culture of African Americans. . . . My argument here is that inscribing the BaKongo cosmogram on the center of clay bowls was one of those elements."[42] Ferguson was able to put the pieces together at a symposium in Williamsburg, Virginia, "Symposium on African American Culture," in February 1987, when Wythe Dornman and Elaine Nichols helped him make the connection to the Bakongo cosmogram. In *Uncommon Ground,* Ferguson develops the complex spiritual lineage of the Bakongo marks:

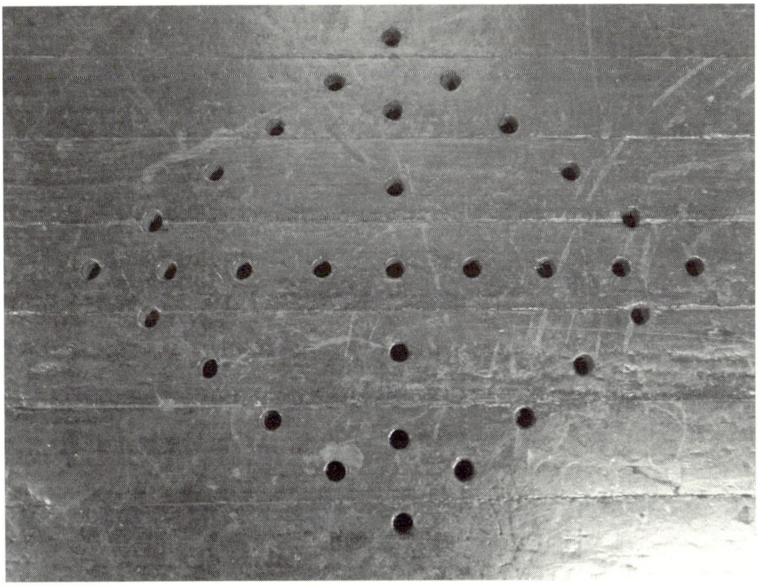

FIGURE 35
Pattern of a Bakongo cosmogram formed by the holes drilled into the subfloor of the First African Baptist Church, Savannah, Georgia. These holes were used as breathing holes for fugitive slaves hiding in the subfloor. (Courtesy of First African Baptist Church, Savannah, Georgia)

> The marks on bowls picked up from river bottoms in the Carolina lowcountry strongly resemble Bakongo cosmograms. The association of marks with earthenware vessels, ring bases, and underwater sites also fits the general West African model. . . . Overall, the traditional African association of medicines or charms with earthenware vessels, and the exclusive archaeological association of marks with handbuilt earthenware bowls, and not with imported European ware, suggests an interpretation of the bowls as receptacles for minkisi or for use in a ritual similar to those involving minkisi.[43]

According to Ferguson, archaeologists have not just found Bakongo cosmograms on pottery in South Carolina; they have also identified these marks on pocket knives at a plantation in Creswell, North Carolina, on pewter spoons at plantations in Maryland, on pipes and spoons in Virginia, on a subfloor in a slave cabin on the Levi Jordan plantation in Brazoria, Texas, between the doorways and hearths in the Brice house in Annapolis, Maryland, and on the subfloor of the First African Baptist Church in Savannah, Georgia (fig. 35). As Ferguson and

Thompson make clear, more than half of the people captured and sold as slaves in South Carolina in the first half of the eighteenth century came from the area in West Africa where the Bakongo cosmogram originated. The subfloor in the First African Baptist Church is particularly intriguing because the holes served as breathing holes for enslaved people waiting to take the Underground Railroad out of Savannah. As breathing holes, the markings become lifesavers literally as well as metaphorically.

Also at the First African Baptist Church is one of the most poignant examples of visceral graphism. When enslaved people in Savannah built the church that stands today in the late 1850s, they either crafted beautiful wooden pews for this new building or moved them from the previous church building. The pews are located in the upstairs gallery. On the sides of each pew are markings of a lighter stain that visiting scholars have identified as an African dialect known as cursive Hebrew. No one has yet interpreted these markings as having specific messages, but several researchers are working on this project.

In my opinion, the artisans and craftsmen were not just writing messages in cursive Hebrew on the sides of these benches. They were doing something much more circumspect: they were hiding their messages from violent eyes by mixing decorative patterns with actual lettering. While many of the messages do appear to contain letters, specifically remnants of cursive Hebrew or some other script, many are simply abstract patterns that resemble waves, rain, and grass, markings that do not seem alphabetic. By mixing the "letters" with the marks, I believe, based on my attention to biomorphic markings, that the enslaved people found a way to blend decoration with inscription, thus hiding their true messages. When linguists do read what is obviously a text for future generations, they will find a mixture of markings of liberation and texts of liberation. The First African Baptist Church in Savannah is one of the most important sites of continuous, well-preserved, historical memory. The benches provide a perfect example of the culture of ancestors designing and naming the terms of their own selves, autonomy, and liberation (fig. 36). What is also interesting is the possibility that woodcarvers brought part of the hush harbor, the biomorphic markings, into their church sanctuary.

Hush Harbor, Ring Shout, and Bakongo Cosmogram

The subversive graphic markings discussed above are liberatory and celebrate the brilliant minds of the enslaved graphic artists. But perhaps the story of the libera-

FIGURE 36
Markings (possibly cursive Hebrew) painted on pews made by enslaved parishioners at the First African Baptist Church in Savannah, Georgia. (Courtesy of First African Baptist Church, Savannah, Georgia)

tion of "African" peoples from American slavery belongs most dramatically in the woods and ravines where hush-harbor secret meetings took place. The hush harbor provided a protected space where enslaved people could meet privately. The ring shout, or ritual of patterned dance performed during the hush-harbor gatherings, reveals a direct link between these meetings and African cultural retention. The ring shout traces out the pattern of a cross with a circle superimposed on top that mirrors exactly the Bakongo cosmography.

Enslaved people used the term *hush harbor* to refer to a meeting place, usually hidden in the woods or heavy foliage, where they convened to conduct rituals and "prayers" and to plan for escape. The meetings were secret meetings, and there was always someone looking out for the master or overseer. Robert Peppers, an

African American artist, understood the power of the hush harbors when he built a series of crosses to represent the churches burned in the 1990s in South Carolina. Each piece in Peppers's series, which he titled "Hush Harbor," includes fragments of burnt wood, charcoal, sticks, and rocks, as well as images of leaves, trees, and branches. Like Clyde Connell, he unites the spiritual world with the physical environment of leaves and sticks. His act of artistic regeneration counteracts the genocidal attacks on black churches by returning to the secret world of the hush harbor.[44]

These meetings in the deep recesses of the woods brought together spiritual and magical rituals. Most importantly, these secret meetings allowed displaced Africans to join elements of African and Christian religious practices. The hush-harbor meetings were not church meetings in any modern sense. According to Laurie Maffly-Kipp, "In the slave quarters . . . African Americans organized their own 'invisible institution.' Through signals, passwords, and messages not discernible to whites, they called believers to 'Hush Harbors' where they freely mixed African rhythms, singing, and beliefs with evangelical Christianity." The hush harbor allowed men and women in the slave community to begin to practice and perfect their new form of preaching, which was "rhythmic, intoned," and "extemporaneous."[45]

The hush harbor was a place where enslaved Africans stole away to let down the masks they had to wear in front of whites. Stephan Talty insightfully argues that "the blacks pantomimed agreement with the white world, but, come nightfall, they would steal away and either gather themselves in a prayer house or in the woods for an 'arbor. . . . If the mass were to be held in a new place, broken twigs on tree branches would point the way. Coded songs, movement in darkness, markers left by an invisible hand: everything spoke of secrecy, brotherhood." I would only add that these gatherings were as much about sisterhood as they were about brotherhood. Women participated fully and were often the night preachers. Talty writes about gatherings that took place after the grueling sunup-to-sundown labor in the fields that "often an iron pot would be turned upside down and placed at the center of the meeting; it was reputed to deaden the sound. . . . The worshippers would begin by asking each how they felt, 'The state of mind.' Then one member would begin testifying about his sin-sick life, his unworthiness; the pace at the beginning halting and heavy, the absence of the spirit clear to everyone."[46]

The hush harbor gave the exhausted people a chance to pour their hearts out to one another, so that each person felt that he or she was loved and heard and could bear another day. There is a strong oral record from as early as 1837 of free(d) persons discussing their experiences attending hush-harbor meetings. Janet Cornelius cites Sallie Carder, a former bondwoman, who recalled that "at nights dey would slip off and git in ditches and sing and pray." According to Cornelius, "Many slaves reported that although they were allowed to attend church services on plantations, they wanted to hold secret meetings as well in order to share what they remembered of African lore and cultural wisdom and to preserve control of their own practices."[47] Cornelius also cites Susan Rhodes, who spoke about how "we used to steal off to de woods and have church, like de spirit moved us—sing and pray to our own liking and soul satisfaction. . . . We had dem spirit-filled meetings at night on de bank of de river and God met us dere."[48] In the arbor space itself, the broken twigs and codes and markings were a language of resistance that could be read only by enslaved people, who relied on these subtle, almost invisible traces to lead them to a place and moment of freedom outside the restrictions of the plantation. The tree language was hidden, but it was a language nonetheless.

Whether or not they escaped, the hush harbor was freedom. The slaves began the arbor services with lines from European hymnbooks, then turned to spirituals, sermonizing, talking, and often chanting before beginning a ring shout. They did not so much take on Christianity as use Christianity to include the forms and passions of the African rituals and beliefs. The hush harbors were communal, emotional, and, most importantly, circular and egalitarian, allowing people who had been whipped or humiliated during the day to express their sorrow and hope for change. The preacher, often someone who could memorize or read the Bible, would call out the names of those present, so that the personhood of each was recognized and their stories were woven into the Bible stories the preacher told. The hush-harbor meeting ended with the ring shout, in which participants would move in a circle, chanting and stomping particular rhythms that can be traced to the Bakongo pattern of the Bantu Kongo religions.

The Bakongo pattern follows the four stages of the sun—rising, peaking, setting, and absence—and the four stages of human life—conception, birth, maturity, and death. Practitioners mark the pattern as a cross with a circle through the middle or a cross with a circle on each end. This careful dance is the exact inversion of the Currier and Ives supplication. The shouter keeps his feet firmly on the earth, feeling the ground, as every part of the earth is sacred. The dancer's bare feet touch as much of the bare earth as possible. The dancer moves in circles and kneels to the earth, "knee bone in the wilderness," as one ring-shout song tells us. This worldview is the antithesis of the culture of George Washington's head and includes the connections necessary to keep a person from going crazy in the world of the master.

Participants in a ring shout follow this circular pattern representing a life journey through not only the sun's phases but also the male and female elements and the four directions. Archaeologists have found dots that they believe mark a Bakongo pattern for a ring shout in slave cabins in South Carolina. The dots are in two rows that cross in the middle, with an intersecting circle.[49] During a ring shout, practitioners did not actually shout but engaged in a complex circling and singing that the McIntosh County Shouters, from McIntosh County, Georgia, preserve to this day.[50] The McIntosh County Shouters still participate in the ring shout and perform the ritualized movements for educational celebratory events. There are many detailed personal accounts that describe the characteristics of the dance: the short steps, bent knees, African elements, and even probable Native American components.[51]

The McIntosh County Shouters move every part of their bodies—legs, hands, arms—in a circular motion, completing the Bakongo pattern. One of their dances is set to the song "Move Daniel," with the lyrics, "Move, Daniel move." This song tells the story of warning a slave named Daniel, who is stealing from the storage room, that the master is coming. The other slaves create a diversion by singing the song and warning Daniel to move away from the master. They tell the story and say that Daniel knew how to "put it down," meaning to get out of there. The McIntosh County Shouters' interpretation of "Knee Bone in the Wilderness" is that the slaves in the wilderness bent their knees to God. While this may have been true, it is more likely, given our knowledge of African dance, that they were engaging in African martial, religious, and spiritual rituals in the wilderness and that knee bends were a distinctive characteristic of these dances. Almost every gesture in these dances is part of the vocabulary of Africanized movement and an inscription of cultural resistance.[52]

While there is a distinctive Christian overlay to many of the ring-shout songs, they come out of the backwoods style of Christianity. During most of the eighteenth century, Anglican preachers failed to convert enslaved Africans to Christianity because the English preachers sent to indoctrinate the enslaved people of Virginia and South Carolina did not connect in any way with the latter's experience of slavery or their understanding of their personhood. Not surprisingly, because they did not allow enslaved persons to read the Bible but only to experience the teachings of Christianity secondhand, these ministers taught obedience, the gospel of the book as they chose to interpret it, a gospel of rules and not personal enlightenment, they failed to win converts. The enslaved people refused to accept this doctrine, because they were not slaves but captives in a cruel system. If this system was God's plan, it made no sense on an intellectual or emotional level. Only during the Second Great Awakening—when preachers moved from doctrine, script, and the written word to the power of speech and the body, and not until they empowered African American speakers to be preachers—did Christianity really take hold among the former Africans and their descendants.

These two forms of root culture—ring shout and hush harbor—connect the enslaved not just to the spirit of communal healing but to their warrior power and to survival. Many African dance steps originated as the ritualized practice of a warrior preparing for battle. By survival I mean not that of one individual but that of a community of souls connected to their environment over hundreds of years, many of whom might never know physical freedom. The ring shout and the graphic inscription of the Bakongo cosmogram allowed enslaved people and their children to experience an internal, bodily marked freedom that could never be taken away. For those in the second, third, and fourth generations who had never known freedom, participation in these African-inspired rituals was lifesaving. In direct contrast to the iconic image of the whipped "slave," hush harbors, ring shouts, and Bakongo cosmograms enabled enslaved African peoples to imagine themselves into freedom, whether or not they ever left the plantation.

According to Karen Baker-Fletcher, "Hush harbor space is sacred space. It is a space that draws boundaries between peace and violence, life and death, healing and sickness, freedom and captivity, love and hate, faith and fear. It defies the prison of shame and hate, that oppressive forces produce to contain control, break, and destroy the sexual-spiritual lives of the subjugated."[53] Toni Morrison writes about a hush harbor in *Beloved,* when Baby Suggs brings the community together in the clearing. Joy R. Bostic equates this clearing directly with African cultural memories: "Within this ritual space dance functions as the bridge of embodiment that speaks the unspeakable in rhyme so that flesh and spirit become one." Bostic explains that in the hush-harbor space not only could people move freely but they could release emotions, tears, laughter, all that the master forbade. They could be human again.[54]

The hush harbor and the ring shout were radical, because each person who attended the meetings was called on to testify, was made part of the sermonizing and the word of God. The embodied individual is the site of liberation for a community in which slavery has erased individuality. While the Christian notion of God is an all-powerful male figure, the enslaved people transformed Christianity itself into the passionate liberatory rhetoric of communal love. "God" loves each and every one of the people, so if God loved them and they could tell each other, bear witness, and testify, then they were people. Free peoples saw and spoke in oral histories about seeing women put their heads into large pots that would catch the sound of their voices so that they could sing, speak, and cry out loud: "Slaves made hush harbors of poles and brush and sawed rough planks from small logs for seats. Former slaves remembered turning a big pot upside down for noise control; Clara Young remembered that, after a meeting had lasted all day, 'when dark came, de man folks would hang up a wash pot, bottom up'ards, in de little brush church-houses had, so's it would catch de noise an de oberseer wouldn' hear us singin and shoutin.'"[55]

Maffly's phrase "signals, passwords, and messages not discernible to whites" introduces the fully developed language of enslaved Africans in America into the conversation of visceral graphism. Movement was everywhere in the slave community, in every form of work, but mostly in two important realms: in dances and in the thousands upon thousands of attempts, successful or not, to run away—to a free space within one's own body or outside the plantation. Often these two realms were inextricably connected. Once someone started moving, he or she could move right off the plantation. This movement to a free space took the form of the spiritual, martial, and often ritualized patterned footsteps performed under cover of white cultural misunderstanding, within harbors at night, or in broad daylight. The language of personhood in the enslaved community was not one of exceptional "codes" or marks but of bodies, as ciphers, in motion.

And if one could not run away, one could trace the steps of a ritual dance, the ring shout. In direct opposition to the immobility of fetters and chains and whips was the pattern of the steps, all the variations and spin-offs of the ring shout. A poster for a 4 August 2011 performance of the Ladies Ring Shout, a modern-day version of the ring shout, by Honey Pot Performance, with the dancers Abra Johnson, Meida McNeal, and Felicia Holman, shows footprints overlapping and moving in a circle in a graphic inscription (fig. 37).

"Feet Don't Fail Me Now" II

The "dances" that have come to us emphasize the movement of feet tracing the most intricate patterns of survival. When the shuffling feet of Uncle Tom and Lincoln Perry's brilliant performance of Stepin Fetchit moved across our cultural lens, we might have misinterpreted their slow, deliberate, connected-to-the-earth

FIGURE 37
Graphic image for poster for the Ladies Ring Shout, by Jeanne Medina, 2011. (Courtesy of the artist and Meida McNeal, Honey Pot Performance)

movements as subservient, when they might actually have been subversive. They might have been moving their feet slowly, deliberately working out a pattern, tracing the ancient Bakongo cosmogram or other ideograms. With the ability to know exactly where one's arms and legs and feet were located in space at any given time, the enslaved became experts in invisibility, in getting out of the way, in moving in and out of moments of danger, without being seen or heard.

The art of silence became part of the body in motion. When the body is in a space that demands stillness, the motion of that body inscribes freedom on that space. This is the most powerful form of visceral graphism.[56] The moment a trapped person chooses the precise direction and the precise gesture of his or her movement, he or she is no longer a slave but has written an emancipation proclamation. Whether this proclamation leads to escape or death, it is still a moment of liberation. The longer this declaration occupies space, the more likely it functions not just to go beyond the limits of the prison walls that hold it but to dissolve those barriers.

Feet were a slave's escape. Legs and feet were the means to freedom. Without one's feet, both metaphorically and actually, there was no hope, no road, and no path to freedom. Feet carved out paths, and these paths became the script of liberation. Cutting the feet off a slave was the greatest punishment. Writers and songs and stories tell of severed feet[57] and hamstringing. In George Washington Cable's *The Grandissimes* local leaders in New Orleans hamstring the strong African prince Bras Coupe, who refuses to work as a slave in America.

The styles of African American dancing are evidence of the importance of feet on the ground. In tapping, stomping, and stepping, there is a connection to the earth, to all that keeps us grounded as a community of human beings, animals, and plants. If the head drives European civilization, African and African American civilization move from the intelligence of the connection between the head and the whole body. A head disconnected from its body will foul its own nest, as the Jamestown settlers did, or will suppress its own women and devalue the cycle of the growing season. Profound advances in civilization came directly from a circular and spiritually embodied understanding of human life on earth, with heads and bodies working together.

The European domination of head over land and body, a genocidal experiment, has been dramatic and explosive and changed the demographics, the geography, and the environmental balance of the world in immeasurable ways. Our skyscrapers cannot reach the skies, and our planes cannot reach the solar system. But the stomp, shuffle, tap, and drum of other civilizations call us to a council that may, by firmly placing foot to earth, reach the trees, the clouds, even the skies and make visible the constellations of the solar system. This is the knowledge of connection rather than dislocation, of the beat of a constantly moving embodied community rather than an embalmed heroic head of state.

Over the years, African American dance has initiated the stomp, stepping, break dancing, second lining, the ring shout, and tap, to name just a few forms. All of these forms of movement have the incessant demand of the drum behind them and the foot raised or held down to listen to the earth rhythms. The broom, stick, pole, raised fighting pole, or drum helps measure the beat. Drums were extremely important to many West African peoples, as they could use them not just to signal or warn but also to express complex thoughts and messages. The talking drums conveyed a tonal language that could be heard and understood across long distances.[58]

Most elements of moving and drumming that enslaved people practiced were not performative at all but actually spiritual, religious, and, as Richard Cullen Rath explicates, martial:

> Kongolese and Angolan techniques of unarmed combat were learned in the form of a martial art set in time to drum music. In short, the skills were encoded in a form of dance. . . . According to John Thornton, this specialized form of dance, called *sanga* in the Kikongo language, and *sanguar* in Ndongo, valued hand-to-hand combat skills, the use of sticks and other weapons, as well as "the ability to twist, leap, and dodge to avoid arrows or the blows of opponents." . . . Ritualized stick fighting and dancing like that found in Central Africa persisted all over the "new world."[59]

The intricate connection between martial arts, drumming, "dancing" and power dynamics makes these cultural retentions particularly significant. Europeans often did not understand what, exactly, they were seeing:

> One particular type of West African Court music—that radiating from a Kwa ethnic base centered in the region from eastern Nigeria to modern Ghana—was more than a set of signals. It functioned as an immanent and immediate means of representing and communicating ideas in a repeatable form, somewhat similar to a spoken language. Most Kwa languages are tonal: That is words can be differentiated on the basis of pitch change. Kwa drummers, able to rely in part on pitch patterns, could produce, musical representation akin to a language rather than being fixed corpus of signals.[60]

After the Stono Rebellion in 1739, the slave masters in South Carolina made teaching slaves to read and drumming illegal in the Negro Acts of 1740: "And whatsoever master, owner or overseer shall permit or suffer his or their Negro or other slave or slaves, at any time hereafter, to beat drums, blow horns, or use any other loud instruments or whosoever shall suffer and countenance any public meeting or feastings of strange Negroes or slaves in their plantations, shall forfeit ten pounds, current money, for every such offence."[61] According to the critic Ortiz Walton, in *Music, Black and White and Blues,* "The enforcement of anti-drum laws in the United States made it necessary to transfer the function of the drum to the feet, the hands, and body by way of the Spirituals during the slave era and by way of instrumental music after the Civil War in the new form of black music called Jazz."[62] By transferring the function of the drum to the feet and hands, expressing liberation and speaking language became directly visceral and gestural.

Much of the rhythmic beat went into a kind of dancing called "patting Juba" or "Hambone," in which performers would beat the rhythms on their bodies with their hands and feet.[63] People took up the barrel, the butter churn, the cane, the spoon on a hand, the overturned metal washbasin, the hand beating and slapping body parts to keep the rhythm. In an improvised orchestration, the polyrhythmic beat survives. In *The Bluesman,* Julio Finn asserts that enslaved people never let the drums die out: "In spite of the anti-drumming laws promulgated throughout the United States, black people managed to keep the institution of the drum alive, and when they found themselves deprived of those drums which sounded throughout the land of their origin they turned to adapting other instruments to serve as percussive substitutes."[64] Even with strict drum laws, people of African descent managed to maintain these practices. Many people living on South Carolina's Sea Islands in the 1930s could remember people who knew how to play the talking African drums.

Thompson in *Flash of the Spirit* emphasizes the "dominance of a percussive performance style; a propensity of multiple meter, overlapping call and response; inner pulse or keeping a beat indelibly in mind as a rhythmic common denominator in a welter of different meters; suspended accentuation patterning or off-beat phrasing of melodic and choreographic accents; and songs and dances of social allusion."[65] Thompson emphasizes the multiple meter of African dance, as well as its inner pulse and overlapping call and response, which literally creates a boundary crossing in the New World. This is why when a scholars such as Wyatt MacGaffey, in *Modern Kongo Prophets: Religion in a Plural Society,* connect the Bakongo cosmogram to the ring shout and the drum beat, the full significance of cultural retention becomes clear.

The ring shout and the Bakongo cosmogram have received much greater attention recently because of the placement of a modern cosmogram on the floor of the Ted Weiss Federal Building in New York City over an excavated slave burial site. When city officials began to excavate the foundation for the new building in 1991, they found skeletal remains. At first the contractors tried to cover up the discovery, but several investigative reporters leaked the findings, leading to a full-scale archaeological dig. The archaeologists unearthed the remains of more than

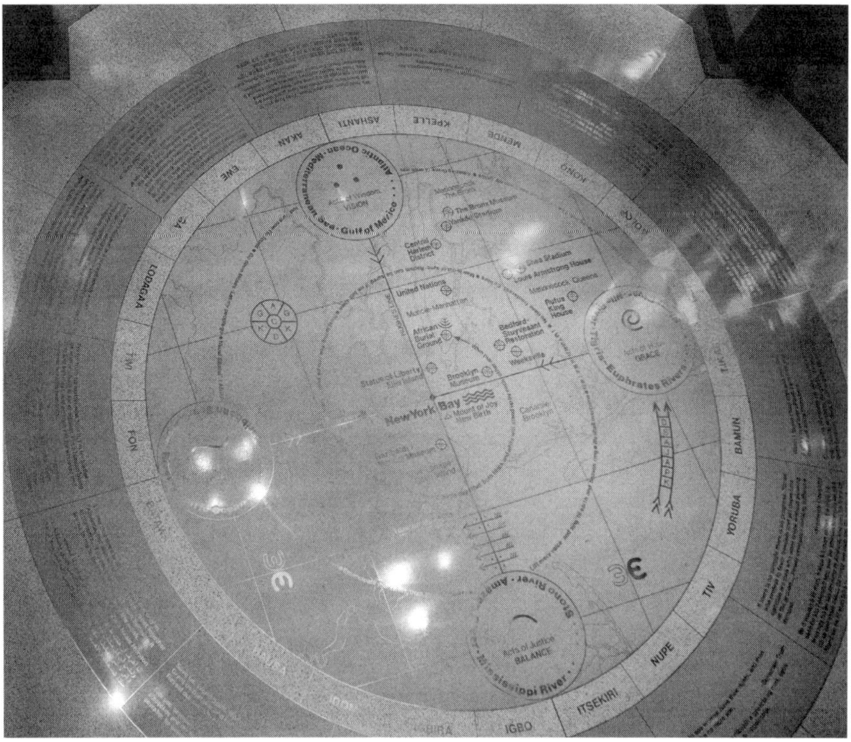

FIGURE 38

The New Ring Shout, designed by Houston Conwill, Joseph DePace, and Estella Conwill Májozo, 1994, African Burial Ground National Monument, Ted Weiss Federal Building, New York. Illuminated terrazzo and polished brass, 40 ft. in diameter. (Prints & Photographs Division, Library of Congress)

four hundred enslaved and free people of African descent buried in a cemetery in the seventeenth and eighteenth centuries.

Activists, academics, and local politicians in the African American community all put pressure on government officials, and eventually the planned Ted Weiss Federal Building was transformed to include a sacred space that houses a museum, a burial site, and a memorial garden. The entire space is named the African Burial Ground National Monument. In the interior of the Ted Weiss Federal Building, the floor contains a circular mosaic measuring forty feet in diameter entitled *The New Ring Shout* (fig. 38). The sculptor Houston Conwill, the architect Joseph DePace, and the poet Estella Conwill Májozo collaborated on the design of this modern version of a Bakongo cosmogram made of terrazzo and polished brass. *The New Ring Shout* includes a cross and a spiral with four circles.

In *The New Ring Shout,* the Bakongo cosmogram's already multilayered symbolic meanings are expanded upon by the inclusion of the names of African cultural groups and quotations from all the ethnic groups represented in America, including words by Marcus Garvey, Zora Neale Hurston, Nelson Mandela, Martin Luther King Jr., Maya Angelou, and Mary McLeod Bethune, as well as many others. The circles contain a new geography of places associated with liberation and words to express compassion and depth of empathy. This striking Bakongo symbol represents one of the most powerful images of cultural retention yet found by archaeologists.

A steady, polyrhythmic African drumbeat, marked pottery, stitched cloth, beads and shells, burial rituals, and remnants found by archaeologists in and around enslaved communities all allow us to follow the thread of personhood, the heartbeat of peoples who never lost their connection to the cultural markings of their home countries.

Icons of Slavery

One reason why we have such difficulty moving from the Currier and Ives supplicant slave to the self-liberated free woman and man is the role the powerful iconography of abolition has played in the cultural imagination. In direct contrast to the subtlety and mystery of Dave's poems scrolled on the large pots, the abolitionist visual images tended to create simple, emblematic icons rather than complex, thought-provoking images of the slave experience. The abolitionist propaganda that so radically transformed American perceptions of slavery, including the work of John Rankin and Harriet Beecher Stowe, inadvertently reduced the slave experience in the white cultural imagination to about ten iconic images. While these images provided a powerful propagandistic tool that cut through the paternalistic myth, they also reified slavery.

Exposing the cruelty of the slave system, almost all these images simultaneously celebrate and, unfortunately, negate the full autonomous personhood of the enslaved people they depict. These stock images often substitute the object for the subject, pity for empathy, and dead flesh for living tissue. For each dehumanized and objectified image of slavery—our iconic cultural "memory"—artists have found alternative visual representations of the active, self-defined free

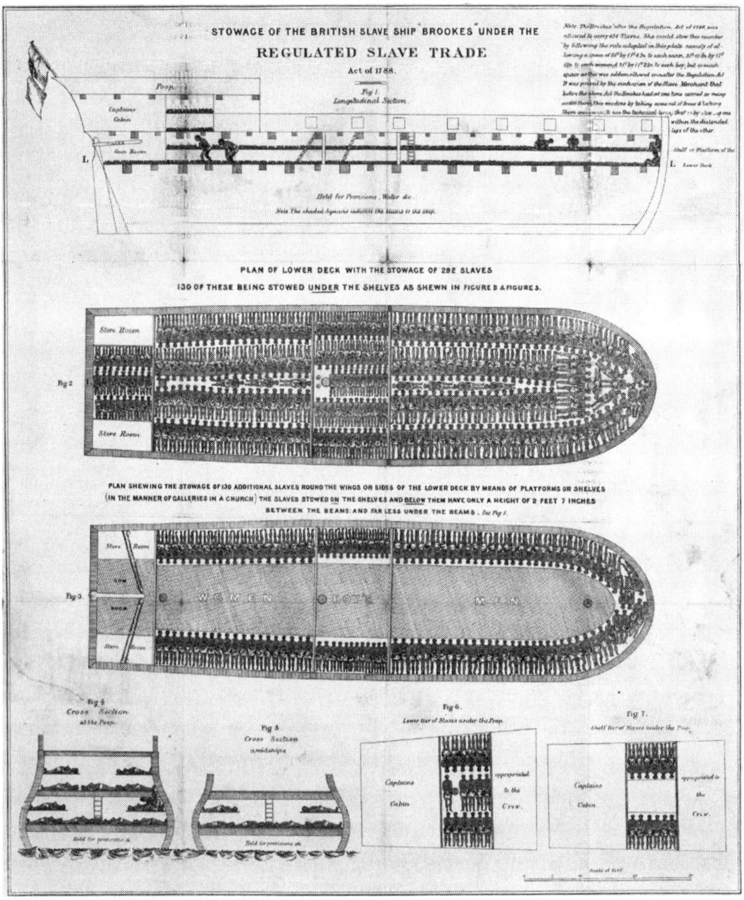

FIGURE 39

Stowage of the British Slave Ship "Brookes" under the Regulated Slave Trade Act of 1788, Fig. 1, Longitudinal Section. (American Memory Digital Collection, Library of Congress)

man and woman. For instance, visual art and archival research have so enlivened and provided a counternarrative to the static image of Thomas Clarkson's diagram of stowage on the British slave ship *Brookes* that we can no longer think of the transatlantic slave trade in the same way (fig. 39). That we have to constantly create new, unsettling images exposes how tenacious ersatz history can be. Johann Moritz Rugendas's 1827 painting *Enslaved Africans in Hold of a Slave Ship* (fig. 40) reveals the humanity of the enslaved people in the hold. Rather than lying half-dead in rows, they are sitting, conversing, suffering, and fully human.

FIGURE 40

Enslaved Africans in Hold of a Slave Ship, by Johann Moritz Rugendas, 1827. (Image reference E109, *The Atlantic Slave Trade and Slave Life in the Americas: A Visual Record,* http://hitchcock.itc.virginia.edu/slavery, compiled by Jerome S. Handler and Michael L. Tuite Jr., sponsored by the Virginia Foundation for the Humanities and the University of Virginia Library)

Joseph Turner's painting *Slave Ship* (formally known as *Slavers Throwing Overboard the Dead and Dying—Typhoon Coming On*), which depicts a tumultuous, intense, ocean scene with a blood-red sky overhead, high waves, and slaves being thrown overboard by the crew, takes the stagnant image of the ship and making it a living horror. Tom Feelings's dramatic and important book of drawings, *The Middle Passage,* enlivens, spiritualizes, and empowers all the African people aboard a ship in the Middle Passage. His exquisite sketches animate the enslaved people, so that they become at once human and larger-than-life, powerful spirit figures; they are quite literally the force of the wind, propelling the ship. They appear as deities, transfigured (fig. 41). Turner and Feelings reclaim the beaten-down slaves of abolitionist rhetoric and transform them into complex human beings with power, desires, and dreams of their own.

Fred D'Aguiar transforms the rows of bodies in Clarkson's diagram of the slave ship when he writes of Mintah's escape from the hold after being thrown overboard in *Feeding the Ghosts.* Mintah is able to climb up the barnacled side of

FIGURE 41
The Middle Passage, by Tom Feelings, from his book by the same name. (Reproduced with permission of the Estate of Tom Feelings; image courtesy of the Beinecke Rare Book and Manuscript Library, Yale University)

the ship and escape from a narrative that in its most iconized form meant death by suicide, murder, starvation, or eventual enslavement. D'Aguiar dismantles the iconic image of stowage by allowing his character to escape the hold and survive.

Marcus Wood devotes an entire chapter in *The Horrible Gift of Freedom* to contemporary imaginative treatments of the *Brookes.*[66] Wood is not as interested in visual representations that simply reproduce or use a gimmick to provide an easy counternarrative as he is in works that take us out of what Adorno would call our barbarous complacency. Willie Cole's *Stowage* depicts a *Brookes*-like slave ship by using the face of an iron to cover the "deck." The whole ship is a print of an ironing board (fig. 42). Over the years, Cole has created a vocabulary of irons that appear in multiple contexts and connect American domestics of the twentieth and twenty-first centuries with African markers of personhood. In one image he prints the outline of an iron as a mask over his face and tattoos his face in paint. The tension within his work is palatable.

The most widely publicized iconic image of slavery in many people's minds is *The Scourged Back,* the 1863 photograph by William D. McPherson and his partner, Mr. Oliver, of New Orleans, of a slave, sometimes called Peter and sometimes Gordon, the skin of whose back is lacerated into a horrible, raised pattern of scars. Abolitionists widely circulated the photograph of this slave from Baton Rouge, Louisiana, who had been whipped by the overseer Artayou Carrier. A

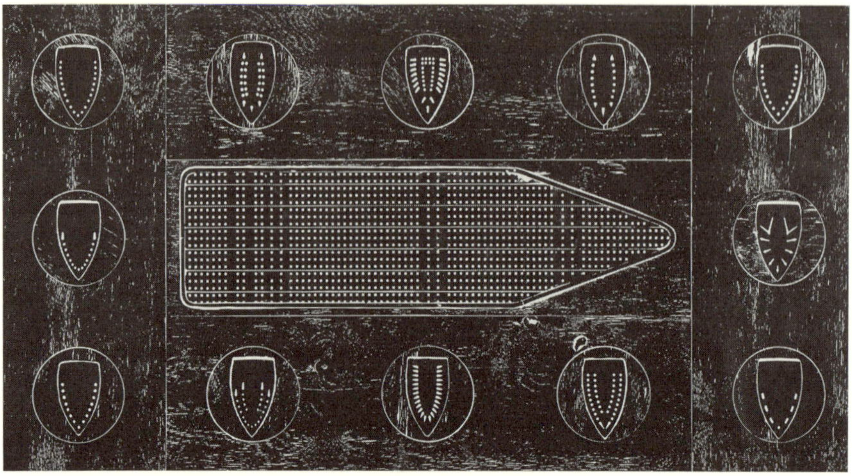

FIGURE 42
Stowage, by Willie Cole, 1997. Relief print on paper, 56 × 104 in. (Collection of the Walker Art Center, Minneapolis; McKnight Acquisition Fund, 1998)

reporter for the *New York Independent* commented: "This Card Photograph should be multiplied by the 100,000 and scattered over the states. It tells the story in a way that even Mrs. (Harriet Beecher) Stowe cannot approach, because it tells the story to the eye."[67] Kathleen Collins, in her essay "The Scourged Back," writes that the photograph "shows a slave named Gordon who escaped his master in Mississippi by rubbing himself with onions to throw off the bloodhounds. He took refuge with the Union Army at Baton Rouge and, in 1863, three engraved portraits of him were printed in *Harper's Weekly,* showing the man 'as he underwent the surgical examination previous to being mustered into the service—his back furrowed and scarred with the traces of a whipping administered on Christmas Day last.' Gordon defined his own positionality and cultural performance by choosing to reveal his back and having the photographer take pictures of him clothed in his military uniform as he transitions from slave to soldier."[68]

The artists who have famously transformed Gordon's back from a symbol of oppression to a symbol of regeneration and empowerment have acknowledged that this was no easy transformation. The most well known is Toni Morrison's extended description in *Beloved* of the chokecherry tree on Sethe's back. When Paul D. asks Sethe about the tree on her back, Sethe replies: "White girl. That's what she called it. I've never seen it and never will. But that's what she said it looked like. A chokecherry tree. Trunk, branches, and even leaves. Tiny little chokecherry leaves. But that was eighteen years ago. Could have cherries too now for all I know."[69]

The first person to read the script on Sethe's back is a white girl, just as the abolitionists who read Gordon's back are white. But now a man who wants to make love to Sethe is reading her back, and Sethe goes beyond Denver's description to imagine the tree growing cherries. The dead, scarified flesh becomes living flesh in Sethe's mouth as she rolls out bread and tells Paul D. the story of the boys' taking her milk. "School teacher made one open up my back, and when it closed it made a tree. It grows there still." Paul D. asks, "They used cowhide on you?"[70] But Sethe will not tell the old story. She is much more concerned with the fact that they took the milk she wanted so desperately to give to her baby. Paul D. knows what to do; he presses his cheek up against her tree, her back, and

> Behind her, bending down, his body an arc of kindness, he held her breasts in the palms of his hands. He rubbed his cheek on her back and learned that way her sorrow, the roots of it; its wide trunk and intricate branches. Raising his fingers to the hooks of her dress, he knew without seeing them or hearing any sigh that the tears were coming fast. And when the top of her dress was around her hips and he saw the sculpture her back had become, like the decorative work of an ironsmith too passionate for display, he could think but not say, "Aw, Lord, girl." And he would tolerate no peace until he had touched every ridge and leaf of it with his mouth, none of which Sethe could feel because her back skin had been dead for years. What she knew was that the responsibility for her breasts, at last was in somebody else's hands.[71]

We know that Paul D. does not yet know the real sorrow or the real nightmare of what those men did to Sethe or what Sethe did to her baby, but he is on the path; his tongue and mouth are where they need to be to sense and learn the deepest secrets. He has Sethe's breasts, her real story, in his hands, and it is the intricate tracings of the chokecherry tree that have led him to this place.

Where Morrison leaves off, Carrie Mae Weems picks up in her exhibit of toned prints, which are prints that she has colored in deep red and black tones. For this exhibit, called *From Here I Saw What Happened and I Cried* (1995–96), Weems selected thirty-three archival prints of African Americans, many of them images of enslaved people, including *The Scourged Back.* She sandblasted texts onto the protective glass that lay over the transformed photographs, which she has made uniform in size and tinted red and black instead of a black and white.

She framed each photo with an oval frame. The poem she sandblasted onto the photograph of Gordon's back reads, in capital letters:

BLACK AND TANNED
YOUR WHIPPED WIND
OF CHANGE HOWLED LOW
BLOWING ITSELF—HA—SMACK
INTO THE MIDDLE OF
ELLINGTON'S ORCHESTRA
BILLIE HEARD IT TOO &
CRIED STRANGE FRUIT TEARS

With the words "whipped wind of change" Weems transforms any vestige of Gordon as victim into Gordon as empowered (fig. 43). Cassandra Jackson writes that Gordon later enlisted in the Union army, when the picture was taken. In *Violence, Visual Culture, and the Black Male Body* Jackson herself reclaims the image of the wounded black man in visual culture.

Gordon escaped to become a Union soldier. He displayed his back to the photographer as a map of where he had been, so he was in many ways in control of the image. Gordon's willingness to reveal his scars becomes an act of rebellion as powerful as his escape. Gordon's scarred back is not the living tree or the deep roots but the cut and torn and dead branches all scattered. It took the imagination of Toni Morrison to piece that torn flesh into a living chokecherry tree on Sethe's back under the loving touch of Paul D.'s lovemaking.

Democracy

That the American democracy has been flawed, violent, and racist says nothing about the aesthetic, moral, and ethical choices of African American culture in the forming of this nation. It says instead that there is a strong conflict in the country, a fight for the soul of Americans, and that the voice of democracy can be found as much in the traces of Africanisms and the belts and strings of the Six Nations as in the Declaration of Independence or the Constitution. Again, the sourcing of democracy, mirroring Rancière's formulations, comes from those breaking down the gates, undermining the rules, fighting against the "police," and demanding movement and change. Slavery ended in America not because of a proclamation and not even, as James McPherson insists, because of a war, but because over time, as peoples of African descent and newly arrived African

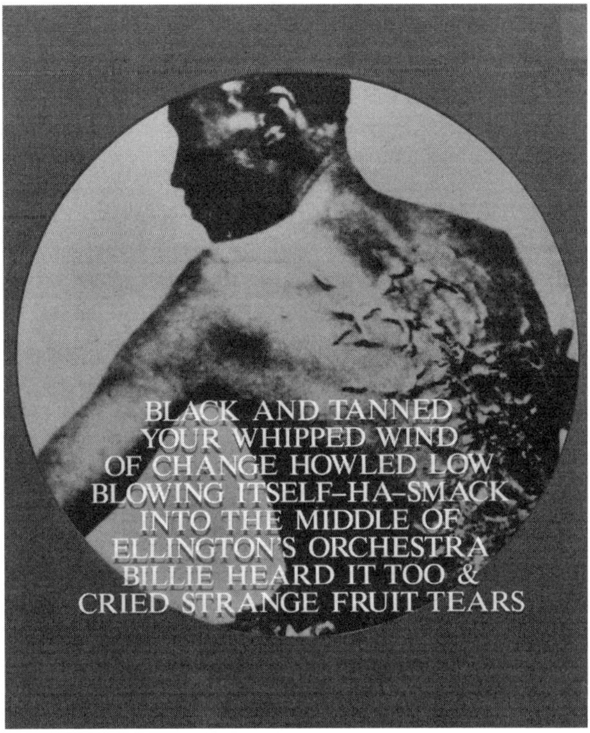

FIGURE 43
BLACK AND TANNED . . ., by Carrie Mae Weems, from *From Here I Saw What Happened and I Cried,* 1995–96. Chromogenic print and sandblasted glass, 59.7 × 49.4 cm. (© Carrie Mae Weems; courtesy of the artist and Jack Shainman Gallery, NY)

peoples wove their sustained cultural expressions into hybridized religious expressions, joined together to create creolized cultures that articulated an African American sustainability against all odds, their liberty as humans broke down the walls of their enslavement. This occurred even on the most practical level. As soon as the war started, enslaved people were escaping from plantations in what became unimaginable numbers, because they knew what freedom meant and they wanted to move their bodies to occupy, quite literally, the space that their hearts and heads and visceral knowledge already inhabited.

Although enslaved people's lives were often severely circumscribed and made unimaginably desperate, although they had little hope and experienced a catastrophic degree of human suffering, even when they were forced to stand still, they were on the move. If enslaved and free people of color had not—from the moment slave drivers demanded that they leave homes, imprisoned them in coastal slave "castles," imposed the horror of being thrown as cargo into the hulls of slave ships, sold them on auction blocks, forced them to pick up hoe and shovel and scythe, to gather, plow, saw, chop, nail, fell, tend, sew, mend, nurse, simmer, boil, roast, sauté, dice, knead, butcher, feed, seed, and build a nation for others—stepped away from their unrelenting work and held on to their souls, they would have died spiritually and physically. As they spoke, wrote, carved, stepped, walked, sewed, drummed, sung, practiced martial-art movements, and moved outside the boundary of their cage, they inscribed their marks and footprints on the landscape, carved words on the benches, houses, and floors, stitched messages on quilts, and marked the woods in which they lived and through which they traveled to liberty. These marks are the counterstory to the Emancipation Proclamation.

One thinks of those in prison who beat out intricate rhythms on the bars in order to communicate. This kind of communication has no formal rules but instead expands upon itself as it creates a field of expectation. Of course it was easy to deceive outsiders because they were just that, outside the group and thus unable to decipher even the most broad slights, jokes, mimicking, plotting, and planning. Though they saw a rebellion brewing under every twig, they missed the broken twig leading to the hush harbor; they missed the important information of the insistent drums, because they did not understand the basic cultural premise that those they called "slaves" were brilliant, determined, intelligent, articulate, literate, talented, clear-thinking, cynical, imaginative human beings with lives, communities, loves, hates, and dreams of their own. To think that one owned a slave was to block human empathy from one's heart and brain.

Since there was no real democracy in America until enslaved people walked freely, the claim can be made that African Americans brought democracy to the nation. Even more unsettling is that if the founding fathers had been able to hear the free(d) men's and women's and enslaved people's polyrhythmic drumbeat instead of being blinded by the revolutionary drumbeat of white male freedom, there most likely would have been no need for either the Emancipation Proclamation or the Civil War.

EPILOGUE

A VIEW OF THE WOODS FROM THE GLASS HOUSE

> She stared across the lot where there was nothing but a profusion of pink and yellow and purple weeds, and on across the red road to the sullen line of black pinewoods fringed on top with green. Behind that line was a narrow gray-blue line of more distant woods and beyond that nothing but the sky, entirely blank except for one or two threadbare clouds. She looked into this scene as if it were a person she preferred to him.—FLANNERY O'CONNOR, "A View of the Woods"

On one research trip to Jamestown while working on the chapter about George Washington's head, I took a detour to a place called Presidents Park, near Williamsburg, to see the two-story, eighteen-foot-high busts of forty-two of the American presidents (fig. 44). I was both amused and horrified by the sheer audacity of these huge hollow busts by David Atickes. Presidents Park is truly the height of ersatz history.

I have since learned that there were actually two Presidents Parks, the one near Williamsburg and one in North Dakota, both now closed. The one near Williamsburg closed before a bust of Obama could be added, so the whiteness of the statues and of the men remained inviolate. Now that the park is closed, presidents' noses are peeling off, ears are breaking, chins sloughing, and cracks forming on cheeks and necks. Branches are growing out of presidential ears, and grass is as high as their shoulders. I would like to think that these deteriorating monstrosities are prescient. I would like to believe that Americans have finally lost their insatiable appetite for ersatz America, that these presidents' heads will

FIGURE 44
Presidents Park, near Williamsburg, Virginia, 2010.
(Photograph by Rebecca Mark)

crumble to rubble, with no ladies of Mount Vernon to save them or restore them to their former glory. I would have liked to call this book *The Death of Ersatz America,* but I am not convinced that we are not even now finding new ways to paralyze and memorialize democracy.

Having grown up in a 1955 version of a Bauhaus-inspired glass house, similar to Philip Johnson's famous glass house but reworked and redesigned by Charles Goodman in the Virginia woods, I find in this experience a metaphor for my inquiry into national authenticity. What could be more real than complete transparency, a clean pane of glass through which anyone could look and see the world of the people inside? Yet as a small child who spent countless hours peering into the night, I knew that the obscure, mysterious trees held far more truths then the well-lit, glassed-in museum case. Glass houses exposed the children of the fifties to the change of seasons, the mysteries of natural light, and the questions about the universe that have plagued humans forever. At a moment in the sixties when the forces of technology and modernism were driving architecture up, up, and away from the earth, the open invitation of Hollin Hills not just to look out into the woods but to live in the woods was permanently changing a generation of American children.

The dirt paths and scrubby underbrush stood as a reminder to me and my siblings of the uncontrollability of our lives; they provided an escape from the frightening realities of an unstable 1960s America. We lived in a labyrinth larger than us, hiding our desires and plots, our indiscretions, and the woods protected and challenged us. We lived in the woods and returned home for an occasional meal, some homework, and a parental nod. Hollin Hills was about liberty from the stifling conformity of fifties America.

Outside my window the trees created a latticed pattern, a language I have been deciphering ever since, the source, as I have said, for the hieroglyphic focus of this book. The visual pattern of the tree branches is stamped on my brain, informing my understanding of everything. The tree branches are a hieroglyphic puzzle never to be solved, comforting in their impenetrable mystery, unsettling in their spiritual demands.

The land of Virginia, the red clay soil, depleted of nutrients after too many years of exploitation, is thick with national memories. While the ladies of Mount Vernon might choose to neglect the oral history that tells West Ford's descendants that he was George Washington's son, I have no such choice. As one who rode her bike through the African American town of Gum Springs, with streets named West and Ford, I do not have the luxury of selective amnesia. The Virginia history that I was subjected to in the fourth, seventh, and eleventh grade was ersatz history writ larger than the heads at Presidents Park. But the history I lived on the streets broke through the distortions.

I learned to recite Patrick Henry's "Give me liberty or give me death!" speech while looking at history books with pictures of happy darkies eating watermelons. I spent days drawing a to-scale picture of the Capitol, but I didn't learn that the land I put my feet down on to walk to school, the creek and the woods of my childhood, had been inhabited by the Dogue and Algonquian Indians and that they had an established town in Mason Neck, not far from my house. I never knew that these peoples had built houses out of branches from the same kinds of beeches and oaks that sheltered my childhood. How different my life might have been had I known. I might have tried to learn the language of the ancestors and decipher the messages that the land whispered to me.

I clearly remember exploring with a friend along a side road between Mount Vernon Parkway and the river and coming upon an abandoned plantation long since hidden by surrounding subdivisions. This plantation was no Mount Vernon, and the rubble slave cabins disturbed our complacency. Our new high school had been built to preserve Spring Hill, an African American community that claimed direct descendants from George Washington's slaves.

In our innocence, we thought nothing of visiting the slave cabins at Mount Vernon. Nothing of the dislocation of feeling that it took to learn in school that George Washington was the father of our country and to realize that he depended for his wealth and livelihood on slaves. A part of our ethical soul must have died in the face of the irony and madness of it all. Growing up in Alexandria, Virginia, I lived with the identity of a border state, neither wholly Confederate nor wholly Union. We played on the battlefields of Manassas and took field trips to Gettysburg and Fredericksburg. History made itself apparent like an old family friend. We lived with and in the monuments to nation.

To this day, when I stand in the Lincoln Memorial and read the words engraved on the walls, they remain larger than life. I look up like a hopeful child at the man who occasionally had the courage to do what was right. The Lincoln Memorial and the Jefferson Memorial were for me neither monumental nor ersatz but living, tragic, joyous, and human spaces. As a child I thought these imposing Romanesque monuments had been there for centuries; I had no idea that they were recently constructed facades, part of a cleverly designed stage set for democracy, or that I was actually acting out the drama of democracy on this political testing ground.

The National Mall was part of my growing up. When I was young, I visited the Smithsonian and the Capitol. When I was older, the Mall was a place for dissent and celebration. On the Mall I listened to Bernice Reagon Johnson and Pete Seeger, and I worked for the Folklife Festival. On the Mall I marched in at least five of the Vietnam War protests in the early seventies and in the gay rights marches of 1987 and 1993, in the latter accompanied by my mother. Standing on the Mall to celebrate the inauguration of the first black president, waving a flag and singing "America the Beautiful," broke a defining cynicism in me. On the Mall we the people, the bodies of people in motion, the steps I took in dissent, became inscriptions of democracy. Especially now that the United States Holocaust Memorial Museum, the National Museum of the American Indian, and the National Museum of African American History promise to change forever the Mall of my childhood—the Mall of patriarchal heroes and of the Smithsonian Institution's pilfered Indian remains—to make it more inclusive, negotiating the minefield of American nation building, I find an even greater potential for unsettling performance.

Children of Hollin Hills, and, for that matter, children of the fifties generally, do not respond well to nostalgia. We are the generation after the Holocaust and World War II. For a brief period before the Vietnam War we lived in a state of shock, an amnesiac state, swallowing whole our parents' and the nation's suspended dream of an American prosperity built on top of a toxic swill pit of rotting bones and silenced voices, the fragmented remains of the hundreds of years of unmourned sacrifice to nationhood.

Any child who grows up in the woods is familiar with paths over hills that lead to nowhere, circles within circles, with no angles, no promenades, a longing for a day when a heavy snow falls weighing down the tree branches, so that one has only a vague idea where home is and a certainty that one is in Narnia, untouched. The unknown is tolerable because it is in the living room; one is not shielded from it. One may, if one can accept this invitation, begin to demand that cultures not be bombed for being different. Having grown up in a land of vast expanses of wilderness, Americans do not just need trees; we depend on the regenerative code of branches. Citizens of a democracy desire the twisted angles, the complexity of a forking, splitting, diverging, dividing intricacy. We need the mystery, the sheltering, the shade, the angles of light, and the dark, hardly perceptible patterns of leaf skeletons. We the people need the shade of the Emancipation Tree in Hampton, Virginia, to understand the hard, long walk toward freedom. We sing of trees. We have known trees.

In "A View of the Woods," written in 1964 by Flannery O'Connor, Mary Fortune Pitts, the granddaughter of Mr. Fortune and the daughter of Mr. Pitts, will not let her grandfather sell the land in front of the family house to a person who will build a gas station and convenience store there. The only thing separating Mary from complete absorption as the property of her father, who whips her, or her grandfather, who thinks she is 100 percent Fortune, is her view of the woods. When her grandfather sells the land and takes away the view of the woods, she fights back against his materialist vision. When she rejects him and his vision of the future, he smashes her head against a rock and kills her. In the final scene he dies of a stroke, but not before he recognizes the mystery of the view of the woods she loved.[1]

The view of the woods is the symbolic line between man-made, reified culture and mysterious unknowns, the cohesive space where the individual lives, the nonhegemonized space, the place where the democratic tension between communal equality and individual freedom resides. The view of the woods does not reflect back the civilized, man-made structures that demand an adherence to ersatz America. From Queequeg to Sethe, the dispossessed in American fiction have had the patterns of violence and biomorphic restoration traced on their skin. Powhatan's mantle, the Six Nations wampum belt, the Bakongo cosmogram, footprints, handprints, drumbeats, stitched and beaded cloths, the Emancipation Tree—all have found a way out of the labyrinth of denial. These are our national scripts of liberation. We should honor them by reading and listening, by making them visible. We should honor them by shouting their message from the rooftops.

NOTES

Introduction

1. See Baudrillard, *Simulacra and Simulation,* 6.
2. Ingold, *Making Anthropology,* 143.
3. Arpad, Botar, and Wünsche, *Biocentrism and Modernism,* 65.
4. Grigson, *Arts Today,* 71–109; Ingold, *Making Anthropology,* 143.
5. Austin, *Taking the Train,* 2–6, 172.
6. DIME139, "Freedom Train Essay."
7. Austin, *Taking the Train,* 2–6.
8. DIME139, "Freedom Train Essay." According to DIME139, several cars did make it into service.
9. Cull, Culbert, and Welch, "Freedom Train (1947–1949)," 138; Hogan, *Cross of Iron,* 430–31.
10. Hogan, *Cross of Iron,* 430–31.
11. Kimball and Emmet, *Complete Lyrics of Irving Berlin,* 406.
12. Hughes, "Freedom Train," 638.
13. "American Freedom Train Display Car #108 'Performing Arts.'"
14. "Story of the American Freedom Train."
15. Lepore, *Tea Party's Revolution.*
16. Haggard, "Here Comes the Freedom Train."
17. Waldman, "Nation Challenged."
18. Nancy Cott, in her 2007 talk "In the Rubble: Women's History as Bulwark," quotes Bab, one of the women in Germany who cleaned up Dresden after the Allied bombing had reduced it to rubble: "There weren't enough men to do this heavy work." Long lines of women on the rubble piles, hammering out stones and handing them down in buckets, were a common sight even years after the war ended. But these so-called *Trümmerfrauen,* or "rubble women," not only tended the wounded, buried the dead, and salvaged belongings; they also began the grueling task of rebuilding war-torn Germany by clearing the country's cities of an estimated 400 million cubic meters of debris, using only basic tools and, above all, their bare hands.
19. Rich, "Jungleland."
20. Benjamin, *Walter Benjamin: Selected Writings,* 541–42.

21. Ibid., 593.

22. Eng and Kazanjian, *Loss,* 23.

23. Ibid., 59–75.

24. Mandel, *Against the Unspeakable,* 39.

25. Rancière, *Politics of Aesthetics,* 3.

26. James Loewen's *Lies My Teacher Told Me,* Howard Zinn's *A People's History of the United States,* David Stannard's groundbreaking *American Holocaust,* and Ward Churchill's *A Little Matter of Genocide* tell unspoken truths and try to correct the wrongs of distortion and omission.

27. See, e.g., White, *Backcountry and the City;* and C. Rosenberg, *Violent Empire,* 228. By uncovering the letters and maps of the backcountry and rural native communities (White, *Backcountry and the City*); by focusing on the interactions between native and European communities (Preston, *Texture of Contact*); by looking at the daily lives of women, children, and families rather than those of great men; and by turning to alternative texts, including poetry, folk songs, cartoons, newspapers, journals, and household artifacts, scholars in many disciplines have resisted the facade of American history.

1. A Riddle to Unfold

1. On 20 July 2012 Congress posthumously awarded Brumidi the Congressional Gold Medal for his work on the *Apotheosis* and the *Frieze of American History.*

2. See Architect of the Capitol, "Apotheosis of Washington." Throughout the text I refer to text and images that appear on websites and not necessarily in books. Although these texts and images are often ephemeral, because this is a book that addresses public art and public access to art, the websites of tourist centers, national parks, museums, etc., are important historical documents.

3. There is much controversy about the politically correct term for the many different peoples who lived on the continent we now call America for thousands of years before the European explorers and colonialists arrived in the fifteenth, sixteenth, and seventeenth centuries. The term *Indian* was Columbus's misnomer for people he thought were from India; however, some American Indians prefer this term because it carries the whole history of contact in its long usage. I use all the following terms throughout the text: *Native Americans, native peoples, First Nations, First Peoples, indigenous peoples,* and *Indian.* Scholars should, whenever possible, call First Peoples by their accurate tribal names.

4. In her influential account *Art and Empire* Vivien Green Fryd provides an analysis of the art in the Capitol, particularly of the depiction of the subjugation of First Peoples and the erasure of African Americans, creating a decidedly Eurocentric vision of America.

5. Precita Eyes, a community mural arts organization based in San Francisco's Mission District, helped Marshall paint the murals for and with Kerry James Marshall. The organization considers painting murals out in public to be a performance as well as visual art.

6. Many video artists interviewed Marshall about his *Visible Means of Support* murals. The best videos are *Kerry James Marshall: Visible Means of Support,* accessed 16 January 2014, http://www.artbabble.org/video/sfmoma/kerry-james-marshall-visible-means-support, and the videos at http://www.sfmoma.org.

7. *Kerry James Marshall on His Use of Games and Puzzles.*

8. Rancière, *Politics of Aesthetics,* 3.

9. Mignolo, *Writing without Words,* 3.

10. Ibid., 78.

11. Deleuze and Guattari, *Anti-Oedipus,* 220.

12. Roland Barthes discusses these phenomena in both *Empire of Signs* and *The Responsibility of Forms.*

13. Barthes, *Responsibility of Forms,* 129.

14. Mignolo, *Writing without Words* and *Darker Side of the Renaissance;* Boone, *Their Way of Writing;* Anzaldúa, *Borderlands/La Frontera;* Salvaggio, *Hearing Sappho in New Orleans;* R. Thompson, *Flash of the Spirit.*

15. Lawrence, *Studies in Classic American Literature,* 55.

16. In *The Future of the Past,* C. Vann Woodward tries valiantly to suggest that America is no longer in any global or national estimation "young," reviewing the four-hundred-year-old obsession with this identity. Woodward argues that not only America's newness but also its innocence is an illusion: "Innocence was much more illusory than security as an endowment of national youth" (109).

17. In the past decade, Toni Morrison's famous call in *Playing in the Dark* for thoroughly interrogated whiteness in America has been answered by many theorists, including Elizabeth Hale, Mike Hill, Robert Jenson, David Roediger, and Ruth Frankenberg.

18. C. Woodward, "Myths of Innocence and Guilt."

19. Lawrence, *Studies in Classic American Literature,* 57, 58.

20. Chatterjee, *Nationalist Thought and the Colonial World.*

21. Johansen and Mann, *Encyclopedia of the Haudenosaunee,* 132.

22. Smithson, "Sedimentation of the Mind," 107.

23. Ibid., 108.

24. Bradford, *Of Plymouth Plantation,* 62.

25. *Oxford English Dictionary Online,* s.v. "savage," accessed 16 January 2014, http://www.oed.com/search?searchType=dictionary&q=savage&_searchBtn=Search.

26. American women's literature follows this trope on a timeline that includes Sarah Orne Jewett's *Country of the Pointed Firs* (1896); Willa Cather's *O Pioneers!* (1913); Zora Neale Hurston's *Their Eyes Were Watching God* (1937); Eudora Welty's *Curtain of Green* (1941); Flannery O'Connor's "A View of the Woods," in *Everything That Rises Must Converge* (1957); Ellen Glasgow's *Barren Ground* (1925); and Marilyn Robinson's *Housekeeping* (1980).

27. Welty, *Collected Stories,* 108.

28. Moser, *Clyde Connell,* 18, 35.

29. Ibid., 35.

30. Barthes, *Responsibility of Forms,* 102.

31. Morley, *Writing on the Wall,* 6.

32. Derrida, *Derrida Reader,* 212.

33. Deleuze, Guattari, and Massumi, *Thousand Plateaus,* 4–5.

2. Pocahontas Fever

1. P. Lee, "Fever." Eddie Cooley and Otis Blackwell wrote the original version of the song, and Peggy Lee wrote the additional "history" verses, including the one about "Capt'n Smith and Pocahontas."

2. Robert Tilton's *Pocahontas* is the best work on this subject and should be consulted in its entirety.

3. It is important when sifting through this vast outpouring to distinguish between journalistic and often fictional accounts, on the one hand, and archival history, on the other. Unfortunately, there is not as much separation between the two as one would like. It would be impossible to list all of the works on Pocahontas, but I include some of the most scholarly and several of the most popular here and in the bibliography.

4. Gleach, *Powhatan's World and Colonial Virginia.*

5. Until 2007, with the publication of Custalow and Daniel's *True Story of Pocahontas,* the entire story came from the colonists' perspective, with few words written or quoted from the living descendants of the Algonquian people.

6. Of the hundreds of significant articles and book-length manuscripts on Pocahontas, I have found particularly useful Appelbaum and Sweet, *Envisioning an English Empire;* Kelso, *Jamestown Rediscovery;* Lamay, *Did Pocahontas Save Captain John Smith?;* Tilton, *Pocahontas;* Townsend, *Pocahontas and the Powhatan Dilemma;* and Seed, "Houses, Gardens, and Fences."

7. Berger, "Indian Policy and the Imagined Indian Woman." According to Berger, "It was Pocahontas' marriage and conversion, however, which best fit the mythology of American nation building. In 1837, the federal government commissioned the . . . *Baptism of Pocahontas at Jamestown, Virginia, 1613,* in which she is separated from her naked compatriots, clothed in the pure white robes of civilization, and illuminated by the light of her conversion to Christianity. In 1840, the finished tableau was hung in the Rotunda of the U.S. Capitol where it remains today" (103).

8. "The bruite of this pretended marriage came soone to Powhatans knowledge, a thing acceptable to him, as appeared by his sudden content thereunto, who some ten daies after sent an olde uncle of hirs, named Opachisco, to give her as his deputy in the Church, and two of his sonnes to see the marriage solemnized, which was accordingly done about the fifth of Aprill and ever since we have had friendly commerce and trade, not onely with Powhatan himselfe, but also with his subjects round about us; so as now I see no reason why the Collonie should not thrive a pace." Hamor, *True Discourse of the Present State of Virginia,* 10.

9. Custalow and Daniel, *True Story of Pocahontas,* 63–65. Historians disagree on whether Thomas was born in or out of wedlock. The Mattaponi oral history challenges that Rolfe was actually the father.

10. A surprising feature of the Jamestown cultural experience is the docudramas with live actors and actresses. From Lew Landers's B movie *Captain John Smith and Pocahontas* (1953) to the docudrama *1607: A Nation Takes Root* to Malick's slick *The New World,* there have been at least eight film attempts to reenact the Pocahontas myth, as well as numerous

stage portrayals. Similar to the early medieval Quem quaeritis plays, which reenacted Mary Magdalene's discovery of Christ's having risen from the grave, these docudramas try to convince viewers of the veracity of the story by showing that real flesh-and-blood bodies can "become" the living legend.

11. Hogan, *Cross of Iron,* 430–31.

12. Colonial Williamsburg Foundation, *Jamestown, Williamsburg, Yorktown,* 127.

13. "New Buildings, Exhibitions, Programs Planned for Jamestown Settlement by 2007."

14. Eng and Kazanjian, *Loss,* 23. In *Archeology as a Tool of Civic Engagement,* Little and Shackel state that "in recent years, interpreters at several of these sites have begun to expand their presentations to include discussions of difficult and complex histories. . . . Where this history is included at heritage locations, it is often subsumed within an overarching national narrative of progress toward a pluralistic, democratic American present" (47).

15. There are sound political reasons why First Peoples activists shy away from the term *genocide.* They believe that for many years the idea that Europeans had killed all the native peoples allowed people to indulge in the fantasy that Indians were extinct. The Smithsonian wax Indian model had so thoroughly engrained in the American psyche the notion that all native peoples, especially those on the East Coast, had been killed off that the surviving native peoples have had to fight hard for visibility. Native peoples have been living in Virginia for twelve thousand years. The state of Virginia recognizes eight Indian tribes: the Mattaponi, Pamunkey, Chickahominy, Eastern Chickahominy, Monacan Indian Nation, Nansemond, Rappahannock, and Upper Mattaponi peoples. Native peoples have fought hard to eradicate the notion that the only real Indian is a dead Indian in articles like Jessup, "We Are Still Here," on the Pamunkey John Miles/Mills, the constant vigilance that cultural critics must pay to honor the living descendants of Indian nations, and their cultural, political, and ethical contributions to their communities. At the same time, the Cherokee historians Ward Churchill, in *A Little Matter of Genocide,* and David Stannard, in *American Holocaust,* have chronicled quite pointedly the genocide of native peoples. Recognizing the massive destruction of native life from the colonial invasion onwards and that direct descendants of the Powhatan people still live in the Virginia area do not need to be mutually exclusive.

16. "Advice of London Council for Virginia to the Colony," 1606, in Southern, *Jamestown Adventure,* 13.

17. On capturing native life in museums, see Huhndorf, *Going Native;* and Luke, *Museum Politics.*

18. John White was a colonist who accompanied Richard Grenville to North Carolina in 1585 and then was appointed governor for Sir Walter Raleigh's second expedition to Roanoke Island in 1587. While White was in England getting supplies, the colony and the colonists disappeared. His seventy-three extant drawings and watercolors are the first known depictions of the New World, and his pictures of Algonquian people were the most often cited for accuracy in the nineteenth century; Roark, *Artists of Colonial America,* 1–3.

19. Ruberton, *Archaeologies of Placemaking,* 222–33.

20. Pratt, *Imperial Eyes,* 1–13.

21. Alphen, *Caught by History.*

22. William Kelso's *Jamestown, the Buried Truth* details the progress of this archaeological dig, and the website Historic Jamestowne: Unearthing America's Birthplace (http://historicjamestowne.org) continues the story.

23. Colonial Williamsburg Foundation, *Jamestown, Williamsburg, Yorktown,* 89.

24. Philip Barbour suggests in *Pocahontas and Her World* that the Pocahontas story might have been edited out of Smith's 1608 *True Relation of Occurrences and Accidents of Note as Hath Hapned in Virginia* and that John Healey, the editor, may have written the replacement material for political reasons. Casey Levinson's article "John Smith and Pocahontas" supports this argument and offers new evidence to corroborate Barbour's conjecture: "That the style and tone of the prose in this section differs distinctly from that which precedes and follows it indeed supports Barbour's argument for editorial interference."

25. One piece of evidence that supports Smith's story is a letter he wrote in 1616 to introduce Pocahontas to the Queen. Unfortunately, many believed that Smith, an aging explorer who liked to make himself the heroic center of attention, only wrote his 1616 letter to the Queen (if he did it at all) to cash in on the stir caused by Pocahontas's trip to London. Since he did not mention Pocahontas saving his life again in any of his writings until his 1624 *General History,* debunkers thought that Smith was vying for the necessary honors to receive his coat of arms and become a gentleman.

26. Lindgren, "Virginia Needs Living Heros," 10.

27. A soldier, Juan Ortiz, who was lost on an expedition to Florida in 1528 and was found there by Hernando de Soto about twelve years later, told about being captured by Indians and saved "at the last second from burning at the stake by the chief's daughter who later came at peril of her life to warn him of her father's plot to kill him." P. Young, *American Fiction, American Myth,* 30. This incident predated John Smith's account by almost a century. A ballad known variously as the Lord Bateman ballad, the Lord Beichan ballad, or the Turkish Lady ballad (and numbered 53 in Francis James Child's collection of ballads) told this story and was widely circulated in Smith's time. That Smith's Pocahontas and the Child ballad 53 appeared at the beginning of a significant period of English colonizing is more than a coincidence.

28. J. Davis, *Travels of Four Years and a Half,* 299.

29. Ibid., 298–99.

30. Jennings, *Invasion of America,* 6. Jennings makes the most thorough argument to date for New World colonization as an extension of feudal and crusading ideologies (3–43). Perry Miller bases his thesis in *Errand in the Wilderness* on the fact that early English colonists were still living in a medieval world: "A great theme, vaster in conception than any of the writers could have framed by himself, elevates even the most ephemeral of these productions into a realm of universal meaning, and the philosophical student may, if he asks the right questions, find in them not only illumination of the pattern of mind out of which America emerged but a profound comment upon the transformation of western European culture from a medieval to a modern (though in 1625 still a bewildered) conception of life and society." He continues: "Examined in this perspective, the literature as it stands tells a strange story, to take it at face value—and to the extent that it is literature we may take it exactly that way—it exhibits a set of principles for guiding not a mercantile investment but a medieval pilgrimage" (100–101). Miller fails to examine whether the two possibilities could be one and the same, the medieval pilgrimage supporting the mercantile investment.

31. Barbour, "April 10, 1606."

32. It is important to remember here that Spain had spent the greater part of the sixteenth century under the Inquisition, whose main purpose was the expulsion of infidels, and that those infidels were in particular Jews, Moors, and Muslims. The ruling elite had devised tortures and procedures to force confessions of heresy from *conversos,* Jewish converts to Catholicism. Being able to prove that one was a good white Christian, not Jewish, not Moorish, ensured that one stayed alive in Spain.

33. "Instructions for the First Colonists," in Southern, *Jamestown Adventure,* 11.

34. Hakluyt, *Discourse Concerning Western Planting,* 71.

35. Gray, *Good Speed to Virginia,* 11.

36. More, *Utopia,* 52.

37. Francis Bacon, *New Atlantis,* in Bacon and Campanella, *"The New Atlantis" and "The City of the Sun,"* 17.

38. More, *Utopia,* 52.

39. See Grizzard, *Jamestown Colony;* Horn, *A Land as God Made It;* Kuppermann, *Jamestown Project;* Price, *Love and Hate in Jamestown;* and Rountree, *Pocahontas, Powhatan, Opechancanough.*

40. Allen, *Pocahontas,* 182.

41. Rountree, *Pocahontas, Powhatan, and Opechancanough,* 161.

42. Ibid., 162.

43. Ibid., 161–62.

44. Abrams, *Pilgrims and Pocahontas,* 20.

45. Southern, *Jamestown Adventure,* 235.

46. Custalow and Daniel, *True Story of Pocahontas,* 62.

47. Vansina, *Oral Tradition,* 9.

48. Thomas, *Skull Wars,* 97.

49. Berger, "Indian Policy and the Imagined Indian Woman," 152.

50. Ibid., 106.

51. Custalow and Daniel, *True Story of Pocahontas,* 63.

52. Billings, *Olde Dominion in the Seventeenth Century,* 35–40.

53. Hamor, *True Discourse of the Present State of Virginia,* 40.

54. Price, *Love and Hate in Jamestown,* 160.

55. Percy, *True Relation,* 290.

56. Lindgren, *Preserving the Old Dominion,* 98.

57. Hazard, *Indians and Pioneers,* 149.

58. Pryor, *Jamestown,* 309.

59. Grizzard, *Jamestown Colony,* 88.

60. Horn, *A Land As God Made It,* 187. When a person is broken upon a wheel, his or her body is literally woven into a wooden wheel, his limbs stretched over the spokes. The torturer turns the wheel until all the victim's bones are broken.

61. Ibid.

62. Southern, *Jamestown Adventure,* 196.

63. Price, *Love and Hate in Jamestown,* 161.

64. The best writing about the inappropriate use of the word *necessary* comes from Sir James MacKintosh, who wrote in 1824, while defending the Reverend John Smith, who

had stood up against the slave trade and was being tried for treason, "The only principle on which the law of England tolerates what is called 'martial law' is necessity. Its continuance requires precisely the same justification of necessity; and if it survives the necessity, in which alone it rests, for a single minute, it becomes instantly a mere exercise of lawless violence." MacKintosh, *Miscellaneous Works,* 540.

65. Randolph, *History of Virginia,* 58, emphasis added.

66. Ibid., 58n.

67. Abrams, *Pilgrims and Pocahontas,* 20.

68. Percy, *True Relation,* 272.

69. Southern, *Jamestown Adventure,* 188.

70. Ibid., 183.

71. G. Woodward, *Pocahontas,* 79.

72. Sharpe, *Jamestown.*

73. *Oxford English Dictionary Online,* s.v. "narrative," accessed 16 January 2014, http://www.oed.com/view/Entry/125146?rskey=nLa86n&result=1#eid.

74. The essays in Appelbaum and Sweet's *Envisioning an English Empire* reflect some of the most important theoretical work on the period.

75. Custalow and Daniel, *True Story of Pocahontas,* 21.

76. Allen writes about the white-feather women throughout the text of *Pocahontas,* referring to Pocahontas specifically on pages 31, 254, and 295. In order to accept Allen's analyses, we have to believe that she could know and interpret Pocahontas's sacred dreams. No scholar could possibly have knowledge of the inner workings of his or her subject's mind unless there was some written or oral record. While Allen's narrative of Pocahontas as spy, entrepreneur, and diplomat is certainly exciting, it is dubious because it is literally too coherent.

77. Gleach, *Powhatan's World and Colonial Virginia,* 114–15. Regarding the Gamwing, Gleach writes: "Such mimetic processes are typical of rituals constituting reality, where ritually created 'maps' can effect change, or maintain the status quo in the 'territory' of the universe" (114).

78. J. Smith, *Complete Works of Captain John Smith,* 2:151.

79. Ibid.

80. Gleach, *Powhatan's World and Colonial Virginia,* 119.

81. Ibid., 117.

82. There are many explanations for how Powhatan's mantle found its way into the collection of John Tradescant. Gregory Waselkov argues that Powhatan may have given Christopher Newport a mantle in one of the many ritualized ceremonies in which the English gave Powhatan military regalia and crowns and he gave them ceremonial robes like the mantle. According to Waselkov, "On March 5 of that year the Spanish ambassador, Don Pedro de Zúñiga, wrote to King Philip III that Powhatan 'has sent a gift to this king,' meaning James I of England. This unspecified gift could have included the mantle presented to Newport, which might then have found its way to the Tradescants." Waselkov, *Powhatan's Mantle,* 308.

83. Bialas, "Ambition and Distortion," 24.

84. Van Duzer, *Sea Monsters,* 73–76; Waldseemüller, *Universalis Cosmographia.*

85. Bialas, "Ambition and Distortion," 24.

86. Edson, *World Map, 1300–1492,* 202; Strathern, *The Artist, the Philosopher, and the Warrior,* 161.

87. Zettel, Review of *The New World.*

88. Smith, *Complete Works of John Smith,* 1:51.

89. Brando, "That Unfinished Oscar Speech."

3. George Washington's Head

1. See George Washington's Mount Vernon, accessed 16 January 2014, http://www.mountvernon.org/miscellaneous/news-press/backgrounders/donald-w-reynolds-education-center-galleries.

2. George Washington to Francis Hopkinson, 16 May 1785, in Washington, *Writings of George Washington, Pt. III* (Sparks), 106.

3. Howard, *Painter's Chair,* 99.

4. Cavarero, *Stately Bodies,* 109.

5. The painting was to be the first in a series by Grant Wood depicting American myths. The second was to be titled *John Smith Rescuing Pocahontas.* Garwood, *Artist in Iowa,* 229.

6. "Parson Weems' Fable."

7. Safire, *Lend Me Your Ears,* 185.

8. Weems, *Life of Washington,* 10.

9. See Hageneder, *Meaning of Trees,* 66. In Celtic mythology, hazel trees are associated with enchantment and poetic inspiration.

10. Grimm and Grimm, *Grimm's Complete Fairy Tales,* 81–83.

11. Tatar, *Off with Their Heads!,* 120–39.

12. Grimm and Grimm, *Grimm's Complete Fairy Tales,* 81–83.

13. Risjord, *Jefferson's America,* 318.

14. See the detailed description of the scientific undertaking to create a younger George Washington head in McClafferty, *Many Faces of George Washington.*

15. See George Washington's Mount Vernon.

16. Longmore, *Invention of George Washington,* 102–8; Banta, *Ohio,* 270; Rasmussen and Tilton, *George Washington,* 46, 100.

17. "During George's boyhood, a group of enterprising gentlemen emerged as the dominant force in the economy and politics of the upper Potomac River Valley. They spearheaded British penetration of the Ohio Valley, undertaking to direct the Indian fur trade, land speculation, and white settlement of the interior. To make this imperial dream a reality, they were ready for Britain to make war on both the Indians and the French. . . . One Scheme of this group was a speculative venture called the Ohio Company, a plan to take up half a million acres in the Ohio Valley and settle them with farm families. Lawrence Washington served as president of the company." Longmore, *Invention of George Washington,* 13.

18. Mann, *George Washington's War on Native America,* 34.

19. See Burns and Dunn, *George Washington,* 10.

20. Katheder, *Baylors of Newmarket.*

21. Sulgrave Manor, accessed 16 January 2014, http://www.sulgravemanor.org.uk/pages/57/john.asp.

22. Bragdon, *Ethnographic Overview and Assessment,* 84–85.

23. Thane, *Mount Vernon Is Ours.* In this history of the preservation of Mount Vernon, Thane writes only about servants, never slaves.

24. Casper, *Sarah Johnson's Mount Vernon,* 6–9. Most of the slaves at Mount Vernon belonged to Washington descendants and had not lived on the estate during Washington's lifetime.

25. Thane, *Mount Vernon Is Ours,* 16.

26. Since the Mount Vernon Ladies' Association opened its doors to visitors in 1860, more than 80 million people have toured the house, and at least a million still visit each year. With an entrance ticket priced at fifteen dollars, the association makes $15 million a year on ticket sales, and then there are the numerous donations, large corporate and endowed gifts, and sales of gift items, which are now a major industry in themselves.

27. Vlach, *Planter's Prospect,* 31.

28. Ibid., 18.

29. See http://www.mountvernon.org/.

30. M. Thompson, "Only Unavoidable Subject of Regret." See also by Thompson "Religious Practice in the Slave Quarters at Mount Vernon," "Different People, Different Stories," and "And Procure for Themselves a Few Amenities." Thompson is presently at work on a book about slavery at Mount Vernon.

31. Parkinson, *Tour in America,* 418–20.

32. Hirschfeld, *George Washington and Slavery,* 62–63.

33. M. Thompson, "Only Unavoidable Subject of Regret."

34. Niemcewicz, *Under Their Vine and Fig Tree,* 100–101, as quoted in M. Thompson, "Lives of Enslaved Workers."

35. "Declaration of Independence: A History."

36. See the evidence concerning Venus, George Washington, and West Ford in Wiencek, *Imperfect God.*

37. Schimmel, *Empire of the Great Mughals,* 176; Condra, *Greenwood Encyclopedia of Clothing,* 210; Cohn, *Colonialism and Its Forms of Knowledge,* 116.

38. Accounts of Lee's life can be found in the two most thorough accounts of George Washington and slavery—Henry Wiencek's *An Imperfect God* and Fritz Hirschfeld's *George Washington and Slavery*—which, however, do not discuss the Muslim heritage of any of Washington's slaves. Mary V. Thompson surmises, based on her study of the names, body markings, and clothing of Washington's slaves, that several were of Hausa origin, from "what is now northwestern Nigeria and southern Niger." Thompson, "Islam at Mount Vernon."

39. Diouf, *Servants of Allah,* 2.

40. M. Thompson, "Islam at Mount Vernon," note v.

41. Ibid., notes vi and vii.

42. Putzi, *Identifying Marks,* 99–153 passim.

43. M. Thompson, "Islam at Mount Vernon."

44. Ibid.

45. This does not mean that Washington refrained from going after his runaway slaves.

"It is sad indeed to read of the clandestine and circumspect stratagems that Washington employed to retrieve these wayward slaves," writes Hirschfeld in *George Washington and Slavery*, 5–6.

46. Wiencek, *Imperfect God*, 16–17.

47. Ibid., 310.

48. Washington wrote to John Mercer on 9 September 1786: "I never mean (unless some particular circumstance should compel me to it) to possess another slave by purchase; it being among my first wishes to see some plan adopted, by which slavery in this country may be abolished by slow, sure, and imperceptible degrees." Higginbotham, *George Washington Reconsidered*, 121.

49. Washington, "Last Will and Testament," 1023.

50. Ibid., 1023–37.

51. Burns and Dunn, *George Washington*, 10.

52. Preston, *Texture of Contact*, 219, 218 (quotation).

53. Lengel, *General George Washington*, 38.

54. "George Washington is believed to have been heir to the Seneca title of Caunotaucarius, or Conotocarious, meaning 'Destroyer of Villages,' 'Town Devourer' or 'Town Taker,' a name which was reportedly first given to his great-grandfather, John Washington (1632–1677) by the Susquehannocks, an Iroquoian people. According to George Washington, Tanaghrisson gave him the appellation Conotocarious sometime during November and December 1753. Although apparently receiving his Seneca name by descent, Washington also earned the grim cognomen, Destroyer of Villages, during the War of Independence." Washington, *George Washington Remembers*, 316.

55. Washington, *Writings of George Washington*, vol. 6 (Sparks), 264.

56. Mann, *George Washington's War on Native America*, 47.

57. Cook, *Journals of the Military Expedition of Major General John Sullivan*, 58.

58. W. Lee, *Barbarians and Brothers*, 242.

59. Mann, *George Washington's War on Native America*, 47.

60. Ibid.

61. Gridley, *Centennial Celebration of General Sullivan's Campaign*. This document of the proceedings of the 1879 celebration includes a poem by the Reverend Dwight Williams glorifying Sullivan's actions: "Then Washington with martial ardor / Called Sullivan in haste to go / And cross the Indians forest border / And lay his fields and orchards low / Till charging Brant in ambuscade / He fled from Newtown's fray / And bold Cornplanter swiftly hasted / To warn his villagers of scath / And tell of wigwams burned and wasted / Along the victor's blazing path" (161).

62. Cook, *Journals of the Military Expedition of Major General John Sullivan*, 9.

63. Churchill, *Little Matter of Genocide*, 185.

64. Ibid., 180.

65. "Journal of Sargent Thomas Roberts," in Cook, *Journals of the Military Expedition of Major General John Sullivan*, 244.

66. "Major General Sullivan's Official Report," in Cook, *Journals of the Military Expedition of Major General John Sullivan*, 303.

67. "Journal of Major Jeremiah Fog," in ibid., 97.

68. *Oxford English Dictionary Online,* s.v. "extirpate," accessed 16 January 2014, http://www.oed.com/search?searchType=dictionary&q=extirpate&_searchBtn=Search.

69. Amory, *Military Services and Public Life of Major-General John Sullivan,* 138.

70. "Sullivan-Clinton Interactive Map."

71. See Kalter, *Benjamin Franklin, Pennsylvania, and the First Nations;* and Preston, *Texture of Contact.*

72. See Johansen, *Native America Political Systems;* and Johansen, *Debating Democracy.* The best synopsis of this debate and refutation of the anti-influence arguments can be found in Grinde and Johansen, "Sauce for the Goose."

73. Anderson, *Crucible of War,* 82–85.

74. Kalter, *Benjamin Franklin, Pennsylvania, and the First Nations,* 118–19.

75. Olson, *Benjamin Franklin's Vision of American Community,* 18.

76. Others, including Francis Jennings in *Invasion of America,* argue that one cannot draw an ahistorical line tracing nation building to documents in the 1740s. That argument would hold if we were indeed tracing nation building, but what we are tracing instead is the building of a republic, a democracy, and a confederation of united states.

77. Colden, *History of the Five Indian Nations of Canada.*

78. Johansen and Mann, *Encyclopedia of the Haudenosaunee,* 274.

79. Kalter, *Benjamin Franklin, Pennsylvania, and the First Nations,* 5.

80. Mann, "Lynx in Time."

81. Kalter, *Benjamin Franklin, Pennsylvania, and the First Nations,* 5.

82. Johansen and Mann, *Encyclopedia of the Haudenosaunee,* 136.

83. Hauptman and Wherry, *Pequots in Southern New England.*

84. Muller, "Two Mystery Belts of Grand River," 129.

85. Kalter, *Benjamin Franklin,* 50–374 passim.

86. Palmer, *North American Indians,* 88, 92, 96.

87. John Heckewelder as quoted in Johansen and Mann, *Encyclopedia of the Haudenosaunee,* 327.

88. Beauchamp, *Wampum and Shell Articles,* 327–435 passim; Butterworth, *Wampum Belt.*

89. William Jacob Heller, in *Historic Easton from the Window of a Trolley Car,* 59, describes an interaction between Tokahayo, Teedyuscung, and British negotiators in which Tokahayo commended Teedyuscung for the way he had spoken. For Tokahayo, speaking from the heart meant speaking directly from his body and soul, not from a text.

90. Johansen and Mann, *Encyclopedia of the Haudenosaunee,* 132.

91. Phillips, *Museum Pieces,* 126.

92. Johansen and Ritzker, *Encyclopedia of American Indian History,* 382.

93. Ibid., 111–31 passim.

4. "Blood Marked Every Step"

1. U.S. Bureau of the Census, *Century of Population Growth,* 133 and passim; Clark, *American Economy,* 460–61.

2. The transatlantic slave trade peaked between 1720 and 1780. In communities that established a lucrative cash crop—such as the farmers who grew rice on the sea islands of South Carolina and Georgia in the eighteenth century—enslaved Africans outnumbered whites from as early as the 1730s. The transatlantic slave trade continued long after it was banned in 1807 and 1808. And the interstate slave trade expanded dramatically after 1800 and continued unabated until 1865. Illegal trafficking occurred throughout. The invention of the cotton gin in 1794 increased the profitability of cotton production, and the demand for slaves could not be filled in the cotton states of the Deep South. In Alabama the slave population increased from 41,879 in 1820 to 435,080 in 1860, both through birth and the interstate slave trade. While the number of slaves who survived the Middle Passage and were actually brought to the United States is estimated at 305,326 (a much contested number), by the time the Civil War was over there were 4 million people of African descent in America. U.S. Bureau of the Census, *Century of Population Growth,* 133 and passim.

3. In addition to Rankin's *Letters on American Slavery,* see Douglass, *Narrative of the Life of Frederick Douglass;* and Garrison's newspaper the *Liberator,* published from 1831 to 1865, http://www.theliberatorfiles.com. Garrison founded the New England Anti-Slavery Society in 1833 and the American Anti-Slavery Society in 1834.

4. See, e.g., Aptheker, *American Negro Slave Revolts;* Borrit, Hancock, and Berlin, *Slavery, Resistance, Freedom;* Higginson, *Black Rebellion;* Frey, *Water from the Rock;* Hoffer, *Cry Liberty;* Price and Price, *Maroon Societies;* Rasmussen, *American Uprising;* Rodriquez, *Slavery and Resistance;* Rucker, *River Flows On;* and M. Smith, *Stono.*

5. See, e.g., Guelzo, *Lincoln's Emancipation Proclamation;* Holzer, Medford, and Williams, *Emancipation Proclamation;* Carnahan, *Act of Justice;* Lincoln, *Lincoln on Race and Slavery;* Foner, *Fiery Trial;* Holzer, Simon, and Vogel, *Lincoln Revisited;* Foner, "Lincoln and Colonization"; Magness and Pages, *Colonization after Emancipation;* and Goldfield, *America Aflame.*

6. Howard Pollack, in his biography *Aaron Copland,* 358, lists the full range of cultural and artistic tributes to Lincoln, from poems to symphonies.

7. Fred Child, "Reflections on Aaron Copland's 'Lincoln's Portrait.'"

8. Watson, *Prepare for Saints,* 37–55 and 281–96 passim.

9. From Lincoln, "Annual Message to Congress," 39.

10. From Lincoln-Douglas debate, 15 October 1858, in Lincoln and Douglas, *Complete Lincoln-Douglass Debates of 1858,* 322.

11. From fragment tentatively dated August 1858, in *Lincoln on Lincoln,* 99.

12. Crist, *Music for the Common Man,* 157–58.

13. In this chapter and elsewhere, I use the words *African, Africa, Africanized,* and even *Africanisms* with a complete awareness that there is really no such unified concept as Africa but a large continent with hundreds of cultures, geographic differences, languages, and nation-states.

14. Lincoln, "Speech at New Haven, Connecticut," 137.

15. Crist, *Music for the Common Man,* 159.

16. Ibid.

17. Holloway, *Africanisms in American Culture,* 390; Conway, *African Banjo Echoes in Appalachia,* 60.

18. From Lincoln, "Gettysburg Address," 536.

19. Lincoln, "Address before the Young Men's Lyceum of Springfield, Illinois," 112.

20. Lincoln, *Lincoln on Race and Slavery,* xxv, 321.

21. Lincoln to Miss Mary Speed, 27 September 1841, in *Lincoln on Race and Slavery,* 10.

22. Jefferson, *Notes on the State of Virginia,* 178–80.

23. Lincoln, "Eulogy on Henry Clay and Outline for Speech to the Colonization Society," in *Lincoln on Race and Slavery,* 31. Collected Works, Volume 2:127–29, 130–32, 298–99, 102, 110.

24. See Magness and Pages, *Colonization after Emancipation.*

25. See Guelzo, *Lincoln's Emancipation Proclamation.*

26. For a revisionist appraisal, see DiLorenzo, *Real Lincoln.*

27. For a reading of this image, see the first two chapters of M. Wood, *Horrible Gift of Freedom.*

28. Frederick Douglass, "Oration in Memory Of Abraham Lincoln," delivered at the unveiling of the Freedmen's Monument, 14 April 1876, in *Frederick Douglass: Selected Speeches and Writings,* 624.

29. Free people of color wrote autobiographies, biographies, novels, songs, poems, treatises, and speeches in refined English, French, and Spanish. These educated African American scholars and writers documented and protested the treatment of enslaved people, and their writings often achieved international fame. The best-known of these activists were, of course, Frederick Douglass and Sojourner Truth, but there were hundreds of others, including William Wells Brown, Jupiter Hammon, Phillis Wheatley, Victor Séjour, Harriet E. Wilson, and Solomon Northup. There would not have been abolition or emancipation without African American intellectuals and their rhetorical molding of public opinion.

30. Sachsman, Rushing, and Morris, *Memory and Myth,* 8.

31. Maker, "What Might Have Been in Litchfield."

32. "Litchfield during the Colonial Revival."

33. Loewen, *Lies across America,* 292.

34. See Litchfield Historical Society, accessed 16 January 2014, http://www.litchfieldhistoricalsociety.org/lawschool/index.php.

35. Mason, "Clear Look at the Beecher House."

36. Stowe, *Uncle Tom's Cabin,* 79.

37. Abby Kelley Foster, quoted in Sterling, *Ahead of Her Time,* 268.

38. Hawthorne, *Scarlet Letter,* 4.

39. Ibid., 5.

40. Ibid., 15.

41. Ibid., 50.

42. Ibid., 51.

43. Ibid., 53.

44. Ibid., 54.

45. Ibid.

46. Doyle, "'A' for Atlantic."

47. Ibid.

48. Hawthorne, *Scarlet Letter,* 54.

49. Hawthorne, "Chiefly about War Matters," 414.

50. Hawthorne to William D. Ticknor, 17 February 1854, in *Letters of Hawthorne to William D. Ticknor,* 29.

51. Hawthorne, "Chiefly about War Matters," 414.

52. Emily Dickinson, "No Rack can torture me," poem 384, in *Poems of Emily Dickinson,* 635.

53. See V. Jackson, *Dickinson's Misery;* Mitchell, *Measure of Possibility;* and Werner, *Emily Dickinson's Open Folios.*

54. Sánchez-Eppler, *Touching Liberty,* 107.

55. Fagan, "Emily Dickinson's Unutterable Word," 70.

56. Farr, *Passion of Emily Dickinson,* 326.

57. Wise, "12 Poems of Emily Dickinson."

58. Bervin, "Dickinson Fascicles."

59. Ibid.

60. "Leslie Dill's New Opera Divide Light."

5. "In the Solitude of My Spirit"

1. Johnson, *Soul by Soul;* Feagin, *Racist America.*

2. Berlin et al., *Freedom,* 111.

3. M. Wood, *Horrible Gift of Freedom,* 2.

4. Hahn, Miller, and Rowland, *Freedom.*

5. Berlin, "Who Freed the Slaves?," 111–12. See also Berlin, *Black Military Experience;* Berlin, *Generations of Captivity;* Berlin, *Many Thousands Gone;* Berlin et al., *Freedom;* Berlin and Morgan, *Cultivation and Culture*; and Berlin and Rowland, *Families and Freedom.*

6. See Harding, *There Is a River;* Frey, *Water from the Rock;* Johnson, *Soul by Soul;* Rucker, *River Flows On;* and Borrit, Hancock, and Berlin, *Slavery, Resistance, Freedom.*

7. Harding, *There Is a River,* 40.

8. Frey, "Resistance and Revolts," 2.

9. Jones, *African Americans in Florida,* 15, 143, 172.

10. Harding, *There Is a River,* 41.

11. Walker, *Meridian,* 27–29.

12. Sidbury, *Becoming African in America.*

13. Osburn, "Along the Side of the Road"; Hall, "African Religious Retentions in Florida."

14. Vlach, *Back of the Big House.*

15. P. Wood, *Black Majority:* "In contrast to Europeans, Negroes from the West Coast of African were widely familiar with rice planting. Ancient speakers of a proto-Bantu language in the sub-Sahara region are known to have cultivated the crop. An indigenous variety *(Oryza glaberrima)* was a staple in the western rain-forest regions long before Portuguese and French navigators introduced Asian and American varieties of *O. sativa* in the 1500s" (59); "Indigo and cotton grow in wild exuberance almost everywhere, without culture, and the women collect such quantities as they consider requisite for their families, which they prepare and spin upon a distaff; the thread is woven, by an apparatus of great

simplicity, into fillets, or pieces from six to nine inches broad, which are sewed together to any width, required for use. The indigo, in its indigenous state, and a variety of other plants, colour these cloths, an ell of which will serve as a dress for a Negro of the lower class" (119n).

16. Tobin and Dobard, *Hidden in Plain View;* Fry, *Stitched from the Soul;* Brackman, *Facts and Fabrications.*

17. Obi, *Fighting for Honor.*

18. Bower, *African American Foodways;* Eisnach and Covey, *What the Slaves Ate.*

19. White and White, *Sounds of Slavery;* Floyd, *Power of Black Music.*

20. Gottschild, *Digging.*

21. Holloway, *Africanisms in American Culture,* 240.

22. Mufwene, *Africanisms in Afro-American Language Varieties.*

23. Carney and Rosomof, *In the Shadow of Slavery.*

24. Studies of Africanisms in the culture of enslaved peoples face the difficult task of piecing together a story from the fragments of material history. For this reason, there have been mistakes, miscalculations, and contentious debates about authenticity (particularly in reference to the codes in slave quilts and in the ideograms found on grave markers). It will be many years before historians and anthropologists are able to sift through all the pieces and conclude what is and what is not a remnant of African culture. But scholars whose studies are cited in notes 13–23 above have accumulated enough irrefutable evidence of material and spiritual culture in the Americas that traveled from Senegambia, West Central Africa, Bight of Biafra, and the Gold Coast to argue for definite influence.

25. Brown, "Body Work in the Antebellum United States," 219, 233, 234.

26. Stuckey, *Slave Culture;* Stuckey, *Going through the Storm.*

27. Todd, *Carolina Clay,* 84.

28. Ibid., 228.

29. Livingston, "Routes of Freedom."

30. Tomblin, *Bluejackets and Contrabands,* 31–62.

31. Ibid.

32. Barbara Fields, in "Was it Not Real?," chapter 6 of episode 9, "The Better Angels of Our Nature (1865)," in Burns, *Civil War.*

33. Downs, *Sick from Freedom,* 18–41 and 95–119 passim; Du Bois, *Black Reconstruction in America,* 648.

34. Since Du Bois, scholars in the disciplines of anthropology, history, and cultural studies have explored the many contributions of African Americans to American history and culture. Carter Woodson's *Education of the Negro prior to 1861* (1915), *History of the Negro Church* (1921), *Negro in Our History* (1922), and *African Heroes and Heroines* (1939) reveal the enormous contributions and complexities of African American history in the United States. Since Melville J. Herskovits argued in *The Myth of the Negro Past* (1941) that African cultural forms had survived and could be found in contemporary African American cultures, scholars have explored the complex details of this cultural preservation. The following works provide nuanced accounts of individual Bantu, Fanti-Ashanti, and Yoruba religious contributions: Blassingame, *Slave Community;* Connor, *Imagining Grace;* Cornelius, *Slave Missions;* Cornelius, *"When I Can Read My Title Clear";* D. Davis, *In the Image*

of God; Hoffer, *Sensory Worlds in Early America;* Hopkins, *Cut Loose Your Stammerin Tongue;* Hopkins, *Religion and Black Theology;* Raboteau, *Slave Religion: The "Invisible Institution" in the Antebellum South.* We are still learning and will be asking difficult questions for years concerning what made certain African practices survive and others die out, what power specific rituals had in individual enslaved communities, and the complexities of cultural preservation and creolization throughout the diasporic incarceration. But we have moved beyond questioning whether African cultural forms survived and influenced American culture.

35. Harding, *There Is a River,* 38.

36. I am indebted to Ryan Woodward for bringing these fingerprints to my attention.

37. See the University of Virginia online collection of images "Atlantic Slave Trade and Slave Life in the Americas," accessed 16 January 2014, http://hitchcock.itc.virginia.edu/, image reference schwein–420. The source for the photograph is given as Schweinfurth, *Heart of Africa,* vol. 2, facing p. 420. The description reads: "Head and face of unnamed captured East African woman; shows remnant of coffle rope around her neck." "Married women among the Babuckur," according to Schweinfurth, "pierce the rims of their ears and both their lips, and insert bits of grass stalk about an inch long in the holes. . . . The portrait . . . is that of a Babuckur slave bound by a leather rope" (2:258, 419). This image was reproduced in Knox, *Boy Travellers on the Congo,* 217, which is a condensation of Stanley, *Through the Dark Continent.*

38. M. Thompson, "Islam at Mount Vernon"; R. Thompson, *Flash of the Spirit.*

39. Stuckey, *African Culture and Melville's Art,* 30. See also Putzi, *Identifying Marks;* and Ezekwueche, "Afro Beauty."

40. Robert Farris Thompson devotes an entire chapter of his book *Flash of the Spirit* to *nsibidi* "alphabets," making the idea of visceral graphism a prominent element of cultural retention.

41. R. Thompson, *Flash of the Spirit,* 110, 121; Stuckey, *Slave Culture,* 3–97.

42. Ferguson, "Cross is a Magic Sign," quotation from 117. See also MacGaffey and Janzen, "Nkisi Figures of the BaKongo"; and R. Thompson, *Flash of the Spirit,* 108–31.

43. Ferguson, *Uncommon Ground,* 115.

44. See http://www.ohio.edu/infocus/hushharbors/.

45. Maffly-Kipp, "African American Christianity, Pt. II: To the Civil War."

46. Talty, *Mulatto America,* 45.

47. Cornelius, *Slave Missions,* 9.

48. Ibid.

49. Rosenbaum, *Shout Because You're Free.*

50. "McIntosh County Shouters."

51. Rosenbaum, *Shout Because You're Free,* 19, 31, 45, 127–30.

52. Ibid., 127–30.

53. Baker-Fletcher, "Erotic in Contemporary Black Women's Writing," 205.

54. Bostic, "Flesh that Dances," 286.

55. Cornelius, *Slave Missions,* 9.

56. In *The Shawl,* Cynthia Ozick describes a little girl in a concentration camp who wanders out into the square in front of the Nazi guards as a girl toddling on "pencil legs"

(10): "Again! Magda was wavering in the perilous sunlight of the arena, scribbling on such pitiful little bent shins" (8). The word *scribbling* firmly inscribes Magda as the author of her destiny. Her body writes the script that will define her. She is the pencil, the instrument of inscription. Ozick tells us that Magda lived to walk. When she walks into the square in front of the Nazi guards, away from her mother's arms, it is her moment of freedom. It is also her moment of death, for the guards grab her and throw her against the electric fence.

57. See Rankin, *Letters on American Slavery,* 63–64.

58. Rath, "Drums and Power," 110.

59. Ibid. Rath cites John Thorton's "Art of War in Angola."

60. Rath, "Drums and Power," 107–8.

61. McCord and Cooper, *Statutes at Large of South Carolina,* 410.

62. Walton, *Music, Black and White and Blues,* 21–23.

63. In *Jazz Dance* the historians Marshall and Jean Stearns identified the six basic characteristics of African dance: "1) danced on naked earth with bare feet, often flat-footed, favoring gliding, dragging or shuffling steps, 2) frequently performed from a crouch, knees flexed and body bent at the waist like a hunter crouched for the kill, 3) imitates animals in realistic detail, 4) places great importance upon improvisation, allowing freedom of individual expression, 5) centrifugal, exploding outward from the hips, and 6) performed to a propulsive rhythm, which gives it a 'swinging' quality" (14).

64. Finn, *Bluesman,* 87.

65. R. Thompson, *Flash of the Spirit,* xiii.

66. M. Wood, "Supine in Perpetuity: The *Description* of the *Brookes* in 2007," chap. 5 in Wood, *Horrible Gift of Freedom.*

67. See http://www.civilwar.org/education/history/bound-for-freedoms-light/bound-for-freedoms-light.html.

68. Collins, "Scourged Back," 44.

69. Morrison, *Beloved,* 24.

70. Ibid., 25.

71. Ibid., 26.

Epilogue

1. O'Connor, *Everything That Rises Must Converge,* 70.

BIBLIOGRAPHY

Abrams, Ann Uhry. *The Pilgrims and Pocahontas: Rival Myths of American Origins.* Boulder, CO: Westview, 1999.

Allen, Paula Gunn. *Pocahontas: Medicine Woman, Spy, Entrepreneur, Diplomat.* San Francisco: Harper, 2004.

Alphen, Ernst van. *Caught by History: Holocaust Effects in Contemporary Art, Literature, and Theory.* Palo Alto, CA: Stanford University Press, 1998.

Alter, Ethan. "The New World." *New York Film Critic,* 11 February 2006.

"American Freedom Train Display Car #108 'Performing Arts.'" American Freedom Train. Accessed 16 January 2014. http://www.freedomtrain.org/american-freedom-train-m-k line-o-gauge-trains-lineup.htm.

"American Officer Letter to His Fiancée Before His Death in Battle." September 1779. Sullivan/Clinton Campaign Then and Now. http://www.sullivanclinton.com/archives/000107.php.

Amory, Thomas Coffin. *The Military Services and Public Life of Major-General John Sullivan of the American Revolutionary Army.*Boston: Wiggin & Lunt, 1868.

Anderson, Fred. *Crucible of War: The Seven Years' War and the Fate of Empire in British North America, 1754–1766.* New York: Vintage, 2001.

Anzaldúa, Gloria. *Borderlands/La Frontera: The New Mestiza.* San Francisco: Aunt Lute Books, 2007.

Appelbaum, Robert, and John Wood Sweet, eds. *Envisioning an English Empire: Jamestown and the Making of the North Atlantic World.* Philadelphia: University of Pennsylvania Press, 2005.

Aptheker, Herbert. *American Negro Slave Revolts.* 5th ed. New York: International, 1983.

Architect of the Capitol. "The Apotheosis of Washington." Accessed 16 January 2014. http://www.aoc.gov/capitol-hill/murals/apotheosis-washington.

Arpad, Oliver, Istvan Botar, and Isabel Wünsche, eds. *Biocentrism and Modernism.* London: Ashgate, 2011.

Austin, Joe. *Taking the Train: How Graffiti Art Became an Urban Crisis in New York City.* New York: Columbia University Press, 2002.

Avatar. Directed by James Cameron. Los Angeles: Twentieth Century Fox, 2009.

Bacon, Francis, and Tomasso Campanella. *"The New Atlantis" and "The City of the Sun": Two Classic Utopias.* Mineola, NY: Dover, 2003.

Baker, William Spohn. *Early Sketches of George Washington.* New York: J. B. Lippincott, 1894.

Baker-Fletcher, Karen. "The Erotic in Contemporary Black Women's Writing." In *Loving the Body: Black Religious Studies and the Erotic,* edited by Anthony B. Pinn and Dwight N. Hopkins. Minneapolis: Fortress, 2010.

Banta, R. E. *The Ohio.* 1949. Reprint, Lexington: University Press of Kentucky, 1998.

Barbour, Philip L. "April 10, 1606: James I Grants the First Charter to the Virginia Company." In Smith, *Complete Works of Captain John Smith,* 1:24–34.

———. *The Jamestown Voyages under the First Charter, 1606–1609.* 2 vols. Cambridge: Cambridge University Press, 1969.

———. *Pocahontas and Her World: A Chronicle of America's First Settlement in which is Related the Story of the Indians and the Englishmen, Particularly Captain John Smith, Captain Samuel Argall, and Master John Rolfe.* Boston: Houghton Mifflin, 1970.

Barthes, Roland. *Empire of Signs.* New York: Hill & Wang, 1983.

———. *The Responsibility of Forms: Critical Essays on Music, Art, and Representation.* Berkeley: University of California Press, 1991.

Baudrillard, Jean. *Simulacra and Simulation.* Ann Arbor: University of Michigan Press, 1995.

Beasts of the Southern Wild. Directed by Behn Zeitlin. New Orleans: Court 13 Films, 2012.

Beauchamp, William Martin. *A History of the New York Iroquois, Now Commonly Called the Six Nations.* Bulletin of the New York State Museum No 78. Albany: University of the State of New York, 1905.

———. *Wampum and Shell Articles Used by the New York Indians.* Bulletin of the New York State Museum No. 41, vol. 8. Albany: University of the State of New York, 1901.

Benjamin, Walter. *Walter Benjamin: Selected Writings, Volume 2, Part 2, 1931–1934.* Translated by Rodney Livingstone. Edited by Gary Smith, Michael W. Jennings, and Howard Eiland. Cambridge, MA: Harvard University Press, 2005.

Berger, Bethany. "Indian Policy and the Imagined Indian Woman." *Kansas Journal of Law and Public Policy* 14 (Fall 2004).

Berlin, Ira. *The Black Military Experience.* Cambridge: Cambridge University Press, 1985.

———. *Generations of Captivity: A History of African American Slaves.* Cambridge, MA: Harvard University Press, 2003.

———. *Many Thousands Gone: The First Two Centuries of Slavery in North America.* Cambridge, MA: Harvard University Press, 1998.

———. "Who Freed the Slaves? Emancipation and Its Meaning." In *Union and Emancipation: Essays on Politics and Race in the Civil War Era,* edited by David Blight and Brooks D. Simpson. Kent, OH: Kent State University Press, 1997.

Berlin, Ira, Barbara J. Fields, Thavolia Glymph, Joseph P. Reidy, and Leslie S. Rowland, eds. *Freedom: A Documentary History of Emancipation Selected from the Holdings of the National Archives of the United States.* Cambridge: Cambridge University Press, 1986.

Berlin, Ira, and Philip D. Morgan, eds. *Cultivation and Culture: Labor and the Shaping of Slave Life in the Americas.* Charlottesville: University of Virginia Press, 1993.

Berlin, Ira, and Leslie Rowland, eds. *Families and Freedom: A Documentary History of African-American Kinship in the Civil War Era.* New York: New Press, 1998.

Bervin, Jen. "The Dickinson Fascicles." Accessed 16 January 2014. http://jenbervin.com/html/dickinson.html.

Bialas, Zbigniew. "Ambition and Distortion: An Ontological Dimension in Colonial Cartography." In *Borderlands,* edited by M. Reif-Hulser. Amsterdam: Rodopi, 1999.

Billings, Warren M., ed. *The Olde Dominion in the Seventeenth Century: A Documentary History of Virginia, 1606–1700.* Chapel Hill: University of North Carolina Press, 2007.

Blassingame, John. *The Slave Community: Plantation Life in the Antebellum South.* Oxford: Oxford University Press, 1979.

Boone, Elizabeth. *Their Way of Writing: Scripts, Signs, and Pictographies in Pre-Columbian America.* Washington, DC: Dumbarton Oaks Research Library and Collection, 2011.

Borrit, G. S., Scott Hancock, and Ira Berlin. *Slavery, Resistance, Freedom.* Oxford: Oxford University Press, 2007.

Bostic, Joy R. "'Flesh that Dances': A Theology of Sexuality and the Spirit in Toni Morrison's *Beloved.*" In *The Embrace of Eros: Bodies, Desires, and Sexuality in Christianity,* edited by Margaret D. Kamitsuka. Minneapolis: Fortress, 2010.

Bower, Anne. *African American Foodways: Explorations of History and Culture.* Chicago: University of Illinois Press, 2007.

Brackman, Barbara. *Facts and Fabrications: Unraveling the History of Quilts and Slavery.* Lafayette, CA: C&T, 2006.

Bradford, William. *Of Plymouth Plantation: 1620–1647.* Edited by Samuel Eliot Morison. New Brunswick, NJ: Rutgers University Press, 1952.

Bragdon, Kathleen J. *Ethnographic Overview and Assessment: George Washington Birthplace National Monument.* Prepared under Cooperative Agreement with The College Of William and Mary. Boston: Northeast Region Ethnography Program, National Park Service, 2009.

Brando, Marlon. "That Unfinished Oscar Speech." *New York Times,* 30 March 1973.

Brown, Kathleen. "Body Work in the Antebellum United States." In *Haunted by Empire: Geographies of Intimacy in North American History,* edited by Ann Laura Stoler. Durham, NC: Duke University Press, 2006.

Bruce, Mason. "A Clear Look at the Beecher House." *Voice News,* 4 October 2002.

Bryant, Linda Allen. *I Cannot Tell a Lie: The True Story of George Washington's African American Descendants.* Bloomington, IN: iUniverse Star, 2004.

Burns, James MacGregor, and Susan Dunn. *George Washington.* New York: Henry Holt, 2004.

Burns, Ken. *Civil War.* PBS, 1990.

Butler, William J. *Another City upon a Hill: Litchfield, Connecticut, and the Colonial Revival.* Newark: University of Delaware Press, 1983.

Butterworth, Hezekiah. *The Wampum Belt.* New York: Appleton, 1897.

Cable, George Washington. *The Grandissimes: A Story of Creole Life.* New York: Penguin Classics, 1988.

Cameron, Verney Lovett. *Across Africa.* New York: Harper & Brothers, 1877.

Captain John Smith and Pocahontas. Directed by Lew Landers. Los Angeles: United Artists, 1953.

Carnahan, Burrus M. *Act of Justice: Lincoln's Emancipation Proclamation and the Law of War.* Lexington: University Press of Kentucky, 2007.
Carney, Judith, and Richard Nicholas Rosomof. *In the Shadow of Slavery: African's Botanical Legacy in the Atlantic World.* Berkeley: University of California Press, 2011.
Casper, Scott J. *Sarah Johnson's Mount Vernon: The Forgotten History of an American Shrine.* New York: Macmillan, 2009.
Cather, Willa. *O Pioneers!* 1913. Reprint, New York: Barnes & Noble, 2004.
Cavarero, Adriana. *Stately Bodies: Literature, Philosophy, and the Question of Gender.* Ann Arbor: University of Michigan Press, 2002.
Chatterjee, Partha. *Nationalist Thought and the Colonial World: A Derivative Discourse.* Minneapolis: University of Minnesota Press, 1993.
Child, Francis James. *The English and Scottish Popular Ballads.* 5 vols. Mineola, NY: Dover, 2003.
Child, Fred. "Reflections on Aaron Copland's 'Lincoln's Portrait.'" *Performance Today.* American Public Media, 12 February 2009. http://www.publicradio.org.
Churchill, Ward. *A Little Matter of Genocide: Holocaust and Denial in the Americas, 1492 to the Present.* San Francisco: City Lights Books, 1998.
Clark, Cynthia L. *The American Economy: A Historical Encyclopedia.* Vol. 1. Santa Barbara, CA: ABC-CLIO, 2011.
Clarkson, Thomas. *Letters on the Slave-Trade.* London, 1791.
Cohn, Bernard S. *Colonialism and Its Forms of Knowledge: The British in India.* Princeton, NJ: Princeton University Press, 1996.
Colden, Cadwallader. *History of the Five Indian Nations of Canada Which Are Dependent on the Province of New York.* 1727. Reprint, Whitefish, MT: Kessinger, 2005.
Collette, Mark. "The New World." *Tyler (TX) Morning Telegraph,* 13 February 2006.
Collins, Kathleen. "The Scourged Back." *History of Photography* 9, no. 1 (January 1985): 43–45.
Colonial Williamsburg Foundation. *Jamestown, Williamsburg, Yorktown: The Official Guide to America's Historic Triangle.* Winston-Salem, NC: John F. Blair, 2007.
Condra, Jill, ed. *The Greenwood Encyclopedia of Clothing through World History.* Vol. 2, *1501–1800.* Westport, CT: Greenwood, 2008.
Connor, Kimberly Rae. *Imagining Grace: Liberating Theologies in the Slave Narrative Tradition.* Urbana: University of Illinois Press, 2000.
Conway, Cecelia. *African Banjo Echoes in Appalachia: A Study of Folk Traditions.* Knoxville: University of Tennessee Press, 1995.
Cornelius, Janet Duitsman. *Slave Missions and the Black Church in the Antebellum South.* Columbia: University of South Carolina Press, 1999.
———. *"When I Can Read My Title Clear": Literacy, Slavery, and Religion in the Antebellum South.* Columbia: University of South Carolina Press, 1991.
Cook, Frederick. *Journals of the Military Expedition of Major General John Sullivan against the Six Nations of Indians in 1779: With Records of Centennial Celebrations; Prepared Pursuant to Chapter 361, Laws of the State of New York, of 1885 by Frederick Cook, Secretary of State.* Auburn, NY: Knapp, Peck & Thomson, 1887.
Cott, Nancy. "In the Rubble: Women's History as Bulwark." Paper presented at "Edu-

cating Women for a World in Crisis," Newcomb College Institute Summit, New Orleans, 10 February 2007.

Crist, Elizabeth Bergman. *Music for the Common Man: Aaron Copland during the Depression and War.* New York: Oxford University Press, 2009.

Crumbley, Paul. *Inflections of the Pen: Dash and Voice in Emily Dickinson.* Lexington: University Press of Kentucky, 1996.

Cull, Nicholas J., David Culbert, and David Welch. "Freedom Train (1947–1949)." In *Propaganda and Mass Persuasion: A Historical Encyclopedia, 1500 to the Present.* Santa Barbara, CA: ABC-CLIO, 2003.

Custalow, Dr. Linwood "Little Bear," and Angela L. Daniel. "Silver Star." *The True Story of Pocahontas: The Other Side of History.* Golden, CO: Fulcrum, 2007.

D'Aguiar, Fred. *Feeding the Ghosts.* New York: Ecco, 2000.

Davis, David Brion. *In the Image of God: Religion, Moral Values, and Our Heritage of Slavery.* New Haven, CT: Yale University Press, 2001.

Davis, John. *Travels of Four Years and a Half in the United States.* 1803. Reprint, London: British Library, Historical Print Editions, 2011.

"Declaration of Independence: A History." National Archives. Accessed 16 January 2014. http://www.archives.gov/exhibits/charters/declaration_history.html.

Deleuze, Gilles, and Félix Guattari. *Anti-Oedipus: Capitalism and Schizophrenia.* Minneapolis: University of Minnesota Press, 1983.

Deleuze, Gilles, Félix Guattari, and Brian Massumi. *A Thousand Plateaus: Capitalism and Schizophrenia.* Minneapolis: University of Minnesota Press, 1987.

Derrida, Jacques. *The Derrida Reader: Writing Performances.* Lincoln: University of Nebraska Press, 1998.

Dickinson, Emily. *The Poems of Emily Dickinson.* Edited by R. W. Franklin. Vol. 2. Variorum Edition. Cambridge, MA: Belknap Press of Harvard University Press, 1998.

DiLorenzo, Thomas J. *The Real Lincoln: A New Look at Abraham Lincoln, His Agenda, and an Unnecessary War.* New York: Three Rivers, 2003.

DIME139. "Freedom Train Essay." 2002. Accessed 15 January 2014. http://www.at149st.com/dime139.html.

Diouf, Sylviane. *Dreams of Africa in Alabama: The Slave Ship "Clotilda" and the Story of the Last Africans Brought to America.* New York: Oxford University Press, 2007.

———. *Servants of Allah: African Muslims Enslaved in the Americas.* New York: New York University Press, 1998.

Douglass, Frederick. *Frederick Douglass: Selected Speeches and Writings.* Chicago: Chicago Review Press, 2000.

———. *The Narrative of the Life of Frederick Douglass, An American Slave.* 1845. Reprint, Mineola, NY: Dover, 1995.

Downs, Jim. *Sick from Freedom: African American Illness and Suffering during the Civil War and Reconstruction.* Oxford: Oxford University Press, 2012.

Doyle, Laura. "'A' for Atlantic: The Colonizing Force of Hawthorne's *The Scarlet Letter.*" *American Literature* 79, no. 2 (June 2007): 243–73.

Du Bois, W. E. B. *Black Reconstruction in America.* 1935. Reprint, New York: Free Press, 1998.

———. *The Negro.* 1915. Reprint, New York: Cosimo, 2007.
Edson, Evelyn. *The World Map, 1300–1492: The Persistence of Tradition and Transformation.* Baltimore: John Hopkins University Press, 2007.
Eisnach, Dwight, and Herbert C. Covey. *What the Slaves Ate: Recollections of African American Foods and Foodways from the Slave Narratives.* Santa Barbara, CA: ABC-CLIO, 2009.
Eng, David, and David Kazanjian, eds. *Loss: The Politics of Mourning.* Berkeley and Los Angeles: University of California Press, 2003.
Ezekwueche, Nneka. "Afro Beauty: African Body Art." *Afrostyle,* 22 December 2010.
Faery, Rebecca Blevins. *Cartographies of Desire: Captivity, Race, and Sex in the Shaping of an American Nation.* Norman: University of Oklahoma Press, 1999.
Fagan, Deirdre. "Emily Dickinson's Unutterable Word." *Emily Dickinson Journal* 14, no. 2 (March 2005): 70–75.
Farr, Judith. *The Passion of Emily Dickinson.* Cambridge, MA: Harvard University Press, 1998.
Feagin, Joe R. *Racist America: Roots, Current Realities, and Future Reparations.* New York: Routledge, 2009.
Feelings, Tom. *The Middle Passage: White Ships, Black Cargo.* New York: Dial, 1995.
Fenton, William Nelson. *The False Faces of the Iroquois.* Ohsweken, ON: Iroqrafts, 2005.
Ferguson, Leland. "'The Cross Is a Magic Sign': Marks on Eighteenth Century Bowls in South Carolina." In *"I, Too, Am American": Archaeological Studies of African-American Life,* edited by Teresa A. Singleton, 116–31. Charlottesville: University of Virginia Press, 1999.
———. *Uncommon Ground: Archaeology in Early America, 1650–1800.* Washington, DC: Smithsonian Institution Press, 1992.
Finn, Julio. *The Bluesman: The Musical Heritage of Black Men and Women in the Americas.* Northhampton, MA: Interlink, 1992.
Floyd, Samuel A., Jr. *The Power of Black Music: Interpreting Its History from Africa to the United States.* New York: Oxford University Press, 1996.
Foner, Eric. *The Fiery Trial: Abraham Lincoln and American Slavery.* New York: Norton, 2010.
———. "Lincoln and Colonization." In *Our Lincoln: New Perspectives on Lincoln and His World,* edited by Eric Foner. New York: Norton, 2008.
Frey, Sylvia R. "Resistance and Revolts in North American Slave Societies." Slavery, Abolition and Social Justice, Digital Slavery Program, 1490–2007. 2010. Accessed 16 January 2014. http://www.amdigital.co.uk.
———. *Water from the Rock: Black Resistance in a Revolutionary Age.* Princeton, NJ: Princeton University Press, 1993.
Fry, Gladys-Marie. *Stitched from the Soul: Slave Quilts from the Antebellum South.* Chapel Hill: University of North Carolina Press, 2002.
Fryd, Vivien Green. *Art and Empire: The Politics of Ethnicity in the United States Capitol, 1815–1860.* Athens: Ohio University Press, 2001.
Fuller, Thomas. *The History of Worthies of England, 1662.* London: Thomas Tegg, 1840.

Garwood, Darrell. *Artist in Iowa: A Life of Grant Wood.* Westport, CT: Greenwood, 1971.

George-Kanentiio, Doug. "Iroquois Seek to End Outrage of Sacred Objects Being Sold." *Syracuse Herald–American,* 17 September 1995.

Glasgow, Ellen. *Barren Ground.* Orlando: Harcourt Brace, 1985. First published 1925.

Gleach, Frederic. *Powhatan's World and Colonial Virginia: A Conflict of Cultures.* Lincoln: University of Nebraska Press, 1997.

Glory. Directed by Ed Zwick. Culver City, CA: TriStar Pictures and Freddy Field Productions, 1989.

Goldfield, David. *America Aflame: How the Civil War Created a Nation.* London: Bloomsbury, 2011.

Gordon, Lynda. *Lives Like Loaded Guns: Emily Dickinson and Her Family's Feuds.* New York: Viking, 2010.

Gottschild, Brenda Dixon. *Digging: The African Presence in American Dance.* Westport, CT: Greenwood, 1996.

Gray, Robert. *A Good Speed to Virginia.* London: Felix Kyngston for William Welbie, 1609.

Gridley, Samuel H. *The Centennial Celebration of General Sullivan's Campaign against the Iroquois, in 1779 held at Waterloo September 3, 1879.* Waterloo, NY: Waterloo Library and Historical Society, 1880.

Grigson, Geoffrey. *The Arts Today.* London: Bodley Head, 1935.

Grimm, Jacob, and Wilhelm Grimm. *Grimm's Complete Fairy Tales.* Garden City, NY: Nelson Doubleday, 1974.

Grinde, Donald A., Jr., and Bruce E. Johansen. "Sauce for the Goose: Demand and Definitions for 'Proof' Regarding the Iroquois and Democracy." *William and Mary Quarterly,* 3rd ser., 53, no. 3 (Summer 1996): 621–36.

Grizzard, Frank E. *Jamestown Colony: A Political, Social, and Cultural History.* Santa Barbara, CA: ABC-CLIO, 2007.

Groening, Matt. "The Day the Earth Stood Stupid." *Futurama,* season 3, episode 7. Fox Broadcasting Company. 18 February 2001.

Guelzo, Allen C. *Lincoln's Emancipation Proclamation: The End of Slavery in America.* New York: Simon & Schuster, 2004.

Hageneder, Fred. *The Meaning of Trees: Botany, History, Healing Lore.* San Francisco: Chronicle Books, 2005.

Haggard, Merle. Vocal performance of "Here Comes the Freedom Train," by Stephen Lemberg. *On My Love Affair with Trains.* BGO, 1976.

Hahn, Steven, Steven Miller, and Leslie Rowland, eds. *Freedom: A Documentary History of Emancipation, 1861–1867.* Series II, *The Black Military Experience.* Cambridge: Cambridge University Press, 1983.

Hakluyt, Richard. *A Discourse Concerning Western Planting.* 1584. Reprint, Cambridge: Press of John Wilson and Son, 1877.

Hall, Robert L. "African Religious Retentions in Florida." In *Africanisms in American Culture,* edited by Joseph E. Holloway, 98–118. Bloomington: Indiana University Press, 1990.

Hamor, Ralph. *A True Discourse of the Present State of Virginia.* 1615. Reprint, Richmond: Virginia State Library, 1957.
Harding, Vincent. *There Is a River: The Black Struggle for Freedom in America.* New York: Harcourt Brace Jovanovich, 1981.
Hashaw, Tim. *The Birth of Black America: The First African Americans and the Pursuit of Freedom.* New York: Carol & Graf, 2007.
"Haudenosaunee Confederacy Announces Policy on False Face Masks." *Akwesasne Notes* 1, no. 1 (Spring 1995): 39.
Hauptman, Laurence M., and James D. Wherry, eds. *The Pequots in Southern New England: The Fall and Rise of an American Indian Nation.* Norman: University of Oklahoma Press, 1990.
Hawthorne, Nathaniel. "Chiefly about War Matters." In *Nathaniel Hawthorne: Miscellaneous Prose and Verse,* edited by Thomas Woodson, Claude M. Simpson, and L. Neal Smith. Columbus: Ohio State University Press, 1994. First published in the *Atlantic Monthly,* July 1862.
———. *Letters of Hawthorne to William D. Ticknor, 1851–1864.* Newark, NJ: Carteret Book Club, 1910.
———. "Rappucini's Daughter." In *The Portable Hawthorne,* edited by William C. Spengemann, 95–119. New York: Penguin, 2005.
———. *The Scarlet Letter.* Boston: Samuel E. Cassino, 1892.
Hazard, Blanche E. *Indians and Pioneers: An Historical Reader for the Young.* New York: Morse, 1897.
Heller, William Jacob. *Historic Easton from the Window of a Trolley Car.* Lititz, PA: Express, 1912.
Herskovits, Melville J. *The Myth of the Negro Past.* 1941. Reprint, Boston: Beacon, 1990.
Higginbotham, Don. *George Washington Reconsidered.* Charlottesville: University of Virginia Press, 2001.
Higginson, Thomas Wentworth. *Black Rebellion: Five Slave Revolts.* New York: Arno, 1969.
Hirschfeld, Fritz. *George Washington and Slavery: A Documentary Portrayal.* Columbia: University of Missouri Press, 1997.
Hoffer, Peter Charles. *Cry Liberty: The Great Stono River Slave Rebellion of 1739.* Oxford: Oxford University Press, 2011.
———. *Sensory Worlds in Early America.* Baltimore: Johns Hopkins University Press, 2003.
Hogan, Michael J. *A Cross of Iron: Harry S. Truman and the Origins of the National Security State, 1945–1954.* Cambridge: Cambridge University Press, 2000.
Holloway, Joseph E. *Africanisms in American Culture.* 2nd ed. Bloomington: Indiana University Press, 2005.
Holzer, Harold, Edna Greene Medford, and Frank J. Williams. *The Emancipation Proclamation: Three Views.* Baton Rouge: Louisiana State University Press, 2006.
Holzer, Harold, John Y. Simon, and Dawn Vogel. *Lincoln Revisited: New Insights from the Lincoln Forum.* New York: Fordham University Press, 2007.
Hopkins, Dwight. *Cut Loose Your Stammerin Tongue: Black Theology in the Slave Narratives.* Louisville: Westminster John Knox, 2003.

———. *Religion and Black Theology.* Minneapolis: Fortress, 2000.
Horn, James. *A Land as God Made It: Jamestown and the Birth of America.* New York: Basic Books, 2005.
Howard, Hugh. *The Painter's Chair: George Washington and the Making of American Art.* New York: Bloomsbury, 2009.
Hughes, Langston. "Freedom Train." 1947. In *The Collected Works of Langston Hughes,* vol. 6, *Gospels, Plays, Operas and Other Dramatic Works.* Columbia: University of Missouri Press, 2004.
Huhndorf, Shari Michelle. *Going Native: Indians in the American Cultural Imagination.* Ithaca, NY: Cornell University Press, 2001.
Hurston, Zora Neale. *Their Eyes Were Watching God.* 1937. Reprint, New York: Harper Collins, 2010.
Ingold, Tim. *Making Anthropology, Archaeology, Art and Architecture.* New York: Routledge, 2013.
Jackson, Cassandra. *Violence, Visual Culture, and the Black Male Body.* London: Taylor & Francis, 2010.
Jackson, Virginia. *Dickinson's Misery: A Theory of Lyric Reading.* Princeton, NJ: Princeton University Press, 2005.
James, William. *The Letters of William James.* Edited by Henry James. Vol. 2. Boston: Atlantic Monthly Press, 1920.
Jefferson, Thomas. *Notes on the State of Virginia.* 1781. Reprint, Boston: Bedford/St. Martin's, 2002.
Jennings, Francis. *The Invasion of America.* Chapel Hill: University of North Carolina Press, 2010.
Jessup, Georgia Mills. "We Are Still Here." Powhatan Museum. http://www.powhatanmuseum.com/Powhatan_People.
Jewett, Sarah Orne. *The Country of the Pointed Firs.* 1896. Reprint, Piscataway, NJ: Transaction, 1997.
Johansen, Bruce Elliot. *Debating Democracy: The Iroquois Legacy of Freedom.* Santa Fe, NM: Clear Light, 1996.
———. *Native America Political Systems and the Evolution of Democracy: An Annotated Bibliography.* Westport, CT: Greenwood, 1996.
Johansen, Bruce Elliot, and Barbara Alice Mann, eds. *Encyclopedia of the Haudenosaunee.* Westport, CT: Greenwood, 2000.
Johansen, Bruce Elliot, and Barry Ritzker, eds. *Encyclopedia of American Indian History.* Santa Barbara, CA: ABC-CLIO, 2007.
Johnson, Walter. *Soul by Soul: Life inside the Antebellum Slave Market.* Cambridge, MA: Harvard University Press, 2001.
Jones, Maxine D. *African Americans in Florida.* Sarasota, FL: Pineapple, 1993.
Jordan, Don, and Michael Walsh. *White Cargo: The Forgotten History of Britain's White Slaves in America.* Edinburgh: Mainstream, 2007.
Kalter, Susan. *Benjamin Franklin, Pennsylvania, and the First Nations: The Treaties of 1736–62.* Champaign: University of Illinois Press, 2006.
Katheder, Thomas. *The Baylors of Newmarket: The Decline and Fall of a Virginia Planter Family.* Bloomington, IN: iUniverse, 2009.

Katz, William Loren. *Breaking the Chains: African American Slave Resistance.* New York: Simon Pulse, 1998.
Kay, Marvin L., and Lorin Cary. *Slavery in North Carolina, 1748–1775.* Chapel Hill: University of North Carolina Press, 1999.
Kelso, William. *Jamestown Rediscovery, 1994–2004.* Richmond: APVA Preservation Virginia, 2004.
———. *Jamestown, the Buried Truth.* Charlottesville: University of Virginia Press, 2008.
Kerry James Marshall on His Use of Games and Puzzles. Art in the Atrium. April 2009. Accessed 16 January 2014. http://www.sfmoma.org/explore/multimedia/videos/350.
Kimball, Robert, and Linda Emmet. *The Complete Lyrics of Irving Berlin.* New York: Knopf, 2001.
Knox, Thomas W. *The Boy Travelers on the Congo.* New York: Harper Brothers, 1888.
Kupperman, Karen Ordahl. *The Jamestown Project.* Cambridge, MA: Harvard University Press, 2007.
Lamay, J. A. Leo. *Did Pocahontas Save Captain John Smith?* Athens: University of Georgia Press, 1992.
Lawrence, D. H. *Studies in Classic American Literature.* Vol. 2. 1923. Reprint, Cambridge: Cambridge University Press, 2003.
Lee, Peggy. Vocal performance of "Fever," by Eddie Cooley, Otis Blackwell (John Davenport), and Peggy Lee. Recorded 19 May 1958 on *Fever.* Capitol Records, 1958.
Lee, Wayne. *Barbarians and Brothers: Anglo-American Warfare, 1500–1865.* Oxford: Oxford University Press, 2011.
Lengel, Edward G. *General George Washington: A Military Life.* New York: Random House, 2005.
Lepore, Jill. *The Tea Party's Revolution and the Battle over American History.* Princeton, NJ: Princeton University Press, 2010.
"Leslie Dill's New Opera Divide Light." *e-flux,* 27 February 2008. Accessed 16 January 2014. http://www.e-flux.com/announcements/lesley-dills-new-opera-divide-light/.
Levinson, Casey. "John Smith and Pocahontas: A Review of the 'Sometimes Governor' of Jamestown's Works and Reputation." *Eighteenth-Century Reading Room* (blog), 14 June 2007. Accessed 16 January 2014. http://18thcenturyreadingroom.wordpress.com.
Lincoln, Abraham. "Address before the Young Men's Lyceum of Springfield, Illinois." In *The Collected Works of Abraham Lincoln,* edited by Roy P. Basler, 1:108–15. 9 vols. New Brunswick, NJ: Rutgers University Press, 1953.
———. "Annual Message to Congress." 1 December 1862. In *Abraham Lincoln: His Speeches and Writings,* edited by Roy Basler and Carl Sandburg. 1946. Reprint, Cambridge, MA: Da Capo, 2001.
———. "The Gettysburg Address." In *Lincoln: Speeches and Writings, 1859–1865.* Edited by Don E. Fehrenbacher. New York: Library of America, 1989.
———. *Lincoln on Lincoln.* Edited by Paul M. Zall. Lexington: University Press of Kentucky, 2003.
———. *Lincoln on Race and Slavery.* Edited by Henry Louis Gates and Donald Yacovone. Princeton, NJ: Princeton University Press, 2009.

———. "Speech at New Haven, Connecticut: March 6, 1860." In *Lincoln: Speeches and Writings, 1859–1865,* edited by Don E. Fehrenbacher. New York: Library of America, 1989.

Lincoln, Abraham, and Stephen A. Douglas. *The Complete Lincoln-Douglas Debates of 1858.* Edited by Paul M. Angle. Chicago: University of Chicago Press, 1958.

Lindgren, James M. *Preserving the Old Dominion: Historic Preservation and Virginia Traditionalism.* Charlottesville: University of Virginia Press, 1993.

———. "Virginia Needs Living Heros: Historic Preservation in the Progressive Age." *Public Historian* 13, no. 1 (Winter 1991).

"Litchfield during the Colonial Revival." Litchfield Historical Society. Accessed 16 January 2016. http://www.litchfieldhistoricalsociety.org/history/revival.php.

Little, Barbara J., and Paul A. Shackel. *Archeology as a Tool of Civic Engagement.* Lanham, MD: Altamira, 2007.

Liu, Alice, and Missing Chunk. "a.k.a. Pocahontas." *The Resemblance is Uncanny.* New York, 1998.

Livingston, Judy. "Routes of Freedom: Slave Resistance and the Politics of Literary Geography." PhD diss., Louisiana State University, 2005.

Livingstone, David, and Charles Livingstone. *Narrative of an Expedition to the Zambesi and its Tributaries.* London, 1865.

Loewen, James W. *Lies across America: What Our Historic Sites Get Wrong.* New York: Simon & Schuster, 2007.

———. *Lies My Teacher Told Me: Everything Your American History Textbook Got Wrong.* 1995. Reprint, New York: Simon & Schuster, 2007.

Longmore, Paul. *The Invention of George Washington.* Charlottesville: University of Virginia Press, 1999.

Luke, Timothy W. *Museum Politics: Power Plays at the Exhibition.* Minneapolis: University of Minnesota Press, 2002.

MacGaffey, Wyatt. *Modern Kongo Prophets: Religion in a Plural Society.* Bloomington: Indian University Press, 1983.

MacGaffey, Wyatt, and John Janzen. "Nkisi Figures of the BaKongo." *African Arts* 7 (1974): 87–89.

MacKintosh, James. *Miscellaneous Works by Sir James MacKintosh.* Boston: Phillips Sampson, 1858.

Maffly-Kipp, Laurie F. "African American Christianity, Pt. II: To the Civil War." Accessed 16 January 2014. http://nationalhumanitiescenter.org/tserve/nineteen/nkeyinfo/aarcwgm.htm.

———. "An Introduction to the Church in the Southern Black Community." In *Documenting the American South.* May 2001. Magness, Phillip W., and Sebastian M. Pages. *Colonization after Emancipation: Lincoln and the Movement for Black Resettlement.* Columbia: University of Missouri Press, 2011.

Maker, Elizabeth. "What Might Have Been in Litchfield." *New York Times,* 20 August 2000.

Mandel, Naomi. *Against the Unspeakable: Complicity, the Holocaust, and Slavery in America.* Charlottesville: University of Virginia Press, 2006.

Mann, Barbara Alice. *George Washington's War on Native America.* Westport, CT: Greenwood, 2009.

———. "The Lynx in Time: Haudenosaunee Women's Traditions and History." *American Indian Quarterly* 21, no. 3 (Summer 1997): 433–37.

Mann, Sarah. Interview by Geo. H. Conn. *Born in Slavery: Slave Narratives from the Federal Writers Project, 1936–1938.* Ohio Narratives, vol. 12. Federal Writer's Project, United States Works Progress Administration, Manuscript Division, Library of Congress. Accessed 16 January 2014. http://memory.loc.gov/cgi-bin/ampage?collId=mesn&fileName=120/mesn120.db&recNum=73&itemLink=S?ammem/mesnbib:@field%28AUTHOR+@od1%28Mann,+Sarah%29%29.

McClafferty, Carla Killough. *The Many Faces of George Washington: Remaking a Presidential Icon.* Minneapolis: Carolrhoda Books, 2011.

McCord, David, and Thomas Cooper. *The Statutes at Large of South Carolina: Acts Relating to Charleston, Courts, Slaves, and Rivers.* Columbia, SC: A. S. Johnston, 1840.

"McIntosh County Shouters: Gullah Geechee Ring Shout." YouTube video, 57:07, from a concert at the Library of Congress, 12 April 2011. Accessed 16 January 2014. https://www.youtube.com.

Melville, Herman. *Moby-Dick.* New York: Signet Classic, 1998.

Mignolo, Walter D. *The Darker Side of the Renaissance: Literacy, Territoriality, and Colonization.* Ann Arbor: University of Michigan Press, 2003.

———. *Writing without Words.* Durham, NC: Duke University Press, 1994.

Miller, Perry. *Errand in the Wilderness.* Cambridge, MA: Harvard University Press, 1956.

Minta, Max M. *Seeds of Empire: The American Revolutionary Conquest of the Iroquois.* New York: New York University Press, 1999.

Mitchell, Domhnall. *Measures of Possibility: Emily Dickinson's Manuscripts.* Amherst: University of Massachusetts Press, 2005.

Mitnick, Barbara J., and William S. Ayres. *George Washington: American Symbol.* Manchester, VT: Hudson Hills, 1999.

More, Thomas. *Utopia.* 1516. Reprint, Madison, WI: Cricket House Books, 2010.

Morley, Simon. *Writing on the Wall: Word and Image in Modern Art.* Berkeley: University of California Press, 2005.

Morrison, Toni. *Beloved.* New York: Random House, 2004. First published 1987.

———. *Playing in the Dark: Whiteness and the Literary Imagination.* New York: Vintage, 1993.

Moser, Charlotte. *Clyde Connell: The Art and Life of a Louisiana Woman.* Austin: University of Texas Press, 1991.

Mossiker, Frances. *Pocahontas: The Life and the Legend.* Boston: Da Capo, 1996.

Mott, Frank L. *Golden Multitudes.* New York: Macmillan, 1947.

Mufwene, Salikoko S., ed. *Africanisms in Afro-American Language Varieties.* Athens: University of Georgia Press, 1993.

Muller, Kathyrn V. "The Two Mystery Belts of Grand River: A Biography of the Two Row Wampum and the Friendship Belt." *American Indian Quarterly* 31, no. 1 (Winter 2007): 129–64.

Murray, Aife. *Maid as Muse.* Lebanon, NH: University Press of New England, 2009.

"New Buildings, Exhibitions, Programs Planned for Jamestown Settlement by 2007." Jamestown Settlement. Accessed 16 January 2014. http://www.historyisfun.org/New-Buildings-Exhibitions.htm.

The New World. Directed by Terrence Malick. Los Angeles: New Line Cinema, 2005.

Niemcewicz, Julian Ursyn. *Under Their Vine and Fig Tree.* Elizabeth, NJ: Grassman, 1965.

Obi, Thomas J. Desch. *Fighting for Honor: The History of African Martial Art in the Atlantic World.* Columbia: University of South Carolina Press, 2008.

O'Connor, Flannery. *Everything That Rises Must Converge.* 1957. Reprint, New York: Macmillan, 1965.

Ogunleye, Tolagbe. "Àrokò, Mmomomme Twe, Nsibidi, Ogede, Tusona: Africanisms in Florida's Self-Emancipated Africans' Resistance to Enslavement and War Stratagems." *Journal of Black Studies* 36, no. 3 (January 2006): 396–414.

Olson, Lester C. *Benjamin Franklin's Vision of American Community: A Study in Rhetorical Iconology.* Columbia: University of South Carolina Press, 2004.

Osburn, Margaret. "Along the Side of the Road: Crafting Sea Grass Baskets." *American Visions* 3, no. 2 (April 1988).

Ozick, Cynthia. *The Shawl.* New York: Vintage, 1990.

Palmer, Rose A. *The North American Indians: An Account of the American Indians North Of Mexico, Compiled form the Original Sources.* Smithsonian Scientific Series, vol. 4. New York: Smithsonian Institution Series, 1929.

Parker, Arthur C. *The Code of Handsome Lake, the Seneca Prophet.* Bulletin of the New York State Museum No. 163, Education Department Bulletin No. 530. Albany: University of the State of New York, 1913.

Parkinson, Richard. *A Tour in America in 1798, 1799, and 1800.* London: Printed for J. Harding and J. Murray, 1805.

"'Parson Weems' Fable': Grant Wood Paints George Washington and Cherry Tree." *Life,* 19 February 1940, 33.

Percy, George. *A True Relation of the Proceedings and Occurences of Moment which have happened in Virginia from the Time Sir Thomas GATES was shipwrecked upon the BERMUDES the year of our lord 1609 until my departure out of the Country which was in the year of our lord 1612,* Virtual Jamestown. Accessed 16 January 2014. http://etext.lib.virginia.edu/etcbin/ot2www-jamestown?specfile=/web/data/subjects/jamestown/persnarr.o2w&act=surround&offset=4340250&tag=A+True+Relation&query=quene.

Phillips, Ruth B. "Disappearing Acts: Traditions of Enclosure and Iroquois Masks." In *Questions of Tradition,* edited by Mark Salber Phillips and Gordon Schochet. Toronto: University of Toronto Press, 2004.

———. *Museum Pieces: Toward the Indigenization of Canadian Museums.* Montreal: McGill-Queen's University Press, 2011.

Pocahontas. Directed by Mike Gabriel and Eric Goldberg. Los Angeles: Walt Disney Studios, 1995. DVD.

Pollack, Howard. *Aaron Copland: The Life and Work of an Uncommon Man.* New York: Henry Holt, 1999.

Pratt, Mary. *Imperial Eyes: Travel Writing and Transculturation.* New York: Routledge, 2008.

Preston, David L. *The Texture of Contact: European and Indian Settler Communities on the Frontiers of Iroquoia, 1667–1783.* Lincoln: University of Nebraska Press, 2009.

Price, David. *Love and Hate in Jamestown.* New York: Vintage, 2005.

Price, Richard, and Sally Price. *Maroon Societies: Rebel Slave Communities in America.* Edited by Richard Price. Baltimore: Johns Hopkins University Press, 1996.

Pryor, Sara. *Jamestown: The Birth of the Nation, 1607.* New York: MacMillan, 1907.

Putzi, Jennifer. *Identifying Marks: Race, Gender, and the Marked Body in Nineteenth Century America.* Athens: University of Georgia Press, 2006.

Raboteau, Albert J. *Slave Religion: The "Invisible Institution" in the Antebellum South.* New York: Oxford University Press, 1978.

Rancière, Jacques. *The Politics of Aesthetics.* New York: Continuum, 2004.

Randolph, Edmund. *The History of Virginia.* 1809. Edited by Arthur H. Shaffer. Charlottesville: University of Virginia Press for Virginia Historical Society, 1970.

Rankin, John. *Letters on American Slavery.* 1837. Reprint, London: Greenwood, 1970.

Rasmussen, Daniel. *American Uprising: The Untold Story of America's Largest Slave Revolt.* 2011. Reprint, New York: Harper Perennial, 2012.

Rasmussen, William Meade Stith, and Robert Tilton. *George Washington: The Man behind the Myths.* Charlottesville: University of Virginia Press, 1999.

Rath, Richard Cullen. "Drums and Power: Ways of Creolizing Music in Coastal South Carolina and Georgia 1730–90." In *Creolization in the Americas,* by David Buisseret, Daniel H. Usner Jr., Mary L. Gavin, Richard Cullen Rath, and J. L. Dillard, edited by David Buisseret and Steven G. Reinhardt. College Station: University of Texas Press at Arlington, 2000.

Rediker, Marcus. *The Slave Ship: A Human History.* New York: Penguin, 2008.

Rich, Nathaniel. "Jungleland: The Lower Ninth Ward in New Orleans Gives New Meaning to Urban Growth." *New York Times,* 21 March 2012.

Risjord, Norman. *Jefferson's America, 1760–1815.* 3rd ed. Washington, DC: Rowman & Littlefield, 2009.

Roark, Elizabeth Louise. *Artists of Colonial America.* Westport, CT: Greenwood, 2003.

Robinson, Marilyn. *Housekeeping.* New York: Farrar, Straus, & Giroux, 1980.

Rodriguez, Junius P. *Slavery and Resistance: Encyclopedia of Slave Resistance and Rebellion.* Westport, CT: Greenwood, 2006.

Rosenbaum, Art. *Shout Because You're Free: The African American Ring Shout Tradition in Coastal Georgia.* Athens: University of Georgia Press, 1998.

Rosenberg, Carroll Smith. *The Violent Empire: The Birth of an American National Identity.* Chapel Hill: University of North Carolina Press, 2010.

Rountree, Helen C. *Pocahontas, Powhatan, and Opechancanough: Three Indian Lives Changed by Jamestown.* Charlottesville: University of Virginia Press, 2006.

Ruberton, Patricia E. *Archaeologies of Placemaking: Monuments, Memories, and Engagement in Native North America.* Walnut Creek, CA: Left Coast, 2009.

Rucker, Walter C. *The River Flows On: Black Resistance, Culture and Identity.* Baton Rouge: Louisiana State University Press, 2006.

Sachsman, David B., S. Kittrell Rushing, and Roy Morris, eds. *Memory and Myth: The*

Civil War in Fiction and Film from "Uncle Tom's Cabin" to "Cold Mountain." West Lafayette, IN: Purdue University Press, 2007.
Safire, William. *Lend Me Your Ears: Great Speeches in History.* New York: Norton, 1992.
Salvaggio, Ruth. *Hearing Sappho in New Orleans: The Call of Poetry from Congo Square to the Ninth Ward.* Baton Rouge: Louisiana State University Press, 2012.
Sánchez-Eppler, Karen. *Touching Liberty: Abolition, Feminism and the Politics of the Body.* Berkeley: University of California Press, 1993.
Schimmel, Annemarie. *The Empire of the Great Mughals: History, Art, and Culture.* London: Reaktion Books, 2004.
Schweinfurth, Georg. *The Heart of Africa.* Translated by Ellen Frewer. 2 vols. New York: Harper & Brothers, 1874.
Seed, Patricia. "Houses, Gardens, and Fences: Signs of English Possession in the New World." In *Ceremonies of Possession in Europe's Conquest of the New World, 1492–1640,* 16–40. Cambridge: Cambridge University Press, 1995.
Sharpe, Matthew. *Jamestown.* Brooklyn: Soft Skull, 2007.
Sidbury, James. *Becoming African in America: Race and Nation in the Early Black Atlantic.* New York: Oxford University Press, 2007.
Sims, Paterson. *Anxious Objects: Willie Coles' Favorite Brands.* New Brunswick, NJ: Rutgers University Press, 2000.
1607: A Nation Takes Root. Whittier, CA: Finley Holiday Films, 2011.
Slenes, Robert W. "African Abrahams, Lucretias, and Men of Sorrows: Allegory and Allusion in the Brazilian Anti-slavery Lithographs (1827–1835) of Johann Moritz Rugendas." *Slavery and Abolition* 23 (2002).
Smith, Anna. Interview by Geo. H. Conn. *Born in Slavery: Slave Narratives from the Federal Writers Project, 1936–1938.* Ohio Narratives, vol. 12. Federal Writer's Project, United States Works Progress Administration, Manuscript Division, Library of Congress. Accessed 16 January 2014. http://memory.loc.gov/cgi-bin/ampage?collId=mesn&fileName=120/mesn120.db&recNum=85&itemLink=S?ammem/mesnbib:@field(AUTHOR+@od1(Smith,+Anna)).
Smith, John. *The Complete Works of Captain John Smith (1580–1631) in Three Volumes.* Edited by Philip L. Barbour. 3 vols. Chapel Hill: University of North Carolina Press, 1986.
———. *The General History of Virginia, New England, and the Summer Isles.* London: Printed by I.D. and I.H. for Michaels Sparks, 1624.
———. *A True Relation of Such Occurrences and Accidents of Note as Hath Hapned in Virginia Since the First Planting of that Colony.* 1608. In Smith, *Complete Works of Captain John Smith,* 1:23–116.
Smith, Mark M., ed. *Stono: Documenting and Interpreting a Southern Slave Revolt.* Columbia: University of South Carolina Press, 2005.
Smithson, Robert. "A Sedimentation of the Mind: Earth Projects." 1968. In *Robert Smithson: The Collected Writings,* edited by Jack Flam. Berkeley: University of California Press, 1996.
Southern, Ed, ed. *The Jamestown Adventure: Account of the Virginia Colony, 1605–1614.* Winston-Salem, VA: John F. Blair, 2004.
Stanley, H. M. *Through the Dark Continent.* New York: Harper Brothers, 1878.

Stannard, David. *American Holocaust: Columbus and the Conquest of the New World.* New York: Oxford University Press, 1992.
Stearns, Marshall, and Jean Stearns. *Jazz Dance: The Story of American Vernacular Dance.* Cambridge, MA: Da Capo, 1994.
Sterling, Dorothy. *Ahead of Her Time: Abby Kelley Foster and the Politics of Anti-Slavery.* New York: Norton, 1991.
"The Story of the American Freedom Train." American Freedom Train. Accessed 16 January 2014. http://www.freedomtrain.org/american-freedom-train-home.htm.
Stowe, Harriet Beecher. *Uncle Tom's Cabin; or, Life Among the Lowly.* 1852. Reprint, New York: Norton, 2010.
Strathern, Paul. *The Artist, the Philosopher, and the Warrior: The Intersecting Lives of Da Vinci, Machiavelli, and Borgia and the World They Shaped.* New York: Random House, 2009.
Stuckey, Sterling. *African Culture and Melville's Art.* New York: Oxford University Press, 2008.
———. *Going through the Storm: The Influence of African American Art in History.* New York: Oxford University Press, 1994.
———. *Slave Culture: Nationalist Theory and the Foundations of Black America.* New York: Oxford University Press, 1988.
"The Sullivan-Clinton Interactive Map." Sullivan/Clinton Campaign Then and Now. Accessed 16 January 2014. http://sullivanclinton.com/maps/.
Sundquist, Eric. *To Wake the Nations: Race and the Making of American Literature.* Cambridge, MA: Harvard University Press, 1993.
Talty, Stephan. *Mulatto America: At the Crossroads of Black and White Culture; A Social History.* New York: HarperCollins, 2003.
Tatar, Maria. *Off with Their Heads! Fairy Tales and the Culture of Childhood.* Princeton, NJ: Princeton University Press, 1992.
Thane, Elyswyth. *Mount Vernon Is Ours: The Story of Its Preservation.* New York: Duel, Sloan, & Pearce, 1966.
Thomas, David H. *Skull Wars: Kennewick Man Archeology and the Battle for Native American Identity.* Foreword by Vine Deloria Jr. New York: Basic Books, 2000.
Thompson, Mary V. "'And Procure for Themselves a Few Amenities': The Private Life of George Washington's Slaves." *Virginia Cavalcade* 48, no. 4 (Autumn 1999): 178–90.
———. "Different People, Different Stories: The Life Stories of Individual Slaves from Mount Vernon and Their Relationships with George and Martha Washington." Talk given at the symposium "George Washington and Slavery," Mount Vernon, VA. Updated 10 November 2006.
———. "Islam at Mount Vernon." Accessed 16 January 2014. http://www.mountvernon.org/educational-resources/encyclopedia/islam.
———. "The Lives of Enslaved Workers on George Washington's Outlying Farms." Talk, Neighborhood Friends of Mount Vernon, 16 June 1999.
——— "The Only Unavoidable Subject of Regret: George Washington and Slavery." Talk given at the symposium "George Washington and Alexandria, Virginia: Ties That Bind," Masonic Memorial, Alexandria, VA, 20 February 1999.

———. “Religious Practice in the Slave Quarters at Mount Vernon.” *Colonial Williamsburg Interpreter* 21, no. 1 (Spring 2000): 10–14.

Thompson, Robert Farris. *Flash of the Spirit: African and Afro-American Art and Philosophy.* New York: Random House, 1983.

Thornton, John. “The Art of War in Angola.” *Comparative Studies in Society and Culture* 30 (April 1988): 362–65.

Tilton, Robert. *Pocahontas: The Evolution of an American Narrative.* Cambridge: Cambridge University Press, 1994.

Tobin, Jacqueline L., and Raymond G. Dobard. *Hidden in Plain View: A Secret Story of Quilts and the Underground Railroad.* New York: Random House, 1999.

Todd, Leonard. *Carolina Clay: The Life and Legend of the Slave Potter Dave.* New York: Norton, 2008.

Tomblin, Barbara, *Bluejackets and Contrabands: African Americans and the Union Navy.* Lexington: University Press of Kentucky, 2009.

Tooker, Elisabeth. *The Iroquois Ceremonial of Midwinter.* Syracuse, NY: Syracuse University Press, 1970.

Townsend, Camilla. *Pocahontas and the Powhatan Dilemma.* American Portrait Series. New York: Hill & Wang, 2004.

Twelve Years a Slave. Directed by Steve McQueen. Los Angeles: Fox Searchlight, 2013.

U.S. Bureau of the Census. *A Century of Population Growth from the First Census of the United States to the Twelfth, 1790–1900.* Washington, DC: Government Printing Office, 1909.

Van Duzer, Chet. *Sea Monsters on Medieval and Renaissance Maps.* London: British Library, 2013.

Vansina, Jan. *Oral Tradition: A Study in Historical Methodology.* Chicago: Aldine Transaction, 1965.

Virtual Jamestown. Ed. Crandall A. Shifflett. 1996. Accessed 16 January 2014. http://www.virtualjamestown.org/.

Vlach, John Michael. *Back of the Big House: The Architecture of Plantation Slavery.* Chapel Hill: University of North Carolina Press, 1993.

———. *The Planter's Prospect: Privilege and Slavery in Plantation Paintings.* Chapel Hill: University of North Carolina Press, 2001.

Waldman, Amy. “A Nation Challenged: The Fliers; Posters of the Missing Now Speak of Losses.” *New York Times,* 29 September 2001.

Waldseemüller, Martin. *Universalis Cosmographia Secundum Ptholomaei Traditionem et Americi Vespucii Alioru[m]que Lustrationes.* St. Dié, 1507. Accessed 16 January 2014. http://www.loc.gov/rr/geogmap/waldexh.html.

Walker, Alice. *Meridian.* New York: Open Road Integrated Media, 2011.

Walton, Ortiz. *Music, Black and White and Blues: A Sociological Survey of the Use and Misuse of Afro-American Music.* New York: Morrow Quill, 1980.

Waselkov, Gregory. *Powhatan's Mantle: Indians in the Colonial Southeast.* Lincoln: University of Nebraska Press, 2006.

Washington, George. *George Washington Remembers: Reflections on the French and Indian War.* Edited by Fred Anderson. Lanham, MD: Rowman & Littlefield, 2004.

———. "Last Will and Testament of George Washington of Mount Vernon." In *George Washington: Writings*. Edited by John H. Rhodehamel. New York: Library of America, 1997.

———. *The Writings of George Washington*. Collected and edited by Worthington Chauncey Ford. Vol. 7, *1778–1779*. New York: G. P. Putnam's Sons, 1890.

———. *The Writings of George Washington; Being his Correspondence, Addresses, Messages, and Other Papers, Official and Private, Selected and Published from the Original Manuscripts with a Life of the Author*. Edited by Jared Sparks. Vol. 6. Boston: Russell, Odiorne, & Metcalf, Hilliard, Gray, 1834.

———. *The Writings of George Washington, Pt. III: Private Letters from the Time Washington Resigned His Commission as Commander-in-Chief of the Army to That of His Inauguration as President of the United States, December, 1783–April, 1789*. Edited by Jared Sparks. Boston: Russell, Odiorne, & Metcalf, Hilliard, Gray, 1835.

Watson, Steven. *Prepare for Saints: Gertrude Stein, Virgil Thompson and the Mainstreaming of American Modernism*. New York: Random House, 2012.

Weems, Mason Locke. *The Life of Washington*. Introduction by Peter S. Onuf. New York: M. E. Sharpe, 1996. First published 1809.

Welty, Eudora. *The Collected Stories of Eudora Welty*. New York: Harcourt, 1965.

———. *A Curtain of Green: And Other Stories*. New York: Mariner Books, 1979. First published 1941.

Werner, Marta. *Emily Dickinson's Open Folios: Scenes of Reading, Surfaces of Writing*. Ann Arbor: University of Michigan Press, 1995.

White, Ed. *The Backcountry and the City: Colonization and Conflict in Early America*. Minneapolis: University of Minnesota Press, 2005.

White, Shane, and Graham J. White. *The Sounds of Slavery: Discovering African American History*. Boston: Beacon, 2005.

Wiencek, Henry. *An Imperfect God: George Washington, His Slaves, and the Creation of America*. New York: Farrar, Straus & Giroux, 2003.

Wilks, Ivor. "Abu Bakr Al-Siddiq of Timbuktu." In *Africa Remembered: Narratives by West Africans from the Era of the Slave Trade*, edited by Philip D. Curtin. Madison: University of Wisconsin Press, 1967.

Williams, Julia. Interview by Geo. H. Conn. *Born in Slavery: Slave Narratives from the Federal Writers Project, 1936–1938*. Ohio Narratives, vol. 12. Federal Writer's Project, United States Works Progress Administration, Manuscript Division, Library of Congress. Accessed 16 January 2014. http://memory.loc.gov/cgi-bin/ampage?collId=mesn&fileName=120/mesn120.db&recNum=105&itemLink=D?mesnbib:2:./temp/~ammem_kAi5::.

Wise, Brian. "12 Poems of Emily Dickinson." In *All Music Guide to Classical Music*. Classical Archives. Accessed 16 January 2014. http://www.classicalarchives.com/work/48041.html#tvf=tracks&tv=about.

Wood, Marcus. *The Horrible Gift of Freedom*. Athens: University of Georgia Press, 2010.

Wood, Peter H. *Black Majority: Negroes in Colonial South Carolina from 1670 through the Stono Rebellion*. New York: Knopf, 1975.

Woodson, Carter Godwin. *The African Background Outlined: Or, Handbook for the Study of the Negro.* New York: Negro Universities Press, 1936.
———. *African Heroes and Heroines.* Washington, DC: Associated Publishers, 1939.
———. *The Education of the Negro prior to 1861: A History of the Education of the Colored People of the United States from the Beginning of Slavery to the Civil War.* New York: Putnam's, 1915.
———. *The History of the Negro Church.* Washington, DC: Associated Publishers, 1921.
———. *The Negro in Our History.* Washington, DC: Associated Publishers, 1922.
Woodward, C. Vann. *The Future of the Past.* New York: Oxford University Press, 1991.
———. "Myths of Innocence and Guilt: The Fall of the American Adam." *New Republic,* 16 August 2012. http://www.newrepublic.com/book/review/myths-innocence-and-guilt-the-fall-the-american-adam.
Woodward, Grace Steele. *Pocahontas.* Norman: University of Oklahoma Press, 1969.
Young, Neil. Vocal performance of "Pocahontas," by Neil Young. *Rust Never Sleeps.* Rhino Records, 1979.
Young, Phillip. *American Fiction, American Myth: Essays by Phillip Young.* University Park: Pennsylvania State University Press, 2000.
Zettel. Review of *The New World,* directed by Terrence Malick. *Write Words* (blog), 31 January 2006. Accessed 16 January 2014. http://www.writewords.org.uk/forum/93_60760.asp.
Zinn, Howard. *A People's History of the United States.* 1980. Reprint, New York: Harper Perennial Modern Classics, 2005.

INDEX